Beginning
XML Databases

Beginning
XML Databases

Gavin Powell

Wiley Publishing, Inc.

Beginning XML Databases

Published by
Wiley Publishing, Inc.
10475 Crosspoint Boulevard
Indianapolis, IN 46256
www.wiley.com

Copyright © 2007 by Wiley Publishing, Inc., Indianapolis, Indiana

Published simultaneously in Canada

ISBN-13: 978-0-471-79120-1
ISBN-10: 0-471-79120-2

Manufactured in the United States of America

10 9 8 7 6 5 4 3 2 1

1MA/ST/RQ/QW/IN

Library of Congress Cataloging-in-Publication Data is available from the publisher.

About the Author

Gavin Powell has a BSc. in Computer Science, along with numerous professional accreditations and skills. He has had a lot of practice with things like XML, Oracle, Ingres, and MSAccess, as well as a multitude of application development languages and platforms. He has almost 20 years of contracting, consulting, and hands-on educating experience—in both software development and database administration roles. He has lived, studied, and worked on three different continents, and is now scratching a living as a writer, musician, and family man. He can be contacted at creativemusician@bellsouth.net or info@oracledbaexpert.com.

Credits

Senior Acquisitions Editor
Jim Minatel

Development Editor
Kenyon Brown

Technical Editor
Todd Meister

Production Editor
Pamela Hanley

Copy Editor
Nancy Rapoport

Editorial Manager
Mary Beth Wakefield

Production Manager
Tim Tate

Vice President and Executive Group Publisher
Richard Swadley

Vice President and Executive Publisher
Joseph B. Wikert

Project Corrdination
Ryan Steffen

Graphics and Production Specialists
Brook Graczyk
Denny Hager
Barbara Moore
Lynsey Osborn
Jill Proll
Heather Ryan
Alicia B. South

Quality Control Technicians
Amanda Briggs
John Greenough
Christy Pingleton
Brain H. Walls

Proofreading and Indexing
Techbooks

My thanks to all those who waited so very patiently for this one.

Contents

Contents

Contents

Contents

Contents

Contents

Introduction

XML may very well be the wave of the future in the computing world, both with respect to applications programming on the Internet, and with that of database storage. In fact, XML is so flexible that it can even be used to transfer information between two completely different databases. Those databases could reside on different types of computers, even in multiple companies, and on opposite sides of the world.

As with all of my previous books, I strive to make something complex into something that is easy to understand. I make extensive use of examples. The idea is to make it an interesting read. Lots of examples and pretty pictures can help to keep things interesting. This type of approach can be useful to beginners but can sometimes also present new ideas to the more experienced eye. If you don't like books with lots of examples and pictures, or you are an expert in the subject matter, then this book may not suit your taste.

Who Should Read This Book

This book is for beginners, beginning with both XML and databases as a merged subject. Some XML knowledge can be gained from this book, as can some database knowledge. However, the focus of this book is on the combination of the topics of XML and databases.

The target audience of this book is anyone wishing to know brief details of XML and database technology, as applied to both XML and relational database technology working hand in hand.

Anyone involved with either XML or database technology, from the novice all the way through to the expert, would benefit from reading this book. This includes database administrators, developers, data modelers, systems or network administrators, technical managers, marketers, advertisers, forecasters, planners—anyone who actually uses XML and database data for any application type.

What This Book Covers

The aim of this book is to teach you, the reader, about the confluence of two technologies: XML and relational databases. How do XML and relational databases combine to form a more powerful tool? If you want specific information about either XML or some particular database (relational, object, or native XML) then once again, you might be reading the wrong book. This book packs a lot of information, about some very complex and detailed topics, into a brief introductory beginner's guide. As already stated, this book is purely about the confluence, juncture, or meeting point of two topics: relational databases and XML.

This book does not focus on XML, the XML DOM, XSL, or any other XML application programming technology, unless that technology is directly related to database technology. This book also does not focus on any particular database engine. This book does, however, explore how XML is used with the Oracle and SQL Server relational databases. There is also a small amount of coverage of native XML databases, and even a brief summary of DB2 database XML capabilities.

Chapters covering the basics of topics, such as XML and XSL, are intended as introductory. If further detail on these topics is required then another book in this series might be useful to you (see, for example, *Beginning XML* by David Hunter et. al., [Wiley, 2004]).

Some database engines allow complete processing of XML documents through a database-embedded, fully capable XML data type structure. XML data types are explored deeply in this book, as they are considered the most critical confluence between XML and a relational database.

How This Book Is Organized

One of the biggest challenges in writing a book such as this is to maintain focus on the subject at hand. Of course, one has to introduce some of the basic facts of XML and database technology in order to achieve a sensible merging of these two very widely scoped topics. This is precisely why this book focuses on XML in the first three chapters. Chapter 4 focuses on relational database technology by introducing the basics of SQL—so important for understanding database structure and reading a relational database. Chapters 5 and 6 attempt to begin the merging process of XML and databases by describing the ways that Oracle and SQL Server are including XML capabilities. Chapter 7 attempts to demonstrate not only the platform-independence capability of XML, but also the database vendor-independence of XML. Chapters 8 and 9 go back into database technology. Chapter 8 explains XML as the equivalent of an object database model. Chapter 9 presents XML, and any XML document, each as being a database in itself. Chapters 10 through 13 describe some of the most advanced features of XML, further expanding the concept of an XML document as a database. Chapter 14, the final chapter in this book, wraps it all up by describing some applications, tools, and implementations of XML in modern industry.

Within most chapters are Try It Out sections where you get to try out various concepts, summary sections, and exercise sections at the end. The entire book includes as much example material as possible. I have attempted, wherever possible, to reuse the same data set throughout the entire book in order to maintain consistency and provide a sense of reality. The objective is to include as much diverse material as possible. This should help to give a better overall understanding of the topics at hand.

This book contains a glossary, which allows you to look up terms rapidly and avoid having to page through the index, and the entire book, searching for explicit definitions of frequently used terms.

❑ **Chapter 1, What Is XML?** This chapter gives you a brief summary of eXtensible Markup Language (XML). XML is extensible or changeable. HTML (HyperText Markup Language), on the contrary, is a non-extensible language.

❑ **Chapter 2, The XML Document Object Model (DOM):** This chapter tells you all about the XML Document Object Model (XML DOM). The XML DOM allows complete dynamic access to all the bits and pieces within an XML document. The XML DOM allows programmatic change to an XML document at run-time.

❑ **Chapter 3, Extending the Power of XML with XSL:** This chapter covers eXtensible Style Sheets (XSL). XSL is used to template and filter XML data. This chapter briefly touches on using database data directly.

❑ **Chapter 4, Relational Database Tables and XML:** This chapter examines how data is accessed within a relational database using Structured Query Language (SQL). SQL is a language used for reading data from a relational database. Specialized commands are used to change data: INSERT, UPDATE, and DELETE.

❑ **Chapter 5, Oracle Database and XML:** There is immense capability in Oracle Database and Oracle SQL for utilizing the power of XML. This chapter covers XML only as directly related to Oracle Database and Oracle SQL. You examine how XML documents can be created, accessed, and manipulated directly from within an Oracle database. You will be presented with various specialized techniques and facilities available in an Oracle Database, including embedded XML data types.

❑ **Chapter 6, SQL Server and XML:** There is also immense capability in SQL Server database for utilizing the power of XML. This chapter covers XML only as it directly relates to SQL Server. You examine how XML documents can be created, accessed, and manipulated directly from within a SQL Server database. You are presented with various specialized techniques and facilities available in a SQL Server database, including embedded XML data types.

❑ **Chapter 7, Using XML in Heterogeneous Environments:** The structure of XML documents is an established and widely accepted standard. XML is also very easy to use and understand. Passing XML documents between different database engines, different operating systems, and different hardware platforms is easy! This chapter demonstrates how to transfer XML easily between different computer architectures. One of the central tenets of XML is to allow for sharing of data without regard to whatever is at either end of a transfer.

❑ **Chapter 8, Understanding XML Documents as Objects:** This chapter is included to give you an understanding of the object data model because XML document structure is hierarchical. XML documents can be flat structured but best utilize XML when they are hierarchically structured. XML document structure is similar to that of object data model structure.

❑ **Chapter 9, What Is a Native XML Database?** Chapters 5 and 6 cover specifics of Oracle and SQL Server databases respectively. This chapter attempts to conceptually refine some of the details covered in those chapters, and also to expand on much of what is covered in previous chapters. This chapter begins the process of describing native XML databases. A native XML database describes an XML document as a database by itself.

❑ **Chapter 10, Navigating XML Documents Using XPath:** This chapter briefly covers XPath technology, including XPath 1.0 and XPath 2.0. XPath is a specialized expression language, used to parse through XML node hierarchies and retrieve chunks of data from XML documents. XPath is a major part of the scripting language eXtensible Style Sheet Transformations (XSLT). XSLT is the transformation subset of XSL. Many of the other tools, such as XPointer and XQuery, are based on XPath.

❑ **Chapter 11, Reading XML Documents Using XQuery:** XPath is used to navigate through XML documents, based on an absolute or relative position of a node in an XML document. XQuery makes extensive use of XPath expressions in order to build XQuery query commands. XQuery is to XML as SQL is to relational databases. So, XQuery is used to read XML documents. XQuery is designed to query anything appearing as XML data, even XML data type structures (or otherwise) and XML stored in a database as XML data types.

❑ **Chapter 12, Some Advanced XML Standards:** Many of the advanced standards of XML are not essentially database specific, but more front-end application coding specific. Where your database stores your data, your front-end application is made up of the screens you use to communicate with that database. Advanced XML standards such as XLink, XPointer, and XForms may not at first seem quite relevant to this text. However, in order to do XML justice, I have to at least touch on both database and application XML capabilities. And as you shall see in this chapter, front-end applications can sometimes be very closely related to database content. The fact is, XML is often generated dynamically from data. This generated XML often includes use of tools such as XLinks, XPointers, and XForms.

❑ **Chapter 13, Data Modeling and XML:** This chapter ties together the conceptual application and the database aspects of XML. Document Type Definitions (DTD) and XML Schema Definitions (XSD) can both be used to impose structure onto XML data. The overall message of this chapter is critical to the understanding of the confluence of XML and relational databases. This chapter conveys the concept that a rigid structure can be applied to any XML document. This is very much the same conceptually as tables and schemas that apply rigid structure to a relational database. The result is that a relational database model can be applied to any XML document that conforms to the logical structure of that relational database model. XML documents and relational databases can be fit together structurally using DTDs and XSDs.

❑ **Chapter 14, Applying XML Databases in Industry:** The purpose of this chapter is to give you, the reader, a brief picture of the *how and what* of XML use in industry today. What is being used? What is it being used for? How is it being used? What are some of the products? What are their basic capabilities? This book focuses on concepts with respect to native XML databases. It does not provide details for any specific native XML database. Additionally, both Oracle and SQL Server databases include an XML data type. This makes both of these databases quite capable as native XML databases through the application and use of their contained XML data types.

What You Need to Use This Book

Some programming knowledge, formal training, or Internet scripting language experience is probably extremely useful. For example, Internet scripting languages such as HTML, JavaScript, VBScript, and ASP could all be very useful for reading this book. Relational database modeling experience and use of at least one relational database and XML use would help, too.

In-depth knowledge of computer programming and relational database modeling theory are probably not absolutely essential. There is no denying that these skills would certainly help. If there is something you do not understand you can always look it up elsewhere.

Future Editions of This Book

DB2 Database does allow a form of XML data type inclusion using something called the DB2 Extender. The DB2 Extender allows for full storage and functionality of XML data types into the DB2 relational database. However, it was decided during the process of writing this book that the DB2 Extender was not within the scope of this book. Additionally, many other relational databases do allow some form of XML use. Even MS Access database does. Future editions will include additional database vendor software as XML inclusion is added by the various database vendors, and as database vendor XML implementations become easier to use.

If you want to find further information on the Internet: Search for a term such as "XML DOM" or "XSL" in search engines such as Yahoo!. Be aware that not all information will be current and might be incorrect. Verify by cross-checking between multiple references. If no results are found using Yahoo! then try the full detailed listings on Google.

Search Amazon.com and Barnesandnoble.com, where other titles can be found.

I have also written the following books, which you will find useful:

- ❑ *Beginning Database Design* (ISBN: 0764574906)
- ❑ *Oracle Data Warehouse Tuning for 10g* (ISBN: 1555583350)
- ❑ *Oracle 9i: SQL Exam Cram 2 (1Z0-007)* (ISBN: 0789732483)
- ❑ *Oracle SQL: Jumpstart with Examples* (ISBN: 1555583237)
- ❑ *Oracle Performance Tuning for 9i and 10g* (ISBN: 1555583059)
- ❑ *ASP Scripting* (ISBN: 1932808450)
- ❑ *Oracle Performance Tuning* (ISBN: 1932808345)
- ❑ *Oracle Database Administration Fundamentals II* (ISBN: 1932072845)
- ❑ *Oracle Database Administration Fundamentals I* (ISBN: 1932072535)
- ❑ *Introduction to Oracle 9i and Beyond: SQL & PL/SQL* (ISBN: 1932072241)

My website at www.oracledbaexpert.com contains a lot of information. Included there are details covering anything and everything I have worked with and written about over the last 20 years. A lot of this information on my website is out-of-date.

Software accreditations for this book include:

- ❑ Microsoft Word, PowerPoint, Excel, Win2K
- ❑ ERWin
- ❑ PaintShop
- ❑ Oracle Database
- ❑ Microsoft SQL Server Database
- ❑ IBM DB2 relational database
- ❑ Numerous freeware and shareware XML tools

As a final note, if this book included full descriptions of relational database model and XML, in addition to its current content, you might need a truck to carry the book around with you. The following two titles might help with specifics on the two topics of this book:

- ❑ *Beginning XML*, David Hunter, et. al., Wrox, 2004, ISBN: 0764570773
- ❑ *Beginning Database Design*, Gavin Powell, Wrox, 2005, ISBN: 0764574906

There are a multitude of other books covering both of these topics, both in bookstores and online.

Let's get started.

Conventions

To help you get the most from the text and keep track of what's happening, I've used a number of conventions throughout the book.

> **Boxes like this one hold important, not-to-be-forgotten information that is directly relevant to the surrounding text.**

Tips, hints, tricks, and asides to the current discussion are offset and placed in italics like this.

```
In code examples, I highlight new and important code with a gray background.
```

```
The gray highlighting is not used for code that's less important in the present
context, or has been shown before.
```

Source Code

As you work through the examples in this book, you may choose either to type in all the code manually or to use the source code files that accompany the book. All of the source code used in this book is available for download at `http://www.wrox.com`. Once at the site, simply locate the book's title (either by using the Search box or by using one of the title lists) and click the Download Code link on the book's detail page to obtain all the source code for the book.

Because many books have similar titles, you may find it easiest to search by ISBN; this book's ISBN is 0-471-79120-2 (changing to 978-0-471-79120-1 as the new industry-wide 13-digit ISBN numbering system is phased in by January 2007).

Once you download the code, just decompress it with your favorite compression tool. Alternately, you can go to the main Wrox code download page at `http://www.wrox.com/dynamic/books/download.aspx` to see the code available for this book and all other Wrox books.

Errata

We make every effort to ensure that there are no errors in the text or in the code. However, no one is perfect, and mistakes do occur. If you find an error in one of our books, such as a spelling mistake or faulty piece of code, we would be very grateful for your feedback. By sending in errata you may save another reader hours of frustration and at the same time you will be helping us provide even higher quality information.

To find the errata page for this book, go to `http://www.wrox.com` and locate the title using the Search box or one of the title lists. Then, on the book details page, click the Book Errata link. On this page you can view all errata that has been submitted for this book and posted by Wrox editors. A complete book list including links to each book's errata is also available at `www.wrox.com/misc-pages/booklist.shtml`.

If you don't spot "your" error on the Book Errata page, go to www.wrox.com/contact/techsupport .shtml and complete the form there to send us the error you have found. We'll check the information and, if appropriate, post a message to the book's errata page and fix the problem in subsequent editions of the book.

p2p.wrox.com

For author and peer discussion, join the P2P forums at p2p.wrox.com. The forums are a Web-based system for you to post messages relating to Wrox books and related technologies and interact with other readers and technology users. The forums offer a subscription feature to e-mail you topics of interest of your choosing when new posts are made to the forums. Wrox authors, editors, other industry experts, and your fellow readers are present on these forums.

At http://p2p.wrox.com you will find a number of different forums that will help you not only as you read this book, but also as you develop your own applications. To join the forums, just follow these steps:

1. Go to p2p.wrox.com and click the Register link.

2. Read the terms of use and click Agree.

3. Complete the required information to join as well as any optional information you wish to provide and click Submit.

4. You will receive an e-mail with information describing how to verify your account and complete the joining process.

You can read messages in the forums without joining P2P but in order to post your own messages, you must join.

Once you join, you can post new messages and respond to messages other users post. You can read messages at any time on the Web. If you would like to have new messages from a particular forum e-mailed to you, click the Subscribe to this Forum icon by the forum name in the forum listing.

For more information about how to use the Wrox P2P, be sure to read the P2P FAQs for answers to questions about how the forum software works as well as many common questions specific to P2P and Wrox books. To read the FAQs, click the FAQ link on any P2P page.

What Is XML?

This chapter provides a brief summary of what XML is. The abbreviation "XML" refers to eXtensible Markup Language, which means that XML is extensible or changeable. HTML (Hypertext Markup Language), on the contrary, is a non-extensible language and is the default language that sits behind many of the web pages in your web browser, along with numerous other languages.

HTML does not allow changes to web pages. HTML web pages are effectively frozen in time when they are built and cannot be changed when viewed in a browser.

> Internet Explorer and Netscape are browsers used for viewing websites on the Internet.

XML, on the other hand, allows generation of web pages on the fly. XML allows storage of changeable data into web pages that can be altered at any time besides runtime. XML pages can also be tailored in look, feel, and content, and they can be tailored to any specific user looking at a web page at any point in time.

In this chapter you learn:

- ❑ What XML is
- ❑ What XSL is
- ❑ The differences between XML and HTML
- ❑ Basic XML syntax
- ❑ The basics of the XML DOM
- ❑ Details about different browsers and XML
- ❑ The basics of the DTD (Document Type Definition)
- ❑ How to construct an XML document
- ❑ Reserved characters in XML
- ❑ How to ignore the XML parser

❏   What XML namespaces are

❏   How to handle XML for multiple languages

Let's begin by comparing XML with HTML, the Hypertext Markup Language.

Comparing HTML and XML

XML can, in some respects, be considered an extensible form of HTML. This is because HTML is restrictive in terms of the tags it is allowed to use. In the following sample HTML document, all tags, such as <HTML>, are predefined:

```
<HTML>
<HEAD><TITLE>This is a simple HMTL page</TITLE></HEAD>
<BODY>

<P>
Once more unto the breach, dear friends, once more; or close the wall up with
our English dead. In peace there's nothing so becomes a man as modest stillness
and humility; but when th' blast of war blows in our ears, then imitate the action
of the tiger: stiffen the sinews, summon up the blood, disguise fair nature with
hard-favour'd rage; then lend the eye a terrible aspect.

<P>
Cry 'Havoc !' and let slip the dogs of war, that this foul deed shall smell above
the earth with carrion men, groaning for burial.
</P>

</BODY>
</HTML>
```

Figure 1-1 shows the execution of this script in a browser. You can see in the figure that none of the tags appear in the browser, only the text between the tags. In the preceding sample HTML page code, the tags are all predefined and enclosed within angle brackets (< . . . >). An HTML document will always begin with the tag <HTML> and end with the corresponding closing tag </HTML>. Other tags shown in the above script are <HEAD>, <TITLE>, <BODY>, and <P>. The <P> tag is used for paragraphs.

Unlike HTML, XML is extensible and thus is capable of being extended or modified by changing or adding features. XML can have tags of its own created (customized) that are unique to every XML document created. An XML document when embedded into an HTML page needs the predefined tag that an HTML page does, such as <HTML> and <P>, but XML can also make up its own tags as it goes along.

An important restriction with respect to the construction of XML documents that is not strictly applied in HTML code is that all tags must be contained within other tags. The root node tag is the only exception. Examine the previous HTML coding example and you will see that in the source code the first paragraph does not have a terminating </P> tag (using the / or forward slash character). HTML does not care about this. XML does!

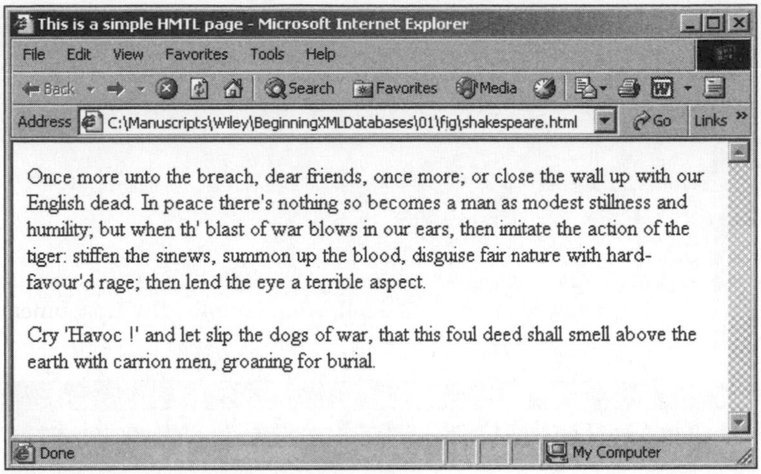

Figure 1-1: A simple sample HTML page

What Is XML Capable Of?

So, XML is not limited to a predefined set of tags as HTML is, but allows the creation of customized tags. The advantages of using XML could loosely be stated as follows:

❑ **Flexibility with data:** Any information can be placed into an XML page. The XML page becomes the data rather than the definitional container for data, as shown in Figure 1-1.

❑ **Web page integration:** This becomes easier because building those web pages becomes more generic. Web pages are data driven (based on content in the web page) rather than relying on the definition of the tags (programming language–driven) and where the tags are placed.

❑ **Open standards:** XML is completely flexible. No single software company can control and define what tags are created, what each tag means, and where in a document tags should appear. XML is a little like a completely generic programming language.

❑ **Enhanced scalability and compression:** When sending web pages over the Internet, XML pages can contain just data. All the coded programming tags required for HTML are not needed.

❑ **Irrelevant order of data:** The order in which data appears in an XML page is unimportant because it is data. Data can have things applied to it at the client site (in a browser) to change it, if you use something like eXtensible Style Sheets (XSL).

What Is XSL?

XSL is a formatting language that applies templating to consistent data repetitions inside XML documents. For example, an XML page containing a listing of clients and their addresses could be formatted into a nice looking table field using an XSL style sheet that showed each different client on a single row in the table, as shown in Figure 1-2.

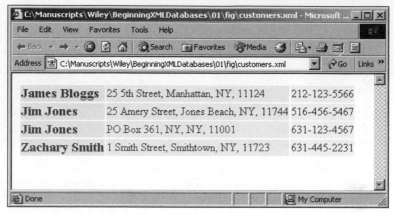

Figure 1-2: XSL can be used to apply templates to XML documents.

The HTML equivalent of XSL is cascading style sheets (CSS).

Creating and Displaying a Simple XML Document

Following is a sample XML document. The only required predefined tag is on the first line, which describes that the version of the XML parser used is version 1.0:

```
<?xmlversion="1.0"?>
<WeatherForecast date="2/1/2004">
    <city>
        <name>Frankfurt</name>
        <temperature>
        <min>43</min>
            <max>52</max>
        </temperature>
    </city>
    <city>
        <name>London</name>
        <temperature>
            <min>31</min>
            <max>45</max>
        </temperature>
    </city>
    <city>
        <name>Paris</name>
        <temperature>
            <min>620</min>
            <max>74</max>
        </temperature>
    </city>
</WeatherForecast>
```

A parser is a program that analyzes and verifies the syntax of the coding of a programming language. An XML- capable browser parses XML code to ensure that is syntactically correct. As already mentioned, one parser function is to ensure that all starting and ending tags exist, and that there is no interlocking of XML tags within the document. Interlocking implies that a new tag of the same type, such as <city>, cannot be started, until the ending tag of the previous city (</city>), has been found.

In a browser, the XML document looks as shown in Figure 1-3. The callouts in Figure 1-3 show that in addition to being flexible for a web pages programmer, XML is even flexible to the end user. End users are unlikely to see an XML document in this raw state, but Figure 1-3 helps to demonstrate the flexibility of XML.

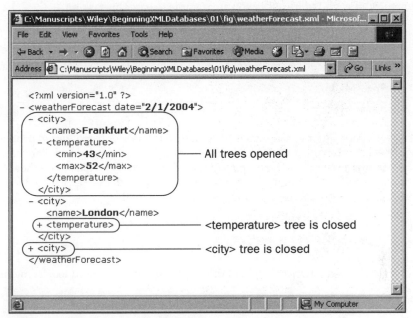

Figure 1-3: A simple sample XML page

The primary purpose of HTML is for display of data. XML is intended to describe data. XML is the data and thus describes itself. When HTML pages contain data, they must be explicitly generated. For every web page weather report written in HTML, a new HTML page must be created. This includes both the weather report data and all HTML tags. When regenerating an XML-based weather report, only the data is regenerated. Any templates using something like XSL remain the same. And those templates are probably only downloaded once. The result is that XML occupies less network bandwidth and involves less processing power.

XML is also a very capable medium for bulk data transfers that are platform and database independent. This is because XML is a universal standard. In short, XML does not do as much processing as HTML does. XML is structure applied to data. Effectively XML complements HTML rather than replaces it. XML was built to store and exchange data; HTML is designed to display data. XSL, on the other hand, is designed to format data.

Try It Out   **Creating a Simple XML Document**

The data shown below represents three regions containing six countries:

```
Africa          Zambia
Africa          Zimbabwe
Asia            Burma
Australasia     Australia
Caribbean       Bahamas
Caribbean       Barbados
```

Here, you are going to create a single hierarchy XML document. The example shown in Figure 1-3, and its preceding matching XML data, gives you an example to base this task on.

Create the XML document as follows:

1. Use an appropriate editor to create the XML document text file (Notepad in Windows).

2. Create the XML tag:

```
<?xml version="1.0"?>
```

3. Create the root tag first. The data is divided up as countries listed within continents (regions). Countries are contained within regions. There are multiple regions so there has to be a tag, which is a parent tag of the multiple regions. If there was a single region there could be a single `<region>` tag as the root node. So create a root node such as `<regions>`, indicating multiple regions. The XML document now looks something like this:

```
<?xml version="1.0"?>
<regions>
</regions>
```

4. Now add each region in as a child of the `<regions>` tag. It should look something like this:

```
<?xml version="1.0"?>
<regions>
    <region>Africa</region>
    <region>Asia</region>
    <region>Australasia</region>
    <region>Caribbean</region>
</regions>
```

5. Next you can add the individual countries into their respective regions by creating individual `<country>` tags:

```
<?xml version="1.0"?>
<regions>
    <region>Africa</region>
        <country>Zambia</country>
        <country>Zimbabwe</country>
```

```
    <region>Asia</region>
        <country>Burma</country>
    <region>Australasia</region>
        <country>Australia</country>
    <region>Caribbean</region>
        <country>Bahamas</country>
        <country>Barbados</country>
</regions>
```

6. When executed in a browser, the result will look as shown in Figure 1-4.

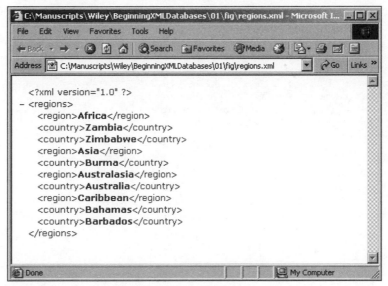

Figure 1-4: Creating a simple XML document

How It Works

You opened a text editor and created an XML document file. The XML document begins with the XML tag, identifying the version of XML is use. Next you added the root node called `<regions>`. All XML documents must have a single root node. Next you added four `<region>` nodes representing four regions into the root node. Next you added countries into the four different regions. Last, you viewed the XML document in your browser.

Embedding XML in HTML Pages (Data Islands)

XML documents can also be displayed in a browser using an XML data island. An *XML data island* is an XML document (with its data) directly or indirectly embedded inside an HTML page. An XML document can be embedded inline inside an HTML page using the HTML `<XML>` tag. It can also be referenced with an HTML SRC attribute.

This first example uses the XML tag to embed XML document data within an HTML page:

```
<HTML><BODY>

<XML ID="xmlParts">
    <?xml version="1.0" ?>
    <parts>
        <part>
            <partnumber>X12334-125</partnumber>
            <description>Oil Filter</description>
            <quantity>$24.99</quantity>
        </part>
        <part>
            <partnumber>X44562-001</partnumber>
            <description>Brake Hose</description>
            <quantity>$22.45</quantity>
        </part>
        <part>
            <partnumber>Y00023-12A</partnumber>
            <description>Transmission</description>
            <quantity>$8000.00</quantity>
        </part>
    </parts>
</XML>

<TABLE DATASRC=#xmlParts>
<TR>
    <TD><DIV DATAFLD="partnumber"></DIV></TD>
    <TD><DIV DATAFLD="$text"></DIV></TD>
</TR>
</TABLE>

</BODY></HTML>
```

HTML and XML tags can have attributes or descriptive values. In the HTML code `<IMG SRC="image.jpg" BORDER="1">` *the tag is an* `<IMG>` *or image tag for referencing an image. The* `SRC` *attribute tells the HTML* `<IMG>` *tag where to find the image, and the* `BORDER` *tag tells HTML to put a "1" pixel wide border around the image.*

The second example allows a reference to a separate XML file using the `SRC` attribute of the XML tag.

The XML source file is stored externally to the HTML page. In this case, the parts.xml file is stored in the operating system and not stored within the HTML file as in the previous example:

```
<HTML><BODY>

<XML ID="xmlParts" SRC="parts.xml"></XML>

<TABLE DATASRC=#xmlParts>
    <TR><TD><DIV DATAFLD="partnumber"></DIV></TD>
        <TD><DIV DATAFLD="$text"></DIV></TD>
    </TR>
</TABLE>

</BODY></HTML>
```

Both of these examples look as the screen does in Figure 1-5.

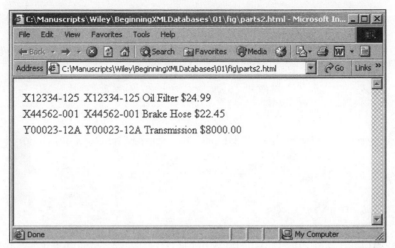

Figure 1-5: Using the XML tag to embed XML data islands into an HTML page

There are always different ways to do things.

Try It Out   XML Data Islands

The XML document that follows represents the three regions and six countries created in the Try It Out exercise presented earlier in this chapter:

```xml
<?xml version="1.0"?>
<regions>
   <region>Africa</region>
      <country>Zambia</country>
      <country>Zimbabwe</country>
   <region>Asia</region>
      <country>Burma</country>
   <region>Australasia</region>
      <country>Australia</country>
   <region>Caribbean</region>
      <country>Bahamas</country>
      <country>Barbados</country>
</regions>
```

Here we will create a simple HTML page, containing the preceding XML document as a data island. Assume that the XML document is called countries.xml. Don't worry about a full path name. The example shown in Figure 1-5 and its preceding matching XML data island HTML pages give you an example to base this task on.

Create the HTML page as follows:

1. Use an appropriate editor to create a text file.

2. Begin by creating the `<HTML>` tags for the start and end of the HTML page:

```
<HTML>
</HTML>
```

3. You could add a `<HEAD>` tag, allowing inclusion of a title into the browser. Begin by creating the `<HTML>` tags for the start and end of the HTML page:

```
<HTML>
<HEAD><TITLE>Regions and Countries</TITLE></HEAD>
</HTML>
```

4. Add the body section for the HTML page by enclosing it between the `<BODY>` tags:

```
<HTML>
<HEAD><TITLE>Regions and Countries</TITLE></HEAD>
<BODY>
</BODY>
</HTML>
```

5. Now add the `<XML>` tag into the body of the HTML page, which references the externally stored XML document:

```
<HTML>
<HEAD><TITLE>Regions and Countries</TITLE></HEAD>
<BODY>
<XML ID="xmlCountries" SRC="countries.xml"></XML>
</BODY>
</HTML>
```

6. Add a table field (`<TABLE>` tag) to the HTML page. The table field references the `<XML>` tag, by the ID attribute, as shown in the code that follows. The SRC in the `<XML>` tag allows direct access from the HTML page to XML tags as stored in the countries.xml file. In other words, the countries.xml file is referenced from the HTML page as a referenced data island:

```
<HTML>
<HEAD><TITLE>Regions and Countries</TITLE></HEAD>
<BODY>

<XML ID="xmlCountries" SRC="countries.xml"></XML>

<TABLE DATASRC=#xmlCountries>
<TR>
    <TD><DIV DATAFLD="region"></DIV></TD>
    <TD><DIV DATAFLD="$text"></DIV></TD>
</TR>
</TABLE>
</BODY>
</HTML>
```

7. The result will look as shown in Figure 1-6, when executed in a browser.

Figure 1-6: Creating a simple HTML page containing an XML data island

How It Works

You created an HTML page that referenced an XML document from the HTML page as a data island. The data island is referenced from the HTML page, to the XML document, using the XML tag as defined in the HTML page. Data is scrolled through in the HTML page using an HTML table field, using the DATASRC attribute of the HTML <TABLE> tag.

Introducing the XML Document Object Model

Another factor when using XML is that built into the browser used to display XML data, is a structure behind the XML data set. Look again at Figure 1-3 and you should see that everything is very neatly structured into a hierarchy. This entire structure can be accessed programmatically using something called the Document Object Model, or XML DOM. Using the XML DOM a programmer can find, read, and even change anything within an XML document. Those changes can also be made in two fundamental ways:

❑ **Explicit data access:** A program can access an XML document explicitly. For example, one can find a particular city by using the <city> tag and the name of the city.

❑ **Dynamic or generic access:** A program can access an XML document regardless of its data content by using the structure of the document. In other words, a program can scroll through all the tags and the data no matter what it is. That is what the XML DOM allows. An XML page can be a list of cities, weather reports, or even part numbers for an automobile manufacturer. The data set is somewhat irrelevant because the XML DOM allows direct access to the program within the browser, which displays the XML data on the screen, as shown in Figure 1-3. In other words, a program can find all the tags by passing up and down the tree of the XML DOM.

A browser uses the XML DOM to build a picture of an XML document, as shown in Figure 1-3. The browser contains a parser that does not care what the data is, but rather how data is constructed. In other words, the DOM contains a multiple dimensional (hierarchical) array structure. That array structure allows access to all tags and all data, without the programmer having to know the contents of the tags within it and even the names of the tags. An XML document is just data and so any data can be contained within it.

When creating weather reports for people in different parts of the world, the underlying templates that make the web pages look nice are all exactly the same; only the data is different. This is where this book comes into being. Data stored in databases as traditional relation tables can be used to create XML documents that can also be stored in a database. The XML DOM allows programmatic access into XML documents stored in a database. In other words, you can create XML documents, stuff them in a database, and then use database software to access the documents either as a whole or in part using the XML DOM.

That is really what this book is about. It is, however, necessary to explain certain facets of XML before we get to the meat of databases and XML. You need to have a basic picture of things such as XML and XSL first.

XML Browsers and Different Internet Browsers

There are varying degrees of support for XML in different Internet browsers. In general the latest versions of Internet Explorer or Netscape will do nicely. Using an older version of a software tool can sometimes be asking for trouble.

Using a non-mainstream browser might also be limited in scope but this is unlikely if you use the latest version. There are, however, some very specific technologies used by specific vendors. Microsoft's Internet Explorer falls into this category. Then again, Internet Explorer is probably now the most widely used browser. So, for browser-based examples, I've used Microsoft technology.

Database technology being used in this book will primarily be Oracle Database from Oracle Corporation and SQL-Server Database from Microsoft. Once again, bear in mind that the focus of this book is on using XML as a database, or in other databases.

The Document Type Definition

The Document Type Definition (DTD) is a method of defining consistent structure across all XML documents within a company, an installation, and so on. In other words, it allows validation of XML documents, ensuring that standards are adhered to even for XML data where the source of the XML data is external to the company.

From an XML in databases perspective, DTD could provide a method of structural validation, which is of course very important to any kind of database structure. However, it could also be superfluous and simply get in the way. It may depend on how XML documents are created or generated as being sources of both metadata and data. If XML documents are manually created then something like DTD could be very useful. Of course, once data is created, it is possible that only one round of validation is required for at least static data.

Static data in a database is data that does not change very often, if at all. In a database containing customers and invoices, your customers are relatively static (their names don't change — at least not very often). Transactional or dynamic data such as invoices is likely to change frequently. However, it is extremely likely that any creation of XML documents would be automatically generated by application programs. Why validate with the DTD when applications generating data (XML documents) will do that validation for you?

The DTD will be covered in a later chapter in detail, where you will deal with schemas and XML Schemas. XML Schemas are a more advanced form of the DTD. XML Schemas can be used to define what and how everything is to be created in an XML document.

XML Syntax

The basic syntax rules of XML are simple but also very strict. This section goes through those basic syntax rules one by one:

❑ **The XML tag:** The first line in an XML document declares the XML version in use:

```
<?xml version="1.0"?>
```

❑ **Including style sheets:** The optional second line contains a style sheet reference, if a style sheet is in use:

```
<?xml:stylesheet type="text/xsl" href="cities.xsl"?>
```

❑ **The root node:** The next line will contain the root node of the XML document tree structure. The root node contains all other nodes in the XML document, either directly or indirectly (through child nodes):

```
<root>
```

❑ **A single root node:** An XML document must have a single root tag, such that all other tags are contained within that root tag. All subsequent elements must be contained within the root tag, each nested within its parent tag.

An XML tag is usually called an element.

❑ **The ending root tag:** The last line will contain the ending element for the root element. All ending elements have exactly the same name as their corresponding starting elements, except that the name of the node is preceded by a forward slash (/):

```
</root>
```

❑ **Opening and closing elements:** All XML elements must have a closing element. Omitting a closing element will cause an error. Exceptions to this rule is the XML definitional element at the beginning of the document, declaring the version of XML in exceptions, and an optional style sheet:

```
<root>
    <branch_1>
        <leaf_1>
        </leaf_1>
    </branch_1>
    <branch_2>
    </branch_2>
</root>
```

HTML tags do not always require a closing tag. Examine the first HTML code example in this chapter in the section "Comparing HTML and XML." The first paragraph does not have a </P> paragraph end tag. The second paragraph does have a </P> paragraph eng tag. Some closing tags in HTML are optional, meaning that a closing tag can be included or not.

❑ **Case sensitive:** XML elements are case sensitive. HTML tags are not case sensitive. The XML element <root> in the previous example is completely different than the XML element <Root> in the next example. The following example is completely different than the previous XML document shown in the previous point. Even though all the elements are the same, their case is different for the <Root> and <BRANCH_1> elements:

```
<Root>
    <BRANCH_1>
        <leaf_1>
        </leaf_1>
    </BRANCH_1>
    <branch_2>
    </branch_2>
</Root>
```

HTML does not require proper nesting of elements, such as in this example:

```
<FONT COLOR="red"><B><I>This is bold italic text in red</FONT></B></I>
```

XML on the other hand, produces an error using the preceding code. For example, in XML the following code is invalid because </tag2> should appear before </tag1>:

```
<tag1><tag2>some tags</tag1></tag2>
```

❑ **Element attributes:** Like HTML tags, XML elements can have attributes. An element attribute refines the aspects of an element. Attributes and their values are called name-value pairs. An XML element can have one or more name-value pairs, and the value must always be quoted. HTML attribute values do not always have to be quoted, although it is advisable. In the following XML document sample (the complete document is not shown here), populations for continents (including the name of the continent) are contained as attributes of the <continent> element. In other words, the continent of Africa had a population of 748,927,000 people in 1998 (748 million people where the population in thousands is the total divided by 1,000, or 748,927).

It follows that projected populations for the African continent are 1.3 billion (1,298,311) for the year 2025, and 1.8 billion (1,766,082) for the year 2050. Also in this example, the name of the country is stored in the XML document as an attribute of the `<country>` element:

```
<?xml version="1.0"?>
<?xml:stylesheet type="text/xsl" href="791202 fig0105.xsl" ?>
<populationInThousands>
   <world>
      <continents>
         <continent name="Africa" year1998="748,927" year2025="1,298,311"
year2050="1,766,082">
            <countries>
               <country name="Burundi">
                  <year1998>6457</year1998>
                  <year2025>11569</year2025>
                  <year2050>15571</year2050>
               </country>
               <country name="Comoros">
                  <year1998>658</year1998>
                  <year2025>1176</year2025>
                  <year2050>1577</year2050>
               </country>
               . . .
            </country>
            . . .
         </continent>
         . . .
      </continents>
      . . .
   </world>
   . . .
</populationInThousands>
```

XML element and attribute names can have space characters included in those names, as in the
`<continent>` *element shown in the preceding sample XML document.*

❑   As shown in Figure 1-7, the previous sample XML document does include a style sheet, making the XML document display with only the names of continents and countries.

❑   And here is an HTML equivalent of the XML document for the previous example—as shown in Figure 1-7. Notice how much more raw code there is for each population region and country:

```
<HTML><BODY>
<TABLE CELLPADDING="2" CELLSPACING="0" BORDER="1">
   <TR>
      <TH BGCOLOR="silver">Continent
      <TH BGCOLOR="silver">Country
      <TH BGCOLOR="silver">1998
      <TH BGCOLOR="silver">2025
      <TH BGCOLOR="silver">2050
   </TR>
```

```
    <TR ALIGN="right">
        <TD BGCOLOR="#D0FFFF" ALIGN=left>Africa</TD>
        <TD BGCOLOR=#FFFFD0> </TD>
        <TD>748,927</TD>
        <TD>1,298,311</TD>
        <TD>1,766,082</TD>
    </TR>
    <TR ALIGN="right">
        <TD BGCOLOR="#D0FFFF"> </TD>
        <TD BGCOLOR=#FFFFD0 ALIGN=left>Burundi</TD>
        <TD>6,457</TD>
        <TD>11,569</TD>
        <TD>11,571</TD>
    </TR>
    <TR ALIGN="right">
        <TD BGCOLOR="#D0FFFF"> </TD>
        <TD BGCOLOR=#FFFFD0 ALIGN=left>Comoros</TD>
        <TD>658</TD>
        <TD>1,176</TD>
        <TD>1,577</TD>
    </TR>
    ...
</TABLE>
</BODY></HTML>
```

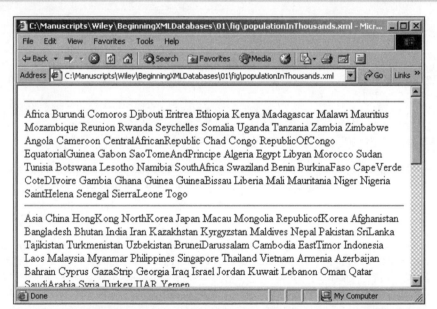

Figure 1-7: Using XML element attributes to change the display of an XML document

Figure 1-8 shows the HTML display of the preceding HTML coded page, and the XML displayed document in Figure 1-7 (the previous example).

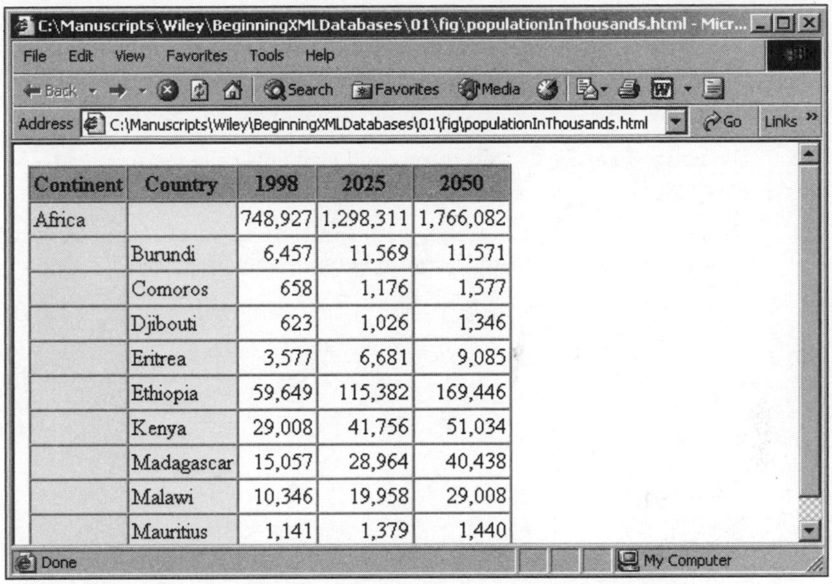

Continent	Country	1998	2025	2050
Africa		748,927	1,298,311	1,766,082
	Burundi	6,457	11,569	11,571
	Comoros	658	1,176	1,577
	Djibouti	623	1,026	1,346
	Eritrea	3,577	6,681	9,085
	Ethiopia	59,649	115,382	169,446
	Kenya	29,008	41,756	51,034
	Madagascar	15,057	28,964	40,438
	Malawi	10,346	19,958	29,008
	Mauritius	1,141	1,379	1,440

Figure 1-8: HTML embeds the code and is less flexible than XML.

❑ **Comments**: Both XML and HTML use the same character strings to indicate commented out code:

```
<!-- This is a comment and will not be processed by the HTML or XML parser -->
```

Elements

As you have already seen in the previous section, an XML element is the equivalent of an HTML tag. A few rules apply explicitly to elements:

❑ **Element naming rules:** The names of elements (XML tags) can contain all alphanumeric characters as long as the name of the element does not begin with a number or a punctuation character. Also, names cannot contain any spaces. XML delimits between element names and attributes using a space character. Do not begin an element name with any combination of the letters XML, in any combination of uppercase or lowercase characters. In other words, XML_1, xml_1, xML_1, and so on, are all not allowed. It will not produce an error to use multiple operative characters, such as + (addition) and – (subtraction), but their use is inadvisable. Elements least likely to cause any problems are those containing only letters and numbers. Stay away from odd characters.

17

❑ **Relationships between elements:** The root node has only children. All other nodes have one parent node, as well as zero or more child nodes. Nodes can have elements that are related on the same hierarchical level. In the code example that follows, the following apply:

  ❑ The root node element is called `<root>`.

  ❑ The root node has two child node elements: `<branch_1>` and `<branch_2>`.

  ❑ The node `<branch_1>` has one child element called `<leaf_1_1>`.

  ❑ The node `<branch_2>` has three child elements called `<leaf_2_1>`, `<leaf_2_2>`, and `<leaf_2_3>`.

  ❑ The nodes `<leaf_2_1>`, `<leaf_2_2>`, and `<leaf_2_3>` are all siblings, having the same parent node element in common (node `<branch_2>`):

```
<root>
    <branch_1>
        <leaf_1_1>
        </leaf_1_1>
    </branch_1>
    <branch_2 name="branch two">
        <leaf_2_1>
        </leaf_2_1>
        <leaf_2_2>
        </leaf_2_2>
        <leaf_2_3>This is a leaf</leaf_2_3>
    </branch_2>
</root>
```

❑ **The content of elements:** XML elements can have simple content (text only), attributes for the element concerned, and can contain other child elements. Node `<branch_2>` in the preceding example has an attribute called name (with a value of *branch two*). The node `<leaf_1>` contains nothing. The node `<leaf_2_3>` contains the text string *This is a leaf*.

❑ **Extensible elements:** XML documents can be altered without necessarily altering what is delivered by an application. Examine Figure 1-7. The following is the XSL code used to apply the reduced template for get the result shown in Figure 1-7:

```
    <xsl:template>
        <xsl:apply-templates select="@*"/>
            <xsl:if test="@name[.='Africa']"><HR/></xsl:if>
            <xsl:if test="@name[.='Asia']"><HR/></xsl:if>
            <xsl:if test="@name[.='Europe']"><HR/></xsl:if>
            <xsl:if test="@name[.='Latin America and the Caribbean']"><HR/></xsl:if>
            <xsl:if test="@name[.='North America']"><HR/></xsl:if>
            <xsl:if test="@name[.='Oceania']"><HR/></xsl:if>
            <xsl:value-of select="@name"/>
        <xsl:apply-templates/>
    </xsl:template>
</xsl:stylesheet>
```

Looking at the preceding XSL script, yes, we have not as yet covered anything about eXtensible Style Sheets (XSL). The point to note is that the boldface text in the preceding code finds only the name attribute values, from all elements, ignoring everything else. Therefore all population numbers are discarded and only the names of continents and countries are returned. It is almost as if the XML document might as well look like that shown next, with all population numbers removed. The result in Figure 1-7 will still be exactly the same:

```
<?xml version="1.0"?>
<?xml:stylesheet type="text/xsl" href="791202 fig0107.xsl" ?>

<populationInThousands>
   <world>
      <continents>
         <continent name="Africa">
            <countries>
               <country name="Burundi"></country>
               <country name="Comoros"></country>
            </countries>
            ...
         </continent>
      </continents>
   </world>
</populationInThousands>
```

Attributes

Elements can have attributes. An element is allowed to have zero or more attributes that describe it. Attributes are often used when the attribute is not part of the textual data set of an XML document, or when not using attributes is simply awkward. Store data as individual elements and metadata as attributes.

> Metadata is the data about the data. In a database environment the data is the names of your customers and the invoices you send them. The metadata is the tables you define which are used to store records in customer and invoice tables. In the case of XML and HTML metadata is the tags or elements (< . . . > ... < . . . >) contained within a web page. The values between the tags is the actual data.

Once again, the now familiar population example:

```
<populationInThousands>
   <world>
      <continents>
         <continent name="Africa" year1998="748,927" year2025="1,298,311"
year2050="1,766,082">
            <countries>
               <country name="Burundi">
                  <year1998>6457</year1998>
                  <year2025>11569</year2025>
                  <year2050>15571</year2050>
               </country>
```

```
            <country name="Comoros">
                <year1998>658</year1998>
                <year2025>1176</year2025>
                <year2050>1577</year2050>
            </country>
            ...
        </countries>
        ...
    </continent>
    ...
  </continents>
  ...
 </world>
 ...
</populationInThousands>
```

Attributes can also be contained within an element as child elements. The example you just saw can be altered as in the next script, removing all element attributes. The following script just looks busier and perhaps a little more complex for the naked eye to decipher. The more important point to note is that the physical size of the XML document is larger because additional termination elements are introduced. In very large XML documents this can be a significant performance factor:

```
<populationInThousands>
    <world>
        <continents>
            <continent>
                <name>Africa</name>
                <year1998>748,927</year1998>
                <year2025>1,298,311</year2025>
                <year2050>1,766,082</year2050>
                <countries>
                    <country>
                        <name>Burundi</name>
                        <year1998>6457</year1998>
                        <year2025>11569</year2025>
                        <year2050>15571</year2050>
                    </country>
                    <country>
                        <name>Comoros</name>
                        <year1998>658</year1998>
                        <year2025>1176</year2025>
                        <year2050>1577</year2050>
                    </country>
                    ...
                </countries>
                ...
            </continent>
            ...
        </continents>
        ...
```

```
        </world>
    ...
</populationInThousands>
```

From a purely programming perspective, it could be stated that attributes should not be used because of the following reasons:

❑   Elements help to define structure and attributes do not.

❑   Attributes are not allowed to have multiple values whereas elements can.

❑   Programming is more complex using attributes.

❑   Attributes are more difficult to alter in XML documents at a later stage.

As already stated, the preceding reasons are all sensible from a purely programming perspective. From a database perspective, and XML in databases, the preceding points need some refinement and perhaps even some contradiction:

❑   **Elements define structure and attributes do not.** I prefer not to put too much structure into data, particularly in a database environment because the overall architecture of data can become too complex to manage and maintain, both for administrators and the database software engine. Performance can become completely disastrous if a database gets large because there is simply too much structure to deal with.

❑   **Attributes are not allowed multiple values.** If attributes need to have multiple values then those attributes should probably become child elements anyway. This book is after all about XML databases (and XML in databases). Therefore it makes sense to say that an attribute with multiple values is effectively a one-to-many relationship.

You send many invoices to your customers. There is a one-to-many relationship between each customer and all of their respective invoices. A one-to-many relationship is also known as a master-detail relationship. In this case the customer is the master, and the invoices are the detail structural element. The many sides of this relationship are also known as a collection, or even an array, in object methodology parlance.

❑   **Attributes make programming more complex.** Programming is more complex when accessing attributes because code has to select specific values. Converting attributes to multiple contained elements allows programming to scan through array or collection structures. Once again, performance should always be considered as a factor. Scrolling through a multitude of elements contained within an array or collection is much less efficient than searching for exact attributes, which are within exact elements. It is much faster to find a single piece of data, rather than searching through lots of elements, when you do not even know if the element exists or not. An XML document can contain an element, which can be empty, or the element can simply not exist at all. From a database performance perspective, avoiding use of attributes in favor of contained, unreferenced collections (which are what a multitude of same named elements is)/is suicidal for your applications if your database gets even to a reasonable size. It will just be too slow.

❑ **Attributes are not expansion friendly.** It is more difficult to change metadata than it is to change data. It should be. If you have to change metadata then there might be data structural design issues anyway. In a purely database environment (not using XML), changing the database model is the equivalent of changing metadata. In commercial environments metadata is usually not altered because it is too difficult and too expensive. All application code depends on database structure not being changed. Changing database metadata requires application changes as well. That's why it can get expensive. From a perspective of XML and XML in databases, you do not want to change attributes because attributes represent metadata, and that is a database modeling design issue — not a programming issue. Changing the data is much, much easier.

Try It Out   **Using XML Syntax**

The following data represents three regions, containing six countries, as in the previous Try It Out sections in this chapter. In this example, currencies are now added:

```
Africa          Zambia          Kwacha
Africa          Zimbabwe        Zimbabwe Dollars
Asia            Burma
Australasia     Australia       Dollars
Caribbean       Bahamas         Dollars
Caribbean       Barbados        Dollars
```

In this example, you use what you have learned about the difference between XML document elements and attributes.

The following script is the XML document created in the first Try It Out section in this chapter:

```xml
<?xml version="1.0"?>
<regions>
    <region>Africa</region>
        <country>Zambia</country>
        <country>Zimbabwe</country>
    <region>Asia</region>
        <country>Burma</country>
    <region>Australasia</region>
        <country>Australia</country>
    <region>Caribbean</region>
        <country>Bahamas</country>
        <country>Barbados</country>
</regions>
```

You will use the preceding XML document and add the currencies for each country. Do not create any new elements in this XML document.

Change the XML document as follows:

1. Open the XML document. You can copy the existing XML text into a new text file if you want.

2. All you do is add an attribute name-value pair to each opening <country> tag:

```
<country currency="Kwacha">Zambia</country>
```

3. The final XML document looks something like this:

```
<?xml version="1.0"?>
<regions>
    <region>Africa</region>
        <country currency="Kwacha">Zambia</country>
        <country currency="Zimbabwe Dollars">Zimbabwe</country>
    <region>Asia</region>
        <country>Burma</country>
    <region>Australasia</region>
        <country currency="Dollars">Australia</country>
    <region>Caribbean</region>
        <country currency="Dollars">Bahamas</country>
        <country currency="Dollars">Barbados</country>
</regions>
```

4. Figure 1-9 shows the result when executed in a browser.

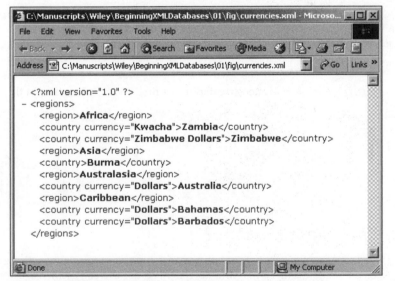

Figure 1-9: Adding attributes to elements in an XML document

How It Works

All you did was to edit an XML document containing the XML tag, a single root node, and various regions of the world that contained some of their respective countries. You then proceeded to add currency attributes into some of the countries.

Reserved Characters in XML

Escape characters are characters preventing execution in a programming language or parser. Thus the < and > characters must be escaped (using an escape sequence) if they are used in an XML document anywhere other than delimiting tags (elements). In XML, an escape sequence is a sequence of characters known to the XML parser to represent special characters. This escape sequence is exactly the same as that used by HTML. The following XML code is invalid:

```
<country name="Germany">West < East</country>
```

The preceding code can be resolved into XML by replacing the < character with the escape sequence string < as follows:

```
<country name="Germany">West &lt; East</country>
```

The <, >, and & characters are illegal in XML and will be interpreted. Quotation characters of all forms are best avoided and best replaced with an escape sequence.

Ignoring the XML Parser with CDATA

There is a special section in an XML document called the CDATA section. The XML parser ignores anything within the CDATA section. So no errors or syntax checking will be performed in the CDATA section. The CDATA section can be used to include scripts written in other languages such as JavaScript. The CDATA section is the equivalent of a <SCRIPT> ... </SCRIPT> tag enclosed section in an HTML page. The CDATA section begins and ends with the strings, as highlighted in the following script example:

```
<SCRIPT>
<![CDATA[
function F_To_C
{
   return ((F - 32) * (5 / 9))
}
]]>
</SCRIPT>
```

What Are XML Namespaces?

Two different XML documents containing elements with the same name, where those names have different meanings, could cause conflict. This XML document contains weather forecasts for three different cities. The <name> element represents the name of each city:

```
<?xml version="1.0"?>
<WeatherForecast date="2/1/2004">
   <city>
      <name>Frankfurt</name>
      <temperature><min>43</min><max>52</max></temperature>
   </city>
```

```
    <city>
        <name>London</name>
        <temperature><min>31</min><max>45</max></temperature>
    </city>
    <city>
        <name>Paris</name>
        <temperature><min>20</min><max>74</max></temperature>
    </city>
</WeatherForecast>
```

This next XML document also contains <name> elements but those names are of countries and not of cities. Adding these two XML documents together could cause a semantic (meaning) conflict between the <name> elements in the two separate XML documents:

```
<?xml version="1.0"?>
<WeatherForecast date="2/1/2004">
    <country>
        <name>Germany</name>
        <temperature><min>22</min><max>45</max></temperature>
    </country>
    <country>
        <name>England</name>
        <temperature><min>24</min><max>39</max></temperature>
    </country>
    <country>
        <name>France</name>
        <temperature><min>22</min><max>85</max></temperature>
    </country>
</WeatherForecast>
```

Namespaces can be used to resolve this type of conflict by assigning a separate prefix to each XML document, adding the prefix to tags in each XML document as follows for the XML document containing cities:

```
<?xml version="1.0"?>
<i:WeatherForecastxmlns:i="http://www.mywebsite.com/nsforcities" date="2/1/2004">
    <i:city>
        <i:name>Frankfurt</i:name>
        <i:temperature><i:min>43</i:min><i:max>52</i:max></i:temperature>
    </i:city>
    <i:city>
        <i:name>London</i:name>
        <i:temperature><i:min>31</i:min><i:max>45</i:max></i:temperature>
    </i:city>
    <i:city>
        <i:name>Paris</i:name>
        <i:temperature><i:min>20</i:min><i:max>74</i:max></i:temperature>
    </i:city>
</i:WeatherForecast>
```

And for the XML document containing countries, you use a different prefix:

```xml
<?xml version="1.0"?>
<o:WeatherForecastxmlns:o="http://www.mywebsite.com/nsforcities" date="2/1/2004">
    <o:city>
        <o:name>Frankfurt</o:name>
        <o:temperature><o:min>43</o:min><o:max>52</o:max></o:temperature>
    </o:city>
    <o:city>
        <o:name>London</o:name>
        <o:temperature><o:min>31</o:min><o:max>45</o:max></o:temperature>
    </o:city>
    <o:city>
        <o:name>Paris</o:name>
        <o:temperature><o:min>20</o:min><o:max>74</o:max></o:temperature>
    </o:city>
</o:WeatherForecast>
```

Creating the preceding XML documents using prefixes has actually created separate elements in separate documents. This is done by using an attribute and a URL. Also when using a namespace, you don't have to assign the prefix to every child element, only the parent node concerned. So with the first XML document previously listed you can do this:

```xml
<?xml version="1.0"?>
<WeatherForecast xmlns:i="http://www.mywebsite.com/nsforcities" date="2/1/2004">
 <city>
    <name>Frankfurt</name>
    <temperature><min>43</min><max>52</max></temperature>
</city>
 <city>
    <name>London</name>
    <temperature><min>31</min><max>45</max></temperature>
</city>
<city>
    <name>Paris</name>
    <temperature><min>20</min><max>74</max></temperature>
</city>
</WeatherForecast>
```

You could also use a namespace for the weather forecast for the countries.

XML in Many Languages

Storing XML documents in a language other than English requires some characters not used in the English language. These characters are encoded if not stored in Unicode. Notepad allows you to store text files, in this case XML documents, in Unicode. In Notepad on Win2K, select the Encoding option under the Save As menu option.

When reloading the XML document in a browser you simply have to alter the XML tag at the beginning of the script, to indicate that an encoding other than the default is used. Win2K (SP3) Notepad will allow storage as ANSI (the default), Unicode, Unicode big endian, and UTF-8. To allow the XML parser in a browser to interpret the contents of an XML document stored as UTF-8 change the XML tag as follows:

```xml
<?xml version="1.0" encoding="UTF-8"?>
```

Summary

In this chapter you learned that:

❑   HTML is the Hypertext Markup Language and its set of tags is predetermined.

❑   XML is the eXtensible Markup Language.

❑   XML is extensible because its metadata (set of tags) is completely dynamic and can be extended.

❑   XSL stands for eXtensible Style Sheets.

❑   XSL allows for consistent formatting to be applied to repeated groups stored in XML documents.

❑   XML namespaces allow for the making of distinctions between different XML documents that have the same elements.

❑   XML can utilize character sets of different languages by using Unicode character sets.

❑   The XML DOM (Dynamic Object Model) allows run-time (dynamic) access to XML web pages.

❑   Different browsers and browser versions will behave differently with XML.

❑   For examples in this book, I've used Microsoft Internet Explorer version 6.0, running in Win2K (Windows 2000).

❑   The DTD (Document Type Definition) allows enforcement of structure across XML documents.

This chapter has given you a brief picture of what XML is, including a comparison with HTML and a brief summary of XSL. HTML creates web pages with fixed data and metadata. XML allows creation of web pages with adaptable data and metadata content.

The next chapter examines the XML DOM or the Document Object Model for XML. The XML DOM, like the HTML DOM, allows dynamic (run-time) access to both the data and metadata in a web page.

Exercise

1.   Which line in this HTML script contains an error?

```
1. <HTML>
2. <HEAD><TITLE>Title</TITLE></HEAD>
3. <BODY>
4. <P>This is a paragraph.
5. <P>This another paragraph.</P>
6. </BODY></HTML>
```

a.   1

b.   3

c.   4

d.   5

e.   None of the above

2. How many errors are present in this XML script?

```
<?xml>
<customers>
    <customer>
        <name>Zachary Smith</name>
        <address>
            <street>1 Smith Street</street>
            <town>Smithtown</town>
            <state>NY</state>
            <zip>11723</zip>
        </address>
        <phone>631-445-2231</phone>
    </customer>
    <customer>
</customers>
```

3. What kind of a web page is this?

```
<HTML><BODY>
<XML ID="xmlParts" SRC="cookies.xml"></XML>
<TABLE DATASRC=#xmlCookies>
    <TR>
        <TD><DIV DATAFLD="cookietype"></DIV></TD>
        <TD><DIV DATAFLD="$cookiedescription"></DIV></TD>
    </TR>
</TABLE>
</BODY></HTML>
```

4. What does XSL do for XML?

    a. Allows changes to data in XML pages at run-time

    b. Allows changes to metadata in XML pages at run-time

    c. Allows regeneration of entire XML pages at run-time

    d. All of the above

    e. None of the above

The XML Document Object Model

This chapter tells you all about the XML Document Object Model, or XML DOM for short. The XML DOM allows complete dynamic access to all the bits and pieces within an XML document. The XML DOM allows the programmer not only to get the metadata of an XML document at run-time, but also to change an XML document at run-time.

The XML DOM is similar in nature and function to that of the HTML document object model, or HTML DOM. Typically the HTML DOM is accessed using programming languages such as JavaScript, VBScript, ASP, PHP, and many others. JavaScript for instance allows access to all the parts and pieces that make up an HTML page from the document as a whole, right down to all the buttons and pieces of text — anything and everything making up an HTML web page.

> *You do not have to have a deep understanding of the HTML DOM in order to comprehend the material in this book or the XML DOM. It would help but it is unimportant. The HTML DOM simply allows dynamic access to HTML pages in a similar way that the XML DOM allows dynamic access to XML documents. In fact, the XML DOM is probably a lot easier to grasp because it is that much simpler than the HTML DOM. One of the primary advantages of using XML is its simplicity.*

In essence, the XML DOM allows programmatic manipulation of all the contents of an XML document, even allowing programmers to build an XML document from scratch and this is without ever directly accessing the XML text and elements, but merely by accessing the structure that comprises that XML document (the metadata or defining structure). This is what allows for complete dynamic access to everything in an XML document.

In this chapter you learn about the following:

- ❑ What the XML DOM is
- ❑ The primary classes of the XML DOM
- ❑ The Node and NodeList class
- ❑ The Document class

- ❑ The `Element`, `Attr`, and `Text` classes
- ❑ The `parseError` class
- ❑ The `HTTPRequest` class
- ❑ Generating XML pages

Basic XML DOM Structure

Unlike the HTML DOM, the real beauty of the XML DOM is that the XML DOM is language- and platform-independent. This makes the XML DOM exactly the same for all those languages and platforms. Just like an XML document itself, the XML DOM is a hierarchical structure of objects. In the case of an XML document, those objects are called nodes.

The word "node" is used in many fields to describe what is essentially a joint in a structure of some kind, such as the joints in a tree between branches. In computer jargon a node is often a terminal on a computer network, even down to a web browser, on any computer anywhere on the Internet. An XML document is a hierarchical structure, a little like an upside down tree. So, every single tag (element) in an XML document is a node, which is a potential branch or connection to other child nodes.

The only problem with the XML DOM is that there is a lot to it, and more than one way to get at the same thing, using different browsers from different vendors. This book focuses mostly on Microsoft products because they are the most widely used. For the purposes of this book and focusing on XML and databases, I am going to keep it simple. The first thing we need to do is examine the general structure of the DOM for an XML document, from a purely structural perspective. This structure is shown in Figure 2-1.

The actual class structure of the XML DOM is quite different from that shown in Figure 2-1. This book is not about XML, but rather about XML as it pertains to databases. So the intention is to introduce the parts of XML simply to begin with and then expand as needed as you go through the entire book. The only classes within the XML DOM that are important to this book at present are those shown in Figure 2-2.

Please understand that I am not attempting to explain the diagrams shown in Figure 2-1 and Figure 2-2. This is deliberate. For now, all I am trying to do is to give you a mental picture that is easy to imagine and remember.

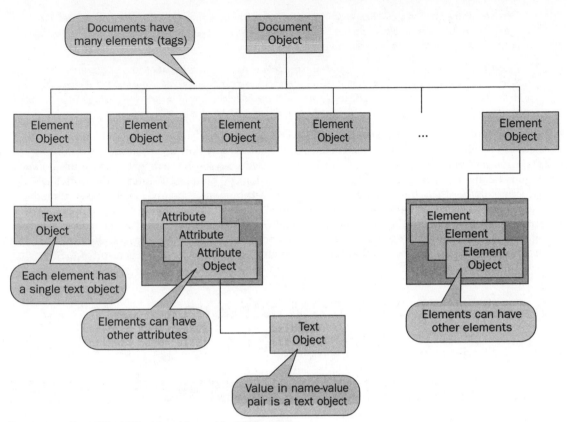

Figure 2-1: The XML DOM object hierarchical structure

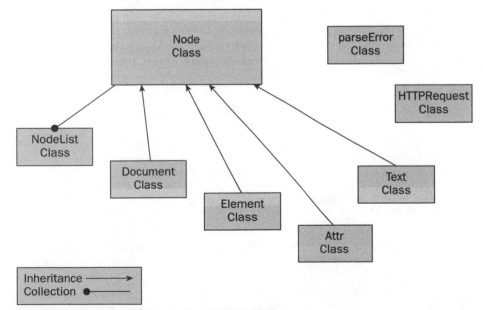

Figure 2-2: The XML DOM class hierarchical structure

Inheritance means that a child class can inherit all the attributes and methods of its parent class. For example, the Document *class inherits all attributes and methods contained in the* Node *class, unless overridden by the same named methods or attributes in the* Document *class.*

A collection is an inclusion of an array or a repetition of one class within another. For example, the NodeList *class is a repetition contained within the* Node *class, and thus a collection of nodes within a node. The word "collection" is essentially an object methodology term for the word "array" in programmatic parlance. The terms "collection" and "array" are synonymous.*

When it comes to object structure and the XML DOM, it is important to understand the difference between an object and a class. A class defines programmatically how an application is built. An object is the instantiation of the class structure at run-time. As you can see in the diagrams in Figure 2-1 and Figure 2-2, there is quite a difference between the XML DOM object structure and the XML DOM class structure. Rather than draw a complex picture of all attributes and methods in all classes, it might be best to examine each of those represented in Figure 2-2 one by one. There are parts I will omit in the interests of simplicity and because I do not think those pieces pertain directly to the material of this book. After all, this book is primarily about XML and databases, and more specifically how XML can be used both as a database and in other databases, such as Oracle Database or Microsoft SQL Server.

The Primary XML DOM Classes

The most significant XML DOM classes — the Document class, the Element class, the Attr (or Attribute) class, and the Text class — are shown in Figure 2-3.

Class	Description	Child Classes	Example	Method nodeName()	Method nodeValue()	Method nodeType()
Node	Abstraction of other classes	NodeList (Node collection)				
Document	Root node	Element collection	<populationInThousands>			9 (DOCUMENT_NODE)
Element	Element or tag	Text	<country>	country		1 (ELEMENT_NODE)
Attr	An attribute name-value pair	Text	<country name="Germany">	name	Germany	2 (ATTRIBUTE_NODE)
Text	Textual value in element or attribute		<country> <pop>24 mill</pop> </country>	population	24 million	3 (TEXT_NODE)

Figure 2-3: The most significant XML DOM classes

The classes shown in Figure 2-3 generally perform the following functions:

❑   Node **class and** NodeList **class:** The Node class is an abstract of many other classes in the XML DOM, including the Document, Element, Attr, and Text classes. The NodeList class contains a collection of Node class objects within each node object instantiation of the Node class.

❑   Document **class:** Contains the entire XML document including all elements (tags) and text. Elements are metadata and text is data. So, the Document class contains all structural metadata and data.

It is important to remember that the XML DOM provides direct programmatic (or dynamic) access to both metadata and data.

❑ Element **class:** Every tag in an XML document is represented by an iteration of (a copy of or an object of) the Element class. Within every element are zero or more child elements.

❑ Attr **class:** Every element can have attributes helping to refine the behavior of specific Element class objects.

❑ Text **class:** The data (not the metadata) is contained within Text class iteration objects.

All details in figures in this chapter are deliberately sparse because the names of attributes and nodes are assumed to be intuitive. In others words, a method's name describes exactly what its function is. Anything not detailed is self-explanatory. It is what it is, nothing more, nothing less. Also, less cluttered diagrams are so much easier to read.

The Node Class

The Node class is essentially an abstraction of all inherited classes. The Node class contains abstracted definitions of classes inherited from it. The Document class is a good example of a class inheriting attributes and methods from the Node class. However, all the primary XML DOM classes inherit attributes and methods from the Node class. Thus the Node class is an abstraction of the Document, Element, Attr, and Text classes.

An abstracted class is a little like a generalized class as it takes all the attributes and methods common to its child classes, and removes them to itself as a single abstracted class. The child classes then inherit those attributes and methods from the abstracted parent class. In this case, the parent class is the Node class, which is of course the abstracted class. Use of the word "abstract" defines the Node class as a summary or abstract of all the important points about other classes in the XML DOM. Essentially, it's the same thing as the abstract of a document such as a scientific paper summarizing all the key points of that paper.

Because the Node class is an abstraction, it contains attributes and methods that can be used by all inherited classes, as shown in Figure 2-4.

Attribute	
attributes	
childNodes	
firstChild	
lastChild	
namespaceURL	
nextSibling	
nodeName	
nodeType	
nodeValue	
ownerDocument	The root node (Document object)
parentNode	
prefix	Returns the namespace prefix of a node
previousSibling	
text	
xml	Returns the XML of a node and all its children

Method	
appendChild(newnode)	
cloneNode(boolean)	True clones all child nodes as well
hasChildNodes()	
insertBefore(newnode,beforenode)	
removeChild(nodename)	
replaceChild(newnode,oldnode)	
selectNodes(pattern)	
selectSingleNode(pattern)	
transformNode(XSL)	Transforms XML using XSL

Figure 2-4: The XML DOM Node class attributes and methods that are inherited by child classes within the XML DOM

In Figure 2-4 inheritance implies, for example, that the attributes collection can be accessed at the Node class level, as shown in the following example:

```
Node.attributes
```

And at the inherited level for the Document class, as in:

```
Document.attributes
```

And similarly as applied to the Element class, as in:

```
Element.attributes
```

The same does not apply to the Attr class because each instantiation of the Attr class creates a single attribute object. A single attribute is not a collection of attributes. In other words, attributes do not have attribute collections of their own.

The same applies to both attributes and methods. So, for the Node class method appendChild(newnode) the same applies as shown here:

```
Node.appendChild("newChildNode")
```

And for the Document class:

```
Document.appendChild("newChildNode")
```

And the Element class:

```
Element.appendChild("newChildNode")
```

The NodeList Class

The NodeList class is a little like an array or collection contained within the Node class. The NodeList class can be very useful for iterating through objects contained within the Node class structure.

Iterating through an array implies scrolling through an array one by one, programmatically. This gives complete access to all child objects contained within each node of an XML document.

The NodeList class can be used to retrieve an entire XML document, or a subset thereof, including the nodes and all child nodes contained within that node. Figure 2-5 shows the attributes and methods for the NodeList class.

Attribute		Method	
length	Number of nodes	item(index)	Returns the referenced node at the array subscript
		nextNode()	
		reset()	Sets the list of node objects back to the first node

Figure 2-5: The XML DOM NodeList class is an array or collection of nodes within an XML document.

The NodeList class could be accessed as a part of the childNodes Node class collection as follows:

```
xmlDoc.documentElement.childNodes.item(0)
```

The preceding example uses the Node class childNodes collection, and finds all the text values within the first element of the root node of an XML document.

The NamedNodeMap Class

Unlike the NodeList class, which is an ordered collection, the NamedNodeMap class is an unordered collection. All this means is that it has to access as an iteration through an array. The only attribute of a NamedNodeMap class is length, determining the number of items in the collection. The Node class attributes property is a NamedNodeMap class object.

Try It Out   Using the Node Class

This is an XML document representing all states in the United States and some of the provinces in Canada. The data in this XML document is intentionally unsorted. Assume that this file is called countries.xml:

```
<?xml version="1.0" ?>
<countries>
   <country name="Canada">
      <state name="Alberta">AB</state>
      <state name="Nova Scotia">NS</state>
      <state name="British Columbia">BC</state>
      <state name="Quebec">QB</state>
      <state name="Ontario">ON</state>
   </country>
   <country name="United States">
      <state name="Colorado">CO</state>
      <state name="Connecticut">CT</state>
      <state name="Delaware">DE</state>
      <state name="Florida">FL</state>
      <state name="Georgia">GA</state>
      <state name="Hawaii">HI</state>
      <state name="Iowa">IA</state>
      <state name="Idaho">ID</state>
      <state name="Illinois">IL</state>
      <state name="Indiana">IN</state>
      <state name="Kansas">KS</state>
      <state name="Kentucky">KY</state>
      <state name="Louisiana">LA</state>
      <state name="Massachusetts">MA</state>
      <state name="Maryland">MD</state>
      <state name="Maine">ME</state>
      <state name="Minnesota">MN</state>
      <state name="Missouri">MO</state>
      <state name="Mississippi">MS</state>
      <state name="Montana">MT</state>
      <state name="North Carolina">NC</state>
      <state name="North Dakota">ND</state>
      <state name="New Hampshire">NH</state>
      <state name="New Jersey">NJ</state>
```

```
            <state name="Nebraska">NE</state>
            <state name="New Mexico">NM</state>
            <state name="Nevada">NV</state>
            <state name="New York">NY</state>
            <state name="Ohio">OH</state>
            <state name="Oklahoma">OK</state>
            <state name="Oregon">OR</state>
            <state name="Pennsylvania">PA</state>
            <state name="Rhode Island">RI</state>
            <state name="South Carolina">SC</state>
            <state name="South Dakota">SD</state>
            <state name="Tennessee">TN</state>
            <state name="Texas">TX</state>
            <state name="Utah">UT</state>
            <state name="Vermont">VEM</state>
            <state name="Virginia">VA</state>
            <state name="Washington">WA</state>
            <state name="Wisconsin">WI</state>
            <state name="West Virginia">WV</state>
            <state name="Wyoming">WY</state>
            <state name="California">CA</state>
            <state name="Arizona">AZ</state>
            <state name="Arkansas">AR</state>
            <state name="Alabama">AL</state>
            <state name="Alaska">AK</state>
            <state name="Michigan">MI</state>
       </country>
    </countries>
```

Find the type, name, and value of the node for the second to last state in the XML document. Do not use the `Node` class `nodeValue` attribute. The type, name, and value of a node can be found using the `Node` class `nodeType`, `nodeName`, and `text` attributes.

Follow these steps to create an HTML file that includes a JavaScript `<SCRIPT>` tag section and that includes the appropriate XML DOM scripting commands in order to retrieve the required values:

1. Create an HTML file as follows:

```
<HTML><BODY>
<SCRIPT LANGUAGE="JavaScript">
</SCRIPT>
</BODY></HTML>
```

2. Create the XML document object in the XML DOM and load the XML document into the variable:

```
<HTML><BODY>
<SCRIPT LANGUAGE="JavaScript">
var xmlDoc = new ActiveXObject("Microsoft.XMLDOM");
xmlDoc.load("countries.xml");
</SCRIPT>
</BODY></HTML>
```

3. Add a variable to find the targeted element, the second to last state in the XML document, which happens to be in the second country, the United States, and is the state of Alaska:

```
<HTML><BODY>
<SCRIPT LANGUAGE="JavaScript">
var xmlDoc;
xmlDoc = new ActiveXObject("Microsoft.XMLDOM");
xmlDoc.load("countries.xml");
var root = xmlDoc.documentElement.lastChild.lastChild.previousSibling;
</SCRIPT>
</BODY></HTML>
```

In the preceding code, the variable called `root` is set to the `lastChild` (the last element in the root node), which is the last country (the United States). The `lastChild.lastChild` is the last state in the United States. `previousSibling` finds the second to last state in the United States (the second to last state in the XML document).

4. Last but not least, return the node type, node name, and value using the `Node` class `nodeType`, `nodeName`, and `text` attributes:

```
<HTML><BODY>
<SCRIPT LANGUAGE="JavaScript">
var xmlDoc = new ActiveXObject("Microsoft.XMLDOM");
xmlDoc.load("countries.xml");
var root = xmlDoc.documentElement.lastChild.lastChild.previousSibling;
document.write("nodeType  :" + root.nodeType + "<BR>");
document.write("nodeName  :" + root.nodeName + "<BR>");
document.write("text :" + root.text + "<BR>");
</SCRIPT>
</BODY></HTML>
```

The final result looks as shown in Figure 2-6.

Figure 2-6: Working with the XML DOM Node class

How It Works

You created an HTML file that included a JavaScript section. You then created an XML document variable object, loading an XML document into that document object variable. Next you created a variable and set it to the previous sibling of the last child, of the last child. In other words, you parsed (scanned through) the XML document and found the last child element in the root node, which is the United States. Within the last element you found its last node and you found Michigan. Then you found the node previous to Michigan, which is Alaska. Once again, the elements in this document are not sorted in any particular order — this is intentional. Later on in this book you learn ways to sort data that do not include manually rearranging an XML document in a text editor. It is much easier to let a computer do things such as sorting for you. In the last step you used various attributes of the node you had found (Alaska) to dump information onto the browser display. This demonstrates programmatic access to an XML document, regardless of its specific data content, or even whether or not it is sorted.

There is a possibility that some of the scripts here may not run on your computer, depending on your operating system, the browser you are using, the version of the browser you are using, and even some of the security settings in your browser. I do not suggest changing any security settings, or anything else on your computer, just to get examples running. Most examples are displayed in working order in figures anyway.

The Document Class

The Document class attributes and methods are shown in Figure 2-7. The grayed out sections show all the attributes and methods that are inherited from the Node class. Inherited attributes and methods can be executed against a node object (instantiation of a Node class) or against a document object (instantiation of the Document class) because they are inherited. Inheritance means that a document object automatically has access to all the goodies in the Node class, plus anything overriding the Node class by the Document class. By definition this also makes the Node class an abstracted class of the Document class. That is what inheritance is.

Again, most attributes and methods are self-explanatory.

> **Grayed out attributes and methods are inherited from a parent class but are still applicable to, and usable on, document objects instantiated from this class.**

The following is an XML document representing a group of customers:

```
<?xml version="1.0" ?>
<customers>
    <customer>
        <name phone="631-445-2231">Zachary Smith</name>
        <address>
            <street>1 Smith Street</street>
            <town>Smithtown</town>
            <state>NY</state>
```

```
            <zip>11723</zip>
        </address>
    </customer>
    <customer>
        <name phone="516-456-5467">Jim Jones</name>
        <address>
            <street>25 Amery Street</street>
            <town>Jones Beach</town>
            <state>NY</state>
            <zip>11744</zip>
        </address>
    </customer>
    <customer>
        <name phone="631-123-4567">Joe Bloggs</name>
        <address>
            <street>PO Box 4261</street>
            <town>New York</town>
            <state>NY</state>
            <zip>22451</zip>
        </address>
    </customer>
    <customer>
        <name phone="212-123-5566">James Bloggs</name>
        <address>
            <street>25 5th Street</street>
            <town>Manhattan</town>
            <state>NY</state>
            <zip>11124</zip>
        </address>
    </customer>
</customers>
```

Attribute		Method	
documentElement	Root element	abort()	Abort an XML document
parseError		createAttribute("name")	
preserveWhiteSpace	True if default of white space preservation is set	createElement("name")	
readyState	XML document current state	createNode(type,name,ns)	
url	Most recently loaded XML	createTextNode("text")	
attributes		getElementById("id")	Get element with ID
childNodes		getElementsByTagName("name")	Get node as a NodeList object
firstChild		load("URL" | "text")	Load an XML document
lastChild			
namespaceURL		nodeFromID(id)	Get node with ID
nextSibling		save(obj)	Store an XML document
nodeName		appendChild(newnode)	
nodeType		cloneNode(boolean)	True clones all child nodes as well
nodeValue		hasChildNodes()	
ownerDocument	The root node (Document object)	insertBefore(newnode,beforenode)	
parentNode		removeChild(nodename)	
prefix	Returns the namespace prefix of a node	replaceChild(newnode,oldnode)	
previousSibling		selectNodes(pattern)	
text		selectSingleNode(pattern)	
xml	Returns the XML of a node and all its children	transformNode(XSL)	Transforms XML using XSL

Figure 2-7: The XML DOM Document class

Figure 2-8 shows the same group of customers as before, but from within a browser.

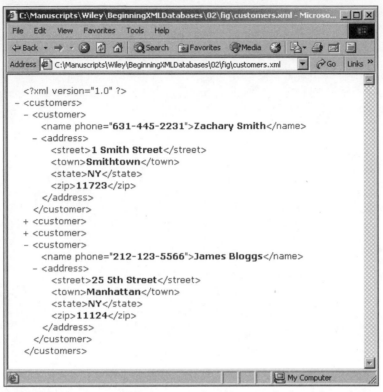

```
C:\Manuscripts\Wiley\BeginningXMLDatabases\02\fig\customers.xml - Microso...
File   Edit   View   Favorites   Tools   Help
⇐ Back ▾  ⇒ ▾  ⊗  ⁑  ⌂   ⚲ Search  ⭐ Favorites  ⧉Media  ⊚  ⬚▾ ⬚ ⬚ ⬚
Address  ⬚ C:\Manuscripts\Wiley\BeginningXMLDatabases\02\fig\customers.xml  ▾  ⬚ Go  Links »

  <?xml version="1.0" ?>
- <customers>
  - <customer>
      <name phone="631-445-2231">Zachary Smith</name>
    - <address>
        <street>1 Smith Street</street>
        <town>Smithtown</town>
        <state>NY</state>
        <zip>11723</zip>
      </address>
    </customer>
  + <customer>
  + <customer>
  - <customer>
      <name phone="212-123-5566">James Bloggs</name>
    - <address>
        <street>25 5th Street</street>
        <town>Manhattan</town>
        <state>NY</state>
        <zip>11124</zip>
      </address>
    </customer>
  </customers>

⬚                                          🖳 My Computer
```

Figure 2-8: Viewing an XML document in a browser shows a clear picture of hierarchical structure

Now let's build an HTML page using JavaScript in order to access parts of the XML document. Start by creating the initial tags for an HTML page:

```
<HTML>
<HEAD><TITLE>The XML DOM in JavaScript</TITLE></HEAD>
<BODY>
</BODY></HTML>
```

Next, create the JavaScript tag and open the XML document as an ActiveX object and using the Document class load method:

```
<HTML>
<HEAD><TITLE>The XML DOM in JavaScript</TITLE></HEAD>
<BODY>

<SCRIPT LANGUAGE="JavaScript">

var xmlDoc;
```

```
xmlDoc = new ActiveXObject("Microsoft.XMLDOM");
xmlDoc.load("customers.xml");

</SCRIPT>

</BODY></HTML>
```

Finally, put the Document class object into a variable using the documentElement attribute, the Node class childNodes attribute (inherited), and the NodeList class item collection (inherited). This example finds the first element within the root node and displays it:

```
<HTML>
<HEAD><TITLE>The XML DOM in JavaScript</TITLE></HEAD>
<BODY>

<SCRIPT LANGUAGE="JavaScript">

var xmlDoc;
xmlDoc = new ActiveXObject("Microsoft.XMLDOM");
xmlDoc.load("customers.xml");

var root = xmlDoc.documentElement.childNodes.item(0);
document.write(root.xml);

</SCRIPT>

</BODY></HTML>
```

Figure 2-9 shows the result of running the preceding HTML code.

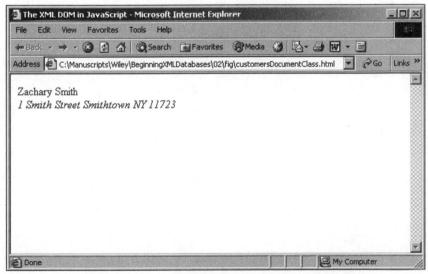

Figure 2-9: Using JavaScript and the XML DOM to view an XML document

The Document class also has something specific to Document class instantiated objects called *events*. An event is a function or process that executes when the specified events occur to an XML document. These functions can have custom code in them (programmed specifically by a programmer for each XML document):

❑ `Document.OnDataAvailable="GoDoThis"`: Executes when an XML document becomes available.

❑ `Document.OnReadyStateChange="GoDoThis"`: Executes when an XML document `ReadyState` attribute changes.

❑ `Boolean = OnTransformNodeBoolean`: Executes before a node is transformed by an XSL transformation.

Demonstrating Document class events is beyond the scope of this book.

The Element Class

The Element class comprises the definitional structure for all the elements or tags created and placed into an XML document. Figure 2-10 shows all the interesting attributes and methods for the Element class. Once again, all is self-explanatory and including examples at this stage would probably just be excess.

Attribute		Method	
tagName	The name of the element (the tag)	getAttribute(name)	Uses an attribute name to find a value
attributes		getAttributeNode(name)	Finds an Attr object containing a name-value pair
childNodes		hasAttribute()	
firstChild		item()	
lastChild		normalize()	Combines all subtrees in a tree
namespaceURL		removeAttribute(name)	Destroys the value of an attribute
nextSibling		removeAttributeNode(name)	Destroys an attribute node
nodeName		setAttribute(name,value)	Sets an attribute value
nodeType		setAttributeNode(name)	Adds an attribute to an element
nodeValue		appendChild(newnode)	
ownerDocument	The root node (Document object)	cloneNode(boolean)	True clones all child nodes as well
parentNode		getElementByTagName("name")	
prefix	Returns the namespace prefix of a node	hasChildNodes()	
previousSibling		insertBefore(newnode,beforenode)	
text		removeChild(nodename)	
xml	Returns the XML of a node and all its children	replaceChild(newnode,oldnode)	
		selectNodes(pattern)	
		selectSingleNode(pattern)	
		transformNode(XSL)	Transforms XML using XSL

Figure 2-10: The XML DOM Element class contains all the tags in an XML document.

> **Grayed out attributes and methods are inherited from a parent class but are still applicable to, and usable on, document objects instantiated from this class.**

Using the previous example again, we can use the Element class tagName attribute to return the names of elements:

```
<HTML>
<HEAD><TITLE>The XML DOM in JavaScript</TITLE></HEAD>
<BODY>

<SCRIPT LANGUAGE="JavaScript">

//Create the object:

var xmlDoc;
xmlDoc = new ActiveXObject("Microsoft.XMLDOM");
xmlDoc.load("customers.xml");

//Put the object into a variable
var root = xmlDoc.documentElement.childNodes.item(0);

document.writeln("Root : " + root.tagName + "<BR>");

for (i = 0; i < root.childNodes.length; i++)
{
   document.writeln("   Parent " + i + ": "
      + root.childNodes.item(i).tagName + "<BR>");
   child = root.childNodes.item(i);
   for (j = 0; j < child.childNodes.length; j++)
   {
      document.writeln("      Child " + j + ": "
         + child.childNodes.item(j).tagName + "<BR>");
   }
}

</SCRIPT>

</BODY></HTML>
```

The result of the preceding script is shown in Figure 2-11.

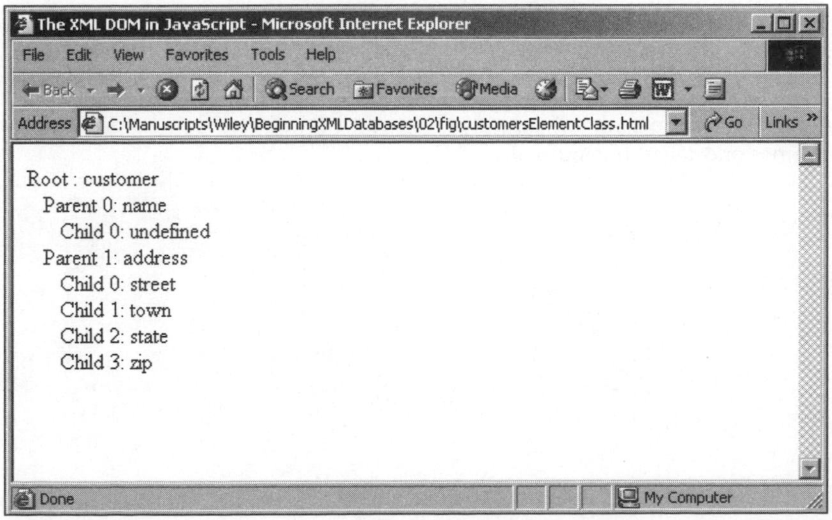

Figure 2-11: Using JavaScript and the XML DOM to view XML document elements

The Attr Class

The Attr (Attribute) class is nice and easy, having only three attributes (one is irrelevant to this text) and no methods. The two relevant attributes are shown in Figure 2-12.

Attribute	
name	Attribute name
value	Attribute value

Figure 2-12: The XML DOM Attr (attribute) class *has no* inherited attributes *or* methods.

It is important to understand that XML document Attr class objects are name-value pairs attached to an element:

<address **phone="631-445-2231"**>

Attr class objects are not part of the XML document hierarchical structure itself. In other words, Attr class objects do not define metadata structures within an XML document because they are not tags (elements). Elements make up structure. Attr class objects refine only properties of elements, which is the semantics of the word attributes in this context. The result is that the Attr class does not inherit attributes and methods from the other classes.

> *The* Attr *class does not inherit attributes and methods from other classes in the XML DOM, such as* Node, Document, *and* Element *classes.*

Attr class attributes can be utilized as follows:

❑ Attr.Name: The name of an attribute as in the boldface section here:

```
<country name="Germany">
```

❑ Attr.Value: Allows recovery of or setting of the value of an attribute:

```
<country name="Germany">
```

Using the previous example again, you can use the Attr (attribute) class name and value attributes to return the names and telephone numbers:

```
<HTML>
<HEAD><TITLE>The XML DOM in JavaScript</TITLE></HEAD>
<BODY>

<SCRIPT LANGUAGE="JavaScript">

//Create the object:

var xmlDoc;
```

```
xmlDoc = new ActiveXObject("Microsoft.XMLDOM");
xmlDoc.load("customers.xml");

var names = xmlDoc.getElementsByTagName("name");

for (i = 0; i < names.length; i++)
{
   document.write(names.item(i).attributes(0).name + " "
      + names.item(i).attributes(0).value + "<BR><BR>");
}

</SCRIPT>

</BODY></HTML>
```

The result of the preceding script is shown in Figure 2-13.

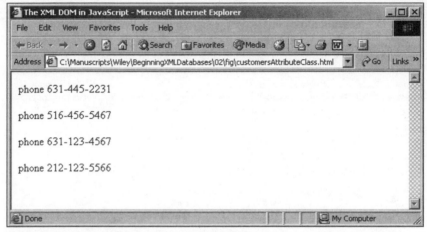

Figure 2-13: Using JavaScript and the XML DOM to view an XML document's element attributes

The Text Class

The Text class gives structure and access to the data (textual parts) within an XML document. Figure 2-14 shows all the interesting attributes and methods for the Text class.

> **Grayed out attributes and methods are inherited from a parent class but are still applicable to, and usable on, document objects instantiated from this class.**

Attribute		Method	
data	Text value	appendData(string)	Appends a value to the end of a text object
length	Character length of text data	deleteData(offset,count)	Deletes a substring from a text object
attributes		insertData(offset,string)	Adds to a text object at an offset
childNodes		splitText(offset)	Splits a node into two text objects
firstChild		substringData(offset,count)	Gets a substring from a text object
lastChild		appendChild(newnode)	
namespaceURL		cloneNode(boolean)	True clones all child nodes as well
nextSibling			
nodeName		getElementByTagName("name")	
nodeType		hasChildNodes()	
nodeValue		insertBefore(newnode,beforenode)	
ownerDocument	The root node (Document object)	removeChild(nodename)	
parentNode		replaceChild(newnode,oldnode)	
prefix	Returns the namespace prefix of a node	selectNodes(pattern)	
previousSibling		selectSingleNode(pattern)	
text			
xml	Returns the XML of a node and all its children		

Figure 2-14: The XML DOM Text class contains values between tag elements.

And yet again, using the previous example I have added another line to the JavaScript for loop to display the Text class object for the customer <name> element:

```
<HTML>
<HEAD><TITLE>The XML DOM in JavaScript</TITLE></HEAD>
<BODY>

<SCRIPT LANGUAGE="JavaScript">

//Create the object:

var xmlDoc;
xmlDoc = new ActiveXObject("Microsoft.XMLDOM");
xmlDoc.load("customers.xml");

var names = xmlDoc.getElementsByTagName("name");

for (i = 0; i < names.length; i++)
{
   document.write(names.item(i).text + ": "
      + names.item(i).attributes(0).name + " "
      + names.item(i).attributes(0).value + "<BR><BR>");
}

</SCRIPT>

</BODY></HTML>
```

The result of the preceding script is shown in Figure 2-15.

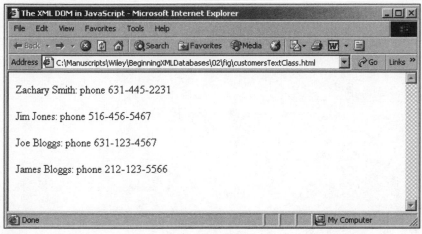

Figure 2-15: Using JavaScript and the XML DOM to view an XML document's element text values

More Obscure XML DOM Classes

In this section you read about and experiment with non-structural and somewhat non-central XML DOM classes. Let's begin with the parseError class.

The parseError Class

The parseError class is exclusive to Microsoft and Internet Explorer. It can be used to get details of what an error is, should one have occurred, as an XML document is loaded and parsed in the browser. Figure 2-16 shows all the interesting attributes and methods for the parseError class.

Attribute	
errorCode	An integer error code
reason	
line	XML document error line number
linepos	Position of error in the line
srcText	The code of the line causing the error
url	URL of the erroneous XML document
filepos	Error position in file

Figure 2-16: The XML DOM parseError class can contain error details.

Here is an example XML document containing a very simple error. The start element <World> does not match the ending element <world> because the case of the two element names is different:

```
<?xml version="1.0"?>
<WORLD>
    <countries>
        <country>
            <name>Canada</name>
            <states>
                <state>
                    <name>Quebec</name>
                    <cities>
                        <city>
                            <name>Montreal</name>
                            <type>French</type>
                        </city>
                    </cities>
                </state>
                <state>
                    <name>British Columbia</name>
                    <cities>
                        <city>
                            <name>Vancouver</name>
                            <type>Nice</type>
                        </city>
                    </cities>
                </state>
            </states>
        </country>
        <country>
            <name>United States</name>
            <states>
                <state>
                    <name>New York</name>
                    <cities>
                        <city>
                            <name>New York City</name>
                            <type>Commercial</type>
                        </city>
                        <city>
                            <name>Buffalo</name>
                            <type>Big Snow Balls</type>
                        </city>
                    </cities>
                </state>
                <state>
                    <name>California</name>
                    <cities>
                        <city>
                            <name>San Francisco</name>
                            <type>Silicon Valley</type>
                        </city>
                        <city>
                            <name>Los Angeles</name>
                            <type>Polluted</type>
```

```
                </city>
                <city>
                    <name>San Diego</name>
                    <type>Sunny</type>
                </city>
            </cities>
        </state>
      </states>
    </country>
  </countries>
</world>
```

In order to access information placed into a parseError object by the most recent error produced, the parseError class can be as in the following HTML and JavaScript code:

```
<HTML><BODY>

<SCRIPT LANGUAGE="JavaScript">

var xmlDoc = new ActiveXObject("Microsoft.XMLDOM");
xmlDoc.async = false;
xmlDoc.load("cities.xml");

document.write(xmlDoc.xml);

if (xmlDoc.parseError.errorCode != 0)
{

    document.writeln("Error " + xmlDoc.parseError.errorCode + " on line "
        + xmlDoc.parseError.line + ", position " + xmlDoc.parseError.linepos
        + "<BR><BR>");

    document.writeln(xmlDoc.parseError.reason + "<BR><BR>");

    document.writeln(xmlDoc.parseError.srcText + "<BR><BR>");

}

</SCRIPT>

</BODY></HTML>
```

Setting the preceding async *attribute to false ensures asynchronous download of the XML document. The entire document is parsed prior to executing the rest of this script.*

The result is as shown in Figure 2-17 where in the first browser window (top-left of the diagram) the error is present in the cities.xml file, as shown previously. The second browser window (bottom-right of the diagram) has the error corrected, with both root elements set as <world>.

XML is case sensitive!

Chapter 2

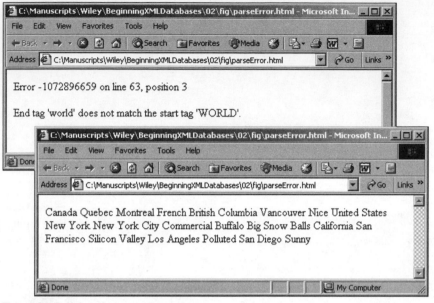

Figure 2-17: Using the parseError class

HTTPRequest Class

An HTTP request allows a web page to be changed without the page being reloaded in the client's browser. Attributes and methods for the HTTPRequest object are shown in Figure 2-18.

Attribute		Method	
onreadystatechange	State change event	abort()	
readyState	0 = not initialized, 1 = loading, 2 = loaded, 3 = interactive, 4 = complete	getAllResponseHeaders()	Get all HTTP headers
responseText	HTTP response string	getResponseHeader("headername")	Get a specific HTTP header
responseXML	HTTP response as XML	open("method","URL",async,"uname","pswd")	Method is GET to get data from the server, and POST to send data to the server
status	Status of an XML document on loading and parsing	send(content)	Send request to server
statusText	Text string equivalent of above	setRequestHeader("label","value")	Request header setting

Figure 2-18: The XML DOM HTTPRequest class passes data between XML documents and the server.

This following example tests for a URL to see if it exists:

```
<HTML><BODY>

<SCRIPT LANGUAGE="JavaScript">

var url = "http://www.oracledbaexpert.com/xml/parts.xml";
var xmlHTTP = new ActiveXObject("Microsoft.xmlHTTP");

xmlHTTP.open("HEAD", url, true);
```

```
xmlHTTP.onreadystatechange = function()
{
   if (xmlHTTP.readyState == 4)
   {
      if (xmlHTTP.status == 200) { alert (url + " OK"); }
      else if (xmlHTTP.status == 404) { alert (url + " not found"); }
      else { alert (xmlHTTP.status + ": " + xmlHTTP.statusText); }
   }
}

xmlHTTP.send();

</SCRIPT>

</BODY></HTML>
```

The parts.xml page does exist on my website at that URL address, as shown in the top left of the diagram in Figure 2-19. In the bottom right of the diagram in Figure 2-19, I set the URL variable in the preceding script to a URL that does not exist.

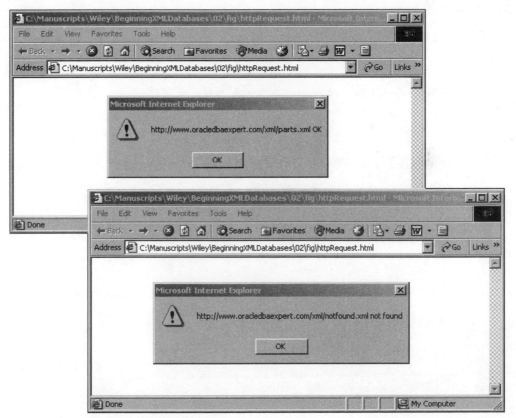

Figure 2-19: Using the HTTPRequest class

Other Classes

Various other XML DOM classes can sometimes be useful:

❑ CDATA Section **class:** Used to create structure for the CDATA section in an XML document. The CDATA section is ignored by the XML parser.

❑ Comment **class:** Comment nodes in XML documents are ignored by the parser as being part of the XML document structure. Comment nodes have a textual value but no node name.

❑ ProcessingInstruction **class:** This class contains the processing instructions in an XML document, such as the XML tag at the beginning of all XML documents (<?xml version="1.0"?>).

The ProcessingInstruction class is required when building an XML document from scratch.

Generating XML Using ASP

The following example shows you the process by which a server-side scripting language, in this can be used to generate an XML document. The scripting language is called ASP (Active Server Pages) and uses the XML DOM:

```
<%

Set XMLDoc = Server.CreateObject ("Microsoft.XMLDOM")

rem Create the root element weatherForceast and attach it to the XML document
Set weatherForecast = XMLDoc.createElement ("weatherForecast")

Set dateAttr = XMLDoc.createAttribute ("date")
dateAttr.Text = "3/2/99"
weatherForecast.attributes.setNamedItem (dateAttr)
Set XMLDoc.documentElement = weatherForecast

rem Add the first vacation resort to a list of resorts
Set resort = XMLDoc.createElement ("resort")
weatherForecast.appendChild (resort)
set name = XMLDoc.createElement ("name")
name.Text = "Meribel"
resort.appendChild (name)

rem Create the temperature element within the first resort
Set temperatures = XMLDoc.createElement ("temperatures")
resort.appendChild (temperatures)

rem Create the minimum temperatute
Set min = XMLDoc.createElement ("min")
```

```
min.Text = "80"
temperatures.appendChild (min)

rem Create the maximum temperatute
Set max = XMLDoc.createElement ("max")
max.Text = "105"
temperatures.appendChild (max)

Response.Write "<?xml version=""1.0""?>"
Response.Write XMLDoc.xml

%>
```

The preceding example consists of only a single resort because it is all hard coded and written directly into a browser by ASP. The browser response is shown in Figure 2-20.

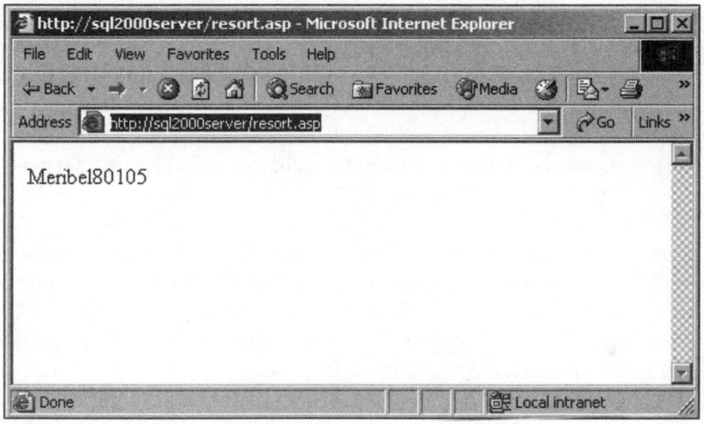

Figure 2-20: The results of a processed ASP script

If you go into the source for your browser page after you have executed the ASP script, you will find that the XML document produced will look like that shown here (I have added new lines and formatting to make it easier to read):

```
<?xml version="1.0"?>
<weatherForecast date="3/2/99">
   <resort>
      <name>Meribel</name>
      <temperatures>
         <min>80</min>
         <max>105</max>
      </temperatures>
   </resort>
</weatherForecast>
```

Summary

In this chapter you learned the following:

❑ The basic syntax of an XML document is a hierarchical tree structure containing a single root node, which contains zero or more child nodes. Every child node can have a child node tree of its own.

❑ XML tags are known as elements. Elements are marked as tags using < . . . > characters where values for those tags are enclosed within a beginning and an ending tag: `<country>Germany</country>`.

❑ The XML DOM is the XML Document Object Model, the equivalent of the HTML DOM.

❑ The XML DOM can be used to access XML documents dynamically, and at run-time, regardless of the data content of those XML pages.

❑ The most important classes in the XML DOM are the `Node` class, the `NodeList` class, the `Document` class, the `Element` class, the `Attr` (attribute) class, and the `Text` class.

❑ Other classes that can sometimes be useful are the `parseError` class and the `HTTPRequest` class.

❑ XML documents can be generated from scratch, typically using a server-side scripting language such as ASP.

The intention of this chapter has been to introduce you to the XML DOM, not provide a detailed dissertation on the subject. To find out more about using the XML DOM there are numerous other available texts. To find out more about using the XML DOM, check out *Beginning XML, Third Edition*, by David Hunter, et al. (Wiley, 2004). The next chapter digs a little deeper into the basic tools and facets of XML by examining usage of eXtensible Style Sheets, or XSL.

Exercises

1. Which of these classes is an abstracted class?

    a. `Node` class

    b. `Document` class

    c. `NodeList` class

    d. All of the above

    e. None of the above

2. What is the difference between an object and a class?

    a. There is no difference between the two.

    b. A class is a structural definition.

    c. An object is a copy of a class.

      d.   An object is an iteration of a class.

      e.   All of the above.

3.   What's wrong with this script?

```
<HTML><BODY>

var xmlDoc;
xmlDoc = ActiveXObject("Microsoft.XMLDOM");
xmlDoc.load("customers.txt");

</BODY></HTML>
```

      a.   There is nothing wrong with this script.

      b.   It's loading a .txt file.

      c.   A HEAD tag section, including a TITLE tag, is required.

      d.   The keyword *new* is missing before ActiveXObject.

      e.   None of the above.

      f.   All of the above.

4.   Which of the following commands returns a Document class object?

```
a. xmlDoc.getElementsByTagName("name");
b. xmlDoc.documentElement.childNodes.item(0);
c. xmlDoc.documentElement;
d. xmlDoc.getElementsByTagName("name").item(1).attributes(0).name
e. xmlDoc.getElementsByTagName("name").item(1).attributes(0).name
```

Extending the Power of XML with XSL

This chapter covers eXtensible Style Sheets (XSL). The intention is to keep this discussion of XSL very basic, as was done with XML and the XML DOM in previous chapters. The goal is to retain simplicity of presentation of various facets of XML, and to avoid going into enormous detail on these various topics. Once again, the motivation for this approach is to focus on XML and the way XML is used with databases, both specific vendor databases, and the use of XML itself as a native XML database.

This chapter focuses primarily on using XSL templating and filtering, which can be applied to relational databases. Data can be contained within a database in tables or native XML in a database, or outside of a database in XML document form. This chapter touches briefly on using database data directly, but mostly focuses on the use and application of XSL itself. Subsequent chapters will begin in earnest the study of XML documents and relational databases.

In this chapter you learn about:

- ❑ What XSL is
- ❑ The roots of XSL and where it is now
- ❑ Basic XSL syntax, including all elements such as processing instructions, transformations, node creation, data retrieval, and control structures
- ❑ Some advanced XSL syntax including functions, methods, and pattern matching
- ❑ Combining XSL with the XML DOM

What Is XSL?

As you saw in Chapter 1, XSL is essentially a formatting or text parsing language. Formatting refers to applying consistent pictures to XML data where repeated element structures of XML data can be displayed in a consistent manner. For example, a set of rows from a relational database table stored as an XML document can be very easily displayed by applying the same template to each row (see Chapter 1, Figure 1-2). A text parsing language is a programming or scripting language that can be used to filter in (or out) both wanted and unwanted data. In terms of XML documents, XSL can be used to dig down into the hierarchical tree structure of an XML document and retrieve only the elements you want to see displayed. In other words, using XSL as an XML document text parser allows you to select parts of an XML document to retrieve. For example, Figure 1-7 in Chapter 1 used an XSL style sheet templating operation to format and apply filtering, returning only the names of continents and countries, ignoring all population data.

The Roots of XSL

XSL began as just XSL. Now it seems to be called XSL, XSLT, XPath, and even XSL-FO. What are all these things?

❑ **XSL:** eXtensible Style Sheet Language, which is essentially an XML-based style sheet language exclusively for applying styles to XML documents. XSL is similar to CSS in function, where CSS applies styles to HTML files.

❑ **XSLT:** eXtensible Style Sheet Language Transformations allows transformations of XML documents into other formats, such as HTML or XHTML.

XHTML is a more restrictive and cleaner version of HTML.

❑ **XSL-FO:** XML Format is used to apply consistent formatting to XML documents. In some respects, XSL and XSL-FO (including XPath) are both essentially one and the same. The initial World Wide Web Consortium (W3C at www.w3c.com) defined all expression pattern matching (see XPath next) and formatting (XML-FO) as being part and parcel of XSL. Essentially, XML-FO and XPath are splits and refinements on the original expression pattern matching and formatting contained within the original W3C definition of XSL.

❑ **XPath:** A scripting language that can be used to navigate through XML documents. XPath is used to apply expressions to the elements and attributes in XML documents, allowing for pattern matching filtering on the contents of XML documents. Like XML-FO, XPath is essentially a W3C definition split and refinement on the original definition of XSL.

This chapter will not cover XML-FO and XPath specifically. This chapter is all about the basics of XSL formatting and parsing of XML documents. Thus the original form of the W3C XSL definition will be used with a Microsoft bent. Once again, the subject matter of this book is XML as it relates to relational databases and native XML databases. Therefore, any coverage of XML, the XML DOM, XSL, and other tools is kept as simple as possible. This forces the focus on the database aspect of XML technology.

The objective is to demonstrate how XSL can be used to format and filter XML documents. The objective is not to describe all the miniscule details of XML and all its related tools, toys, and scripting languages. Some of these extra scripting languages are covered elsewhere in this book, at the appropriate juncture, and if applicable to the topic at hand.

XSL syntax can be divided into three general sections: elements, methods, and pattern matching characters. Let's begin with the syntax of XSL elements.

Basic XSL Elements Syntax

XSL can be used to manipulate, sort, and filter XML data. Transformations can include well-formed HTML. Well-formed means that any HTML tag can be used, subject to the stricter syntax rules of XML. All start tags are paired with end tags and are nested correctly. Well-formed HTML can be displayed by the browser, or further manipulated by XML tools.

XSL enables you to define templates for your output into which data from the XML source is delivered. Each template defines a pattern that identifies elements in the source tree and defines the resulting output subtree to be generated. The XSL transformation processor merges data from the XML source document with the template. By combining a set of template fragments into a style sheet, XSL can be used to perform transformations driven by XML document data. These transformations are useful for making XML data and XML documents much more presentable and refinable.

A very small set of XML elemental functionality can be used to define all the formatting and filtering functionality of XSL, as shown in Figure 3-1.

Element	Element Category	Description
*xsl:processing-instruction	Processing instruction	Create a processing instruction. Previously called xsl:pi
xsl:stylesheet	Processing instruction	XSL processing instructions element
xsl:comment	Processing instruction	Comments are ignored by the XSL parser
xsl:script	Processing instruction	Insert a script in a language such as JavaScript, into an XSL page
xsl:template	Transformation	Create a formatting template
xsl:apply-templates	Transformation	Apply a formatting template
*xsl:call-template	Transformation	Execute a named template with outside parameters
xsl:element	Node creation	Create an element
xsl:attribute	Node creation	Create an attribute
xsl:copy	Node creation	Makes a duplicate of an existing node, excluding subtrees
*xsl:copy-of	Node creation	As for xsl:copy, except including subtrees
xsl:value-of	Data retrieval	Get the text for a node
*xsl:output	Data retrieval	Produce output in a specific format, such as XML or HTML
*xsl:text	Data retrieval	Dumps a text string to the output
xsl:if	Control structure	An IF statement
xsl:for-each	Control structure	A loop construct executing repeated processing to items in a collection
xsl:choose xsl:when xsl:otherwise	Control structure	Case statement
*xsl:sort	Control structure	Sort by a specified node
*xsl:variable	Control structure	Declare a variable
*xsl:parameter	Control structure	Declare a parameter

*Included in W3C definition of XSLT, not original XSL definition. XSL is Internet Explorer 5 (IE5). XSLT is IE6.Most

Figure 3-1: The XSL elements

The order and division of XSL elements shown in Figure 3-1 are sorted to allow for easiest explanation. In some cases elements not yet explained have to be included in order to facilitate explaining a particular element.

The fundamental structures of XSL syntax consist of the elements that make up XSL style sheets, as shown in Figure 3-1. Let's go through these elements one by one, as they are displayed in Figure 3-1.

Processing Instruction Elements

A node processing instruction includes a processing instruction, such as an <xsl: . . . > tag in the output. As shown in Figure 3-1, the node processing instruction elements are xsl:processing-instruction, xsl:stylesheet, xsl:comment, and xsl:script.

xsl:processing-instruction

The xsl:processing-instruction element can be used to place a processing instruction into an XSL script as follows:

```
<xsl:processing-instruction name="xml-stylesheet" xmlns=" http://www.w3.org/TR/WD-
xsl"> </xsl:processing-instruction>
```

The preceding command produces the following output:

```
<xsl:stylesheet xmlns:xsl="http://www.w3.org/TR/WD-xsl">
```

In fact, it is easier simply to hard code the specific processing instruction element, such as the xsl:stylesheet element.

The xsl:processing-instruction element has also been called the xsl:pi element in the past.

xsl:stylesheet

The root element of an XSL style sheet is the xsl:stylesheet or the xsl:transform elements.

The xsl:transform element is ignored for the purposes of simplicity in this book as it is the same semantically as xsl:stylesheet.

XSL style sheets containing HTML code do not require the xsl:stylesheet element.

The basic syntax for the xsl:stylesheet element is as follows:

```
<xsl:stylesheet version="1.0" xmlns="http://www.w3.org/TR/WD-xsl" language="
language">
```

Attributes for the xsl:stylesheet element are as follows:

❑   version: Typically this can be included in the XML document that the XSL style sheet is to be applied to, but it can be included in the XSL style sheet's xsl:stylesheet element as well.

❑   xmlns: This attribute determines the default namespace, generally pointing to the W3C definition.

❑   language: Apply a scripting language as a default for an entire XSL style sheet.

Other more obscure attributes are default-space and indent-result, both preserving white space. There is also a language attribute that can define a scripting language as applied to the entire XSL style sheet. Finally there is a result-ns attribute that defines if the output is to be parsed as HTML, XML, or otherwise. These additional parameters are a little beyond the scope of this book.

Remember this for now: the xsl:stylesheet *element can contain zero or more* xsl:template
elements. The root template contains the "/" pattern in the xsl:template *match attribute.*
When applying templates to an XML document, each template is applied as an individual container,
within the root template.

xsl:comment

The comment element causes the parser to ignore text enclosed within the xsl:comment element
like this:

```
<xsl:comment>
Place comments into an XSL script like this
</xsl:comment>
```

xsl:script

Various XSL script elements can place scripting language code blocks into XSL style sheets. Where the
xsl:stylesheet element language attribute applies a specific scripting language to an entire XSL file,
the xsl:script element allows insertion of a language-specific script into an XSL style sheet. The syntax is as follows:

```
<xsl:script language="JavaScript">
for (n in collection)
{
    document.writeln ("Subscript: " + n);
    document.writeln ("Value: " + collection[n]);
}
</xsl:script>
```

Transformation Elements

Transformation elements allow for transformations of XML data, formatting one or more parts of an
XML document into a variable output display. As shown in Figure 3-1, the transformation elements are
xsl:template, xsl:apply-templates, and xsl:call-template.

xsl:template

The xsl:template is used to define a template that can be applied to nodes of a particular type and
context. This means that one can pattern match a specific tag within an XML file, and then designate that
a tag and its contents are displayed in a manner specified by the template. This also implies that differ-
ing tags accessed within the same XSL style sheet can even have different templates applied in the same
style sheet. The result is multiple possible display formats for the same XML tree. This means that the
same data (in the same XML document) can be made to appear differently on the web, depending on
what template is applied. The syntax is as follows:

```
<xsl:template language="language" match="context">
```

Attributes for the xsl:template element are as follows:

❏ language: A template can use a different scripting language. Thus, one can change the scripting language within a specific template. As you already know, a template can apply a specific transformation to a specific part of an XML document. This attribute will be ignored at this stage as being too fiddly and complicated. I thought it was interesting to mention it.

❏ match: This attribute allows pattern matching in an XML document. Pattern matching allows the template to select those certain parts of an XML document as already mentioned.

What is really interesting about the xsl:template tag is that not only can a consistent format be applied across an entire XML document, but also you can even find separate parts of an XML document within each template, and then apply those different templates to the XML document as it is parsed.

Figure 3-2 shows an XML document containing comments about cities, within states, within countries.

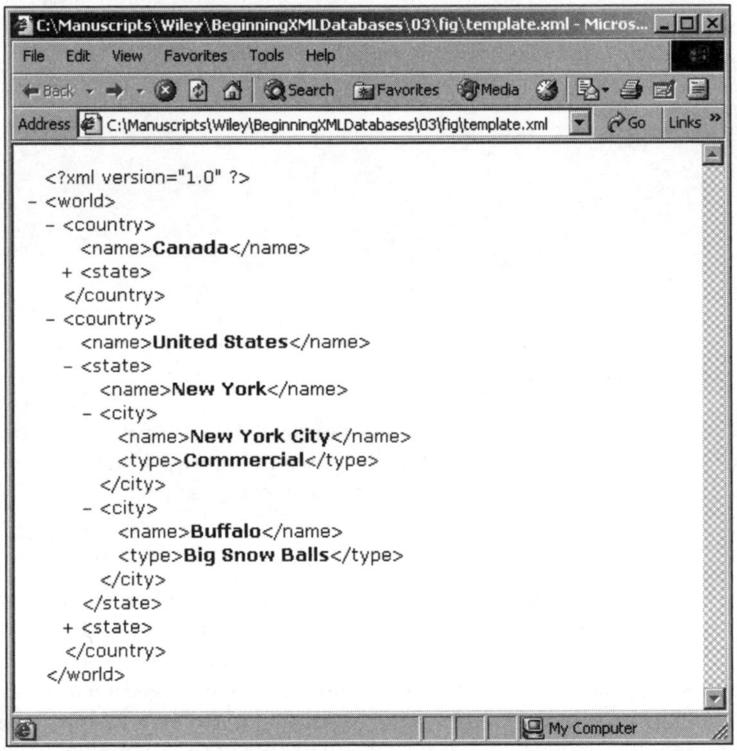

Figure 3-2: An XML document containing commentary, within cities, within states, within countries

The xsl:template element can be used to match and retrieve specific nodes. In the XSL style sheet that follows, the template is set to "/", representing the root node of the XML document. In the case of Figure 3-2, the root node is the <world> node. The xsl:value element is used to select all text values within the subtree referenced as world/countries (everything in the XML document):

```
<xsl:stylesheet xmlns:xsl="http://www.w3.org/TR/WD-xsl">
   <xsl:template match="/">
      <xsl:value-of select="world/country"/>
   </xsl:template>
</xsl:stylesheet>
```

The <xsl:value-of> *element extracts text values from a node and is covered in detail in the next section.*

The result of the previous script is as shown in Figure 3-3, where the xsl:template is digging down into the first <country> node, within the root node (<world>). It finds all the text values for <name> and <type> elements within the country of Canada. This is not too useful.

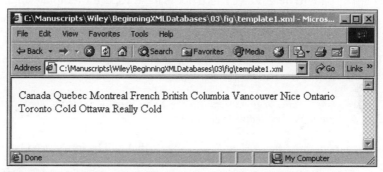

Figure 3-3: A single xsl:template finds all text values within the first matched node

The next example, as shown in the script that follows, finds all text items in the entire XML document. The result is shown in Figure 3-4.

```
<xsl:stylesheet xmlns:xsl="http://www.w3.org/TR/WD-xsl">
   <xsl:template match="/">
      <xsl:value-of select="*"/>
   </xsl:template>
</xsl:stylesheet>
```

The example shown in Figure 3-4 finds all text items, both <name> and <type> elements, for both Canada and the United States.

Figure 3-4: A single xsl:template finds all element text values within the entire XML document

xsl:apply-templates

The xsl:apply-templates element applies a template to all or part of an XML document sometimes based on a pattern match. This is the syntax for the xsl:apply-templates element:

```
<xsl:apply-templates order-by="sort-criteria-list" select="pattern">
```

Attributes for the xsl:apply-templates element are as follows:

❑   order-by: A semicolon separated list. A plus (+) sign denotes ascending order and a minus (–) sign denotes descending order.

❑   select: The pattern determines which nodes have a specific template applied to them.

At this stage the xsl:template element does not seem too useful. Combining the xsl:template element with the xsl:apply-templates element gets interesting. Remember that during the description of the xsl:stylesheet element earlier, you were told that multiple templates can be applied to individual parts of an XML document. This allows for multiple display formats across the same XML document.

The xsl:stylesheet element can have multiple xsl:template elements. The root template, indicated by the " pattern, is the first template processed.

The following script contains a few XSL syntax elements that will be introduced later on in this chapter:

```
<xsl:stylesheet xmlns:xsl="http://www.w3.org/TR/WD-xsl">

<xsl:template match="/">
   <HTML><BODY>
   <xsl:for-each select="world/country/state/city">
      <xsl:apply-templates select="name"/>
      <xsl:apply-templates select="type"/>
   </xsl:for-each>
   </BODY></HTML>
</xsl:template>

<xsl:template match="name">
   <B><U><xsl:value-of select="name"/><xsl:apply-templates/></U></B>
</xsl:template>

<xsl:template match="type">
   <I><xsl:value-of select="type"/><xsl:apply-templates/></I>
</xsl:template>

<xsl:template match="text()"><xsl:value-of/></xsl:template>

</xsl:stylesheet>
```

Unlike in previous examples where the xsl:value-of element was used to retrieve a single node, the xsl:for-each element applies a looping construct to the entire XML document. The for-each loop scans the entire XML document for all matching city names and types.

The text() method on the second to last line of the script retrieves the node text values within the <name> and <type> nodes.

HTML tags are added to the preceding XSL script, turning the application of XSL transformations to XML documents into an HTML document. Additionally, HTML tags can be added allowing for simplistic display formatting features such as colors, underline, bold, and italic fonts: essentially, anything that HTML can do.

The point of the preceding script is shown in Figure 3-5, where two templates are defined within the same XML document, and different formatting is applied within each template.

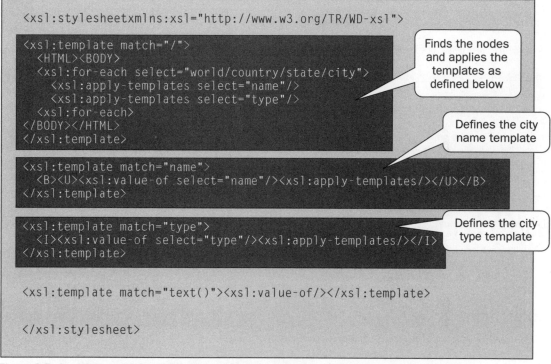

```
<xsl:stylesheetxmlns:xsl="http://www.w3.org/TR/WD-xsl">

<xsl:template match="/">
  <HTML><BODY>
  <xsl:for-each select="world/country/state/city">
    <xsl:apply-templates select="name"/>
    <xsl:apply-templates select="type"/>
  <xsl:for-each>
</BODY></HTML>
</xsl:template>
```
Finds the nodes and applies the templates as defined below

```
<xsl:template match="name">
  <B><U><xsl:value-of select="name"/><xsl:apply-templates/></U></B>
</xsl:template>
```
Defines the city name template

```
<xsl:template match="type">
  <I><xsl:value-of select="type"/><xsl:apply-templates/></I>
</xsl:template>
```
Defines the city type template

```
<xsl:template match="text()"><xsl:value-of/></xsl:template>

</xsl:stylesheet>
```

Figure 3-5: Applying multiple xsl:template elements using the xsl:apply-templates elements

Figure 3-6 shows the example script in Figure 3-5 executed in a browser. The names of cities appear with underline and bold. The `<type>` nodes containing commentary on a city appear as italicized text.

Figure 3-6: xsl:template and xsl:apply-template elements apply varying formats

xsl:call-template

The `xsl:template` allows formatting from XSL onto XML documents. The `xsl:apply-templates` element allows application of multiple templates into a single XML document. The `xsl:call-template` goes one small step further, allowing explicit naming of templates and access to templates. It also allows the ability to pass parameters into those named templates from outside of the XSL style sheet coding. Using the `xsl:call-template` without a parameter looks like this:

```
<xsl:template name="template name">
   ... template contents ...
</xsl:template>
```

And the template is executed like this:

```
<xsl:call-template name="template name">
```

Similarly, with a parameter it looks something like this:

```
<xsl:template name="template name">
   <xsl:with-param name="parameter name"/>
   ... template contents ...
</xsl:template>
<xsl:call-template name="template name" parameter="parameter name">
```

Node Creation Elements

Node creation elements allow generation of new nodes into XML documents when executed including an XSL style sheet transformation. As shown in Figure 3-1, the node creation elements are `xsl:element`, `xsl:attribute`, `xsl:copy`, and `xsl:copy-of`.

xsl:element

The `xsl:element` element creates a named element.

A named element can be accessed directly by the name of that element.

The syntax is as follows:

```
<xsl:element name="element">
```

In the above example, `name` is the name of the element to be created.

The < . . . > angle brackets are part of XSL syntax and thus the syntax line `<xsl:element name="element">` is not Backus-Naur syntax notation.

The following sample XSL code snippet creates an HTML form `<INPUT>` tag field (for data entry). This code snippet will ultimately be part of a web page using XML and XSL formatting, where the XSL code includes HTML tags, which you will see shortly:

```
<xsl:element name="INPUT">
...
</xsl:element>
```

The HTML equivalent of the preceding sample script snippet is something like this:

```
<HTML><BODY>
...
<INPUT ... >
...
</BODY></HTML>
```

There are no attributes in the preceding example yet, so let's examine attributes next.

xsl:attribute

The xsl:attribute element adds attributes to elements. The syntax is as follows:

```
<xsl:attribute name="attribute">
```

The previous sample, in the previous section "xsl:element," is enhanced using the xsl:attribute element. This sample code snippet adds attributes to the HTML <INPUT> tag. Again, this code snippet will ultimately become part of a web page using XML and XSL formatting, where the XSL code includes HTML tags:

```
<xsl:element name="INPUT">
    <xsl:attribute name="VALUE"></xsl:attribute>
    <xsl:attribute name="SIZE">40</xsl:attribute>
</xsl:element>
```

Once again, the HTML equivalent of the preceding sample script snippet is something like this:

```
<HTML><BODY>
...
<INPUT VALUE="" SIZE="40">
...
</BODY></HTML>
```

So, our example as shown previously now has both an HTML form <INPUT> tag (an input field), plus two attributes. The first attribute is called VALUE and the second attribute is called SIZE. HTML form <INPUT> tags can have both value and size attributes. The VALUE attribute determines a default value for an input field. The SIZE attribute determines the width of the field on the screen.

xsl:copy

The xsl:copy element duplicates a node to a new node having the same name, namespace, and type as the duplicated node. Attributes and child nodes of the source node will not be copied automatically. The syntax is as follows:

```
<xsl:copy>
```

The highlighted section of code shows that all text values, in all elements in an XML document, are included when the new node is being created. The `xsl:copy` element simply duplicates all the textual contents of an XML document:

```
<xsl:stylesheet xmlns:xsl="http://www.w3.org/TR/WD-xsl">
    <xsl:template>
        <xsl:copy>
            <xsl:apply-templates select="@*"/>
            <xsl:apply-templates/>
        </xsl:copy>
    </xsl:template>
</xsl:stylesheet>
```

The XML document used in this example is shown in Figure 3-2, and contains comments about cities, within states, within countries. Figure 3-7 shows the result of placing the preceding example template formatting style sheet, shown in Figure 3-2, into the XML document.

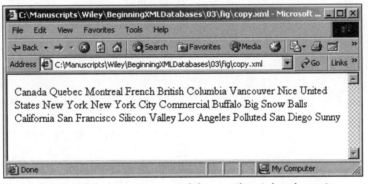

Figure 3-7: An XML document containing continental and country populations

Figure 3-7 is identical to Figure 3-4 except Figure 3-4 uses the `xsl:value-of` *element, as opposed to the* `xsl:copy` *element.*

The example in Figure 3-7 is not really doing very much but simply selecting all text values within the XML document and copying all those values to the browser.

xls:copy-of

The `xls:copy-of` element duplicates nodes including subtree nodes and all descendant nodes and attributes. Basic syntax performs a pattern match:

```
<xsl:copy-of select="pattern">
```

Following is an example application of the `xls:copy-of` element using the same XML document shown in Figure 3-2 again:

```
<xsl:template match="world/country/state/city">
    <xsl:copy-of select="name"/>
    <xsl:text> </xsl:text>
    <xsl:copy-of select="type"/>
</xsl:template>
```

Data Retrieval Elements

A data retrieval element is used to extract data from an XML document and also push data to the output. As shown in Figure 3-1, the node data retrieval elements are `xsl:value-of`, `xsl:output`, and `xsl:text`.

xsl:value-of

The `xsl:value-of` allows the extraction of text values from a node. The syntax is as follows:

```
<xsl:value-of select="pattern">
```

Here, *pattern* is a pattern matching a node. Specific details of all patterns are covered later in this chapter. Any specific patterns used before that section will be very briefly described. The default value for pattern is ".". This finds the text value of the current node.

In addition, the now fully functional XSL script shown in the following code will create an HTML form `<INPUT>` tag field (for data entry). Also, this time all the text values in the XML document will be set into the input field as a default value, as shown in Figure 3-8.

```
<?xml version="1.0"?>
<HTML xmlns:xsl="http://www.w3.org/TR/WD-xsl"><BODY>
    <xsl:element name="INPUT">
        <xsl:attribute name="VALUE">
            <xsl:value-of select="*"/>
        </xsl:attribute>
        <xsl:attribute name="SIZE">40</xsl:attribute>
    </xsl:element>
</BODY></HTML>
```

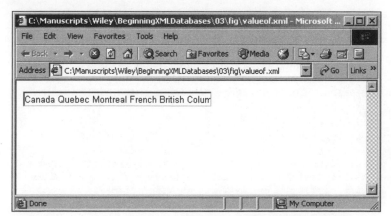

Figure 3-8: An XML document containing an HTML form input field

The HTML equivalent of the preceding sample script snippet would be something like this:

```
<HTML><BODY>
...
<INPUT VALUE="Canada Quebec Montreal French British Columbia Vancouver Nice United
States New York New York City Commercial Buffalo Big Snow Balls California San
Francisco Silicon Valley Los Angeles Polluted San Diego Sunny" SIZE="40">
...
</BODY></HTML>
```

xsl:output

The xls:output element allows production of output in a specific format, such as XML, HTML, or even text. The syntax is as follows:

```
<xsl:output select="method">
```

In the preceding line of code, method *is set to values such as* xml, html, *or* text.

xsl:text

The xsl:text element quite literally places raw text into the output. The syntax is as follows:

```
<xsl:text> this is some text </xsl:text>
```

Control Structure Elements

Control structure elements allow for a certain amount of programmatic decision-making control for XSL style sheet, as well as XML document transformations and formatting. As shown in Figure 3-1, the control structure elements are xsl:if, xsl:for-each, xsl:choose (including xsl:when and xsl:otherwise), xsl:sort, xsl:variable, and xsl:parameter.

xsl:if

The xsl:if element allows optional selection of execution paths. The syntax is as follows:

```
<xsl:if test="conditional expression">
```

If conditional expression evaluates to true, whatever is contained between the <xls:if> and </xls:if> tags will be executed. In the following example, a line is drawn using the HTML <HR> tag whenever there is a change in the name of the continent in the XML document:

```
<xsl:stylesheet xmlns:xsl="http://www.w3.org/TR/WD-xsl">
    <xsl:template>
        <xsl:apply-templates select="@*"/>
            <xsl:if test="@name[.='Africa']"><HR/></xsl:if>
            <xsl:if test="@name[.='Asia']"><HR/></xsl:if>
            <xsl:if test="@name[.='Europe']"><HR/></xsl:if>
            <xsl:if test="@name[.='Latin America and the Caribbean']"><HR/></xsl:if>
            <xsl:if test="@name[.='North America']"><HR/></xsl:if>
```

```
            <xsl:if test="@name[.='Oceania']"><HR/></xsl:if>
            <xsl:value-of select="@name"/>
        <xsl:apply-templates/>
    </xsl:template>
</xsl:stylesheet>
```

The preceding script is the same example used in Figure 1-7 from Chapter 1.

xsl:for-each

The xsl:for-each element can be used to apply a template, looping repeatedly through an XML document. In terms of XML structure, it is a little like a collection iterator, applying the same transformation and formatting to repetitive groups. A repetitive group would be each item in the collection. The syntax is as follows:

```
<xsl:for-each select="pattern" order-by="sort-criteria-list">
```

❑   select: A pattern used to find all the nodes to be looped through.

❑   order-by: A semicolon-separated list of nodes names to sort by. An ascending sort is the default and indicated by a plus sign (optional +). A descending sort is indicated by a minus sign (–).

The order-by *parameter is obsolete in favor of the* xsl:sort *element.*

The example that follows shows iteration through a loop, contained within a loop, within a loop. The outer for-each loop iterates through countries, the next inner one through states within countries, and the innermost loop within cities within states. Note how each successive loop does not have to parse for what its parent loop parses for. Each loop provides each enclosed loop with its iterative object. In other words, when you parse for cities you parse for *cities/city* within each *states/state*, and not *world/countries/country/ states/state/cities/city*:

```
<?xml version="1.0"?>
<HTML xmlns:xsl="http://www.w3.org/TR/WD-xsl">
<BODY STYLE="font-family:Arial, helvetica, sans-serif; font-size:12pt; background-
color:#EEEEEE">

<UL><xsl:for-each select="world/countries/country">
    <LI><FONT COLOR="red"><xsl:value-of select="name"/></FONT></LI>
    <UL><xsl:for-each select="states/state">
        <LI><FONT COLOR="green"><xsl:value-of select="name"/></FONT></LI>
        <UL><xsl:for-each select="cities/city">
            <LI><FONT COLOR="blue"><xsl:value-of select="name"/></FONT>
                is <xsl:value-of select="type"/></LI>
        </xsl:for-each></UL>
    </xsl:for-each></UL>
</xsl:for-each></UL>
</BODY></HTML>
```

Figure 3-9 shows the result of the XSL style sheet applied to the XML document. The XML document used in Figure 3-9 is the same example used earlier in this chapter, in Figure 3-2.

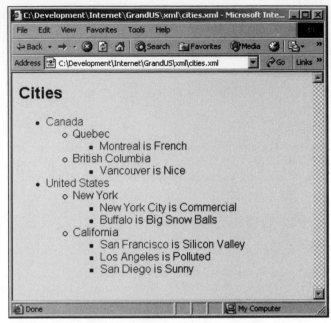

Figure 3-9: An XML document using the xls:if element

xsl:choose, xsl:when and xsl:otherwise

The xsl:choose, xsl:when and xsl:otherwise elements constitute a case statement. The xsl:choose element creates the code block. One or more xsl:when elements allow for explicit pattern matches. xsl:otherwise executes a block of code if all xsl:when conditional expressions have failed. There must be at least one xsl:when element and the xsl:otherwise element is optional. The syntax is as follows:

```
<xsl:choose>
   <xsl:when test="conditional expression">
      ...
   </xsl:when>
   <xsl:when test="conditional expression">
      ...
   </xsl:when>
   <xsl:otherwise>
      ...
   </xsl:otherwise>
</xsl:choose>
```

The following XSL style sheet breaks up the populations by the sizes of those populations, and highlights those that are excessive:

```
<HTML xmlns:xsl="http://www.w3.org/TR/WD-xsl">
<BODY STYLE="font-family:Arial, helvetica, sans-serif; font-size:12pt; background-
color:#EEEEEE">
<H2>Populations</H2><TABLE>
<xsl:for-each order-by="@name" select="populationInThousands/world/continents/
continent/countries/country">
```

```
    <TR>
      <xsl:choose>
        <xsl:when test="year1998[. $gt$ 1000000]">
          <TD><xsl:value-of select="@name"/> is <SPAN STYLE="font-weight:bold;
color:red"><xsl:value-of select="year1998"/></SPAN></TD>
        </xsl:when>
        <xsl:when test="year1998[. $gt$ 100000]">
          <TD><xsl:value-of select="@name"/> is <SPAN STYLE="font-weight:bold;
color:green"><xsl:value-of select="year1998"/></SPAN></TD>
        </xsl:when>
        <xsl:otherwise>
          <TD><xsl:value-of select="@name"/> is <xsl:value-of
select="year1998"/></TD>
        </xsl:otherwise>
      </xsl:choose>
    </TR>
</xsl:for-each>
</TABLE></BODY></HTML>
```

Figure 3-10 shows the result of running the preceding XSL style sheet script.

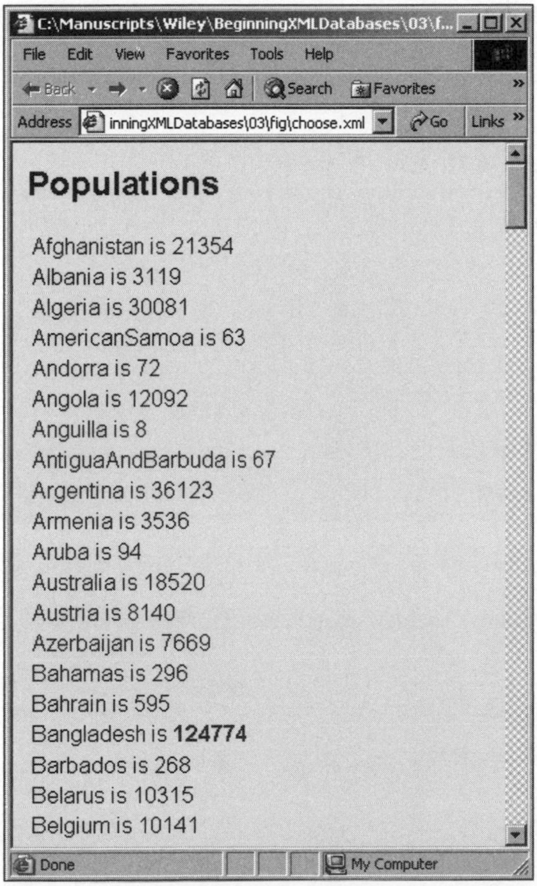

Figure 3-10: An XML document using the xls:choose,
xls:when, and xls:otherwise elements

Figure 3-11 shows a portion of the XML document used for the formatting and transformation shown in Figure 3-10.

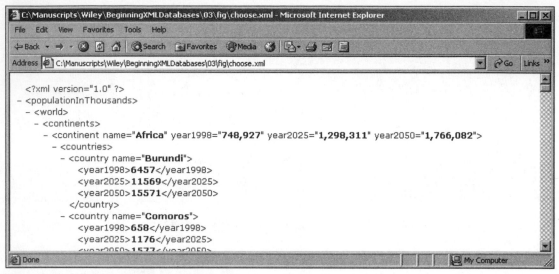

Figure 3-11: Countries and their populations

xsl:sort

The xls:sort element is used to sort the output, with either an xls:for-each or xls:apply-templates elements. There are numerous parameters, of which only the most significant are shown in the following syntax:

```
<xsl:sort select="pattern" order="ascending | descending">
```

The following example XSL style sheet uses the xsl:for-each element, and an order-by attribute to impose sorting on XML document nodes:

```
<xsl:for-each order-by="@name" select="root/ ...">
    ...
</xsl:for-each>
```

The xsl:sort elements can be used to replace the order-by attribute, as shown in the following:

```
<HTML xmlns:xsl="http://www.w3.org/1999/XSL/Transform">
<BODY>
<TABLE>
<xsl:for-each select ="root/ ...">
    ...
    <xsl:sort select="@name"/>
</xsl:for-each>
...
</TABLE></BODY></HTML>
```

The namespace for the HTML tag xmlns *(XML namespace) attribute is changed in the preceding script. This applies to the most recent version of the XSL or XSLT definition from the W3C.*

xsl:variable

The xsl:variable element can be used to declare variables in XSL style sheet scripts. Those variables can be global to the entire style sheet or local to a particular section of that XSL style sheet (within an xsl:template element. The syntax is as follows:

```
<xsl:variable name="variable-name" select="pattern">
```

As you can see from the preceding syntax, a variable can be both declared and set using a pattern match selection from the attached XML document.

A variable is then accessed in the XSL style sheet using a dollar sign ($) reference character as in the following example code snippet:

```
<xsl:stylesheet xmlns:xsl="http://www.w3.org/1999/XSL/Transform">
    <xsl:variable name="foo">funky-foo</xsl:variable>
    <xsl:template match="/">
        <xsl:copy-of select="$foo"/>
    </xsl:template>
</xsl:stylesheet>
```

The only problem with this element is that an xsl:variable *element does not create a true programming variable because* xsl:variable *elements can be set only once within the script.*

xsl:param

The xsl:param element is used to declare parameters in XSL style sheet scripts. As for the xsl:variable element, a parameter is declared locally within an xsl:template element, or globally. The syntax is as follows:

```
<xsl:param name="parameter-name" select="pattern">
```

The xls:param element can be both declared and set using a pattern match selection from the attached XML document.

A parameter is accessed in the XSL style sheet using a dollar sign ($) reference character as in the following example code snippet:

```
<xsl:stylesheet xmlns:xsl="http://www.w3.org/1999/XSL/Transform">
    <xsl:param name="foo">funky-foo</xsl:param>
    ...
    <xsl:template match="/">
        <xsl:value-of select="$foo"/>
    </xsl:template>
</xsl:stylesheet>
```

Advanced XSL Syntax

Some advanced topics of XSL syntax include functions, methods, and pattern matching characters. Most of the content in this section is a little beyond the scope of this chapter but it begins to touch on facets of XSL and XSLT, such as XPath and XQuery. XPath and XQuery are more database-centric than basic XSL formatting and templating and will be covered in later chapters of this book.

Function Versus Method

One simple question should be asked: What is the difference between a function and a method?

A function is a procedural or modular programming construct describing a procedure (built into a language or custom-built), which executes as an expression. The term "expression" suggests that a function can not only be an expression in itself, but can also be embedded within an expression. The general technical programming definition of a function is that it returns a single value.

An expression is a calculation that returns a result. It returns a single value and something that can be used by another expression.

That single value quite often is a Boolean, but not always as functions can essentially return anything because a function is mathematically an expression. A function might look something like this:

```
function ftoc(f integer)
{
    return (f - 32) * 5 / 9;
}
```

The preceding script is intended to be pseudocode and not any particular programming or scripting language.

The preceding function converts temperature readings from degrees Fahrenheit into degrees Celsius and could be expressed something like this:

```
The temperate in $city is ftoc($temperature).
```

A function takes parameters and returns a value, and can be executed independently of the content of a structure (in the case of this book an XML document). A method is different to a function because a method operates on a specific object.

Remember from the previous chapter that "object" is a term that describes an iteration or copy made from a class. A class is a structure and an object is a run-time version of that class.

So where a function is called as part of an expression, a method is called as an inherent part of an object. So, a method has direct access to data. A function can be used for any appropriate data or a function does not have to access any data at all. If you use the previous temperatures example but this time with an object methodology approach, the function becomes a method defined as part of a class:

```
create class CityClass
{
    attribute city string,
```

```
    attribute fahrenheit integer,
    method ftoc
    {
        (this.fahrenheit - 32) * 5 / 9
    }
}
```

The keyword this *means the current class (object created from this class).*

The method would be executed on an object iteration of the previously defined CityClass as something like the following:

```
London.ftoc();
```

In the preceding pseudocode snippet, London is an object created from the class called CityClass. Additionally, the method requires no input as the attribute called Fahrenheit is contained within the object itself. There is no requirement for processing that necessitates venturing outside of the object called London.

Now let's get back to XSL.

XSL Function Syntax

Functions and their syntax are as follows:

❑   current: Gets the current node including all child nodes. Parsing with the "current()" function performs the same task as parsing with ".".

❑   element-available **and** function-available: Returns true if the XSL (XSLT) element or function is available to the XSL parser in use. The following examples will both return false:

```
element-available("xsl:pi")
function-available("idonot-exist")
```

❑   format-number: Formats a number into a string display format. The following example returns 112,102.49:

```
format-number(112102.4900, "#,###.#")
```

❑   generate_id: Unique node identifier.

❑   node-set: Returns a node set, which is the root node plus the specified node only (from an XML document).

❑   system-property: Returns various values for various system properties (XSL or XSLT parser attributes), as extracted from processing instruction elements, such as:

```
system-property("xsl:version")
```

The preceding example returns 1, which represents version 1 or the XML element with <?xml version="1.0"?>

Try It Out   Using an XSL Function

This is an XML document representing all states in the United States and provinces in Canada. Assume
that the XML document is stored in a file called countries.xml:

```
<?xml version="1.0" ?>
<countries>
    <country name="Canada">
        <state name="Alberta">AB</state>
        <state name="Nova Scotia">NS</state>
        <state name="British Columbia">BC</state>
        <state name="Quebec">QB</state>
        <state name="Ontario">ON</state>
    </country>
    <country name="United States">
        <state name="Colorado">CO</state>
        <state name="Connecticut">CT</state>
        <state name="Delaware">DE</state>
        <state name="Florida">FL</state>
        <state name="Georgia">GA</state>
        <state name="Hawaii">HI</state>
        <state name="Iowa">IA</state>
        <state name="Idaho">ID</state>
        <state name="Illinois">IL</state>
        <state name="Indiana">IN</state>
        <state name="Kansas">KS</state>
        <state name="Kentucky">KY</state>
        <state name="Louisiana">LA</state>
        <state name="Massachusetts">MA</state>
        <state name="Maryland">MD</state>
        <state name="Maine">ME</state>
        <state name="Minnesota">MN</state>
        <state name="Missouri">MO</state>
        <state name="Mississippi">MS</state>
        <state name="Montana">MT</state>
        <state name="North Carolina">NC</state>
        <state name="North Dakota">ND</state>
        <state name="New Hampshire">NH</state>
        <state name="New Jersey">NJ</state>
        <state name="Nebraska">NE</state>
        <state name="New Mexico">NM</state>
        <state name="Nevada">NV</state>
        <state name="New York">NY</state>
        <state name="Ohio">OH</state>
        <state name="Oklahoma">OK</state>
        <state name="Oregon">OR</state>
        <state name="Pennsylvania">PA</state>
        <state name="Rhode Island">RI</state>
        <state name="South Carolina">SC</state>
        <state name="South Dakota">SD</state>
        <state name="Tennessee">TN</state>
```

```
        <state name="Texas">TX</state>
        <state name="Utah">UT</state>
        <state name="Vermont">VEM</state>
        <state name="Virginia">VA</state>
        <state name="Washington">WA</state>
        <state name="Wisconsin">WI</state>
        <state name="West Virginia">WV</state>
        <state name="Wyoming">WY</state>
        <state name="California">CA</state>
        <state name="Arizona">AZ</state>
        <state name="Arkansas">AR</state>
        <state name="Alabama">AL</state>
        <state name="Alaska">AK</state>
        <state name="Michigan">MI</state>
    </country>
</countries>
```

Use an XSL function to find all the full text values contained within all the `<country>` nodes of the preceding XML document. This is how:

1. Create an XSL style sheet, including appropriate HTML tags:

```
<?xml version="1.0"?>
<xsl:stylesheet version="1.0">
    <xsl:template match="/">
        <HTML><BODY>
        </BODY></HTML>
    </xsl:template>
</xsl:stylesheet>
```

2. Use the `http://www.w3.org/1999/XSL/Transform` namespace:

```
<?xml version="1.0"?>
<xsl:stylesheet version="1.0" xmlns:xsl="http://www.w3.org/1999/XSL/Transform">
    <xsl:template match="/">
        <HTML><BODY>
        </BODY></HTML>
    </xsl:template>
</xsl:stylesheet>
```

3. Add an XSL `for` loop to parse through the `<countries>` collection:

```
<?xml version="1.0"?>
<xsl:stylesheet version="1.0" xmlns:xsl="http://www.w3.org/1999/XSL/Transform">
    <xsl:template match="/">
        <HTML><BODY>
            <xsl:for-each select="countries/country">
            </xsl:for-each>
        </BODY></HTML>
    </xsl:template>
</xsl:stylesheet>
```

4. Add the xsl:value-of element using the current() function to output the resulting node text values:

```
<?xml version="1.0"?>
<xsl:stylesheet version="1.0" xmlns:xsl="http://www.w3.org/1999/XSL/Transform">
    <xsl:template match="/">
        <HTML><BODY>
            <xsl:for-each select="countries/country">
                <xsl:value-of select="current()"/>
            </xsl:for-each>
        </BODY></HTML>
    </xsl:template>
</xsl:stylesheet>
```

5. Add text and a <BR/> tag into the code to indicate which node is being output:

```
<?xml version="1.0"?>
<xsl:stylesheet version="1.0" xmlns:xsl="http://www.w3.org/1999/XSL/Transform">
    <xsl:template match="/">
        <HTML><BODY>
            <xsl:for-each select="countries/country">
                Country node: <xsl:value-of select="current()"/><BR/>
            </xsl:for-each>
        </BODY></HTML>
    </xsl:template>
</xsl:stylesheet>
```

Figure 3-12 shows the final result.

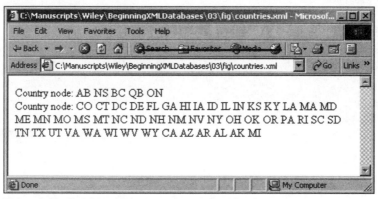

Figure 3-12: Parsing using the current() function is the same as ".".

How It Works

You created a new XSL style sheet and added HTML elements and a namespace. Then you added a for loop to scroll through all countries in the XML document. Next you pulled the text of each node within the for loop, and retrieve as the data is scrolled through. Last, you added a little more HTML text just to make it look nice.

XSL Method Syntax

Methods and their syntax are as follows:

❑ `absoluteChildNumber ("node-name")`: Collection iteration number representing the sequence of a node within a set of siblings.

Siblings are all nodes within the same parent node.

A collection iteration number is the same as a subscript number in an array.

❑ `ancestorChildNumber ("parent-node-name")`: Collection iteration number representing the sequence of the parent node (ancestor) with the parent node's set of siblings.

❑ `childNumber ("parent-node-name")`: Collection iteration number for the nodes of a parent node, relative to the parent node's siblings, where all of those parent siblings have the same node name. In other words, where parent nodes have varying names, only the specified node name is included.

❑ `depth ("node-name")`: XML document hierarchical tree depth number.

❑ `formatXXXX methods`: `formatDate`(date), `formatIndex`(integer), `formatNumber`(number) and `formatTime`(time) all format specific data type values into more readable and user-friendly formats. For output.

❑ `uniqueID ("node-name")`: An XML document is an object structure and therefore every node in an XML document has a unique identifier as a number. This function returns the unique identifier for a node within an XML document.

These methods are all inherited from the XML DOM and require the creation of XML DOM objects in order to execute. The XML DOM is already covered in Chapter 2.

XSL Pattern Matching Syntax

So far in this chapter you have seen very simple pattern matching. Figure 3-13 shows various pattern matching options available when using XSL.

Pattern	Description
/	Child operator, which selects children of the specified collection where "/" selects from the root node
//	Searches a child node recursively
.	Finds the current node
*	Wildcard selecting all elements where * will find all nodes and ba* will find all nodes beginning with the letters ba
@	Attribute prefix name allowing access to attribute string values
@*	Retrieves all attributes regardless of name
:	Separates the namespace element from the element or attribute name
!*	Applies a method to a reference node
()*	Enforcement of precedence by grouping of operations
[]	Filtering pattern
[]*	Collection indexing subscript operator

Precedence order is (), [], and // (grouping, filtering, and pattern matching)

Figure 3-13: Parsing pattern matching options for XSL

Combining the XML DOM and XSL

XSL can be used to transform XML documents into HTML web pages. XSL allows format definitions, data filtering, manipulation, sorting, and use of output template definitions. Templates can be used to display the XML document (or parts thereof) in specific ways. Multiple templates can even be used to display separate parts and subsets of an XML document in different ways. It is also possible to combine the adaptability of the XML DOM, and the formatting capabilities of XSL to produce more flexibility in the application of XML document data. This section covers a simple example just to demonstrate.

All files are stored on the server side in a web server computer called sql2000server.

The term "server side" implies the back-end servers. When you connect over the Internet to a web site, your computer connects to other computers. Those other computers are servers of one type or another, and can be web servers (servicing the web), database servers (providing database access), or other types of servers. The computer you use to connect to the Internet, running a browser, is known as a client-side computer.

There is an XML document (population.xml), an XSL style sheet (population.xsl), and an ASP script (population.asp). This is the XML document:

```
<?xml version="1.0"?>
<?xml:stylesheet type="text/xsl" href="population.xsl" ?>

<populationInThousands>
    <world>
        <areas>
            <area region="Global">
                <years>
                    <year time="1998">5,901,054</year>
                    <year time="2025">7,823,703</year>
                    <year time="2050">8,909,095</year>
                </years>
            </area>
            <area region="FirstWorld">
                <years>
                    <year time="1998">1,182,184</year>
                    <year time="2025">1,214,890</year>
                    <year time="2050">1,155,403</year>
                </years>
            </area>
            <area region="Second World">
                <years>
                    <year time="1998">4,718,869</year>
                    <year time="2025">6,608,813</year>
                    <year time="2050">7,753,693</year>
                </years>
```

```
          </area>
          <area region="Third World">
             <years>
                <year time="1998">614,919</year>
                <year time="2025">1,092,623</year>
                <year time="2050">1,494,925</year>
             </years>
          </area>
      </areas>
   </world>
</populationInThousands>
```

Next is the XSL style sheet script, as applied to the preceding XML document:

```
<?xml version="1.0"?>

<HTML xmlns:xsl="http://www.w3.org/TR/WD-xsl">
<HEAD><TITLE>Regional Global Population in Thousands</TITLE></HEAD>
<BODY>

<CENTER><FORM><TABLE CELLPADDING="5" CELLSPACING="1" BORDER="1">

<TH BGCOLOR="silver">Region</TH><TH BGCOLOR="silver">1998</TH>
<TH BGCOLOR="silver">2025</TH><TH BGCOLOR="silver">2050</TH>

<xsl:for-each select="populationInThousands/world/areas/area"><TR>
   <TD><xsl:value-of select="@region"/></TD>
   <xsl:for-each select="years/year">
   <TD>
      <xsl:element name="INPUT">
      <xsl:attribute name="TYPE">text</xsl:attribute>
      <xsl:attribute name="NAME"><xsl:value-of select="@time"/></xsl:attribute>
      <xsl:attribute name="VALUE"><xsl:value-of select="."/></xsl:attribute>
      <xsl:attribute name="SIZE">10</xsl:attribute>
      </xsl:element>
   </TD>
   </xsl:for-each></TR>
</xsl:for-each>

</TABLE></FORM></CENTER></BODY></HTML>
```

Finally, there is a server side using Active Server Pages (ASP) and VBScript (a Microsoft counterpart to JavaScript). ASP is a scripting language that executes on a server, and thus has direct access to everything on that server and everything that server has access to. For obvious security reasons, end users running an application through a browser over the Internet do not have direct access to database servers and web servers in general. End-user access is strictly controlled, particularly for OLTP databases. The controlling software is often custom-written application code.

```
<% @LANGUAGE = VBScript %>
<% Option Explicit %>
<HTML><HEAD><TITLE>The XML DOM and XSL</TITLE></HEAD>
<BODY BGCOLOR="#FFFFFF">
<%
  Dim XMLDoc, XSLDoc
  Set XMLDoc = Server.CreateObject ("Microsoft.XMLDOM")
  Set XSLDoc = Server.CreateObject ("Microsoft.XMLDOM")
  XMLDoc.async = false
  XMLDoc.load (Server.MapPath("population.xml"))
  XSLDoc.async = false
  XSLDoc.load (Server.MapPath("population.xsl"))
  Response.Write (XMLDoc.transformNode (XSLDoc))
%>
</BODY></HTML>
```

Figure 3-14 shows the result of the preceding script.

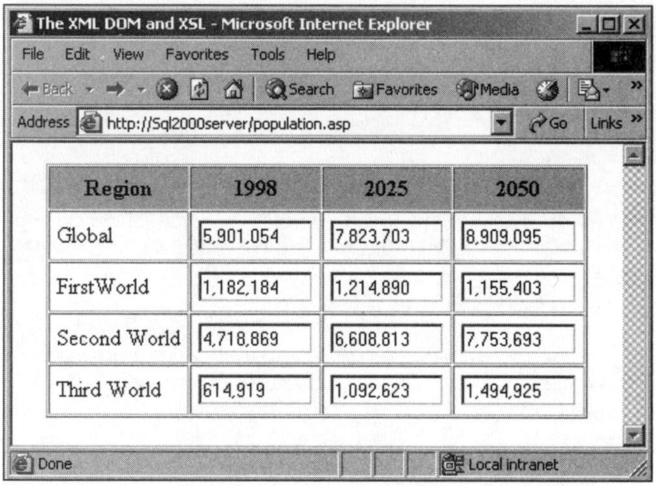

Figure 3-14: Applying XSL to the XML DOM, using ASP on a web server

Summary

In this chapter you learned about:

❑   What XSL is

❑   The roots of XSL and where it is now

❑   Basic XSL syntax including all elements such as processing instructions, transformations, node creation, data retrieval, and control structures

- ❑ XSL processing instruction elements including `xsl:processing-instruction`, `xsl:stylesheet`, `xsl:comment`, and `xsl:script`

- ❑ XSL transformation elements including `xsl:template`, `xsl:apply-templates`, and `xsl:call-template`

- ❑ XSL node creation elements including `xsl:element`, `xsl:attribute`, `xsl:copy-of`, and `xsl:copy-of`

- ❑ XSL data retrieval elements including `xsl:value-of`, `xsl:output`, and `xsl:text`

- ❑ XSL control structure elements including `xsl:if`, `xsl:for-each`, `xsl:choose`, `xsl:sort`, `xsl:variable`, and `xsl:param`

- ❑ The difference between a function and a method

- ❑ Some advanced XSL syntax including functions, methods, and pattern matching

- ❑ Combining XSL with the XML DOM using ASP

Once again, the intention of this chapter, as with the previous two chapters, is to provide a brief introduction. The primary focus of this book is XML as applied to relational databases. To find out more about using the XML DOM, numerous other texts are available, including *Beginning XML, Third Edition*, by David Hunter, et al. (Wiley 2004). The next chapter goes off on what is seemingly a little bit of a tangent, discussing SQL (Structured Query Language) database access, and then reverting back to XML. The meaning to this madness is that SQL is generally the primary programmatic tool for relational database access. The first three chapters in this book look at various ways to use XML (and related tools). Using SQL is essential to database access. In subsequent chapters use of XML, XSL, the XML DOM, and SQL will effectively be joined together into a single set of tools and tricks for access to relational databases.

Exercises

1. Which of these is `xsl:text`?

    a. Processing instruction element

    b. Node creation element

    c. Transformation element

    d. Control structure element

    e. None of the above

2. Which of these are correct?

    a. XSL stands for eXtendable Style Sheets.

    b. XML stands for eXecutable Markup Language.

    c. HTML stands for HyperText Markup Language.

    d. XSL-FO stands for XML Format.

    e. XSLT stands for eXtensible Style Sheet Language Transformations.

    f. All of the above.

3. Which of these are valid XSL elements?

    a.   `xsl:if`

    b.   `xsl:foreach`

    c.   `xsl:choose`

    d.   `xsl:sort`

    e.   `xsl:when`

    f.   `xsl:otherwise`

    g.   All of the above

Relational Database Tables and XML

This book is essentially about XML and databases. In other words, how can XML documents be used with a relational database? XML can be stored in a database as an XML document or as a text document, and can even perhaps be built into table structures. An XML document is a repository for data. A database is also a repository for data. Therefore, it makes perfect sense to state that the two are one and the same in some respects.

Previous chapters have dealt purely with XML and various ways of handling XML documents. Those methods of handling XML documents are completely unrelated to a relational database. This chapter begins by changing the direction of this book completely, examining how data is accessed within a relational database without using XML. That topic is SQL (Structured Query Language). SQL is a language used for reading data from a relational database. Additionally, when writing data to a relational database, special commands are used. These commands in their most basic forms are known as INSERT, UPDATE, and DELETE commands.

In short, because you've dealt with the basics of XML, the beginning of this chapter deals with the basics of accessing a relational database, without any involvement of XML at all. The latter part of this chapter then takes what has been covered in the previous chapters (XML, the XML DOM, XSL) and applies it to relational database technology (using SQL). The result will be access of a relational database to both produce XML documents and edit XML documents to change relational database content.

In this chapter you learn about:

- ❑   What a query is
- ❑   How to use the SELECT statement
- ❑   Filtering records with the WHERE clause
- ❑   Sorting records with the ORDER BY clause
- ❑   Summarizing records with the GROUP BY clause

❑   Getting records from two tables with the JOIN clause

❑   Nesting SELECT statements as subqueries

❑   Merging two record sets with the UNION clause

❑   How to change data in a database

❑   How to generate XML documents using basic SQL

Using SQL for Database Access

So, you need to know how to access a database using SQL. SQL is the most common form of database access. Additionally, SQL can be used to cater to merging relational databases with XML documents and other XML technology. Let's first briefly describe the basics of the SQL language.

SQL works by reading records from the tables in a relational database.

A table is the structure applied to repetitions of some data item. For example, in order to store customers in a database, you need to create a table for those customers. Those customers have names and addresses. A customer table consists of a field for the customer name and a field for the address of the customer.

A record is the name and address of each customer. Each record is a repetition of the structure of the table (the name and address fields).

SQL consists of a number of sections:

❑   **Queries:** The SELECT command is used to read data from a relational database. There are various options when using the SELECT command, which can be used to alter a query:

   ❑   SELECT **command:** Retrieve all records from a single table.

   ❑   WHERE **clause:** Retrieve some records from a table by filtering the records using a WHERE clause. The filter can be used to include a subset of a table's rows, or exclude a subset of a table's rows, or both.

   ❑   ORDER BY **clause:** Retrieve records from a table, but change the order that those records are stored in, using the ORDER BY clause.

   ❑   GROUP BY **clause:** Before returning records from a database, summarize them into fewer rows using the GROUP BY clause. You can also use the HAVING clause to filter grouped records.

   ❑   JOIN **clause:** The JOIN clause can be used to query records from more than one table. The JOIN clause allows you to merge records from two tables based on common values. There are various types of joins creating intersections, outer joins, and various other types of joins.

   ❑   Subquery: A subquery allows one query to be embedded within another query, such that one query is the calling query, and the other query is executed by the calling query. It is also possible to pass values from the calling query to the subquery. Passing values from calling query to subquery allows the calling query to determine the records that the subquery retrieves from the database, for each record retrieved by the calling query.

- ❏ UNION **clause**: The UNION clause can be used to create a composite of two queries where all records are returned from both queries as a merge of the data in two tables. Unlike a join or a subquery, both of which allow matching of values between two tables, a composite query does not allow any matching.

- ❏ **Changing data**: INSERT, UPDATE, and DELETE commands can be used to change data in a database:

  - ❏ INSERT **command**: Add new records to a table using the INSERT command.

  - ❏ UPDATE **command**: Change existing records in a table using the UPDATE command.

  - ❏ DELETE **command**: Delete existing records in a table using the DELETE command.

- ❏ **Metadata change commands**: Records stored in database tables are the actual data stored in the database, such as the names of customers. The metadata in a relational database is the structure of that data, such as the customer table. The table is the box used to store the customers in. In my example, the customer table contains a field for the customer name and a field for the address of the customer. So the metadata is the data about the data. There are various commands that allow changes to metadata. For example, to create a table for customers you would use a CREATE TABLE command. To change the customer table you could use an ALTER TABLE command. To drop a customer table you would use a DROP TABLE command.

Metadata commands are not covered in this book as they are too far removed from the topic of XML. This book is about XML and databases. XML documents are all about data, not changing the structure of data.

Let's go into some detail on the use of relational database access commands. Let's begin by examining queries.

Queries

A query is a question asked of a database. The answer to the question is that records are returned from tables stored in that database. There are various methods of querying data.

The SELECT Command

The simplest method of writing a query is using a basic SELECT statement, consisting of a SELECT statement and a FROM clause. The SELECT statement determines what is retrieved. The FROM clause determines where data is retrieved from, enhancing the SELECT statement. This is the syntax of the SELECT statement:

```
SELECT { [alias.]field | expression | [alias.]* [, field ] }
FROM table [alias];
```

This query finds all records in a table called COUNTRY, in the demographics database:

```
SELECT * FROM COUNTRY;
```

*The * in the SELECT statement fields list finds all fields in a table.*

See Appendix B for details of the demographics database, which is used for examples throughout this book.

This is a partial result of the preceding query (both records and fields have been removed from the output):

```
COUNTRY_ID  REGION_ID  COUNTRY                            CO  POPULATION       AREA
----------  ---------  -------------------------------    --  ----------  ----------
         1          1  Algeria                            AG    32930091     2381741
         2          1  Angola                             AO    12127071     1246699
         3          1  Benin                              BN     7862944      110619
         4          1  Botswana                           BC     1639833      585371
         5          1  Burkina Faso                       UV    13902972      273799
         6          1  Burundi                            BY     8090068       25649
         7          1  Central African Republic           CT     4303356      622980
         8          1  Congo                              CG    62660551     2267599
         9          1  Djibouti                           DJ      486530       21979
        10          1  Equatorial Guinea                  EK      540109       28050
        11          1  Ethiopia                           ET    74777981     1119683
```

You can also get a single field using a query like this:

```
SELECT COUNTRY FROM COUNTRY;
```

And this is a partial result:

```
COUNTRY
-------------------------------
Afghanistan
Albania
Algeria
American Samoa
Angola
Argentina
Armenia
Australia
Austria
Azerbaijan
Bahamas
```

Or you can specify to retrieve a number of fields:

```
SELECT COUNTRY, POPULATION, AREA FROM COUNTRY;
```

Again, this is the partial result:

```
COUNTRY                          POPULATION       AREA
-------------------------------  ----------  ----------
Algeria                            32930091     2381741
Angola                             12127071     1246699
Benin                               7862944      110619
Botswana                            1639833      585371
Burkina Faso                       13902972      273799
Burundi                             8090068       25649
Central African Republic            4303356      622980
Congo                              62660551     2267599
Djibouti                             486530       21979
Equatorial Guinea                    540109       28050
Ethiopia                           74777981     1119683
```

You can even execute an expression, as shown previously in the syntax definition of the SELECT statement. This query finds the population density, or the number of people per square kilometer, for each country and rounds it up to zero decimal places:

```
SELECT COUNTRY, ROUND (POPULATION / AREA, 0) "Population Density" FROM COUNTRY;
```

The result is shown here. The division by zero error is caused because some of the AREA values in the table are zero. Dividing any number by zero is impossible and thus mathematically undefined:

```
COUNTRY                            Population Density
---------------------------------- --------------------
Algeria                                          14
Angola                                           10
Benin                                            71
Botswana                                          3
Burkina Faso                                     51
Burundi                                         315
Central African Republic                          7
Congo                                            28
Djibouti                                         22
Equatorial Guinea                                19
Ethiopia                                         67
Gabon                                             6
Gambia                                            0
Ghana                                            97
Guinea                                           39
ERROR:
ORA-01476: divisor is equal to zero
```

In the preceding query and query result, the field header is renamed using the quoted string Population Density, *appearing after the expression. The quoted value changes the name of the header and not the field name in the query. The AS clause can be used to change a field name, within the current query. The AS clause will be discussed later on in this chapter when it is appropriate.*

Before going further it seems sensible to find a simple resolution for the division by zero issue. If you are executing these examples against a database add a function something like this:

```
CREATE OR REPLACE FUNCTION ZD(pINT IN INTEGER) RETURN VARCHAR2 IS
BEGIN
    RETURN NVL(NULLIF(pINT, 0), 1);
END;
/
```

The preceding function will compile for an Oracle database. If using SQL Server or a different relational database, you may have to recode for appropriate syntax.

The query result using the ZD function is as follows:

```
SELECT COUNTRY, ROUND (POPULATION / ZD(AREA)) "Population Density"
FROM COUNTRY;
```

91

And a partial query result using the ZD function is as follows:

```
COUNTRY                              Population Density
----------------------------------   ------------------
Algeria                                              14
Angola                                               10
Benin                                                71
Botswana                                              3
Burkina Faso                                         51
Burundi                                             315
Central African Republic                              7
Congo                                                28
Djibouti                                             22
Equatorial Guinea                                    19
Ethiopia                                             67
```

The SELECT statement can also use what is called an *alias*. An alias allows renaming a table during the execution of a query. An alias is defined in the FROM clause, and then used in the list of fields selected to refer to the table found by the FROM clause:

```
SELECT C.COUNTRY, ROUND (C.POPULATION / C.AREA, 0) "Population Density"
FROM COUNTRY C;
```

The division by zero error should appear again.

In the preceding query, the COUNTRY table is aliased as the letter C. Each of the fields retrieved from the COUNTRY table is then referenced using an alias.field notation. The result of the preceding query will be identical to the previous example. You will learn the real usefulness of using aliases when you read about join queries later on in this chapter.

A join query is a query that joins fields and records together between two tables, returning records from both tables.

The WHERE Clause

The WHERE clause enhances a SELECT statement by filtering out unwanted records returned by a SELECT statement. This is the basic syntax of the WHERE clause:

```
SELECT ...
FROM ...
[
    WHERE [table.|alias.] { field | expression }
            comparison
          [table.|alias.] { field | expression }
];
```

The SELECT statement and the FROM clause are mandatory. The WHERE clause is optional and is thus enclosed in square brackets as in [WHERE ...].

This query finds all countries with a population of over 100 million people:

```
SELECT COUNTRY, TO_CHAR(POPULATION, '9,999,999,990') "Population"
FROM COUNTRY
WHERE POPULATION > 100000000;
```

The preceding query uses a special `TO_CHAR` *function in order to format the output of the large numbers into a more readable format.*

Also in the preceding query, note the use of the single quote (') *character. Which types of quotation characters are used, and in which types of commands, varies from one database engine to another.*

This is the result of the preceding query:

```
COUNTRY                           Population
-------------------------------- --------------
Nigeria                             131,859,731
Mexico                              107,449,525
China                             1,313,973,713
Indonesia                           245,452,739
Japan                               127,463,611
Bangladesh                          147,365,352
India                             1,095,351,995
Pakistan                            165,803,560
United States                       298,444,215
Russia                              142,893,540
Brazil                              188,078,227
```

The `WHERE` clause can apply multiple filters to selected records. Multiple filters are placed into the same query by joining the two filters together using logical operators called `AND`, `OR`, and `NOT`. Logical operators are shown in the following syntax:

```
SELECT ...
FROM ...
[
    WHERE filter
    [
        { AND | OR } [ NOT ]
            [table.|alias.] { field | expression }
                comparison
            [table.|alias.] { field | expression }
        [ { AND | OR } [ NOT ] ...
    ]
];
```

This query finds all countries with a population over 100 million people and a population density of over 100 people per square kilometer. The two different comparisons are joined together using the `AND` logical operator (or conjunction):

```
SELECT COUNTRY, TO_CHAR(POPULATION, '9,999,999,990') "Population",
    ROUND(POPULATION / ZD(AREA)) "Population Density"
FROM COUNTRY
WHERE POPULATION > 100000000
AND ROUND(POPULATION / ZD(AREA) , 0) > 100;
```

Notice how the expression `ROUND (POPULATION / ZD(AREA) , 0)` *is used in the* `WHERE` *clause as well as retrieved by the* `SELECT` *clause. Also, the division by zero error is removed using the* `AREA` *field filter.*

This is the result of the preceding query:

```
COUNTRY                            Population    Population Density
-------------------------------    ----------    ------------------
Nigeria                           131,859,731                   145
China                           1,313,973,713                   141
Indonesia                         245,452,739                   135
Japan                             127,463,611                   323
Bangladesh                        147,365,352                  1100
India                           1,095,351,995                   368
Pakistan                          165,803,560                   213
```

And here's another example using the OR operator in addition to the AND operator:

```
SELECT COUNTRY, TO_CHAR(POPULATION, '9,999,999,990') "Population", AREA "Km sq.",
    ROUND(POPULATION / ZD(AREA), 0) "Population Density"
FROM COUNTRY
WHERE ((POPULATION > 100000000 AND (ROUND(POPULATION / ZD(AREA), 0) > 100))
OR (POPULATION < 100000000 AND (ROUND(POPULATION / ZD(AREA), 0) > 500)));
```

This query finds heavily populated countries based on population density, or just high density (a smaller country with a high population density). For example, Singapore has a relatively low population but is a very small country, more like a city-state. Singapore is very densely populated because all of its people are packed like sardines onto a small island:

```
COUNTRY                            Population     Km sq.  Population Density
-------------------------------    ----------  ---------  ------------------
Mauritius                           1,240,827       1849                 671
Nigeria                           131,859,731     910771                 145
Barbados                              279,912        430                 651
Bermuda                                65,773         49                1342
Malta                                 400,214        321                1247
China                           1,313,973,713    9326411                 141
Indonesia                         245,452,739    1811831                 135
Japan                             127,463,611     394744                 323
Singapore                           4,492,150        624                7199
Taiwan                             23,036,087      32261                 714
Bahrain                               698,585        619                1129
Bangladesh                        147,365,352     133911                1100
India                           1,095,351,995    2973190                 368
Pakistan                          165,803,560     778720                 213
```

There are also types of comparisons you can use as shown in the following query, including <=, >=, BETWEEN n AND m, LIKE 'pattern', and of course = for equality:

```
SELECT REGION_ID, COUNTRY, TO_CHAR(POPULATION, '9,999,999,990') "Population",
    AREA "Km sq.", ROUND(POPULATION / ZD(AREA), 0) "Population Density"
FROM COUNTRY
WHERE ((POPULATION <= 1000000 AND ROUND(POPULATION / ZD(AREA), 0) <= 100)
OR (ROUND(POPULATION / ZD(AREA), 0) BETWEEN 0 AND 10))
AND REGION_ID = 1 AND COUNTRY LIKE '%a%';
```

The preceding query finds heavily populated countries in region 1 (the continent of Africa), as long as the country name contains a letter *a* somewhere in its name. The result is this:

```
REGION_ID COUNTRY                  Population      Km sq. Population Density
--------- ------------------------ --------------- ---------- --------------------
        1 Angola                   12,127,071      1246699                      10
        1 Botswana                  1,639,833       585371                       3
        1 Central African Republic  4,303,356       622980                       7
        1 Equatorial Guinea           540,109        28050                      19
        1 Gabon                     1,424,906       257669                       6
        1 Gambia                            0        10000                       0
        1 Ivory Coast                       0            0                       0
        1 Libya                     5,900,754      1759540                       3
        1 Mali                     11,716,829      1219999                      10
        1 Mauritania                3,177,388      1030400                       3
        1 Namibia                   2,044,147       823291                       2
        1 Zaire                             0            0                       0
12 records
```

Precedence in SQL

Another important factor to consider in SQL at this stage is the concept of precedence. Precedence of execution is the sequence in which the different filters are applied to the records retrieved by the SELECT statement. The previous query is duplicated here but formatted slightly differently, with everything spread out more clearly according to precedence of execution established by use of the round brackets:

```
SELECT REGION_ID, COUNTRY, TO_CHAR(POPULATION, '9,999,999,990') "Population",
   AREA "Km sq.", ROUND(POPULATION / ZD(AREA), 0) "Population Density"
FROM COUNTRY
WHERE
(
   (
         POPULATION <= 1000000
      AND ROUND
         (
               POPULATION / ZD(AREA)
         , 0
         ) <= 100
   )
   OR
   (
      ROUND
      (
            POPULATION / ZD(AREA)
      , 0
      ) BETWEEN 0 AND 10
   )
)
AND REGION_ID = 1
AND COUNTRY LIKE '%a%';
```

This is the sequence in which the preceding query WHERE clause comparisons are executed, based on the way that the round brackets determine precedence of execution:

1. The top-most ROUND function against the <= 100 comparison is executed:

The ROUND function is executed first as determined by expression precedence. At this point, I am discussing WHERE clause filtering comparison precedence.

```
AND ROUND
    (
          POPULATION / ZD(AREA)
    , 0
    ) <= 100
```

2. The second comparison (BETWEEN 0 AND 10), containing the ROUND function is executed:

```
ROUND
(
      POPULATION / ZD(AREA)
, 0
) BETWEEN 0 AND 10
```

3. The POPULATION <= 1000000 is then logically combined with the result of the comparison in Step 1:

```
(
      POPULATION <= 1000000
AND ROUND
    (
          POPULATION / ZD(AREA)
    , 0
    ) <= 100
)
```

4. The results of the comparisons in Steps 3 and 2 are then combined using the OR logical operator, meaning that either Step 2 or Step 3 can be true to produce a true result:

```
(
  (
        POPULATION <= 1000000
  AND ROUND
      (
            POPULATION / ZD(AREA)
      , 0
      ) <= 100
  )
  OR
  (
    ROUND
    (
          POPULATION / ZD(AREA)
    , 0
    ) BETWEEN 0 AND 10
  )
)
```

5. Finally the two AND logical operators, executed as the AND REGION_ID = 1 comparison, followed by the AND COUNTRY LIKE '%a%' comparison, are executed to produce a resulting true or false result for every record retrieved by the SELECT statement:

```
AND REGION_ID = 1
AND COUNTRY LIKE '%a%'
```

Technically, ZD(AREA) is computed first, but since the ZD function is used everywhere for a population density calculation, I have assumed it a part of the contained expression in this situation. The objective is to give you an overall picture of the process.

Just to demonstrate the use of round brackets and how they apply precedence, the query that follows is the same as the previous query, except that I have removed all the round brackets, which determine the precedence of execution of comparisons in the WHERE clause (excluding those encapsulating the ROUND function as an expression):

```
SELECT REGION_ID, COUNTRY, TO_CHAR(POPULATION, '9,999,999,990') "Population",
    AREA "Km sq.", ROUND(POPULATION / ZD(AREA), 0) "Population Density"
FROM COUNTRY
WHERE POPULATION <= 1000000 AND ROUND(POPULATION / ZD(AREA), 0) <= 100
OR ROUND(POPULATION / ZD(AREA), 0) BETWEEN 0 AND 10
AND REGION_ID = 1 AND COUNTRY LIKE '%a%';
```

In this situation the AND operator has higher precedence than the OR operator and thus all operators are processed as they are encountered (left to right and top to bottom). As shown in the code that follows, the result of the query is completely different. This is a partial result and even this shows extra countries, which are not even in Africa:

REGION_ID	COUNTRY	Population	Km sq.	Population Density
1	Angola	12,127,071	1246699	10
1	Botswana	1,639,833	585371	3
1	Central African Republic	4,303,356	622980	7
1	**Djibouti**	**486,530**	**21979**	**22**
1	Equatorial Guinea	540,109	28050	19
1	Gabon	1,424,906	257669	6
1	Gambia	0	10000	0
1	Ivory Coast	0	0	0
1	Libya	5,900,754	1759540	3
1	Mali	11,716,829	1219999	10
1	Mauritania	3,177,388	1030400	3
1	Namibia	2,044,147	823291	2
1	Zaire	0	0	0
4	**Bahamas**	**0**	**10070**	**0**
6	**Cyprus**	**784,301**	**9241**	**85**
6	**Iceland**	**299,388**	**100251**	**3**
6	**Northern Ireland**	**0**	**0**	**0**
6	**Scotland**	**0**	**0**	**0**
6	**Slovak Republic**	**0**	**48800**	**0**
6	**Yugoslavia**	**0**	**102136**	**0**
10	**Greenland**	**56,361**	**341701**	**0**
11	**Comoros Islands**	**0**	**0**	**0**

In the preceding query, excluding comparison precedence round brackets, there are now 18 records instead of the original 9 records. Djibouti is in Africa but has too low a population, failing the LIKE operator test. The rest of the countries have too low a population, none are in Africa, some fail the LIKE test, and many fail the population density test. However, population density is not a prerequisite because it can be overridden by the low population size comparison. That clearly demonstrates why the round brackets are used to change the precedence of execution, of comparisons, in the WHERE clause.

The only other rule to remember is that the logical operators have an overriding order of precedence. NOT is executed first, followed by AND, and finally by OR. Use of NOT AND or NOT OR requires failure of a test to get a true result.

Precedence in Expressions

The precedence in WHERE clause comparisons determines the sequence in which those comparisons are executed. Mathematically speaking, an expression can be executed in a specific order.

An expression is a single valued, or multiple valued, calculation that when evaluated produces a single result. The number 2 is an expression because its result is 2. The string (5*10)+3 is also an expression because the result is 53. More abstractly, (x*y)+z is also an expression because it equals (x*y)+z.

The expression ((100/((x+y)*z))-5) is an expression in itself, and also contains multiple expressions within it, all producing a single result, where each result is passed back to the calling (or container) expression. This expression can be divided up as follows, where expressions proceed outwards with indentations. It begins with the expression x+y, followed by (x+y)*z, 100/((x+y)*z), (100/((x+y)*z))-5, and finally the round brackets around the entire expression. The round brackets are unnecessary but make the resulting expression look a little easier to read:

```
(
    (
        100/
        (
            (
                x+y
            )
            *z
        )
    )
    -5
)
```

For an example of expression precedence, consider the following:

```
((100/((2+3)*2))-5)  =  ((100/((2+3)*2))-5)
                     =  ((100/(5*2))-5)
                     =  ((100/10)-5)
                     =  (10-5)
                     =  5
```

Now remove all the brackets from the preceding expression and simple rules of mathematical expression apply, where * and / are executed before + and –, but * has equal precedence to /, and + has equal precedence to –. Additionally, the expression is evaluated (calculated) from left to right:

```
100/2+3*2-5 = 50+3*2-5
            = 50+6-5
            = 56-5
            = 1
```

As you see in the preceding code, no round brackets and a different value results. As you saw in queries executed earlier, mathematical expressions are used in SQL, specifically when using the ROUND function in the ROUND (POPULATION / ZD(AREA), 0) calculation. This function executes the division first and then returns a result that is rounded up to the nearest zero. In this query the ROUND function is removed from the fields and expressions retrieved from the table:

```
SELECT COUNTRY, TO_CHAR(POPULATION, '9,999,999,990') "Population", AREA "Km sq.",
    POPULATION / ZD(AREA) "Population Density"
FROM COUNTRY
WHERE ((POPULATION <= 1000000 AND ROUND(POPULATION / ZD(AREA), 0) <= 100)
OR (ROUND(POPULATION / ZD(AREA), 0) BETWEEN 0 AND 10))
AND REGION_ID = 1 AND COUNTRY LIKE '%a%';
```

The resulting query contains a population density figure that is more difficult to read at first glance:

```
COUNTRY                    Population      Km sq. Population Density
------------------------   -------------   ------ -------------------
Angola                     12,127,071      1246699         9.72734477
Botswana                    1,639,833       585371         2.80135675
Central African Republic    4,303,356       622980         6.90769527
Equatorial Guinea             540,109        28050         19.2552228
Gabon                       1,424,906       257669         5.52998615
Gambia                              0        10000                  0
Ivory Coast                         0            0                  0
Libya                       5,900,754      1759540         3.35357764
Mali                       11,716,829      1219999         9.60396607
Mauritania                  3,177,388      1030400         3.08364519
Namibia                     2,044,147       823291          2.4828973
Zaire                               0            0                  0
```

One more point about expression precedence is that any function, such as the ROUND function, has higher precedence than all the arithmetic operators *, /, +, and −. Also some versions of SQL, for some database engines, will use a POWER function. The POWER function raises one number to the power of another. For example $2^3 = 8$, but could also be executed as POWER (2, 3) = 8, depending on the database engine. Some database engines even have a special exponent operator for executing exponents, sometimes using a ^ character, or even a ^^ character sequence. And thus 2^3 or 2^^3 might both be equal to 8, depending on the database engine in use. In this case, the precedence of arithmetic operators would be ROUND (or any other function), followed by ^ or ^^, followed by * and /, and finally + and −.

Mathematically, exponentiation is actually the conversion of large numbers to exponential notation where the number 1,000,000,000,000 can also be represented as $1*10^{12}$, where 12 is the exponent, and the number $1*10^{12}$ is an exponential notational expression of the number 1,000,000,000,000. In all the database engines I have worked with in the past, the term "exponent" is applied to raising a number to the power of another. The exponent is actually the number that another number is raised by, not the entire expression itself. Thus, in the expression 2^3, 2 is the number, and 3 is the exponent.

The ORDER BY Clause

The ORDER BY clause can be used to further enhance a SELECT statement by changing the order in which records are returned. This is the basic syntax of the ORDER BY clause:

```
SELECT ...
FROM ...
[ WHERE ... ]
[ ORDER BY { field | expression [ASC| DESC] [ , ... ] } ];
```

The SELECT statement and the FROM clause are mandatory. The WHERE clause and the ORDER BY clause are both optional and thus enclosed in square brackets as in [ORDER BY ...].

The ORDER BY clause always appears last in a query. The ORDER BY clause is applied to the filtered records after the application of the WHERE clause, not before records are filtered.

This is the same query used before, except that now the records are returned in order of decreasing population density, within increasing REGION_ID value:

```
SELECT REGION_ID, COUNTRY, TO_CHAR(POPULATION, '9,999,999,990') "Population",
    AREA "Km sq.", ROUND(POPULATION / ZD(AREA), 0) "Population Density"
FROM COUNTRY
WHERE ((POPULATION <= 1000000 AND ROUND(POPULATION / ZD(AREA), 0) <= 100)
OR (ROUND(POPULATION / ZD(AREA), 0) BETWEEN 0 AND 10))
AND REGION_ID IN (1, 13) AND COUNTRY LIKE '%a%'
ORDER BY REGION_ID ASC, ROUND(POPULATION / ZD(AREA), 0) DESC;
```

Like the WHERE clause, expressions can be used in the ORDER BY clause, as in ROUND(POPULATION / ZD(AREA), 0) DESC.

A new comparison is introduced in the form of REGION_ID IN (1, 13). *The IN operator allows validation against a list of values. In this case, the REGION_ID can be 1 (Africa), or 13 (South America).*

Here is the result of the preceding query with Equatorial Guinea and Bolivia being the most densely populated countries in Africa and South America, respectively:

REGION_ID	COUNTRY	Population	Km sq.	Population Density
1	**Equatorial Guinea**	540,109	28050	19
1	Angola	12,127,071	1246699	10
1	Mali	11,716,829	1219999	10
1	Central African Republic	4,303,356	622980	7
1	Gabon	1,424,906	257669	6
1	Botswana	1,639,833	585371	3
1	Mauritania	3,177,388	1030400	3
1	Libya	5,900,754	1759540	3
1	Namibia	2,044,147	823291	2
1	Zaire	0	0	0
1	Ivory Coast	0	0	0
1	Gambia	0	10000	0
13	**Bolivia**	8,989,046	1084389	8
13	Guyana	767,245	196850	4
13	French Guiana	199,509	89150	2
13	Surinam	0	161471	0

The AS Clause in the ORDER BY Clause

The AS clause can be used to rename a field within the scope of a running query. In the previous query the quoted strings "Population" and "Population Density" were used to change only the field headers in the output. This next query changes the name of the population density expression ROUND(POPULATION / ZD(AREA), 0), giving the expression a field name of its own. This allows access to the name of the expression in the ORDER BY clause, rather than duplicating the entire expression:

```
SELECT REGION_ID, COUNTRY, TO_CHAR(POPULATION, '9,999,999,990') "Population",
   AREA "Km sq.", ROUND(POPULATION / ZD(AREA), 0) AS DENSITY
FROM COUNTRY
WHERE ((POPULATION <= 1000000 AND ROUND(POPULATION / ZD(AREA), 0) <= 100)
OR (ROUND(POPULATION / ZD(AREA), 0) BETWEEN 0 AND 10))
AND REGION_ID IN (1, 13) AND COUNTRY LIKE '%a%'
ORDER BY REGION_ID ASC, DENSITY DESC;
```

The result of the preceding query is very similar to the previous query's output, as you can see in the code that follows, except that the field name of the calculated expression is now DENSITY as opposed to Population Density:

REGION_ID	COUNTRY	Population	Km sq.	DENSITY
1	Equatorial Guinea	540,109	28050	19
1	Angola	12,127,071	1246699	10
1	Mali	11,716,829	1219999	10
1	Central African Republic	4,303,356	622980	7
1	Gabon	1,424,906	257669	6
1	Botswana	1,639,833	585371	3
1	Mauritania	3,177,388	1030400	3
1	Libya	5,900,754	1759540	3
1	Namibia	2,044,147	823291	2
1	Zaire	0	0	0
1	Ivory Coast	0	0	0
1	Gambia	0	10000	0
13	Bolivia	8,989,046	1084389	8
13	Guyana	767,245	196850	4
13	French Guiana	199,509	89150	2
13	Surinam	0	161471	0

You cannot, however, do as in the following query and replace the density expression in the WHERE clause. The reason is very simple. The ORDER BY clause is always performed after all records have been retrieved from the database. Therefore the calculated expression exists as DENSITY at the point of execution of the ORDER BY clause. The WHERE clause on the other hand is executed as records are retrieved from the database. Consequently, the DENSITY field does not actually exist until after the WHERE clause has been applied to database access. The following query will return an error because the WHERE clause filters cannot find the field called DENSITY:

```
SELECT REGION_ID, COUNTRY, TO_CHAR(POPULATION, '9,999,999,990') "Population",
   AREA "Km sq.", ROUND(POPULATION / ZD(AREA), 0) AS DENSITY
FROM COUNTRY
WHERE ((POPULATION <= 1000000 AND DENSITY <= 100)
OR (DENSITY BETWEEN 0 AND 10))
AND REGION_ID IN (1, 13) AND COUNTRY LIKE '%a%'
ORDER BY REGION_ID ASC, DENSITY DESC;
```

Most database engines allow ORDER BY clause specification not only by field names and expression, but also by the position of a field (or expression), in the list of items retrieved by the SELECT statement. So you could change the ORDER BY clause to that shown in the following query, and get the same result as in the previous query:

```
SELECT REGION_ID, COUNTRY, TO_CHAR(POPULATION, '9,999,999,990') "Population",
    AREA "Km sq.", ROUND(POPULATION / ZD(AREA), 0) AS DENSITY
FROM COUNTRY
WHERE ((POPULATION <= 1000000 AND ROUND(POPULATION / ZD(AREA), 0) <= 100)
OR (ROUND(POPULATION / ZD(AREA), 0) BETWEEN 0 AND 10))
AND REGION_ID IN (1, 13) AND COUNTRY LIKE '%a%'
ORDER BY 1 ASC, 5 DESC;
```

In the preceding query and ORDER BY clause, the REGION_ID field appears in the first position in the SELECT items list, and the population density expression appears fifth in the SELECT statement items list. You can even mix positional values in the ORDER BY clause with field names and expressions. Additionally, some databases do not require that ORDER BY clause items actually be retrieved, as in the following example:

```
SELECT REGION_ID, REGION FROM REGION ORDER BY ROUND(POPULATION / ZD(AREA), 0) DESC;
```

In the query that follows, it is clear to see that the density expression calculation is not returned by the query:

```
REGION_ID REGION
---------- --------------------------------
        9 Near East
        4 Caribbean
        7 Far East
        6 Europe
        2 Asia
        5 Central America
        8 Middle East
        1 Africa
       13 South America
       10 North America
       11 Oceania
       12 Russian Federation
        3 Australasia
```

The ORDER BY clause is simple compared with the WHERE clause.

The GROUP BY Clause

The GROUP BY clause can be used to further enhance a SELECT statement by summarizing records returned from the SELECT statement. This is the basic syntax of the GROUP BY clause:

```
SELECT ...
FROM ...
[ WHERE ... ]
[ GROUP BY expression [, ... ] ]
[ ORDER BY ... ];
```

The SELECT statement and the FROM clause are mandatory. The WHERE clause, the ORDER BY clause, and the GROUP BY clause are all optional and thus enclosed in square brackets as in [GROUP BY ...].

The ORDER BY clause always appears last in a query. Therefore the ORDER BY clause is applied to both filtered and summarized records, after the application of both the WHERE clause and the GROUP BY clause.

The next query reads the COUNTRY table. It finds global population figures, for all countries, in all regions. This particular query produces total regional populations sorted in decreasing order of regional population:

```
SELECT REGION_ID,
   TO_CHAR(SUM(POPULATION)/1000000000, '990.9')||' billion' "Population"
FROM COUNTRY
GROUP BY REGION_ID ORDER BY SUM(POPULATION) DESC;
```

See Appendix B for details of the demographics database, which is used for examples throughout this book.

Here is the result of the preceding query including regions with relatively negligible (zero) populations:

```
REGION_ID Population
---------- --------------
        7    2.1 billion
        9    1.5 billion
        1    0.8 billion
        6    0.5 billion
       13    0.4 billion
       10    0.3 billion
        8    0.3 billion
       12    0.3 billion
        5    0.1 billion
        2    0.0 billion
        4    0.0 billion
        3    0.0 billion
       11    0.0 billion
```

The GROUP BY clause can be further extended by using the HAVING clause. The HAVING clause is applied as a filter to the results of the GROUP BY clause, allowing filtering of resulting summarized records. This is the basic syntax of the GROUP BY clause, this time with the HAVING clause added:

```
SELECT ...
FROM ...
[ WHERE ... ]
[ GROUP BY expression [, ... ] [ HAVING condition ] ]
[ ORDER BY ... ];
```

This query is adapted to remove regions with relatively negligible populations, creating a cut-off point at anything over half a billion people:

```
SELECT REGION_ID,
   TO_CHAR(SUM(POPULATION)/1000000000, '990.99')||' billion' "Population"
FROM COUNTRY
GROUP BY REGION_ID HAVING SUM(POPULATION)/1000000000 >= 0.5
ORDER BY SUM(POPULATION) DESC;
```

Both the GROUP BY *clause and the* HAVING *clause can contain expressions as well as simple field names, as in* SUM(POPULATION).

Here is the result of the preceding query showing the regions of the Far East, the Near East, and Africa:

```
REGION_ID Population
---------- ----------------
        7    2.10 billion
        9    1.50 billion
        1    0.79 billion
```

Some database engines allow specialized clauses for the GROUP BY *clause. These extensions are generally reserved for data warehouse OLAP (Online Application Processing). OLAP functionality is used to produce analytical projection reporting, such as sub-totaling rollups, cubic cross-tabs, and even spreadsheets.*

The JOIN Clause

The JOIN clause is used to merge the records of two separate queries together, based on common field values. This is the basic syntax of the JOIN clause:

```
SELECT ...
FROM table [alias] [ JOIN table [alias] USING (common-field) ]
[ WHERE ... ]
[ GROUP BY ... ]
[ ORDER BY ... ];
```

The common-field element determines that records from two tables are joined together using a field containing values common to records in both tables.

The following query reads both the REGION and COUNTRY tables, joining the two with the JOIN clause:

```
SELECT REGION, COUNTRY
FROM REGION JOIN COUNTRY USING (REGION_ID);
```

The preceding query applies the USING clause to join the REGION and COUNTRY tables based on a REGION_ID value. Every region has a unique value for REGION_ID. Whenever a new record is added to the COUNTRY table, then that country record is allocated a REGION_ID value based on the region the country is in. For example, Cameroon is a country in Africa, Georgia is a country in the Russian Federation, and South Korea is a country in the Far East region.

See Appendix B for details of the demographics database, which is used for examples throughout this book.

Figure B-1 in Appendix B, and the description of Entity Relationship Diagrams (ERDs), also in Appendix B, show that there can be many countries within each region.

Here is a partial result of the preceding query, showing some countries within their respective regions:

```
REGION                   COUNTRY
----------------------   ----------------------
Africa                   Cameroon
Africa                   Cote Divoire
Russian Federation       Georgia
Russian Federation       Kazakhstan
Far East                 Myanmar
Middle East              Palestinian Territories
Europe                   Serbia And Montenegro
Far East                 South Korea
Russian Federation       Ukraine
Middle East              United Arab Emirates
Russian Federation       Uzbekistan
```

The JOIN clause can be expanded upon by joining more than two tables using multiple JOIN clauses. The syntax is expanded upon as shown here:

```
SELECT ...
FROM table [alias] [ JOIN table [alias] USING (common-field)
    [ JOIN table [alias] USING (common-field) ]
]
[ WHERE ... ]
[ GROUP BY ... ]
[ ORDER BY ... ];
```

The following query joins regions to countries, and then countries to states using two JOIN clauses:

```
SELECT REGION, COUNTRY, STATE "State or Province"
FROM REGION JOIN COUNTRY USING (REGION_ID)
    JOIN STATE USING (COUNTRY_ID);
```

Again, the USING clause is applied to join the REGION and COUNTRY tables using REGION ID, plus a second USING clause is applied to join the COUNTRY and STATE tables together.

Figure B-1 in Appendix B, and the description of Entity Relationship Diagrams (ERDs), also in Appendix B, show that there can be many countries within each region and many states within each country.

Here is a partial result of the preceding query, showing some states within the United States and Canada, in North America (only North America has states in this database):

```
REGION                   COUNTRY                   State or Province
----------------------   ----------------------   ----------------------
North America            United States             Washington
North America            United States             Wisconsin
North America            United States             West Virginia
North America            United States             Wyoming
North America            United States             Nebraska
North America            United States             New Jersey
North America            United States             Vermont
North America            Canada                    British Columbia
North America            Canada                    Nova Scotia
North America            Canada                    Ontario
North America            Canada                    Quebec
North America            Canada                    Alberta
```

And going just a little further, the next query joins regions to countries, and then countries to states, followed by states to cities. This time the query uses four JOIN clauses:

```
SELECT REGION, COUNTRY, STATE "State or Province", CITY
FROM REGION JOIN COUNTRY USING (REGION_ID)
    JOIN STATE USING (COUNTRY_ID)
        JOIN CITY USING (STATE_ID);
```

And once again, the USING clause is applied to join the REGION and COUNTRY tables using the REGION ID field. A second USING clause is applied to join the COUNTRY and STATE tables together using the COUNTRY_ID field. A third USING clause is applied to join the STATE and CITY tables together using the STATE_ID field.

Figure B-1 in Appendix B, and the description of Entity Relationship Diagrams (ERDs), also in Appendix B, show that there can be many cities within each state, within each country, within each region.

Here is a partial result of the preceding query, showing some cities within their respective states, in the United States and Canada, in North America:

```
REGION          COUNTRY         State or Province   CITY
--------------  --------------  ------------------  ---------------
North America   United States   Texas               Waco
North America   United States   Utah                Salt Lake City
North America   United States   Virginia            Norfolk
North America   United States   Washington          Seattle
North America   United States   Washington          Spokane
North America   United States   Wisconsin           Madison
North America   United States   Wisconsin           Milwaukee
North America   United States   Wyoming             Cheyenne
North America   Canada          Alberta             Burlington
North America   Canada          Alberta             Calgary
North America   Canada          Alberta             Edmonton
```

Another variation of JOIN clause syntax is the ON clause, substituting for the USING clause. This is the altered syntax of the JOIN clause:

```
SELECT ...
FROM table [alias] [ JOIN table [alias] ON (left-field = right-field)
    [ JOIN table [alias] USING (left-field = right-field) ]
]
[ WHERE ... ]
[ GROUP BY ... ]
[ ORDER BY ... ];
```

The USING clause can be applied when there are common fields between two tables, and those fields contain common values. You use the ON clause when two fields that are named the same in two tables do not contain common values. Or, when using aliases in a join query, the field names on the joined tables are effectively different because they are altered by two different table aliases. For example, alias-1.field1 is not the same as alias-2.field1.

In the following example query, aliases rename fields in tables within the query, effectively giving fields different names. The USING clause would not be able to perform the join because it cannot determine that r.REGION_ID is the same as c.REGION_ID:

```
SELECT r.REGION, c.COUNTRY
FROM REGION r JOIN COUNTRY c ON (c.REGION_ID = r.REGION_ID);
```

This is the resulting query:

```
REGION                   COUNTRY
------------------------ ------------------------
Africa                   Cameroon
Africa                   Cote Divoire
Russian Federation       Georgia
Russian Federation       Kazakhstan
Far East                 Myanmar
Middle East              Palestinian Territories
Europe                   Serbia And Montenegro
Far East                 South Korea
Russian Federation       Ukraine
Middle East              United Arab Emirates
Russian Federation       Uzbekistan
```

Types of Joins

There are various different types of joins in that two tables can be joined together, finding different sets of records for each join type. These join types are generally called natural joins, inner joins, cross-joins, and various subtypes of outer joins.

A natural join uses the NATURAL keyword to allow the database to guess at the correct field to join two tables on. The syntax looks like this:

```
SELECT ...
FROM table [alias] [ NATURAL JOIN table [alias] ... ]
[ WHERE ... ]
[ GROUP BY ... ]
[ ORDER BY ... ];
```

A natural join does not require the ON *or* USING *keywords.*

The following query joins regions to countries, with a best guess using common field names between the two tables:

```
SELECT REGION, COUNTRY
FROM REGION NATURAL JOIN COUNTRY;
```

The preceding query will not return any records. Examine the ERD in Appendix B and you will see that the REGION and COUNTRY tables have three common fields, in the form of the REGION_ID, POPULATION, and AREA fields. Obviously, population and square kilometer values for regions and countries are completely different, and the result is no records found by the preceding query.

The keyword INNER can be used to indicate an inner or intersecting join. All the join queries seen so far in this section are inner joins.

From a mathematical perspective, an intersection is made up of the common elements in two sets of values.

The syntax looks like this where either the USING or ON clause are required:

```
SELECT ...
FROM table [alias]
[
      INNER JOIN table [alias] USING (common-field)
    | INNER JOIN table [alias] ON (left-field = right-field)
]
[ WHERE ... ]
[ GROUP BY ... ]
[ ORDER BY ... ];
```

As already stated, all working example join queries seen so far in this section are inner joins.

The INNER keyword is optional.

A special type of intersecting join is a self-join. A self-join is simply an intersection between records in the same table. You can join records within the same table. Commonly self-joins are used to join records in a table containing hierarchical data.

A cross-join returns all records from two tables, merging regardless of any common values. In other words, every record in one table is joined with every record in another table. A cross-join completely ignores common fields and common values.

Mathematically speaking, a cross-join is a Cartesian product which is a multiplication or product of all the elements in two sets.

The syntax for a cross-join looks like this:

```
SELECT ...
FROM table [alias] [ CROSS JOIN table [alias] ]
[ WHERE ... ]
[ GROUP BY ... ]
[ ORDER BY ... ];
```

The following example, as you can see, does not relate regions with countries:

```
SELECT REGION, COUNTRY
FROM REGION CROSS JOIN COUNTRY;
```

This is the result of the preceding query. The United Kingdom is not in the Near East region, and Afghanistan is definitely not in North America:

```
REGION                    COUNTRY
----------------------    ----------------------
Near East                 United Kingdom
Near East                 United States
Near East                 Uruguay
Near East                 Uzbekistan
```

```
Near East              Venezuela
Near East              Vietnam
Near East              Yemen
Near East              Yugoslavia
Near East              Zaire
Near East              Zambia
Near East              Zimbabwe
North America          Afghanistan
North America          Albania
North America          Algeria
North America          American Samoa
```

Data warehouses sometimes use cross-joins.

An outer join can be used to return both intersecting records, plus records in one or either table, but not in the other table. There are three types of outer joins: a left outer join, a right outer join, and a full outer join.

A left outer join finds all records in the table on the left, plus all records in the table on the right, where records in the left-side table do not have to exist in the right-side table. This is the syntax for a left outer join:

```
SELECT ...
FROM table [alias]
[
      LEFT OUTER JOIN table [alias] USING (common-field)
   |  LEFT OUTER JOIN table [alias] ON (left-field = right-field)
]
[ WHERE ... ]
[ GROUP BY ... ]
[ ORDER BY ... ];
```

The USING *or* ON *clause is required for outer joins.*

This query finds all countries regardless of whether they have states or not:

```
SELECT COUNTRY, STATE "State or Province"
FROM COUNTRY LEFT OUTER JOIN STATE USING (COUNTRY_ID);
```

This is the result of the preceding query. The United States has states, and Canada has provinces. Other countries do not have states, at least not in this database:

```
COUNTRY                  State or Province
------------------------ -------------------
United States            Washington
United States            Wisconsin
United States            West Virginia
United States            Wyoming
Canada                   Alberta
United States            Nebraska
United States            New Jersey
United States            Vermont
South Korea
India
Maldive Islands
Papua New Guinea
```

In an outer join, records without matching field values have non-retrievable field values set to NULL. Thus in the preceding query, `State` or `Province` values for the last four countries are all NULL values.

A right outer join finds all records in the table on the right, plus all records in the table on the left, where records in the right-side table do not have to exist in the left-side table. This is the syntax for a right outer join:

```
SELECT ...
FROM table [alias]
[
    RIGHT OUTER JOIN table [alias] USING (common-field)
  | RIGHT OUTER JOIN table [alias] ON (left-field = right-field)
]
[ WHERE ... ]
[ GROUP BY ... ]
[ ORDER BY ... ];
```

This query simply reverses the sequence of the tables from the previous example query, again finding all countries regardless of whether they have states or not:

```
SELECT COUNTRY, STATE "State or Province"
FROM STATE RIGHT OUTER JOIN COUNTRY USING (COUNTRY_ID);
```

The result for the preceding query is identical to the previous query result.

The last type of outer join is a full outer join. A full outer join finds all intersecting records, plus any records in the left-side table not in the right side, and any records in the right-side table not in the left. This is the syntax for a full outer join:

```
SELECT ...
FROM table [alias]
[
    FULL OUTER JOIN table [alias] USING (common-field)
  | FULL OUTER JOIN table [alias] ON (left-field = right-field)
]
[ WHERE ... ]
[ GROUP BY ... ]
[ ORDER BY ... ];
```

The following query can potentially find all countries regardless of whether they have states or not, and vice versa:

```
SELECT COUNTRY, STATE "State or Province"
FROM COUNTRY FULL OUTER JOIN STATE USING (COUNTRY_ID);
```

The database used in this book does not have any relationship that would demonstrate a full outer join, and thus showing a query result is pointless.

Subqueries

A subquery is a query that is embedded within, and called from, another query. The calling query is known as the calling query or the parent query. Subqueries can be nested to an arbitrary depth, depending usually on the specific database engine in use. Subqueries can return a single scalar value, multiple values, or even multiple records. A subquery can be correlated, passing values passed into a child query, which can affect records retrieved by the subquery, for each parent query record retrieved. There are various different ways that subqueries can be used and built:

❑ The IN and EXISTS operators can contain embedded subqueries.

❑ A subquery can be embedded in the FROM clause of a SELECT statement.

❑ A subquery can be embedded in WHERE, ORDER BY and GROUP BY clauses.

❑ Subqueries can be embedded into INSERT, UPDATE and DELETE statements.

INSERT, UPDATE and DELETE statements are used to add to, change and remove records in tables.

In this first case, a subquery finds all countries, as long as they have a related entry in the REGION table:

```
SELECT * FROM COUNTRY WHERE REGION_ID IN (SELECT REGION_ID FROM REGION);
```

The subquery is used in the WHERE clause in the preceding query.

This is a partial result of the preceding query. Not all fields are included in this result:

```
COUNTRY_ID  REGION_ID  COUNTRY                          CO  POPULATION
----------  ---------- -------------------------------  --  ----------
         1          1  Algeria                          AG    32930091
         2          1  Angola                           AO    12127071
         3          1  Benin                            BN     7862944
         4          1  Botswana                         BC     1639833
         5          1  Burkina Faso                     UV    13902972
         6          1  Burundi                          BY     8090068
         7          1  Central African Republic         CT     4303356
         8          1  Congo                            CG    62660551
         9          1  Djibouti                         DJ      486530
        10          1  Equatorial Guinea                EK      540109
        11          1  Ethiopia                         ET    74777981
```

This next query embeds multiple layers of subqueries:

```
SELECT * FROM CITY WHERE CITY_ID IN
   (SELECT CITY_ID FROM STATE WHERE STATE_ID IN
      (SELECT STATE_ID FROM STATE WHERE COUNTRY_ID IN
         (SELECT COUNTRY_ID FROM COUNTRY WHERE REGION_ID IN
            (SELECT REGION_ID FROM REGION)
         )
      )
   );
```

This is a partial result of the preceding query:

```
CITY_ID  COUNTRY_ID  STATE_ID  CITY                                POPULATION
-------  ----------  --------- ----------------------------------  ----------
    583         127          8 Phoenix                                3800000
    584         127            Richmond                               1175000
    585         127         37 Rochester                              1050000
    586         127          9 San Diego                              3000000
```

```
  587        127        29 St. Louis                                    2800000
  588        127        14 Tampa                                        2650000
  589        127           Virginia Beach                               1675000
  590        127        12 Washington                                   8050000
  591        165           Tashkent                                     2400000
  592        151           Barquisimeto                                 1150000
  593        151           Maracaibo                                    2150000
```

A subquery can return a single scalar value, multiple values, or even multiple records. In this example, the subquery returns the REGION_ID value for North America only:

```
SELECT * FROM COUNTRY WHERE REGION_ID =
    (SELECT REGION_ID FROM REGION WHERE REGION='North America');
```

This is a partial result, finding only countries in North America:

```
COUNTRY_ID  REGION_ID  COUNTRY                              CO POPULATION
----------  ---------  -----------------------------------  -- ----------
       125         10  Canada                               CA   33098932
       126         10  Greenland                            GL      56361
       127         10  United States                        US  298444215
```

In the next subquery the IN operator validates using two fields:

```
SELECT * FROM CITY WHERE (COUNTRY_ID, STATE_ID) IN
    (SELECT COUNTRY_ID, STATE_ID FROM COUNTRY JOIN STATE USING (COUNTRY_ID));
```

This is a partial result:

```
 CITY_ID COUNTRY_ID   STATE_ID CITY                                 POPULATION
---------- ----------  ---------- --------------------------------- ----------
       583        127          8 Phoenix                              3800000
       585        127         37 Rochester                            1050000
       586        127          9 San Diego                            3000000
       587        127         29 St. Louis                            2800000
       588        127         14 Tampa                                2650000
       590        127         12 Washington                           8050000
         1        125          1 Vancouver                            2200000
         2        125          2 Halifax
         3        125          3 Ottawa                               1150000
         4        125          3 Toronto                              5150000
         5        125          4 Montreal                             3600000
```

A subquery can be correlated, using values passed into it from its parent query, which can affect records retrieved by the subquery:

```
SELECT * FROM COUNTRY WHERE REGION_ID IN
    (SELECT REGION_ID FROM REGION WHERE REGION_ID=COUNTRY.REGION_ID);
```

In the preceding query, the subquery's WHERE clause (WHERE REGION_ID=COUNTRY.REGION_ID) takes a value passed from the calling query into the subquery, determining which records the subquery retrieves for every record retrieved by the calling query. In other words, for every country found, the subquery uses the country's REGION_ID value to find that country's region.

This is a partial result:

```
COUNTRY_ID REGION_ID COUNTRY                         CO POPULATION
---------- ---------- ------------------------------- -- ----------
         1          1 Algeria                         AG   32930091
         2          1 Angola                          AO   12127071
         3          1 Benin                           BN    7862944
         4          1 Botswana                        BC    1639833
         5          1 Burkina Faso                    UV   13902972
         6          1 Burundi                         BY    8090068
         7          1 Central African Republic        CT    4303356
         8          1 Congo                           CG   62660551
         9          1 Djibouti                        DJ     486530
        10          1 Equatorial Guinea               EK     540109
        11          1 Ethiopia                        ET   74777981
```

Some database engines allow the use of an EXISTS operator, which can be used as a slight variation on the IN operator. The IN operator returns a value or a set of values. The EXISTS operator returns a true or false result (a Boolean). So the previous correlated query can be changed to this:

```
SELECT * FROM COUNTRY WHERE EXISTS
   (SELECT REGION_ID FROM REGION WHERE REGION_ID = COUNTRY.REGION_ID);
```

The result of the preceding query is the same as the result for the previous example query.

Some databases allow embedding of a subquery into the FROM clause of a SELECT statement. Unlike subqueries in other SQL statements, a FROM clause embedded subquery can return fields and records to the calling query:

```
SELECT r.REGION, c.COUNTRY FROM REGION r,
   (SELECT * FROM COUNTRY) c
WHERE c.REGION_ID = r.REGION_ID;
```

This is the result of the query where the name of the region is pulled from the calling query, and the name of the country from the FROM clause embedded subquery:

```
REGION                            COUNTRY
--------------------------------- ---------------------------------
Africa                            Zambia
Africa                            Zimbabwe
Asia                              Burma
Australasia                       Australia
Australasia                       New Zealand
Caribbean                         Bahamas
Caribbean                         Barbados
Caribbean                         Bermuda
Caribbean                         Costa Rica
```

A subquery can be one of the expressions in a SELECT statement field selection list:

```
SELECT (SELECT r.REGION FROM REGION r WHERE r.REGION_ID = c.REGION_ID)
   ,c.COUNTRY
FROM COUNTRY c;
```

The result of the preceding query will be the same as the previous query.

A subquery can even be placed into the ORDER BY clause of a SELECT statement, helping to determine the sorted order of the output of a query. What this query does is to sort regions and countries based on the currency exchange rate (in descending order), without returning the exchange rate in the query (there are other ways to do this of course):

```
SELECT r.REGION, c.COUNTRY
FROM REGION r JOIN COUNTRY c ON (c.REGION_ID = r.REGION_ID)
ORDER BY (SELECT RATE FROM COUNTRY WHERE COUNTRY_ID = c.COUNTRY_ID);
```

The result is shown here where the same fields are found, as in the previous query output result shown, except the sorted order changes the records returned:

```
REGION                           COUNTRY
-------------------------------- --------------------------------
Europe                           United Kingdom
Europe                           Switzerland
North America                    Canada
Australasia                      Australia
Australasia                      New Zealand
Europe                           Germany
Far East                         Singapore
South America                    Brazil
Far East                         Malaysia
```

The preceding query, like most others in this chapter, is only a partial result of all records found by the query. The resort returns a completely different set of records for the first few records in the query result.

The AS Clause in Subqueries

As with the ORDER BY clause, in some situations, after completion of execution of a subquery, the AS clause can be used to refer to retrieved items using an AS clause field name change. In the following query the subquery changes the names of the COUNTRY_ID field to COUNTRY, and the COUNTRY field to NAME. The renamed COUNTRY and NAME fields are then accessed in the parent query as c.COUNTRY (containing the COUNTRY_ID value), and c.NAME (containing the COUNTRY value):

```
SELECT r.REGION, c.COUNTRY, c.NAME FROM REGION r,
    (SELECT REGION_ID, COUNTRY_ID AS COUNTRY, COUNTRY AS NAME FROM COUNTRY) c
WHERE c.REGION_ID = r.REGION_ID;
```

This is the result showing the field name changes in the header:

```
REGION                           COUNTRY NAME
-------------------------------- ---------- --------------------------------
Africa                                   42 Zaire
Africa                                   43 Zambia
Africa                                   44 Zimbabwe
Asia                                     45 Burma
Australasia                              46 Australia
Australasia                              47 New Zealand
Caribbean                                48 Bahamas
Caribbean                                49 Barbados
```

Caribbean	50 Bermuda
Caribbean	51 Costa Rica
Caribbean	52 Cuba
Caribbean	53 Dominican Republic

Subqueries can also be placed within INSERT, UPDATE, and DELETE statements, which allows changes to records in a database. These types of subqueries are discussed in a later section in this chapter, after the INSERT, UPDATE, and DELETE statements have been examined.

The UNION Clause

The UNION clause returns records from two queries. The resulting records can be treated as a single query in that they can have an ORDER BY clause applied to them, and be resorted. Additionally, each query can contain query clauses such as WHERE and GROUP BY clauses.

The only requirement for a UNION clause is that the number of fields in the two queries are the same, and that data types for each field are at least compatible. This query finds all regions and countries, regardless of any relationship between the two tables:

```
SELECT REGION_ID "ID-1", NULL "ID-2", REGION "Location" FROM REGION
UNION
SELECT REGION_ID "ID-1", COUNTRY_ID "ID-2", COUNTRY "Location" FROM COUNTRY
ORDER BY 1, 2 NULLS FIRST;
```

The NULLS FIRST *modifier is not available in all database engines.* NULLS FIRST *returns all null values before any non-null values, thus returning regions at the top of each list of countries, within that particular region.*

The NULLS FIRST *and* NULLS LAST *options will not be available in all database engines.*

This is an interesting use of the UNION clause because it effectively sorts all countries within all regions without using a join, and with all records in the same query. This is the result:

```
    ID-1       ID-2 Location
---------- ---------- --------------------------------
     2            Asia
     2         45 Burma
     3            Australasia
     3         46 Australia
     3         47 New Zealand
     4            Caribbean
     4         48 Bahamas
     4         49 Barbados
     4         50 Bermuda
     4         51 Costa Rica
     4         52 Cuba
     4         53 Dominican Republic
     4         54 Haiti
     4         55 Jamaica
     4         56 Martinique
     4         57 Puerto Rico
     5            Central America
     5         58 El Salvador
```

Try It Out   Using the SELECT Statement

Five of the tables in the demographics database (see Appendix B) are REGION, COUNTRY, LANGUAGE, POPULATION, and POPULATIONBYLANGUAGE. The tables look like this:

```
Table: REGION
Field                             Null?     Datatype
-----------------------------     --------  --------------------
REGION_ID                         NOT NULL  INTEGER
REGION                            NOT NULL  VARCHAR(32)
POPULATION                                  INTEGER
AREA                                        INTEGER
```

An Oracle Database VARCHAR2 data type is the same as VARCHAR. An Oracle Database NUMBER(38)
data type is the same as an INTEGER data type.

```
Table: COUNTRY
Field              Null?     Type
-----------------  --------  ------------
COUNTRY_ID         NOT NULL  NUMBER(38)
REGION_ID          NOT NULL  NUMBER(38)
COUNTRY            NOT NULL  VARCHAR2(32)
CODE               NOT NULL  CHAR(2)
POPULATION                   NUMBER(38)
AREA                         NUMBER(38)
FXCODE                       CHAR(3)
CURRENCY                     VARCHAR2(32)
RATE                         FLOAT(126)

Table: LANGUAGE
Field              Null?     Datatype
-----------------  --------  ------------
LANGUAGE_ID        NOT NULL  INTEGER
LANGUAGE           NOT NULL  VARCHAR(16)

Table: POPULATION
Field                             Null?     Datatype
-----------------------------     --------  ----------
POPULATION_ID                     NOT NULL  INTEGER
COUNTRY_ID                                  INTEGER
YEAR                                        INTEGER
POPULATION                                  INTEGER
BIRTHS_PER_1000                             FLOAT
DEATHS_PER_1000                             FLOAT
MIGRANTS_PER_1000                           FLOAT
NATURAL_INCREASE_PERCENT                    FLOAT
GROWTH_RATE                                 FLOAT

Table: POPULATIONBYLANGUAGE
Field                             Null?     Datatype
-----------------------------     --------  ----------
LANGUAGE_ID                       NOT NULL  INTEGER
POPULATION_ID                     NOT NULL  INTEGER
MALE                                        INTEGER
FEMALE                                      INTEGER
```

Use a SELECT statement to find records in which the female population is greater than the male population. Show both male and female populations in the year 1976, summed up for each language within each region, and sorted by each language within region. You don't need to display the year. You don't need to display the language. You don't need to return any fields from the COUNTRY and POPULATION tables, but you do need to get the name of the region from somewhere. The only numbers you should find are the male and female population values. This is how:

1. Create a SELECT statement with a list of fields:

```
SELECT REGION, LANGUAGE, FEMALE, MALE
```

2. Add the FROM clause with the first table:

```
SELECT REGION, LANGUAGE, FEMALE, MALE
FROM REGION
```

3. Add the second table as a join to the first table:

```
SELECT REGION, LANGUAGE, FEMALE, MALE
FROM REGION JOIN COUNTRY USING (REGION_ID)
```

4. Add a third table to the join:

```
SELECT REGION, LANGUAGE, FEMALE, MALE
FROM REGION JOIN COUNTRY USING (REGION_ID)
    JOIN POPULATION USING (COUNTRY_ID)
```

5. Add fourth and fifth tables to the join:

```
SELECT REGION, LANGUAGE, FEMALE, MALE
FROM REGION JOIN COUNTRY USING (REGION_ID)
    JOIN POPULATION USING (COUNTRY_ID)
        JOIN POPULATIONBYLANGUAGE USING (POPULATION_ID)
            JOIN LANGUAGE USING (LANGUAGE_ID)
```

6. A WHERE clause comparison ensures that you find only records in the year 1976, and where the female population exceeds the male population:

```
SELECT REGION, LANGUAGE, FEMALE, MALE
FROM REGION JOIN COUNTRY USING (REGION_ID)
    JOIN POPULATION USING (COUNTRY_ID)
        JOIN POPULATIONBYLANGUAGE USING (POPULATION_ID)
            JOIN LANGUAGE USING (LANGUAGE_ID)
WHERE FEMALE > MALE AND YEAR = 1976
```

7. Summarize by language within groups by applying the SUM functions to both the FEMALE and MALE fields, and then aggregating in the GROUP BY clause using the REGION and LANGUAGE fields:

```
SELECT REGION, LANGUAGE, SUM(FEMALE), SUM(MALE)
FROM REGION JOIN COUNTRY USING (REGION_ID)
    JOIN POPULATION USING (COUNTRY_ID)
        JOIN POPULATIONBYLANGUAGE USING (POPULATION_ID)
            JOIN LANGUAGE USING (LANGUAGE_ID)
WHERE FEMALE > MALE AND YEAR = 1976
GROUP BY REGION, LANGUAGE
```

8. Sort the record output by language and region:

```
SELECT REGION, LANGUAGE, SUM(FEMALE), SUM(MALE)
FROM REGION JOIN COUNTRY USING (REGION_ID)
   JOIN POPULATION USING (COUNTRY_ID)
      JOIN POPULATIONBYLANGUAGE USING (POPULATION_ID)
         JOIN LANGUAGE USING (LANGUAGE_ID)
WHERE FEMALE > MALE AND YEAR = 1976
GROUP BY REGION, LANGUAGE
ORDER BY REGION, LANGUAGE;
```

9. Last, you need to qualify the field name in the query because with so many tables in the join, SQL will get confused trying to figure out what to join with, and where to select fields from. So you need to add aliases and change all the USING clauses to more explicit joining ON clauses. You can also make the query look a little nicer by changing field names using the AS clause:

```
SELECT r.REGION, l.LANGUAGE, SUM(pl.FEMALE), SUM(pl.MALE)
FROM REGION r JOIN COUNTRY c ON (c.REGION_ID=r.REGION_ID)
   JOIN POPULATION p ON (p.COUNTRY_ID=c.COUNTRY_ID)
      JOIN POPULATIONBYLANGUAGE pl ON (pl.POPULATION_ID=p.POPULATION_ID)
         JOIN LANGUAGE l ON (l.LANGUAGE_ID=pl.LANGUAGE_ID)
WHERE pl.FEMALE > pl.MALE AND p.YEAR = 1976
GROUP BY r.REGION, l.LANGUAGE
ORDER BY r.REGION, l.LANGUAGE;
```

If you are using the demographics database as provided by the database creation process described in Appendix B, and the downloads from my website at the following URL:

```
http://www.oracledbaexpert.com/oracle/beginningxmldatabases/index.html
```

you should get a result like this:

```
REGION                          LANGUAGE           FEMALES      MALES
------------------------------  ----------------  ----------  ----------
Australasia                     English Only       5185387     5096972
Australasia                     French               42750       38236
Australasia                     Russian               4979        3676
North America                   English            7101880     7020890
North America                   Estonian              6205        5770
North America                   Finish               15185       13285
North America                   Flemish               4015        3780
North America                   French             2977060     2910140
North America                   German              239995      236720
North America                   Icelandic             2650        2380
North America                   Japanese              8045        7480
North America                   Lettish               5610        5545
North America                   Russian              12105       11375
North America                   Welsh                 1045        1010
North America                   Yiddish              12325       11115

15 records
```

How It Works

You created a fairly complex SELECT statement that retrieved four fields from four different tables. The four tables were all joined with explicit field comparisons using the ON clause and inner (intersecting) joins. This means you only found records where all matches existed in all four tables. You also applied two filters in a WHERE clause; plus you summarized two integer values using a SUM function. Most database engines have a built-in SUM function for adding simple numbers together. Last, you altered the query by adding aliases.

Changing Data in a Database

Changes are made to fields, in records, in tables, in a database, using the INSERT, UPDATE, and DELETE statements.

The INSERT statement is used to add new records to tables. This is the basic syntax for an INSERT statement:

```
INSERT INTO table [ ( field [, ... ] ) ] VALUES ( expression [ , ... ]);
```

A new region could be added to the REGION table with the following statement:

```
INSERT INTO REGION (REGION_ID, REGION, POPULATION, AREA)
VALUES(100,'A New Region', 1000000, 1000);
```

Some database engines allow omission of the list of fields if the VALUES clause exactly matches the structure of the table:

```
INSERT INTO REGION VALUES (101,'Another New Region', 2000000, 2000);
```

The UPDATE statement is used to change existing records in tables and has the following basic syntax:

```
UPDATE table SET field = expression [, ... ] [ WHERE ... ];
```

The WHERE clause filter determines which records are updated.

If no WHERE clause is present in an UPDATE statement, then all records in the table will be altered with a single UPDATE statement.

In this example, both of the records created in the previous two INSERT statements are updated:

```
UPDATE REGION SET REGION = UPPER (REGION) WHERE REGION_ID IN (100, 101);
```

The DELETE statement is similar in syntax to the UPDATE statement:

```
DELETE FROM table [ WHERE ... ];
```

This statement will DELETE the two records created by the previous INSERT statements and subsequently altered by the single UPDATE statement shown previously:

```
DELETE FROM REGION WHERE REGION_ID IN (100, 101);
```

Subqueries in Database Change Statements

Database change statements are the INSERT, UPDATE, and DELETE statements. Subqueries can be embedded into database change statements in various ways.

A subquery can be embedded into the VALUES clause of an INSERT statement:

```
INSERT INTO REGION (REGION_ID, REGION, POPULATION, AREA)
VALUES (102, 'East '||(SELECT REGION FROM REGION WHERE REGION_ID=1), 1000000, 100);
```

The result is that there is a new region called East Africa, as shown in this query:

```
SELECT * FROM REGION;

REGION_ID REGION                                  POPULATION       AREA
---------- ------------------------------------ ---------- ----------
        1 Africa                                 789548670   26780325
        2 Asia                                    47382633     657741
        3 Australasia                             24340222    7886602
        4 Caribbean                               40417697     268857
        5 Central America                        142653392    2360325
        6 Europe                                 488674441    4583335
        7 Far East                              2100636517   15357441
        8 Middle East                            294625718    6798768
        9 Near East                             1499157105    4721322
       10 North America                          331599508   18729272
       11 Oceania                                  9133256     536238
       12 Russian Federation                     258037209   21237500
       13 South America                          375489788   17545171
      102 East Africa                             1000000        100
```

A subquery can even become the VALUES clause of an INSERT statement:

```
INSERT INTO REGION
    SELECT COUNTRY_ID, COUNTRY, POPULATION, AREA
    FROM COUNTRY WHERE COUNTRY_ID > 150;
```

The UPDATE and DELETE statements can contain a WHERE clause. Thus the same rules apply as for the SELECT statement, such that a subquery can be embedded in the WHERE clause of UPDATE and DELETE statements.

An interesting use of embedding subqueries into an UPDATE statement is that some database engines allow more than a single field to be updated within the same UPDATE statement. The multiple fields updated must be retrieved using a subquery as in the following example:

```
UPDATE REGION SET (POPULATION, AREA) =
(
    SELECT SUM(POPULATION), SUM(AREA)
    FROM COUNTRY
    WHERE REGION_ID = REGION.REGION_ID
    GROUP BY REGION_ID
);
```

The preceding query will quite sensibly sum up all POPULATION and AREA values for each region from the COUNTRY table, and set those values into the same summary fields in the REGION table.

What Is a Transaction?

It is very important to understand what a transaction is with respect to a relational database. In a relational database, a transaction allows you to temporarily store changes. At a later point, you can choose to store the changes permanently using a COMMIT statement. Or you can also completely remove all changes you have made by using a ROLLBACK statement, as long as you have not already committed changes.

You can execute multiple database changes, such as the three INSERT statements shown here:

```
INSERT INTO REGION (REGION_ID, REGION, POPULATION, AREA)
   VALUES (111, 'Region 111', 100000, 100);
INSERT INTO REGION (REGION_ID, REGION, POPULATION, AREA)
   VALUES (112, 'Region 112', 200000, 200);
COMMIT;
INSERT INTO REGION (REGION_ID, REGION, POPULATION, AREA)
   VALUES (113, 'Region 113', 300000, 300);
ROLLBACK;
```

In the preceding example, the first two records will be permanently stored in the database by the COMMIT statement. The third record will be removed by the ROLLBACK statement.

Some general concepts of a relational database transaction are as follows:

❏ A transaction is completed when a COMMIT or ROLLBACK statement is issued.

❏ A COMMIT statement stores changes to a database.

❏ A ROLLBACK statement removes pending changes from a database.

❏ A pending change is a change not yet committed (a transaction not as yet terminated by a COMMIT or ROLLBACK statement).

❏ A transaction can exist for one or more database change statements.

❏ Before a change is committed, only the current session (database connection) can see any changes made within that current session. It follows that database changes made in other sessions (other database connections for other users) cannot be seen by the current session until those other sessions issue COMMIT statements.

❏ The term "transaction control" describes the process of how SQL code can be used to control database changes made by one or more SQL statements.

Changing Database Objects

Database objects such as tables and indexes define how data is stored and accessed in a database. Tables and indexes are known as metadata in that they are the data about the data and not the actual records. So in the demographics database (see Appendix B), the COUNTRY table is metadata and the actual countries are the real data. The COUNTRY table describes the structure of how the countries are stored in the database.

Changing database objects is not really within the scope of this book but it may help to have a very basic picture of some database change statements.

The following CREATE TABLE statement creates a table called MOREREGIONS:

```
CREATE TABLE MOREREGIONS(
    REGION_ID INTEGER PRIMARY KEY NOT NULL,
    REGION VARCHAR2(32) UNIQUE NOT NULL,
    POPULATION INTEGER NOT NULL,
    AREA INTEGER NOT NULL);
```

The next ALTER TABLE statement is used to reset the POPULATION and AREA fields in the MORERE-GIONS table, to nullable:

```
ALTER TABLE MOREREGIONS MODIFY(POPULATION INTEGER, AREA INTEGER);
```

And because the MOREREGIONS table is actually useless for the purposes of the demographics database, the MOREREGIONS table can be dropped with this statement:

```
DROP TABLE MOREREGIONS;
```

Also commonly used in a relational database are database objects called indexes. An index simply creates a physical copy of a small section in a table and creates it in a way that allows for fast searching through the index, such as using a binary tree. In general, an index could be created using a statement like this:

```
CREATE INDEX XAK_REGION_POPULATION ON REGION (POPULATION);
```

Indexes can also be altered and dropped using the ALTER INDEX and DROP INDEX statements.

In general, most relational databases allow metadata change commands that are a lot more comprehensive than just creating, altering, and dropping simple tables and indexes. Any more on this topic is not necessary for the purposes of this book.

Some databases include database object change commands within transactions, and some databases do not. In other words, some databases allow a database object change such as a CREATE TABLE statement to be rolled back and some databases do not. Some databases even automatically commit when executing database object change statements.

Generating XML Pages Using Basic SQL

So how does one now apply what was learned in the first three chapters of this book about XML and all the SQL code learned in this chapter so far? How does one use SQL in a relational database to create XML documents?

First, there are various different tools and toys that allow direct access between a relational database, SQL coding, and XML documents. Some of these toys and tricks are covered in subsequent chapters. What you need to discover now is how simple XML documents can be managed using simple SQL statements and a relational database. This will help tie together all you have learned so far.

The very last section in Chapter 2 contained a brief example showing how to generate an XML document using an ASP script, while connected to a relational database. You don't need to use ASP. You cannot use basic SQL commands to create XML documents because relational database tables are two-dimensional structures, whereas XML documents are three-dimensional. XML is more of an object structure, rather than a relational structure. Let me demonstrate how you can go about creating XML documents using SQL.

This query creates a simple two-dimensional XML structure:

```
SELECT '<region><name>'||REGION||'</name>',
    '<population>'||POPULATION||'</population></region>'
FROM REGION;
```

The result could look something like this:

```
<region><name>Africa</name><population>789548670</population></region>
<region><name>Asia</name><population>47382633</population></region>
<region><name>Australasia</name><population>24340222</population></region>
<region><name>Caribbean</name><population>40417697</population></region>
<region><name>CentralAmerica</name><population>142653392</population></region>
<region><name>Europe</name><population>488674441</population></region>
<region><name>FarEast</name><population>2100636517</population></region>
```

There are two problems with the preceding output: There is no XML tag, and there is no root tag. You can try adding them like this:

```
SELECT '<?xml version="1.0" ?><regions><region><name>'||REGION||'</name>',
    '<population>'||POPULATION||'</population></region></regions>'
FROM REGION;
```

The result is this, duplicating both the XML tag and the root tag for every line (a two-dimensional structure), and is not a valid XML document:

```
<?xml version="1.0" ?><regions><region><name>Africa</name>
<population>789548670</population></region></regions>
<?xml version="1.0" ?><regions><region><name>Asia</name>
<population>47382633</population></region></regions>
<?xml version="1.0" ?><regions><region><name>Australasia</name>
<population>24340222</population></region></regions>
<?xml version="1.0" ?><regions><region><name>Caribbean</name>
<population>40417697</population></region></regions>
<?xml version="1.0" ?><regions><region><name>Central America</name>
<population>142653392</population></region></regions>
<?xml version="1.0" ?><regions><region><name>Europe</name>
<population>488674441</population></region></regions>
```

The problem can possibly be solved using something like this, given the ability in the database you are using to retrieve a string from your query tool without actually reading any tables:

```
SELECT '<?xml version="1.0" ?><regions>' FROM DUAL;
SELECT '<region><name>'||REGION||'</name>',
    '<population>'||POPULATION||'</population></region>'
FROM REGION;
SELECT '</regions>' FROM DUAL;
```

This way, you do get a three-dimensional structure where the root node occurs once, and contains all the regional data:

```xml
<?xml version="1.0"?><regions>
<region><name>Africa</name><population>789548670</population></region>
<region><name>Asia</name><population>47382633</population></region>
<region><name>Australasia</name><population>24340222</population></region>
<region><name>Caribbean</name><population>40417697</population></region>
<region><name>CentralAmerica</name><population>142653392</population></region>
<region><name>Europe</name><population>488674441</population></region>
<region><name>FarEast</name><population>2100636517</population></region>
<region><name>MiddleEast</name><population>294625718</population></region>
<region><name>NearEast</name><population>1499157105</population></region>
<region><name>NorthAmerica</name><population>331599508</population></region>
<region><name>Oceania</name><population>9133256</population></region>
<region><name>RussianFederation</name><population>258037209</population></region>
<region><name>SouthAmerica</name><population>375489788</population></region>
</regions>
```

My SQL coding tool for my database did not preserve the space in the XML tag between the strings `<?xml` *and* `version="1.0"?>`. *I had to manually edit the XML text file to put the space character back in.*

The preceding script is a valid XML document and looks like that shown in Figure 4-1, when executed in a browser.

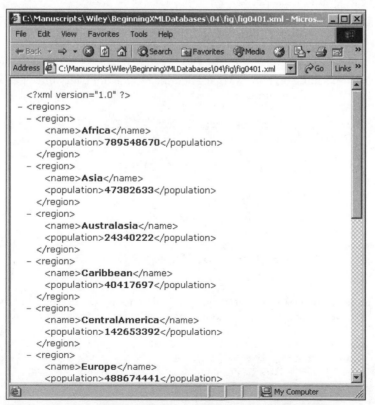

Figure 4-1: Generating a single-layer XML document using SQL

There is one thing that is really, really wrong with using SQL to generate an XML document. It goes back to the relational two-dimensional versus the XML three-dimensional object hierarchy. Getting data from multiple tables — and placing it into multiple layers in an XML document — is more or less impossible with simple SQL because SQL returns two dimensions. This is one possible solution:

```
SELECT '<?xml version="1.0" ?><regions>' FROM DUAL;
SELECT  '<region><name>'||R.REGION||'</name>'
  ||'<population>'||R.POPULATION||'</population>'
  ||'<country><name>'||C.COUNTRY||'</name>'
  ||'<population>'||C.POPULATION||'</population>'
  ||'</country>'
  ||'</region>'
FROM REGION R JOIN COUNTRY C ON (C.REGION_ID = R.REGION_ID)
WHERE R.REGION_ID IN (9,10);
SELECT '</regions>' FROM DUAL;
```

The preceding query is restricted to REGION_ID *values 9 and 10 (Near East and North America) to make the output a little easier to follow.*

As you can see in the preceding query, things are getting a little complicated. The XML output is shown here:

```
<?xml version="1.0" ?><regions>
<region><name>Near
East</name><population>1499157105</population><country><name>Bangladesh</name><popu
lation>147365352</population></country></region>
<region><name>Near
East</name><population>1499157105</population><country><name>India</name><populatio
n>1095351995</population></country></region>
<region><name>Near
East</name><population>1499157105</population><country><name>Pakistan</name><popula
tion>165803560</population></country></region>
<region><name>Near East</name><population>1499157105</population><country><name>Sri
Lanka</name><population>20222240</population></country></region>
<region><name>Near
East</name><population>1499157105</population><country><name>Turkey</name><populati
on>70413958</population></country></region>
<region><name>North
America</name><population>331599508</population><country><name>Canada</name><popula
tion>33098932</population></country></region>
<region><name>North
America</name><population>331599508</population><country><name>Greenland</name><pop
ulation>56361</population></country></region>
<region><name>North
America</name><population>331599508</population><country><name>United
States</name><population>298444215</population></country></region>
</regions>
```

The preceding XML output looks as shown in Figure 4-2, showing countries contained within regions.

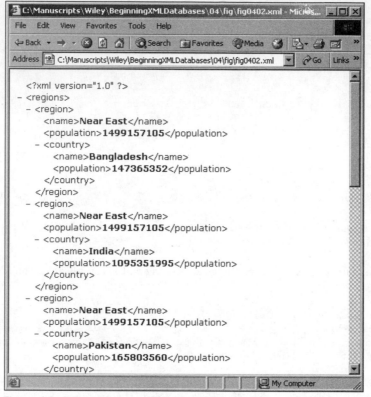

Figure 4-2: Generating a multiple-layer XML document using SQL

You can use multiple SQL statements to contain countries within regions more distinctly, something like that shown here, which is getting really complicated:

```
SELECT '<?xml version="1.0" ?><regions>' FROM DUAL;

SELECT  '<region><name>'||REGION||'</name>'
   ||'<population>'||POPULATION||'</population>'
FROM REGION WHERE REGION_ID=1;

SELECT  '<country><name>'||COUNTRY||'</name>'
   ||'<population>'||POPULATION||'</population>'   ||'</country>'
FROM COUNTRY WHERE REGION_ID = 9;

SELECT '</region>' FROM DUAL;

SELECT  '<region><name>'||REGION||'</name>'
   ||'<population>'||POPULATION||'</population>'
FROM REGION WHERE REGION_ID=2;

SELECT  '<country><name>'||COUNTRY||'</name>'
   ||'<population>'||POPULATION||'</population>'   ||'</country>'
```

```
FROM COUNTRY WHERE REGION_ID = 10;

SELECT '</region>' FROM DUAL;

SELECT '</regions>' FROM DUAL;
```

The output of the preceding script is identical to the previous example except that it might have new lines in more places to break up the XML document a little better:

```
<?xml version="1.0" ?><regions>
<region><name>Africa</name><population>789548670</population>
<country><name>Bangladesh</name><population>147365352</population></country>
<country><name>India</name><population>1095351995</population></country>
<country><name>Pakistan</name><population>165803560</population></country>
<country><name>Sri Lanka</name><population>20222240</population></country>
<country><name>Turkey</name><population>70413958</population></country>
</region>
<region><name>Asia</name><population>47382633</population>
<country><name>Canada</name><population>33098932</population></country>
<country><name>Greenland</name><population>56361</population></country>
<country><name>United States</name><population>298444215</population></country>
</region>
</regions>
```

The point I am trying to make in this section is that you need more of what is called "program control." SQL is a scripting language. SQL sends a single command to a database, where there is no dependence between one command and the next. A proper programming language allows more control, using things such as loops and other programming control structures. In a programming language like C, you can embed the SQL statements shown in the previous example and have better control. However, you would still have individual SQL statements.

There is a better way. Most relational databases contain some kind of procedural language that is intended to create stored procedures. A stored procedure is a procedure that is stored in a database and intended to operate on database data. Some relational databases have very simple stored procedure languages; others allow a lot of sophistication. The code that follows is a specialized stored procedure language (in this case pseudocode), allowing looping constructs to be built for each record retrieved from a parent table. In the case of the demographics database, the REGION table is a parent table of the COUNTRY table, COUNTRY is a parent of STATES, and STATES is a parent of CITIES.

Pseudocode is code that will not work anywhere, in any database or programming language, or for XML. Pseudocode is conceptual in nature and intended to explain or describe a concept, without the nitty-gritty details of actually making coding work in any specific environment.

```
BEGIN
    Regions = SELECT * FROM REGION;
    FOR R IN Regions
        Countries = SELECT * FROM COUNTRY WHERE REGION_ID = R;
        FOR C IN COUNTRIES
            States = SELECT * FROM STATE WHERE COUNTRY_ID = C;
            FOR S IN STATES
                Cities = SELECT * FROM CITY WHERE STATE_ID = S;
            END LOOP
        END LOOP
    END LOOP
END;
```

Now using the same pseudocode example, I have added some of the XML tags and code into the pseudocode script that follows:

```
BEGIN
    print '<?xml version="1.0" ?><regions>'
    Regions = SELECT * FROM REGION;
    FOR R IN Regions
        print
'<region><name>'||REGION||'</name><population>'||POPULATION||'</population>'
        Countries = SELECT * FROM COUNTRY WHERE REGION_ID = R;
        FOR C IN COUNTRIES
            print
'<country><name>'||REGION||'</name><population>'||POPULATION||'</country>'
            States = SELECT * FROM STATE WHERE COUNTRY_ID = C;
            FOR S IN STATES
                print
'<state><name>'||REGION||'</name><population>'||POPULATION||'</population>'
                Cities = SELECT * FROM CITY WHERE STATE_ID = S;
                FOR CI in CITIES
                    print
'<city><name>'||CITY||'</name><population>'||POPULATION||'</city>'
                END LOOP
                print </state>'
            END LOOP
            print </country>'
        END LOOP
        print </region>'
    END LOOP
    print '</regions>'
END;
```

The preceding script is pseudocode. This means it will not function as is — in any programming language, in any database, or on any computer.

Assume in the preceding script that the print *statement dumps whatever literal string is indicated directly to the output.*

There are easier ways to merge relational database and XML technologies, which you will read about in subsequent chapters.

Summary

In this chapter you learned that:

- ❏ Querying tables in a database using a SELECT statement retrieves records that are divided into fields.

- ❏ A table applies structure to data.

- ❏ A record repeats the structure of a table by storing data such as customer names and addresses.

- ❏ A field is used to store an individual value such as the name or address of a customer.

- ❏ The WHERE clause can be used to apply a filter to records retrieved by the SELECT statement.

❏ The `ORDER BY` clause is used to sort records by one or more fields or expressions.

❏ Field headers in queries change only the header of the column in the record output.

❏ The `AS` clause can be used to change a field name, where the new name can be used in some of the other clauses of a query.

❏ The `GROUP BY` clause is used to summarize record output into fewer, aggregated records.

❏ Subqueries can be constructed in various ways.

❏ Subqueries can be nested to many levels.

❏ Subqueries do not always join records as they do not always return values to a calling query.

❏ Records found by a subquery can be filtered by passing values into a subquery from the parent query. This is called a correlated query because a correlation is established between the parent query and the subquery.

❏ The `JOIN` clause merges records from two tables based on matching field values.

❏ The `UNION` clause can be used to retrieve records from two tables, such that all records are retrieved from both tables.

❏ Records can be changed in tables using the `INSERT`, `UPDATE`, and `DELETE` statements.

❏ Subqueries can be used in some parts of `INSERT`, `UPDATE`, and `DELETE` statements.

❏ A transaction begins when `INSERT`, `UPDATE`, and `DELETE` statements are executed.

❏ A transaction is completed when a `COMMIT` or `ROLLBACK` statement is executed.

❏ Database objects are changed with specialized database object `CREATE`, `ALTER`, and `DROP` statements.

Exercises

1. Which of these will sort records in a query?

    a.   `ORDER BY`

    b.   `WHERE`

    c.   `SELECT`

    d.   `FROM`

    e.   None of the above

2. What will the statement `SELECT * FROM CUSTOMER` find?

    a.   All records in the `CUSTOMER` table

    b.   The first record in the `CUSTOMER` table

    c.   The last two records in the `CUSTOMER` table

    d.   All fields in the `CUSTOMER` table

    e.   All records and all fields in the `CUSTOMER` table

3. Which of these statements can be used to make changes to data in a database?

    a.   `UPDATE`

    b.   `SELECT * FROM ...`

    c.   `CREATE TABLE`

    d.   `ALTER TABLE`

    e.   `INSERT`

    f.   All but b.

4. How many tables will this query retrieve records from?

```
SELECT * FROM TABLE1 CROSS JOIN
    INNER JOIN TABLE2 USING (ID1)
        CROSS JOIN TABLE3
            LEFT OUTER JOIN TABLE4 USING (ID2);
```

    a.   1

    b.   2

    c.   3

    d.   4

    e.   5

Oracle Database and XML

There is immense capability in Oracle Database and Oracle SQL for utilizing the power of XML. This chapter covers XML only as it directly relates to Oracle SQL. In other words, you examine how XML documents can be created, accessed, and manipulated directly from within Oracle SQL and Oracle Database. You are presented with various specialized techniques and facilities available to Oracle Database.

> *Oracle Database software can be downloaded from* http://www.oracle.com *and purchased on CD-ROM (for a nominal shipping and handling fee) on a trial basis. You can attempt all the examples in this chapter. There are no Try It Out sections in this chapter as specific database software may not necessarily be available to you at the time of reading this book. Reading this book is not dependent on your having software for any particular database.*

In this chapter you learn about:

❑   The XMLType data type for storing XML documents within an Oracle database

❑   The methods available to the XMLType data type

❑   Creating XML documents using various tools

❑   How XML documents can be created from Oracle Database tables using SQL/XML, the SYS_XMLGEN function, and various methods using PL/SQL

❑   Adding XML document data to an Oracle Database table

❑   Scanning through and retrieving data from XML data stored in an Oracle database

❑   Changing the content of XML data stored in an Oracle database

The Oracle XMLType Data Type

Creating XML documents in any specific database is often all about using the specialized tools available within that database engine. Oracle Database is no exception to this rule. The first thing to do with an Oracle database is to examine what is actually a specialized data type: the XMLType data type.

In its most basic form, XML in Oracle SQL comprises the XMLType data type and a number of methods attached to that data type. (The XMLType is effectively a class.) The XMLType stores the text of XML documents and allows access to the XML document object model. The document object model allows access to all the elements in an XML document programmatically.

The XMLType data type is a specialized data type used for both storing and processing of XML documents in an Oracle database. Additionally, an XMLType can be stored in a specially created table in a binary object field called a CLOB object. A CLOB object in an Oracle database is essentially an internally searchable text object. This means you can search for a single piece of text within the binary object.

XMLTypes are added into tables in Oracle Database in the following ways:

Create a table that is an XML data type in itself:

```
CREATE TABLE XMLDOCUMENT OF XMLTYPE;
```

Or create a table containing an XMLType data type field as follows:

```
CREATE TABLE XML
(
    ID NUMBER NOT NULL, XML XMLTYPE
   ,CONSTRAINT XPK_XML PRIMARY KEY (ID)
);
```

XMLType data types can even be used in the Oracle database programming language—PL/SQL (Programming Language for SQL).

PL/SQL in Oracle Database provides for extensive programming control capabilities in the creation of stored procedures, stored functions, and triggers—within the database.

```
DECLARE
    XML XMLTYPE;
BEGIN
    NULL;
END;
/
```

Oracle XMLType Data Type Methods

There are numerous methods that can be executed against XMLType data types. Oracle Database calls these methods *subprograms*. I am calling them *methods* because they are executed against iterations of the XMLType data type. In other words, these methods are executed something like this:

```
DECLARE
    XML XMLTYPE;
BEGIN
    XML = SELECT * FROM XMLDOCUMENT;
    print XML.GETSTRINGVALUE();
END;
/
```

The preceding script is pseudocode. This means it will not function as is — in any programming language, in any database, or on any computer.

Assume in the preceding script that the print *statement dumps whatever literal string indicated directly to the output.*

This is a brief summary of a few of those methods:

❑ EXISTSNODE(XPath-expression, [namespace]): Uses an XPath expression to see if a node exists in an XMLType. It returns 1 (true) if the node is found, otherwise 0 (false).

XPath is a specialized XSLT tool for parsing XML documents and is discussed later on in this book. An XPath expression is essentially a pattern that can be potentially matched within an XML document. XPath is a specialized scripting language used to scan XML documents.

❑ EXTRACT(XPath-expression): Uses an XPath expression to extract a node (including all children) from an XMLType.

Executing the EXTRACT *function as* XMLType.EXTRACT('/*') *will produce a much more readable display for XML objects.*

❑ GETNAMESPACE(): Retrieves the namespace of an XMLType object.

❑ GETROOTELEMENT(): Retrieves the root element of an XMLType object.

❑ GETSTRINGVAL(): This method is required in order to convert the XML structure (stored in an XMLType) into a readable string.

❑ ISFRAGMENT(): A fragment of an XML document contains no root element (or multiple root elements). Thus 1 (true) is returned for a fragment, 0 (false) for a properly formed XML document.

❑ TRANSFORM(XSL-stylesheet-script): Transforms an XMLType with an XSL stylesheet into a transformed XML document.

You do not need to understand exactly what all these methods do at this point. You just need to know that they exist. You should remember from Chapter 3 how XSL is used to scan through XML documents and apply processing to parts of those XML documents. Of particular note are XSL node creation and templating element categories, which are similar in function to the preceding methods.

You don't need to know anything more about the XMLType data type itself. It is simply a structure for storing an XML document, where the XML document can be worked with as an XML document. In other words, the XMLType data type allows the XML document stored within it to be accessible as any other XML document would be. This includes access to the XML DOM, all sorts of specialized XML features such as XSL and even standardized database access structures such as XQuery.

XQuery is a standard set of tools used for database access of XML documents with any database. It is thus not appropriate for this chapter, which focuses on Oracle Database alone. XQuery is covered from a more generic (non-database vendor-specific) perspective later on in this book.

In short, the XMLType data type has little to do with processing an XML document, or even with SQL in an Oracle database.

All database vendors such as Oracle (Oracle Database), Microsoft (SQL Server), or IBM (DB2), implement a standardized form of SQL. However, they do make changes that are specific to each database engine.

Implementing XML in an Oracle Database

There are a number of things that you need to know about using XML documents in a database:

❑ **Creating XML documents from a database:** This is specialized functionality allowing the creation of XML documents in Oracle Database. Some of this was functionality described generically, using very basic SQL commands, in Chapter 4. This chapter will get a little more sophisticated, and obviously Oracle Database specific, on this particular topic.

❑ **Creating XML documents inside a database:** In this chapter, you examine how to create XML documents within Oracle Database. This involves use of XMLType data types in tandem with Oracle Database–specific functionality to create those XML document structures.

❑ **Retrieving data from XML documents:** Again, there is specialized Oracle Database functionality for retrieving XML Document content from XMLType data types.

❑ **Changing XML document content:** And once again, the XMLType data type comes packaged with specialized functionality. This functionality allows changes to XML documents while they are stored in an Oracle database.

Let's begin.

Creating XML Documents from an Oracle Database

When creating an XML document you are going to read data in an Oracle database. Reading data from any relational database generally involves reading records from tables. There are various Oracle Database–specific methods of doing this:

❑ **The SQL/XML Standard:** There are numerous SQL/XML functions and attributes that adhere to the SQL Standard for XML.

The SQL Standard for XML is a standard created and supported by INCITS (International Committee for Information Technology Standards).

Basic functions create elements (XML tags) and assign attributes to elements (attributes within individual tags), amongst other functionality.

❑ **The DBMS_XMLGEN Package:** This package is complex and creates an XML document based on an entire query.

A package is a programming modular structure used by Oracle PL/SQL. A package is simply a group of stored procedures or functions, grouped together as a single block of code. Thus a package allows access to contained procedures and functions, by referencing procedures or functions as being within that package. This is a programming concept similar to creating class libraries in a language such as Java.

❑ **The SYS_XMLGEN Function:** This function creates an XML document for each record as retrieved by a query to an Oracle database.

❑ **The XSU utility:** This is an XML SQL utility specifically built for Java. This utility is too advanced to be covered in this book. Oracle Database allows for Java-written code to be both stored and executed within an Oracle database. Java can be used to code stored procedures and functions within an Oracle database. Additionally, that Java code can be compiled to a less interpretive form of machine code. This allows Java-created stored procedures and functions to help the overall performance of an Oracle database.

Because the SQL/XML functions are the accepted standard, let's examine these functions in detail.

The SQL/XML Standard

As already stated, SQL/XML as used in Oracle Database, does adhere to INCITS established standards. Let's first of all introduce some of the basic functionality of SQL/XML as it is available in Oracle Database. After that you will see examples to explain it all:

❑ XMLELEMENT: Allows creation of XML tag elements. The syntax is as follows:

```
XMLELEMENT ( [ NAME ] identifier [, attributes ] [, expression [ , ... ] ] )
```

❑ XMLATTRIBUTES: Assigns attribute values to tags. The syntax is as follows:

```
XMLATTRIBUTES ( expression [ AS alias ] [ , ... ] )
```

❑ XMLCONCAT: Concatenates multiple XML element tags. The syntax is as follows:

```
XMLCONCAT ( XMLType object )..
```

❑ XMLAGG: Creates a single column or expression from multiple rows by aggregating them into a single row and XML tag. The syntax is as follows:

```
XMLAGG ( XMLType object [ ORDER BY ... ] )
```

❑ XMLCOLATTVAL: Attempts to standardize for relational tables. Every subset unit is given the tag column and the original name of the tag becomes an attribute of the column tag. For example, <name>Jim Jones</name> becomes <column name = "NAME">Jim Jones</column>.

```
XMLCOLATTVAL ( expression [ AS alias ] [ , ... ] )
```

❑ XMLFOREST: Functions the same way as multiple XMLELEMENT executions where each element is created as a tag, containing their respective values. The syntax is as follows:

```
XMLFOREST ( expression [ AS alias ] [ , ... ] )
```

❑ XMLTRANSFORM: Executes a transformation for repeating groups in an XML document, applying an XSL (eXtensible Style Sheet) to each repeating group item in the XML document. The XMLTRANSFORM method will not be demonstrated in the examples that follow because all it does is apply an XSL style sheet to an XML document. Applying XSL formatting and templating to XML documents is covered in Chapter 3. The syntax is as follows:

```
XMLTRANSFORM (XMLType object, XMLType object )
```

Now let me explain each method by example.

This example uses the XMLELEMENT function to create XML elements (tags) directly from an SQL statement (a much easier method than shown at the end of Chapter 4):

```
SELECT XMLELEMENT("region", REGION) FROM REGION;
```

This is the result:

```
<region>Africa</region>
<region>Asia</region>
<region>Australasia</region>
<region>Caribbean</region>
<region>Central America</region>
<region>Europe</region>
<region>Far East</region>
<region>Middle East</region>
<region>Near East</region>
<region>North America</region>
<region>Oceania</region>
<region>Russian Federation</region>
<region>South America</region>
```

And multiple XMLELEMENT functions can even be embedded within one another to produce a hierarchy of multiple layers, as an XML document should be constructed:

```
SELECT
    XMLELEMENT("region"
        ,XMLELEMENT("name", REGION)
        ,XMLELEMENT("population", POPULATION))
FROM REGION;
```

This is the result:

```
<region><name>Africa</name><population>789548670</population></region>
<region><name>Asia</name><population>47382633</population></region>
<region><name>Australasia</name><population>24340222</population></region>
<region><name>Caribbean</name><population>40417697</population></region>
<region><name>Central America</name><population>142653392</population></region>
<region><name>Europe</name><population>488674441</population></region>
<region><name>Far East</name><population>2100636517</population></region>
<region><name>Middle East</name><population>294625718</population></region>
<region><name>Near East</name><population>1499157105</population></region>
<region><name>North America</name><population>331599508</population></region>
<region><name>Oceania</name><population>9133256</population></region>
<region><name>Russian Federation</name><population>258037209</population></region>
<region><name>South America</name><population>375489788</population></region>
```

In Oracle SQL*Plus tools you may have to execute SET LONG 2000 WRAP ON LINESIZE 5000.

The resulting output, shown in the preceding code, is a little messy but the point is made. The preceding query is much easier than similar queries performed in Chapter 4.

This next example mixes elements and attributes together by adding in the XMLATTRIBUTES function:

```
SELECT
    XMLELEMENT("region", XMLATTRIBUTES(REGION AS "name")
      ,XMLELEMENT("population", POPULATION))
FROM REGION;
```

This is the result with the name attribute highlighted for the first region:

```
<region name="Africa"><population>789548670</population></region>
<region name="Asia"><population>47382633</population></region>
<region name="Australasia"><population>24340222</population></region>
<region name="Caribbean"><population>40417697</population></region>
<region name="Central America"><population>142653392</population></region>
<region name="Europe"><population>488674441</population></region>
<region name="Far East"><population>2100636517</population></region>
<region name="Middle East"><population>294625718</population></region>
<region name="Near East"><population>1499157105</population></region>
<region name="North America"><population>331599508</population></region>
<region name="Oceania"><population>9133256</population></region>
<region name="Russian Federation"><population>258037209</population></region>
<region name="South America"><population>375489788</population></region>
```

And this query places all the fields applicable to each region into the element for each region:

```
SELECT
    XMLELEMENT("region",
      XMLATTRIBUTES(REGION AS "name", POPULATION AS "population"))
FROM REGION;
```

This is the result with the attributes highlighted for the first region again:

```
<region name="Africa" population="789548670"></region>
<region name="Asia" population="47382633"></region>
<region name="Australasia" population="24340222"></region>
<region name="Caribbean" population="40417697"></region>
<region name="Central America" population="142653392"></region>
<region name="Europe" population="488674441"></region>
<region name="Far East" population="2100636517"></region>
<region name="Middle East" population="294625718"></region>
<region name="Near East" population="1499157105"></region>
<region name="North America" population="331599508"></region>
<region name="Oceania" population="9133256"></region>
<region name="Russian Federation" population="258037209"></region>
```

The XML_CONCAT function concatenates multiple XML fragments into a single XML pattern, which will be demonstrated in a roundabout way.

Concatenate means to add multiple strings together into a single string.

This example simply retrieves three fields from the COUNTRY table, all as separate elements:

```
SELECT XMLELEMENT("region", REGION) AS "Region"
   , XMLELEMENT("population", POPULATION) AS "Population"
   , XMLELEMENT("area", AREA) AS "Area"
FROM REGION;
```

The result is just nasty (showing only the first two rows, with huge and ugly long strings representing each XMLELEMENT method. The dots, ..., represent hundreds of space characters:

```
<region>Asia</region>............<population>47382633</population>...........<area
>657741</area>
<region>Australasia</region>............<population>24340222</population>.........
..<area>7886602</area>
```

A TRIM function could be used, where the TRIM function removes all space characters and white space from either side of each of the three separate string values:

```
SELECT TRIM(XMLELEMENT("region", REGION)) AS "Region"
   , TRIM(XMLELEMENT("population", POPULATION)) AS "Population"
   , TRIM(XMLELEMENT("area", AREA)) AS "Area"
FROM REGION;
```

Again, the following shows the two regions in the previous example. This time the space characters are removed:

```
<region>Asia</region>
<population>47382633</population>
<area>657741</area>

<region>Australasia</region>
<population>24340222</population>
<area>7886602</area>
```

Now add the XMLCONCAT method and the benefit is obvious. There are now no spaces:

```
SELECT XMLCONCAT(
    XMLELEMENT("region", REGION)
   ,XMLELEMENT("population", POPULATION)
   ,XMLELEMENT("area", AREA))
FROM REGION;
```

And now it makes sense to display all of the regions again. This is a much neater result:

```
<region>Africa</region><population>789548670</population><area>26780325</area>
<region>Asia</region><population>47382633</population><area>657741</area>
<region>Australasia</region><population>24340222</population><area>7886602</area>
<region>Caribbean</region><population>40417697</population><area>268857</area>
<region>Central America</region><population>142653392</population><area>2360325</
area>
```

```
<region>Europe</region><population>488674441</population><area>4583335</area>
<region>Far East</region><population>2100636517</population><area>15357441</area>
<region>Middle East</region><population>294625718</population><area>6798768</area>
<region>Near East</region><population>1499157105</population><area>4721322</area>
<region>North America</region><population>331599508</population><area>18729272</area>
<region>Oceania</region><population>9133256</population><area>536238</area>
<region>Russian Federation</region><population>258037209</population><area>21237500
</area>
<region>South America</region><population>375489788</population><area>17545171</area>
```

The XMLAGG method aggregates separate lines of output, all into a single string. The XMLAGG method also allows sorting:

```
SELECT XMLELEMENT("demographics", REGION||' '||POPULATION||' '||AREA)
FROM REGION;
```

The result shows multiple lines returned:

```
<demographics>Africa 789548670 26780325</demographics>
<demographics>Asia 47382633 657741</demographics>
<demographics>Australasia 24340222 7886602</demographics>
<demographics>Caribbean 40417697 268857</demographics>
<demographics>Central America 142653392 2360325</demographics>
<demographics>Europe 488674441 4583335</demographics>
<demographics>Far East 2100636517 15357441</demographics>
<demographics>Middle East 294625718 6798768</demographics>
<demographics>Near East 1499157105 4721322</demographics>
<demographics>North America 331599508 18729272</demographics>
<demographics>Oceania 9133256 536238</demographics>
<demographics>Russian Federation 258037209 21237500</demographics>
<demographics>South America 375489788 17545171</demographics>
```

Including the XMLAGG method returns the output as a single string and sorted in order of decreasing population. The POPULATION field is returned first in each demographics element to demonstrate this:

```
SELECT XMLAGG(
    XMLELEMENT("demographics"
    ,POPULATION||' '||REGION||' '||AREA) ORDER BY POPULATION DESC)
FROM REGION;
```

This is the result, containing only the first three regions and clearly showing a single wrapped line in descending order of populations:

```
<demographics>2100636517 Far East 15357441</demographics><demographics>
1499157105 N ear East 4721322</demographics><demographics>789548670 Africa
26780325</demographic s> ...
```

The disadvantage of XMLAGG is that it can only aggregate a single element, and thus fields are concatenated. The only real benefit of the XMLAGG method is to remove new line characters from output and resort. In general, unless XML documents are completely monstrous, or perhaps never viewed by a human eye, then it is not advantageous to remove new line characters. The following query would simply return regions, containing an executable XML document, simply aggregated into a single line:

```
SELECT XMLAGG(
    XMLELEMENT("region", XMLATTRIBUTES(REGION AS "name")
        ,XMLELEMENT("population", POPULATION)
        ,XMLELEMENT("area", AREA)))
FROM REGION;
```

The XMLCOLATTVAL method can be used to generate a form of a relational structure in an XML document format. The following query pulls three fields from the region table generating XML into a relational database recognizable format:

```
SELECT
    XMLELEMENT("region"
        ,XMLCOLATTVAL(REGION, POPULATION, AREA))
FROM REGION;
```

This is the output of the query, containing only the first three regions with each separate line wrapped for the purposes of demonstration:

```
<region><column name = "REGION">Africa</column><column name = "POPULATION">78954867
0</column><column name = "AREA">26780325</column></region>
<region><column name = "REGION">Asia</column><column name = "POPULATION">47382633</
column><column name = "AREA">657741</column></region>
<region><column name = "REGION">Australasia</column><column name = "POPULATION">243
40222</column><column name = "AREA">7886602</column></region>
```

Before going any further let's introduce the use of a function called EXTRACT, which has been mentioned previously in this chapter. This is the same query again but passing the entire resulting XMLType object produced by the SELECT statement through the EXTRACT function:

```
SELECT
    XMLELEMENT("region"
        ,XMLCOLATTVAL(REGION, POPULATION, AREA)).EXTRACT('/*')
FROM REGION;
```

Only the first two regions are shown but the output is so much easier to read in a standard XML document display format:

```
<region>
  <column name="REGION">Africa</column>
  <column name="POPULATION">789548670</column>
  <column name="AREA">26780325</column>
```

```
  </region>

<region>
  <column name="REGION">Asia</column>
  <column name="POPULATION">47382633</column>
  <column name="AREA">657741</column>
</region>
```

In the future, the EXTRACT *function will be used where it is appropriate.*

The XMLFOREST method allows creation of multiple XML elements in a single method. The following query creates multiple elements by selecting fields. It is not creating each field as an individual element:

```
SELECT
   XMLELEMENT("region"
      ,XMLFOREST(REGION AS "name", POPULATION AS "population", AREA AS "area")
).EXTRACT('/*')
FROM REGION;
```

This is the result showing only the first three regions:

```
<region>
   <name>Africa</name>
   <population>789548670</population>
   <area>26780325</area>
</region>

<region>
   <name>Asia</name>
   <population>47382633</population>
   <area>657741</area>
</region>
```

There is really one fundamental problem, which will be demonstrated shortly. You may have already surmised what this problem is. If not, then don't worry about it for it will be explained shortly. The first thing to discuss about this so far possibly unknown problem is the reason why there is a problem. There is a very fundamental disparity between relational database structure and object structures. A relational database and SQL working together output what are called tuples. A tuple is really a two-dimensional structure, where parent values are duplicated. An XML document can duplicate parent values by duplicating parent tags, but it is not supposed to. An XML document is supposed to be a hierarchical structure, where there is only ever one unique copy of each parent tag. This has already been explained in Chapter 2. Let's demonstrate the difference with some examples and show why SQL/XML falls short of the needs of proper XML document hierarchical structure. Examine the following example join query:

```
SELECT R.REGION, R.POPULATION, R.AREA,
   CO.COUNTRY, CO.POPULATION, CO.AREA, CO.CURRENCY, CO.RATE
FROM REGION R JOIN COUNTRY CO ON (CO.REGION_ID=R.REGION_ID)
WHERE R.REGION_ID IN (3,9) ORDER BY R.REGION, CO.COUNTRY;
```

In the partial result that follows, note how the regions are duplicated in all records (there are two occurrences of Australasia and five of Near East):

```
REGION         POPULATION      AREA COUNTRY       POPULATION      AREA CURRENCY
-----------    ----------    -------- -----------   ----------  ---------- --------
Australasia      24340222     7886602 Australia       20264082    7617931 Dollars
Australasia      24340222     7886602 New Zealand      4076140     268671 Dollars
Near East      1499157105     4721322 Bangladesh     147365352     133911 Taka
Near East      1499157105     4721322 India         1095351995    2973190 Rupees
Near East      1499157105     4721322 Pakistan       165803560     778720 Rupees
Near East      1499157105     4721322 Sri Lanka       20222240      64740 Rupees
Near East      1499157105     4721322 Turkey          70413958     770761 New Lira
```

As you see in the preceding result, the parent regions for each country are duplicated. This is the equivalent SQL/XML query:

```
SELECT
    XMLELEMENT("region", XMLATTRIBUTES(R.REGION "name"),
        XMLFOREST(R.POPULATION AS "population", R.AREA AS "area"),
        XMLELEMENT("country", XMLATTRIBUTES(CO.COUNTRY "name"),
            XMLFOREST(CO.POPULATION "population", CO.AREA "area",
                    CO.CURRENCY "currency", CO.RATE "rate")
        )
    ).EXTRACT('/*')
FROM REGION R JOIN COUNTRY CO ON (CO.REGION_ID=R.REGION_ID)
WHERE R.REGION_ID IN (3,9) ORDER BY R.REGION, CO.COUNTRY;
```

And this is the result of the SQL/XML query, showing the first four countries:

```
<region name="Australasia">
  <population>24340222</population>
  <area>7886602</area>
  <country name="Australia">
    <population>20264082</population>
    <area>7617931</area>
    <currency>Dollars</currency>
    <rate>1.30141</rate>
  </country>
</region>

<region name="Australasia">
  <population>24340222</population>
  <area>7886602</area>
  <country name="New Zealand">
    <population>4076140</population>
    <area>268671</area>
    <currency>Dollars</currency>
    <rate>1.42369</rate>
  </country>
</region>

<region name="Near East">
```

```
    <population>1499157105</population>
    <area>4721322</area>
    <country name="Bangladesh">
      <population>147365352</population>
      <area>133911</area>
      <currency>Taka</currency>
      <rate>0</rate>
    </country>
  </region>

  <region name="Near East">
    <population>1499157105</population>
    <area>4721322</area>
    <country name="India">
      <population>1095351995</population>
      <area>2973190</area>
      <currency>Rupees</currency>
      <rate>43.62</rate>
    </country>
  </region>
```

Note how in the preceding XML output the highlighted parts show duplicated information. Imagine an XML document of this nature, where there are many layers of parent-child relationships between tags. The result could be XML data that is physically very much larger than it should be. Physical file sizes can affect performance and scanning efficiency drastically because I/O costs can go up.

I/O means Input/Output and refers to the activity of reading and writing from and to disk. Disk storage is much slower than communication between RAM (Random Access Memory) and the CPU (Central Processing Unit — the processor) of a computer. I/O is very significant and should always be considered seriously.

Of course, a GROUP BY clause could be used in the join query to return only a single record for each region:

```
SELECT R.REGION, R.POPULATION, R.AREA,
    SUM(CO.POPULATION), SUM(CO.AREA)
FROM REGION R JOIN COUNTRY CO ON (CO.REGION_ID=R.REGION_ID)
WHERE R.REGION_ID IN (3,9)
GROUP BY R.REGION, R.POPULATION, R.AREA
ORDER BY R.REGION;
```

But as you can see in the result, the population and area values for each country are summarized, and the currency is completely listed:

```
REGION        POPULATION       AREA SUM(CO.POPULATION) SUM(CO.AREA)
-----------   ----------  ---------- ------------------ ------------
Australasia     24340222     7886602           24340222      7886602
Near East     1499157105     4721322         1499157105      4721322
```

And, of course, the GROUP BY clause could be applied to the SQL/XML query as well:

```
SELECT
    XMLELEMENT(
        "region", XMLATTRIBUTES(R.REGION "name"),
        XMLFOREST(
            R.POPULATION AS "population",
            R.AREA AS "area",
            SUM(CO.POPULATION) AS "populationSum",
            SUM(CO.AREA) AS "areaSum"
        )
    ).EXTRACT('/*')
FROM REGION R JOIN COUNTRY CO ON (CO.REGION_ID=R.REGION_ID)
WHERE R.REGION_ID IN (3,9)
GROUP BY R.REGION, R.POPULATION, R.AREA ORDER BY R.REGION;
```

The following produces unique regions. Again, there are no details on the countries because they have been aggregated into their respective parent regions:

```
<region name="Australasia">
  <population>24340222</population>
  <area>7886602</area>
  <populationSum>24340222</populationSum>
  <areaSum>7886602</areaSum>
</region>

<region name="Near East">
  <population>1499157105</population>
  <area>4721322</area>
  <populationSum>1499157105</populationSum>
  <areaSum>4721322</areaSum>
</region>
```

As you can see in the preceding result, the GROUP BY clause summarizes, removes country records, and becomes something that is not XML. What the XML document should really look like is shown here. The GROUP BY clause does not really help in this situation:

```
<regions>
  <region name="Australasia">
    <population>24340222</population><area>7886602</area>
    <country name="Australia">
      <population>20264082</population><area>7617931</area>
      <currency>Dollars</currency><rate>1.30141</rate>
    </country>
    <country name="New Zealand">
      <population>4076140</population><area>268671</area>
      <currency>Dollars</currency><rate>1.42369</rate>
    </country>
  </region>
  <region name="Near East">
    <population>1499157105</population><area>4721322</area>
    <country name="Bangladesh">
```

```
          <population>147365352</population><area>133911</area>
          <currency>Taka</currency><rate>0</rate>
      </country>
      <country name="India">
          <population>1095351995</population><area>2973190</area>
          <currency>Rupees</currency><rate>43.62</rate>
      </country>
      <country name="Pakistan">
          <population>165803560</population><area>778720</area>
          <currency>Rupees</currency><rate>0</rate>
      </country>
      <country name="Sri Lanka">
          <population>20222240</population><area>64740</area>
          <currency>Rupees</currency><rate>99.4</rate>
      </country>
      <country name="Turkey">
          <population>70413958</population><area>770761</area>
          <currency>New Lira</currency><rate>0</rate>
      </country>
    </region>
  </regions>
```

The preceding example has some start-end tag sets placed onto the same line to keep the output smaller, and perhaps on a single page. The fundamental difference with the preceding XML document is that there is no duplication of regional information. Just imagine how much duplication of parent information would be contained in a join of the REGION, COUNTRY, STATE and CITY tables. The XML document using SQL/XML could easily be thousands of times larger. And Oracle Database does have an XMLROOT function. It does not appear to be much use as of Oracle10*g* Database (10.2.0.1). I took the liberty of manually adding a root tag to the preceding properly structured XML document.

So the problem discussed earlier is essentially that even though relational databases store data in hierarchical table structures, queries return into flattened two-dimensional structures. XML document object hierarchical structure is not really equivalent to a SQL query as it is hierarchical and thus more three-dimensional from a structural perspective. So therefore, SQL and even SQL/XML are of limited use with respect to XML. The only way to produce an XML document like the preceding well-formed XML document is to have full program control with the language querying the database. SQL is a scripting language. A scripting language does not allow full program control because successive commands cannot use the results of previous commands and adapt accordingly. A proper programming language does allow full program control with communication between any two points in a piece of code.

Oracle Database has all sorts of other tricks such as CAST(MULTISET(. . . into nested tables. A nested table allows the creation of a table within a table, a little like an object collection structural relationship. CAST(MULTISET(. . . essentially allows type casting between different object layers of a class hierarchy. The only problem with a solution like this is that one will be attempting to impose an object architecture onto a relational database. That is just as bad as imposing a relational structure onto an object structure. You have already seen this with the previous examples generating potentially tremendous amounts of data duplication from relational queries into XML documents using SQL/XML.

The SYS_XMLGEN Function

The SYS_XMLGEN function returns an XMLType data type object instance, which contains an XML document. Each row in a query is returned as a separate XML document. The following query converts each record retrieved from the REGION table into an XML document:

```
SELECT SYS_XMLGEN(REGION) FROM REGION;
```

This result shows the first two records returned:

```
<?xml version="1.0"?>
<REGION>Africa</REGION>

<?xml version="1.0"?>
<REGION>Asia</REGION>
```

The input to the SYS_XMLGEN function should be a scalar expression. In other words, a list of fields cannot be used. Finding multiple fields requires retrieval of multiple expressions:

```
SELECT SYS_XMLGEN(REGION), SYS_XMLGEN(POPULATION) FROM REGION;
```

This is the result, with a few obvious issues:

```
<?xml version="1.0"?>
<?xml version="1.0"?>
<REGION>Africa</REGION>
<POPULATION>789548670</POPULATION>

<?xml version="1.0"?>
<?xml version="1.0"?>
<REGION>Asia</REGION>
<POPULATION>47382633</POPULATION>
```

A single scalar expression is required for a single SYS_XMLGEN function execution. Thus the fields that are to be retrieved can be structured into new user-defined types. In setting up queries to join regions, countries, and cities, the following user-defined types can be created. The first type is of three fields in the CITY table:

```
CREATE OR REPLACE TYPE tCITY AS OBJECT(CITY VARCHAR2(32), POPULATION INTEGER,
    AREA INTEGER);
/
```

The second type creates a collection of the tCITY type:

```
CREATE OR REPLACE TYPE tCITIES AS TABLE OF tCITY;
/
```

Next create a type to represent some of the fields in the COUNTRY table, and also embed the collection of cities (tCITIES) as a collection structure. Oracle Database allows a fully indexable, single column table data type, called a nested table (TABLE):

```
CREATE OR REPLACE TYPE tCOUNTRY AS OBJECT(COUNTRY VARCHAR2(32), POPULATION INTEGER,
    AREA INTEGER, CURRENCY VARCHAR2(32), RATE FLOAT, CITIES tCITIES);
/
```

It follows that a collection of countries is created, containing multiple countries, where each country contains multiple cities:

```
CREATE OR REPLACE TYPE tCOUNTRIES AS TABLE OF tCOUNTRY;
/
```

Last, create a region type, containing region fields, and a collection of countries, which in turn contain a collection of cities:

```
CREATE OR REPLACE TYPE tREGION AS OBJECT(REGION VARCHAR2(32), POPULATION INTEGER,
    AREA INTEGER, COUNTRIES tCOUNTRIES);
/
CREATE OR REPLACE TYPE tREGIONS AS TABLE OF tREGION;
/
```

If Oracle Database TYPE objects as shown in the preceding code are improperly coded, replacing the TYPE objects requires dropping them in the reverse order that they were created. This is relevant in this case because a three-layer hierarchy of TYPE objects is created:

```
DROP TYPE tREGIONS;
DROP TYPE tREGION;
DROP TYPE tCOUNTRIES;
DROP TYPE tCOUNTRY;
DROP TYPE tCITIES;
DROP TYPE tCITY;
```

To begin with, the following query finds all cities within countries. The CAST function converts one type into another. In object parlance this is called a type-caste. The MULTISET function treats the result as a list, which in this case is a list of cities:

```
SELECT SYS_XMLGEN
(
   tCOUNTRY
   (
      CO.COUNTRY, CO.POPULATION, CO.AREA, CO.CURRENCY, CO.RATE,
      CAST
      (
         MULTISET
         (
            SELECT tCITY(CI.CITY, CI.POPULATION, CI.AREA)
            FROM CITY CI
            WHERE CI.COUNTRY_ID=CO.COUNTRY_ID
         ) AS tCITIES
      )
   )
) AS COUNTRIES
FROM COUNTRY CO;
```

147

If you executed the DROP TYPE *commands shown previously, you will have to recreate the types again as shown prior to the* DROP TYPE *commands. Otherwise, the preceding query will not function.*

The result that follows shows a single XML document for each record. This result shows only the first two countries in the full result of the query, which contains multiple cities within each country, such as Oran and Algiers, both cities in the country of Algeria:

```xml
<?xml version="1.0"?>
<ROW>
 <COUNTRY>Algeria</COUNTRY>
 <POPULATION>32930091</POPULATION>
 <AREA>2381741</AREA>
 <CURRENCY>Algeria Dinars</CURRENCY>
 <RATE>0</RATE>
 <CITIES>
  <TCITY>
   <CITY>Oran</CITY>
   <POPULATION>1200000</POPULATION>
   <AREA>0</AREA>
  </TCITY>
  <TCITY>
   <CITY>Algiers</CITY>
   <POPULATION>4100000</POPULATION>
   <AREA>0</AREA>
  </TCITY>
 </CITIES>
</ROW>

<?xml version="1.0"?>
<ROW>
 <COUNTRY>Angola</COUNTRY>
 <POPULATION>12127071</POPULATION>
 <AREA>1246699</AREA>
 <CURRENCY>Kwanza</CURRENCY>
 <RATE>0</RATE>
 <CITIES>
  <TCITY>
   <CITY>Luanda</CITY>
   <POPULATION>2800000</POPULATION>
   <AREA>0</AREA>
  </TCITY>
 </CITIES>
</ROW>
```

If elements such as <CURRENCY> *do not appear in the preceding script, that is because the default is that an element be omitted if it has no entry in the XML document as stored in the database.*

A record in a table is called a row in Oracle Database.

This next example goes one step further by returning all cities embedded within all parent countries, embedded within all parent regions:

```
SELECT SYS_XMLGEN
(
   tREGION
   (
      R.REGION, R.POPULATION, R.AREA,
      CAST
      (
         MULTISET
         (
            SELECT tCOUNTRY
            (
               CO.COUNTRY, CO.POPULATION, CO.AREA, CO.CURRENCY, CO.RATE,
               CAST
               (
                  MULTISET
                  (
                     SELECT tCITY(CI.CITY, CI.POPULATION, CI.AREA)
                     FROM CITY CI
                     WHERE CI.COUNTRY_ID=CO.COUNTRY_ID
                  ) AS tCITIES
               )
            )
            FROM COUNTRY CO
            WHERE CO.REGION_ID=R.REGION_ID
         ) AS tCOUNTRIES
      )
   )
) AS REGIONS
FROM REGION R;
```

This is once again a partial result, showing the XML document for the region of Australasia. The region Australasia in the demographics database for this book includes only the countries of Australia and New Zealand. This example contains all cities, with the countries, within the region of Australasia:

```
<?xml version="1.0"?>
<ROW>
 <REGION>Australasia</REGION>
 <POPULATION>24340222</POPULATION>
 <AREA>7886602</AREA>
 <COUNTRIES>
  <TCOUNTRY>
   <COUNTRY>Australia</COUNTRY>
   <POPULATION>20264082</POPULATION>
   <AREA>7617931</AREA>
   <CURRENCY>Dollars</CURRENCY>
   <RATE>1.30141</RATE>
   <CITIES>
    <TCITY>
     <CITY>Adelaide</CITY>
     <POPULATION>1125000</POPULATION>
     <AREA>0</AREA>
```

```
  </TCITY>
  <TCITY>
   <CITY>Brisbane</CITY>
   <POPULATION>1775000</POPULATION>
   <AREA>0</AREA>
  </TCITY>
  <TCITY>
   <CITY>Canberra</CITY>
   <POPULATION>0</POPULATION>
   <AREA>0</AREA>
  </TCITY>
  <TCITY>
   <CITY>Darwin</CITY>
   <POPULATION>0</POPULATION>
   <AREA>0</AREA>
  </TCITY>
  <TCITY>
   <CITY>Hobart</CITY>
   <POPULATION>0</POPULATION>
   <AREA>0</AREA>
  </TCITY>
  <TCITY>
   <CITY>Melbourne</CITY>
   <POPULATION>3600000</POPULATION>
   <AREA>0</AREA>
  </TCITY>
  <TCITY>
   <CITY>Perth</CITY>
   <POPULATION>1450000</POPULATION>
   <AREA>0</AREA>
  </TCITY>
  <TCITY>
   <CITY>Sydney</CITY>
   <POPULATION>4300000</POPULATION>
   <AREA>0</AREA>
  </TCITY>
 </CITIES>
</TCOUNTRY>
<TCOUNTRY>
 <COUNTRY>New Zealand</COUNTRY>
 <POPULATION>4076140</POPULATION>
 <AREA>268671</AREA>
 <CURRENCY>Dollars</CURRENCY>
 <RATE>1.42369</RATE>
 <CITIES>
  <TCITY>
   <CITY>Auckland</CITY>
   <POPULATION>1250000</POPULATION>
   <AREA>0</AREA>
  </TCITY>
```

```
   <TCITY>
    <CITY>Christchurch</CITY>
    <POPULATION>0</POPULATION>
    <AREA>0</AREA>
   </TCITY>
   <TCITY>
    <CITY>Wellington</CITY>
    <POPULATION>0</POPULATION>
    <AREA>0</AREA>
   </TCITY>
  </CITIES>
 </TCOUNTRY>
 </COUNTRIES>
</ROW>
```

*If you don't see this output, then scroll up in the SQL*Plus tool.*

Still, you get separate XML documents for each record returned from a query using the SYS_XMLGEN function, but at least you now have properly structured XML documents, containing appropriate XML hierarchical object structures.

PL/SQL and XML

Another option for generating XML documents using Oracle Database is the DBMS_XMLGEN PL/SQL built-in package. This package is somewhat complex so there is only a single example. An example multiple hierarchical layered query is shown here:

```
CREATE TABLE TMP_CLOB(obj CLOB);
```

The CREATE TABLE statement creates a table to contain an XML document in a binary text object.

```
DECLARE
    qry DBMS_XMLGEN.CTXHANDLE;
    obj CLOB;
BEGIN
    DBMS_XMLGEN.SETROWTAG(qry,NULL);
    qry := DBMS_XMLGEN.NEWCONTEXT(
'SELECT tCOUNTRY(CO.COUNTRY, CO.POPULATION, CO.AREA, CO.CURRENCY, CO.RATE,
CAST(MULTISET(
    SELECT CI.CITY, CI.POPULATION, CI.AREA
    FROM CITY CI WHERE CI.COUNTRY_ID=CO.COUNTRY_ID) AS tCITIES)) AS countryXML
FROM COUNTRY CO WHERE CO.COUNTRY IN(''Algeria'',''Angola'')');
    obj := DBMS_XMLGEN.GETXML(qry);
    DELETE FROM TMP_CLOB;
    INSERT INTO TMP_CLOB VALUES(obj);
    COMMIT;
    DBMS_XMLGEN.CLOSECONTEXT(qry);
END;
/
SELECT * FROM TMP_CLOB;
```

The benefit of using the DBMS_XMLGEN package rather than SQL/XML, is that it produces a single root element called `<ROWSET>` and a single XML tag, and thus a complete and usable XML document. This is the result of the preceding query:

```xml
<?xml version="1.0"?>
<ROWSET>
 <ROW>
  <COUNTRYXML>
   <COUNTRY>Algeria</COUNTRY>
   <POPULATION>32930091</POPULATION>
   <AREA>2381741</AREA>
   <CURRENCY>Algeria Dinars</CURRENCY>
   <RATE>0</RATE>
   <CITIES>
    <TCITY>
      <CITY>Oran</CITY>
      <POPULATION>1200000</POPULATION>

      <AREA>0</AREA>
    </TCITY>
    <TCITY>
      <CITY>Algiers</CITY>
      <POPULATION>4100000</POPULATION>
      <AREA>0</AREA>
    </TCITY>
   </CITIES>
  </COUNTRYXML>
 </ROW>
 <ROW>
  <COUNTRYXML>
   <COUNTRY>Angola</COUNTRY>

   <POPULATION>12127071</POPULATION>
   <AREA>1246699</AREA>
   <CURRENCY>Kwanza</CURRENCY>
   <RATE>0</RATE>
   <CITIES>
    <TCITY>
      <CITY>Luanda</CITY>
      <POPULATION>2800000</POPULATION>
      <AREA>0</AREA>
    </TCITY>
   </CITIES>
  </COUNTRYXML>
 </ROW>
</ROWSET>

1 row selected.
```

The preceding method using the DBMS_XMLGEN package creates lots of fluff in the way tags represent user-defined type names, and other tags such as `<ROW>` and `<ROWSET>`. These tags are all essentially meaningless and superfluous to XML. Also generating XML tags in uppercase characters is quite often non-standard. One of the plus sides to using XML is its readability with the human eye. It is also a known fact that mixed case characters are easier to read than just lowercase or uppercase characters. Also, lowercase is better than CAPITALS.

All of the methods for generating XML documents in this chapter so far are either inadequate (not creating completed and usable XML documents), or they are convoluted. So far, the pseudocode example presented at the end of Chapter 4 remains the best method for generating XML documents.

XML and the Database

This section examines XML and Oracle Database in a number of ways. First, you see how to create new XML documents in the database. Second, you see how to retrieve XML documents stored in the database, both in whole and in part. Third and finally, this section explores how to change XML documents stored in the database.

New XML Documents

The following command creates a table to store XML documents, within an Oracle database:

```
CREATE TABLE XML(
    ID NUMBER PRIMARY KEY NOT NULL,
    XML XMLType);
```

There are various methods for adding XML data to a database:

❑   An XML document string can be added as a CLOB object.

❑   It can be type cast as an XMLType data type from a string.

❑   It can be added using SQL/XML functions.

❑   As you saw in the previous section, an XML document was added into a CLOB text binary object in a table called TMP_CLOB, using a procedure containing the DBMS_XMLGEN package.

This command reads the row already stored in the TMP_CLOB table (refer to the last example in the previous section "PL/SQL and XML") into the new table:

```
INSERT INTO XML(ID, XML) SELECT 1, XMLType(OBJ) FROM TMP_CLOB;
```

The preceding INSERT statement has added the CLOB object in the TMP_CLOB table into the XMLType data type field (XML) in the table called XML.

Now let's add the XML document form of the demographics database into the Oracle database (see Appendix B for the document called demographics.xml). It's done as before, by adding the text string of the entire database into a CLOB variable, inserting into the TMP_CLOB table, and finally inserting into the XML table by reading from the TMP_CLOB table.

Appendix B contains a website reference to scripts for generating XML data from the demographics relational tables in an Oracle Database. It also contains a script for generating the demographics.xml XML document, into an Oracle Database XML data type, using a CLOB variable. The script is stored in a zip file on the website. The website belongs to me!

You can expedite examples for this chapter in an Oracle database. Please download and execute Scripts for Oracle Database as indicated in Appendix B. The XML version of the demographics database (demographics.xml) does not include languages and occupations because the XML document would be too large.

```
INSERT INTO XML(ID, XML) SELECT 2, XMLType(OBJ) FROM TMP_CLOB;
COMMIT;
```

Now you have an XML document version of the entire demographics database stored in an XMLType in a table in that database.

Retrieving from XML Documents

Once XML documents are stored inside XMLType fields in tables in the database, they are fairly simple to retrieve using simple SQL with some added functions. A simple query to retrieve the demographics XML document from the database like this next one will dump the data to the display:

```
SELECT XML FROM XML WHERE ID=2;
```

This is a partial result:

```
<?xml version="1.0"?><demographics><region id="1"><name>Africa</name><population
>789548670</population><area>26780325</area><country id="1" code="AG"><name>Alge
ria</name><population><year year="1950" population_id="12009" population="8892718"><births_per_1000>0</births_per_1000><deaths_per_1000>0</deaths_per_1000><migr
ants_per_1000>0</migrants_per_1000><natural_increase_percent>0</natural_increase
_percent><growth_rate>0</growth_rate></year><year year="1951" population_id="120
10" population="9073304"><births_per_1000>0</births_per_1000><deaths_per_1000>0<
/deaths_per_1000><migrants_per_1000>0</migrants_per_1000><natural_increase_perce
nt>0</natural_increase_percent><growth_rate>0</growth_rate></year><year year="19
52" population_id="12011" population="9279525"><births_per_1000>0</births_per_10
00><deaths_per_1000>0</deaths_per_1000><migrants_per_1000>0</migrants_per_1000><
```

Again the EXTRACT function can be used to beautify the output a little with a simple query like this:

```
SELECT X.XML.EXTRACT('/*') AS test FROM XML X WHERE X.ID = 2;
```

Queries using XMLType data type methods do not appear to function properly in Oracle Database unless they are qualified using aliases.

This is a partial result:

```
<demographics>
  <region id="1">
    <name>Africa</name>
    <population>789548670</population>
    <area>26780325</area>
    <country id="1" code="AG">
      <name>Algeria</name>
```

```
<population>
  <year year="1950" population_id="12009" population="8892718">
    <births_per_1000>0</births_per_1000>
    <deaths_per_1000>0</deaths_per_1000>
```

What is really interesting is how to extract parts of an XML document to the display. This can be done by pattern matching and parsing through the XML document, searching for what is required.

"Pattern matching" is a term that refers to searching through text files or objects, trying to find patterns of characters.

The first thing to do is to briefly summarize the syntax of pattern matching in XML documents stored in an Oracle database:

- ❑   `/`: Search from a node, either the root node or a subtree. If the forward slash is omitted at the start of the search path, then the search begins at the root node. For example, `/demographics/ region/country/population/year` will find all countries that have at least one year entry throughout the entire document, regardless of region or country, depending on how the XML document is searched.

- ❑   `text()`: Finds the text value of a node.

- ❑   `//<node>[n]`: Finds the nth child element in a list of elements.

- ❑   `[ ... ]`: Square brackets can be used to qualify expression predicates. What does that mean? For example, `/demographics/region/country[name="Australia" or name="Burma"]/ population/year` will find all year tag subtrees within the countries of Australia or Burma (not both). The fact that these two countries are in two separate regions (Australasia and Asia) is completely irrelevant.

- ❑   `@`: The @ character accesses attribute values as opposed to text values. Australia in the element `<name>Australia</name>` is a text value. In the tag `<country id="46" code="AS">Australia</country>`, id and code are both attributes of the country tag with values of 46 and AS, respectively.

Using XMLType Methods to Read XML Documents

The beginning of this chapter described various methods available to the XMLType data type. Now I shall demonstrate using a few of those methods for retrieving data from XML documents.

The EXISTSNODE method returns 1 if a node exists and 0 if a node does not exist. Its syntax is as follows:

```
EXISTSNODE (<search-path>)
```

The following example returns 1 because Australia exists as a country within a region:

```
SELECT X.XML.EXISTSNODE('/demographics/region/country[name="Australia"]')
FROM XML X WHERE X.ID=2;
```

This query also returns a value of 1 because both countries exist as part of regions, even though they are part of different regions (Australasia and Asia):

```
SELECT X.XML.EXISTSNODE(
    '/demographics/region/country[name="Australia" or name="Burma"]')
FROM XML X WHERE X.ID=2;
```

In contrast, the following query returns a negative result (0) because the and operator implies that both Australia and Burma must exist in the same region:

```
SELECT X.XML.EXISTSNODE(
    '/demographics/region/country[name="Australia" and name="Burma"]')
FROM XML X WHERE X.ID=2;
```

The EXTRACT method returns a string from within an XML document. Where the EXISTSNODE verifies a string's existence, the EXTRACT method returns that string. The string is an XML document tag. That tag can be a single element, the entire document, or a subtree, depending on what is searched for. The syntax is as follows:

```
EXTRACT(<search-path>)
```

This query returns the entire country of Australia, and nothing outside of Australia:

```
SELECT X.XML.EXTRACT('/demographics/region/country[name="Australia"]')
FROM XML X WHERE X.ID=2;
```

This is a partial result:

```
<country id="46" code="AS">
  <name>Australia</name>
  <population>
    <year year="1950" population_id="748" population="8267337">
      <births_per_1000>23.05</births_per_1000>
      <deaths_per_1000>9.46</deaths_per_1000>
      <migrants_per_1000>18.45</migrants_per_1000>
      <natural_increase_percent>1.359</natural_increase_percent>
      <growth_rate>3.204</growth_rate>
    </year>
    <year year="1951" population_id="749" population="8510600">
...
</country>
```

This query finds all states (provinces) in the country of Canada (those that are in this database):

```
SELECT X.XML.EXTRACT('/demographics/region/country[name="Canada"]/state')
FROM XML X WHERE X.ID=2;
```

This is the result:

```
<state id="1">
  <name code="BC">British Columbia</name>
  <population>0</population>
```

```
    </state>
    <state id="2">
      <name code="NS">Nova Scotia</name>
      <population>0</population>
    </state>
    <state id="3">
      <name code="ON">Ontario</name>
      <population>0</population>
    </state>
    <state id="4">
      <name code="QB">Quebec</name>
      <population>0</population>
    </state>
    <state id="53">
      <name code="AB">Alberta</name>
      <population>0</population>
    </state>
```

This query, on the other hand, finds only the <name> tags for each province in Canada:

```
SELECT X.XML.EXTRACT('/demographics/region/country[name="Canada"]/state/name')
FROM XML X WHERE X.ID=2;
```

This is the result:

```
<name code="BC">British Columbia</name>
<name code="NS">Nova Scotia</name>
<name code="ON">Ontario</name>
<name code="QB">Quebec</name>
<name code="AB">Alberta</name>
```

This example uses the text() method to return only the text values within the tags, and excludes the tags:

```
SELECT X.XML.EXTRACT(
    '/demographics/region/country[name="Canada"]/state/name/text()')
FROM XML X WHERE X.ID=2;
```

This is the result showing the names of Canadian provinces, excluding both the <name> tags and the code attributes:

```
British ColumbiaNova ScotiaOntarioQuebecAlberta
```

This query finds the code attributes for each Canadian province:

```
SELECT X.XML.EXTRACT(
    '/demographics/region/country[name="Canada"]/state/name/@code')
FROM XML X WHERE X.ID=2;
```

This is the result showing all Canadian provincial codes, as a single string:

```
BCNSONQBAB
```

And this query finds the code for a single Canadian province (British Columbia):

```
SELECT X.XML.EXTRACT(
'/demographics/region/country[name="Canada"]/
state[name="British Columbia"]/name/@code')
FROM XML X WHERE X.ID=2;
```

The result will be BC for British Columbia.

Also, where more than one attribute exists all can be retrieved using the * (asterisk wildcard) character:

```
SELECT X.XML.EXTRACT('/demographics/region/country[name="Canada"]/@*')
FROM XML X WHERE X.ID=2;
```

The result of the query is 125CA. 125 is the IDD value for Canada, and CA is the country code for Canada, as demonstrated by the following query:

```
SELECT X.XML.EXTRACT('/demographics/region/country[name="Canada"]')
FROM XML X WHERE X.ID=2;
```

This is a partial result, highlighting the ID and CODE attributes:

```
<country id="125" code="CA">
  <name>Canada</name>
  <population>
    <year year="1950" population_id="953" population="14011422">
      <births_per_1000>27.08</births_per_1000>
      <deaths_per_1000>9.04</deaths_per_1000>
      <migrants_per_1000>0</migrants_per_1000>
      <natural_increase_percent>1.804</natural_increase_percent>
      <growth_rate>0</growth_rate>
    </year>
    <year year="1951" population_id="954" population="14330675">
...
</country>
```

You can also find child elements as if they were elements of a collection. The following finds the third province in the list of provinces in Canada:

```
SELECT X.XML.EXTRACT('/demographics/region/country[name="Canada"]/state[3]')
FROM XML X WHERE X.ID=2;
```

This is the result:

```
<state id="3">
  <name code="ON">Ontario</name>
  <population>0</population>
</state>
```

Similarly, collections can be accessed on multiple levels:

```
SELECT X.XML.EXTRACT('/demographics/region[10]/country[3]/state[50]')
FROM XML X WHERE X.ID=2;
```

In the demographics database for this book, the fiftieth state is New Jersey and not Hawaii as shown in this result for the preceding query:

```
<state id="55">
  <name code="NJ" nickname="Garden State">New Jersey</name>
  <population>8115011</population>
</state>
```

There are many other built-in XML-oriented functions and methods (attached to classes) available for use in Oracle Database. These are the most significant ones.

The next thing to discover is how to change XML document content when stored in an Oracle database.

Changing and Removing XML Document Content

There are various methods of changing XML document content in Oracle Database, including some complex built-in functions. Without going into too much detail for Oracle Database (there are other databases to deal with in this book), the UPDATEXML function is the easiest method to use. The UPDATEXML function is not an XMLType method, and thus not presented in the XMLType data type section at the beginning of this chapter.

The UPDATEXML function changes and replaces the entire document. For a large XML document this is inefficient but it is very simple to demonstrate. The syntax is as follows:

```
UPDATEXML(<XMLType-object>, <search-path>, 'replacement-string').
```

Let's go and change the code for a province in Canada:

```
UPDATE XML SET XML = UPDATEXML(XML, '/demographics/region/country[name="Canada"]
/state[name="British Columbia"]/name/@code', 'BU')
WHERE ID = 2;
```

If you run this query, you will see the code changed to BU:

```
SELECT X.XML.EXTRACT(
    '/demographics/region/country[name="Canada"]/state[name="British Columbia"]/name
/@code')
FROM XML X WHERE X.ID=2;
```

It follows that there is no INSERTXML and DELETEXML functionality, apart from within complex built-in functions, which are much too advanced for this book. To delete an element from an XML document, simply find it and set it to NULL. Let's go ahead and delete British Columbia from the XML document. This can be done by setting the entire subtree for the province of British Columbia to NULL, as in the following UPDATE statement:

```
UPDATE XML SET XML = UPDATEXML(XML,
'/demographics/region/country[name="Canada"]/state[name="British Columbia"]', NULL)
WHERE ID = 2;
```

The following query finds all the provinces still remaining for Canada:

```
SELECT X.XML.EXTRACT('/demographics/region/country[name="Canada"]/state')
FROM XML X WHERE X.ID=2;
```

This is the result, indicating a now empty province element (`<state/>`) for British Columbia:

```
<state/>
<state id="2">
  <name code="NS">Nova Scotia</name>
  <population>0</population>
</state>
<state id="3">
  <name code="ON">Ontario</name>
  <population>0</population>
</state>
<state id="4">
  <name code="QB">Quebec</name>
  <population>0</population>
</state>
<state id="53">
  <name code="AB">Alberta</name>
  <population>0</population>
</state>
```

To add the missing node back into the XML document again, I simply update the XML document by adding the entire subtree for British Columbia back into the XML tree again:

```
UPDATE XML SET XML = UPDATEXML(XML,
'/demographics/region/country[name="Canada"]/state[1]', '<state id="1"><name code="
BC">British Columbia</name><population>0</population></state>')
WHERE ID = 2;
```

In the preceding statement, I can no longer find the state by name so I have to use the collection of states. Reading the data again I get the result but now with British Columbia returned as the first province:

```
<state id="1">
  <name code=" BC">British Columbia</name>
  <population>0</population>
</state>
<state id="2">
  <name code="NS">Nova Scotia</name>
  <population>0</population>
</state>
<state id="3">
  <name code="ON">Ontario</name>
  <population>0</population>
</state>
<state id="4">
  <name code="QB">Quebec</name>
  <population>0</population>
</state>
<state id="53">
  <name code="AB">Alberta</name>
  <population>0</population>
</state>
```

Oracle Database also has comprehensive configuration and management facilities in the form of the Oracle Enterprise Manager Console GUI (Graphical User Interface), and the browser-based Database Control tools. Both of these topics are too advanced for this book.

This chapter has introduced the use of XML from directly within Oracle SQL. XML is vastly more complex and detailed than presented in this chapter, both with respect to XML itself and to Oracle software. The intention of this chapter was to introduce the basic scope of using XML documents both with, and within, Oracle Database. The next chapter examines SQL Server database in the same way.

Summary

In this chapter you learned that:

❑   The XMLType data type is a specialized data type, used for storing XML documents within an Oracle database.

❑   XMLType methods include EXISTSNODE and EXTRACT, used for pulling data from XML documents stored in an Oracle database.

❑   The EXISTSNODE XMLType method verifies if a node exists.

❑   The EXTRACT XMLType method retrieves a node including all subtree elements.

❑   There are various other XMLType methods, such as for finding a namespace, an XML root element, XSL transformations, and fragment verification.

❑   XML documents can be created from Oracle Database relational table data using SQL/XML, the DBMS_XMLGEN package, the SYS_XMLGEN function, and the XSH utility.

❑   SQL/XML is The SQL Standard for XML.

❑   SQL/XML is a standard created and supported by INCITS (International Committee for Information Technology Standards).

❑   SQL/XML contains basic functions to create elements (XML tags) and assign attributes to elements (attributes within individual tags), amongst other functionality.

❑   The Oracle Database DBMS_XMLGEN is a complex set of built-in tools used for creating an XML document based on an entire query.

❑   The SYS_XMLGEN function is another option in Oracle Database that creates an XML document for each record, as retrieved by a query to an Oracle database.

❑   The XSU utility is specifically built for Oracle Database, using Java.

❑   XMLType data can be scanned and extracted using specialized extraction functions.

❑   Pattern matching characters are used in extraction functions to find specific nodes and values in XMLType data.

❑   XMLType data can be changed in an Oracle database using the UPDATEXML function.

Exercises

1. Which is the standard established by INCITS?

    a.   XML/SQL

    b.   SQL

    c.   SQL_XMLGEN

    d.   SQL/XML

    e.   None of the above

2. Which of these are tools used to generate XML documents and XML document fragments from Oracle Database tables?

    a.   Oracle Database PL/SQL built-in procedures

    b.   The SYS_XMLGEN function

    c.   The DBMS_XMLGEN package

    d.   The XSU Java utility

    e.   All of the above

3. What does the EXTRACT('/*') method do?

    a.   Finds a specific subtree in an XML document stored outside an Oracle database

    b.   Pulls a specific subtree from an XMLType XML document, stored within an Oracle database

    c.   Retrieves all the content of an XML document from an XMLType stored in an Oracle database

    d.   Retrieves all the content of an XML document from an XMLType stored in an Oracle database, in a more readable, properly organized format

    e.   None of the above

4. England and Japan are both island nations. They are also in different regions of the world. All countries are contained within regions. How many nodes will this query find?

```
SELECT X.XML.EXISTSNODE(
    '/demographics/region/country[name="England" and name="Japan"]')
FROM XML X WHERE X.ID=2;
```

    a.   0

    b.   2

    c.   All nodes within both countries

    d.   All nodes within both their parent regions

    e.   The entire XML document

5. Assume for the following SQL statements that if data can be retrieved for a query that data does exist in the XMLType, as stored in the table called XML. Which statements will retrieve a node and its subtree?

a.

```
SELECT X.XML.EXTRACT('/demographics/region/country[name="China"]')
FROM XML X WHERE X.ID=2;
```

b.

```
UPDATE XML SET XML = UPDATEXML(XML,
'/demographics/region/country[name="United States"]/state[1]', '<state id="1"><name
code=" BC">Arkansas</name><population>0</population></state>')
WHERE ID = 2;
```

c.

```
SELECT X.XML.EXISTSNODE(
    '/demographics/region/country[name="China" or name="Bolivia"]')
FROM XML X WHERE X.ID=2;
```

d.

```
SELECT X.XML.GETROOTELEMENT() FROM XML X WHERE X.ID=2;
```

6

SQL Server and XML

As with Oracle Database, there is immense capability in SQL Server database for utilizing the power of XML. This chapter covers only XML as directly related to SQL Server. In other words, you will examine how XML documents can be created, accessed, and manipulated directly from within an SQL Server database. You will be presented with various specialized techniques and facilities available to SQL Server. And as you will see, having read the previous chapter covering XML in Oracle Database, much of the XML facilities available in SQL Server are common to Oracle Database as well.

> *SQL Server database software can be downloaded from* www.microsoft.com, *or it can be purchased on CD-ROM (for a nominal shipping and handling fee), on a trial basis. You can try out all the examples in this chapter. There are no Try It Out sections in this chapter as specific database software may not necessarily be available to you at the time of reading this book. Reading this book is not dependent on your having software for any particular database.*

In this chapter you learn about:

- ❑ The XML data type for storing XML documents within an SQL Server database
- ❑ The methods available to the XML data type
- ❑ Creating XML documents
- ❑ Relational tables and directly converting into XML structured data
- ❑ Adding XML document data to an SQL Server database table
- ❑ Scanning through and retrieving data from XML data stored in an SQL Server database
- ❑ Changing the content of XML data stored in an SQL Server database
- ❑ Using XSD and SQL Server schema collections to impose structure and relationships into XML data

Chapter 6

The SQL Server XML Data Type

SQL Server 2005 has introduced a new XML data type that allows storage into a database of XML documents, plus direct functional access to that XML document. The first thing to examine is how to create a table in a SQL Server database that contains an XML data type. The easiest way to change metadata in SQL Server 2005 is by using the SQL Server Management Studio tool in SQL Server Express edition. Figure 6-1 shows the creation of a simple table, containing a single XML data type field.

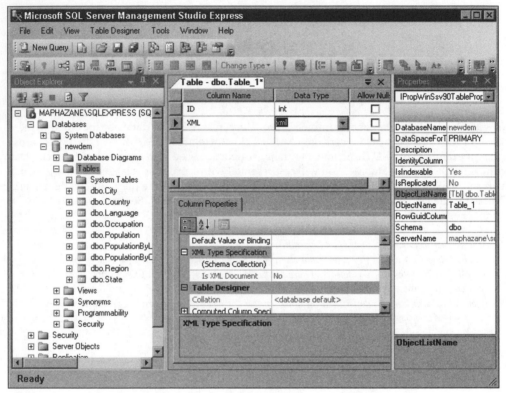

Figure 6-1: Creating a SQL Server table including an XML data type field

At this stage you have to decide a number of things:

❑ Will the XML data type be typed or untyped?

❑ Will it be used to store a complete XML document or just a fragment?

❑ Will one or more schema definitions be associated with the XML data type?

An untyped XML data type is used to contain XML documents that you know are properly formed. A typed XML data type allows specification of conformance according to a schema collection. So, the picture in Figure 6-1 will change to that shown in Figure 6-2, which now contains two XML fields: one untyped (XMLUntyped), and the other typed (XMLType).

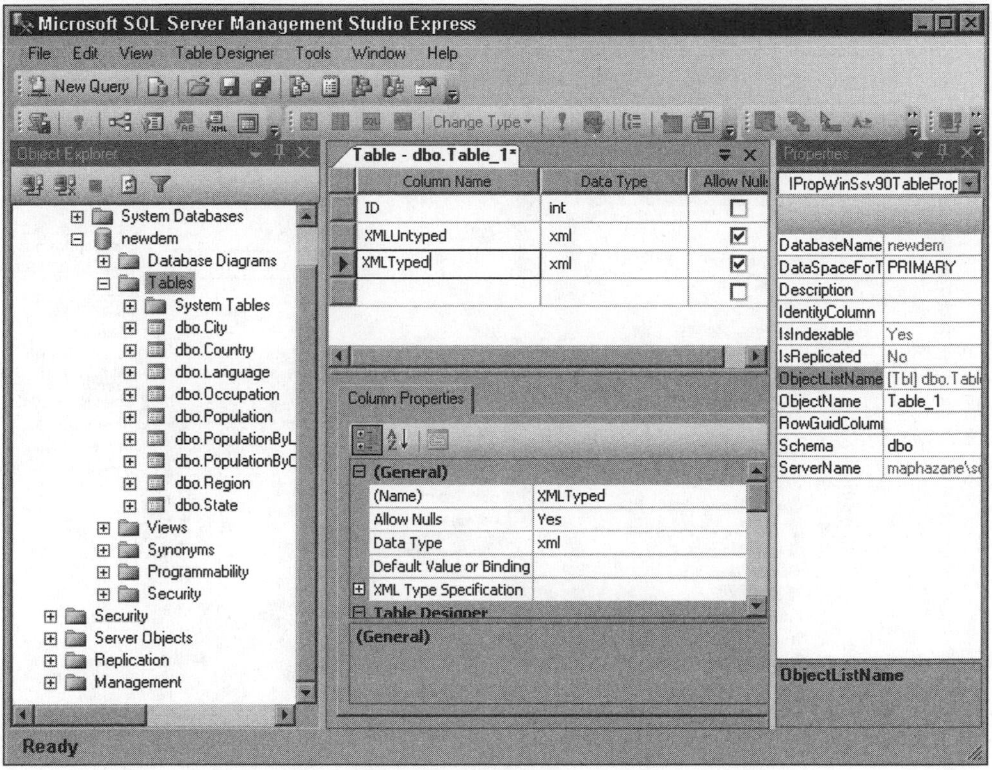

Figure 6-2: Untyped versus typed XML data type fields

For a typed XML data type, a schema collection has to be specified. Typed XML data types go into the topic area of XML Schema Definition schemas (XSD schemas), which are covered later in this chapter. It is best to keep things simple to begin with. For now, only an untyped XML data type is covered. Figure 6-3 shows a new table saved as dbo.XML where only a single XML data type field is stored as an untyped XML data type. The ID field has been set as the primary key for the table.

XML data types can be used to store XML data based on one or more schemas, if the data type will contain complete XML documents or XML document fragments. A fragment is an incomplete XML document in that it contains only a part of an XML document. A fragment does not necessarily have a root element. Without a schema collection defined, an untyped XML data type has its "Is XML Document" option set to No in the management studio, as shown in Figure 6-1. An untyped XML document is not allowed to be set to anything but No and can be either a complete XML document, or an XML fragment.

The demographics XML document used in this book is 4GB in file size, with no white space in the file. SQL Server 2005 has an upper limit of 2GB for an XML data type.

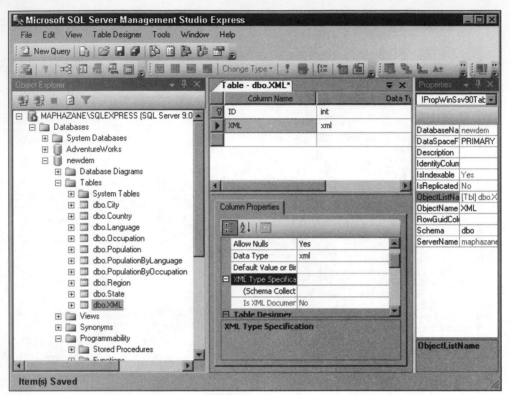

Figure 6-3: A table containing an XML data type

SQL Server XML Data Type Methods

Some will call methods functions, others call them methods. Once again, a function is a procedural programming and relational database term used to describe a process that executes when called. A function can accept parameters and pass back a single value as a returned response. The single returned value of a function allows a function to be embedded as part of an expression. A method, on the other hand, is a chunk of processing that acts on an object, and only on that object. The SQL Server XML data type is effectively a class, where functions operating on that data type are in effect methods. Those methods exist solely to operate on the content of an XML data type object.

Software vendors use all sorts of terminology for all sorts of things. Quite often terms used by different relational database vendors can mean exactly the same thing. In this book I am attempting to standardize terminology a little so that you, the reader, get a little more of a consistent mental picture when reading about the XML capabilities of different databases.

What are the methods allowed for an XML data type in a SQL Server database?

❑ `query(expression [, namespace])`: Extracts nodes from an XML document using a pattern matching string (or expression), and from an XML document stored in an XML data type in a SQL Server database.

❑ `value(expression, typecast-datatype [, namespace])`: Returns a single value of an element or attribute contained within an XML document. The result is type-cast into a specified data type.

❑ `exist(expression [, namespace])`: Returns a Boolean result if an expression finds a value (returns a 1) in an XML document or not (returns a 0).

❑ `nodes(expression [, namespace])`: Returns a relational or flattened structural equivalent of an XML hierarchical node structure.

❑ `modify(expression [, namespace])`: Changes XML document element and attribute values.

The `nodes()` *method is supposed to return a flattened relational structural equivalent of an XML document hierarchy. The* `nodes()` *method is in SQL Server documentation but does not appear to exist as an executable function in my installed version for SQL Server 2005 Express edition in the default namespace.*

The exact details of the preceding methods will be covered later in this chapter. As you can see, the preceding methods allow for both extraction manipulation of XML document data, which is stored within XML data types.

Generating XML: The FOR XML Clause

The FOR XML clause extends a SELECT statement by allowing return of data from relational tables into an XML structured document. The basic syntax of the FOR XML clause is as follows:

```
FOR XML
{
    RAW [('<element>')] [<directives>] [ELEMENTS]
  | AUTO [<directives>] [ELEMENTS]
  | EXPLICIT [<directives>]
  | PATH [('<element>')] [<directives>] [ELEMENTS]
}
<directives> = [ , TYPE ] [, ROOT  ('<root>') ]
```

The FOR XML clause syntax can be described as follows:

❑ RAW: Returns a single XML element for each record returned by a query. Thus a join returns an element for each record returned by the join, regardless of the number of tables in the join query. All fields become attributes with each record-element produced.

❑ AUTO: A nested structure is created when there is more than one table in the query. Thus, for join queries, a nested structure of XML elements is returned. In other words, each table in the query returns a single layer of nested elements. Additionally, the order of fields in the selected list helps to determine XML document structure.

❑ EXPLICIT: This mode allows the most flexibility but also more complex queries. However, explicit definition allows for explicit definition of an XML element hierarchical structure.

❑ `('<element>')`: Allows for an element name change.

❑ ELEMENTS: Fields are returned as child elements as opposed to attribute name-value pairs.

❑ <directives>: Some of these are the TYPE and ROOT directives:

    ❑ TYPE: A query or subquery will return a string typecasted into a SQL Server XML data type.

    ❑ ROOT: Adds a top layer root element to XML document output, creating a properly structured XML document. Not specifying a name creates the root element as <root>.

❑ PATH: Allows more simplistic and comprehensive query construction than the EXPLICIT clause.

❑ Other options are as follows:

    ❑ XMLDATA: Returns an XML-Data Reduced (XDR) schema

    ❑ XMLSCHEMA: Returns an XSD schema

    ❑ BINARY BASE64: Returns binary data

Let's begin with RAW mode.

FOR XML RAW Mode

This is a simple query executed against a single table, displaying regions:

```
USE [newdem]
GO
SELECT * FROM region
GO
```

Figure 6-4 shows the result of the preceding query.

The following query uses RAW mode to return regions. Each record is returned as a single XML element where each field becomes an attribute of each record-element:

```
SELECT * FROM region FOR XML RAW
GO
```

RAW mode produces this:

```
<row region_id="1" region="Africa" population="789548670" area="26780325" />
<row region_id="2" region="Asia" population="47382633" area="657741" />
<row region_id="3" region="Australasia" population="24340222" area="7886602" />
<row region_id="4" region="Caribbean" population="40417697" area="268857" />
<row region_id="5" region="Central America" population="142653392" area="2360325" />
<row region_id="6" region="Europe" population="488674441" area="4583335" />
<row region_id="7" region="Far East" population="2100636517" area="15357441" />
<row region_id="8" region="Middle East" population="294625718" area="6798768" />
<row region_id="9" region="Near East" population="1499157105" area="4721322" />
<row region_id="10" region="North America" population="331599508" area="18729272"
/>
<row region_id="11" region="Oceania" population="9133256" area="536238" />
<row region_id="12" region="Russian Federation" population="258037209"
area="21237500" />
<row region_id="13" region="South America" population="375489788" area="17545171"
/>
```

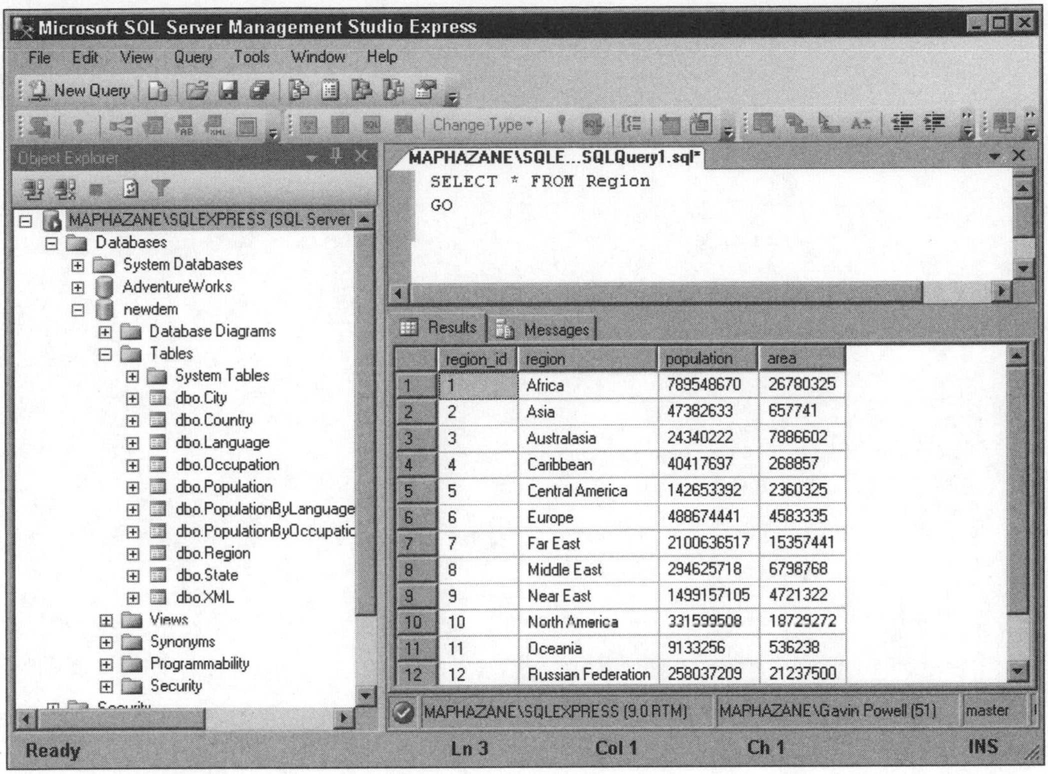

Figure 6-4: A single table query

The element name can be renamed by doing this:

```
SELECT * FROM region FOR XML RAW('region')
GO
```

This is the result showing the name of the element changed to `region`:

```
<region region_id="1" region="Africa" population="789548670" area="26780325" />
<region region_id="2" region="Asia" population="47382633" area="657741" />
<region region_id="3" region="Australasia" population="24340222" area="7886602" />
<region region_id="4" region="Caribbean" population="40417697" area="268857" />
<region region_id="5" region="Central America" population="142653392"
area="2360325" />
<region region_id="6" region="Europe" population="488674441" area="4583335" />
<region region_id="7" region="Far East" population="2100636517" area="15357441" />
<region region_id="8" region="Middle East" population="294625718" area="6798768" />
<region region_id="9" region="Near East" population="1499157105" area="4721322" />
<region region_id="10" region="North America" population="331599508"
area="18729272" />
<region region_id="11" region="Oceania" population="9133256" area="536238" />
<region region_id="12" region="Russian Federation" population="258037209"
area="21237500" />
<region region_id="13" region="South America" population="375489788"
area="17545171" />
```

Use the ELEMENTS clause to convert all attributes produced in RAW mode into child elements:

```
SELECT * FROM region FOR XML RAW('region'), ELEMENTS
GO
```

This is a partial result:

```
<region>
  <region_id>1</region_id>
  <region>Africa</region>
  <population>789548670</population>
  <area>26780325</area>
</region>
<region>
  <region_id>2</region_id>
  <region>Asia</region>
  <population>47382633</population>
  <area>657741</area>
</region>

...

<region>
  <region_id>13</region_id>
  <region>South America</region>
  <population>375489788</population>
  <area>17545171</area>
</region>
```

Now let's do a join without the ELEMENTS clause:

```
SELECT r.region, co.country FROM region AS r JOIN country AS co
ON co.region_id = r.region_id FOR XML RAW
GO
```

This is a partial result:

```
...
<row region="Africa" country="Zambia" />
<row region="Africa" country="Zimbabwe" />
<row region="Asia" country="Burma" />
<row region="Australasia" country="Australia" />
<row region="Australasia" country="New Zealand" />
<row region="Caribbean" country="Bahamas" />
<row region="Caribbean" country="Barbados" />
...
```

And now let's add the ELEMENTS clause and this time join three tables:

```
SELECT r.region, co.country, s.state
FROM region AS r JOIN country AS co ON co.region_id = r.region_id
JOIN state AS s ON s.country_id = co.country_id
FOR XML RAW
GO
```

Here is a partial result showing the three tables joined, returning states, within countries, within regions:

```
<row region="North America" country="Canada" state="British Columbia" />
<row region="North America" country="Canada" state="Nova Scotia" />
<row region="North America" country="Canada" state="Ontario" />
<row region="North America" country="Canada" state="Quebec" />
<row region="North America" country="United States" state="Alaska" />
<row region="North America" country="United States" state="Alabama" />
<row region="North America" country="United States" state="Arkansas" />
<row region="North America" country="United States" state="Arizona" />
...
```

Now the ELEMENTS clause is added back in:

```
SELECT r.region, co.country, s.state
FROM region AS r JOIN country AS co ON co.region_id = r.region_id
JOIN state AS s ON s.country_id = co.country_id
FOR XML RAW('region'), ELEMENTS
GO
```

This is the result. The problem is that there is only a single element layer:

```
<region>
  <region>North America</region>
  <country>Canada</country>
  <state>British Columbia</state>
</region>
<region>
  <region>North America</region>
  <country>Canada</country>
  <state>Nova Scotia</state>
</region>
<region>
  <region>North America</region>
  <country>Canada</country>
  <state>Ontario</state>
</region>
<region>
  <region>North America</region>
  <country>Canada</country>
  <state>Quebec</state>
</region>
<region>
  <region>North America</region>
  <country>United States</country>
  <state>Alaska</state>
</region>
...
<region>
  <region>North America</region>
  <country>United States</country>
  <state>Vermont</state>
</region>
```

At this stage the limits of what RAW mode can do have more or less been reached, and it is better to proceed to using AUTO mode.

FOR XML AUTO Mode

As already stated, AUTO mode allows the creation of a nested XML structure. The previous example in the previous section on RAW mode showed that only a single nested layer could be created using RAW mode. There are two ways in which AUTO mode improves on using RAW mode:

❑ Element names are not called row by default. And they do not have to be set as in FOR XML RAW('region'). With AUTO mode the table names in a query become the XML element names.

❑ The order of tables in a join query, coupled with the order of fields in the selected field list determines the layer of the hierarchy in which elements are displayed.

The following query is the last example used in the previous section covering RAW mode, joining three tables. The query is now changed to return XML in AUTO as opposed to RAW mode:

```
SELECT r.region, r.population, r.area, co.country, co.currency, s.state, s.nickname
FROM region AS r JOIN country AS co ON co.region_id = r.region_id
JOIN state AS s ON s.country_id = co.country_id
FOR XML AUTO
GO
```

Again here is a complete result:

```
<r region="North America" population="331599508" area="18729272">
  <co country="Canada" currency="Dollars">
    <s state="British Columbia" nickname="" />
    <s state="Nova Scotia" nickname="" />
    <s state="Ontario" nickname="" />
    <s state="Quebec" nickname="" />
  </co>
  <co country="United States" currency="">
    <s state="Alaska" nickname="" />
    <s state="Alabama" nickname="" />
    <s state="Arkansas" nickname="The Natural State" />
    <s state="Arizona" nickname="" />
    <s state="California" nickname="Golden State" />
    <s state="Colorado" nickname="Centennial State" />
    <s state="Connecticut" nickname="Nutmeg State" />
    <s state="Dictrict of Columbia" nickname="" />
    <s state="Delaware" nickname="Diamond State" />
    <s state="Florida" nickname="Sunshine State" />
    <s state="Georgia" nickname="Peach State" />
    <s state="Hawaii" nickname="Aloha State" />
    <s state="Iowa" nickname="Hawkeye State" />
    <s state="Idaho" nickname="Gem State" />
```

```
      <s state="Illinois" nickname="Prairie State" />
      <s state="Indiana" nickname="Hoosier State" />
      <s state="Kansas" nickname="Sunflower State" />
      <s state="Kentucky" nickname="Bluegrass State" />
      <s state="Louisiana" nickname="Pelican State" />
      <s state="Massachusetts" nickname="Bay State" />
      <s state="Maryland" nickname="Free State" />
      <s state="Maine" nickname="Pine Tree State" />
      <s state="Michigan" nickname="Wolverine State" />
      <s state="Minnesota" nickname="North Star State" />
      <s state="Missouri" nickname="Show-me State" />
      <s state="Mississippi" nickname="Magnolia State" />
      <s state="Montana" nickname="Treasure State" />
      <s state="North Carolina" nickname="Tar Heel State" />
      <s state="North Dakota" nickname="Sioux State" />
      <s state="New Hampshire" nickname="Granite State" />
      <s state="New Mexico" nickname="Land of Enchantment" />
      <s state="Nevada" nickname="Sagebrush State" />
      <s state="New York" nickname="Empire State" />
      <s state="Ohio" nickname="Buckeye State" />
      <s state="Oklahoma" nickname="Sooner State" />
      <s state="Oregon" nickname="Beaver State" />
      <s state="Pennsylvania" nickname="Keystone State" />
      <s state="Rhode Island" nickname="The Ocean State" />
      <s state="South Carolina" nickname="Palmetto State" />
      <s state="South Dakota" nickname="Mount Rushmore State" />
      <s state="Tennessee" nickname="Volunteer State" />
      <s state="Texas" nickname="Lone Star State" />
      <s state="Utah" nickname="Beehive State" />
      <s state="Virginia" nickname="The Old Dominion" />
      <s state="Washington" nickname="Evergreen State" />
      <s state="Wisconsin" nickname="Badger State" />
      <s state="West Virginia" nickname="Mountain State" />
      <s state="Wyoming" nickname="Equality State" />
    </co>
    <co country="Canada" currency="Dollars">
      <s state="Alberta" nickname="" />
    </co>
    <co country="United States" currency="">
      <s state="Nebraska" nickname="Cornhusker State" />
      <s state="New Jersey" nickname="Garden State" />
      <s state="Vermont" nickname="Green Mountain State" />
    </co>
  </r>
```

A couple of things are odd about the preceding query result:

❑   The ordering is completely messed up.

❑   Table aliases are used to name elements.

These issues can be resolved by including an ORDER BY clause in the query and by removing aliases from the query. I have also changed the attribute names for regions, countries, and states to a generic value in the form of the *name* attributes:

```
SELECT region.region AS name, region.population, region.area,
    country.country AS name, country.currency, state.state AS name, state.nickname
FROM region JOIN country ON country.region_id = region.region_id
JOIN state ON state.country_id = country.country_id
ORDER BY region.region, country.country, state.state
FOR XML AUTO
GO
```

The result is now properly sorted with more sensibly named elements:

```
<region name="North America" population="331599508" area="18729272">
  <country name="Canada" currency="Dollars">
    <state name="Alberta" nickname="" />
    <state name="British Columbia" nickname="" />
    <state name="Nova Scotia" nickname="" />
    <state name="Ontario" nickname="" />
    <state name="Quebec" nickname="" />
  </country>
  <country name="United States" currency="">
    <state name="Alabama" nickname="" />
    <state name="Alaska" nickname="" />
    <state name="Arizona" nickname="" />
    <state name="Arkansas" nickname="The Natural State" />
    <state name="California" nickname="Golden State" />
    <state name="Colorado" nickname="Centennial State" />
    <state name="Connecticut" nickname="Nutmeg State" />
    <state name="Delaware" nickname="Diamond State" />
    <state name="Dictrict of Columbia" nickname="" />
    <state name="Florida" nickname="Sunshine State" />
    <state name="Georgia" nickname="Peach State" />
    <state name="Hawaii" nickname="Aloha State" />
    <state name="Idaho" nickname="Gem State" />
    <state name="Illinois" nickname="Prairie State" />
    <state name="Indiana" nickname="Hoosier State" />
    <state name="Iowa" nickname="Hawkeye State" />
    <state name="Kansas" nickname="Sunflower State" />
    <state name="Kentucky" nickname="Bluegrass State" />
    <state name="Louisiana" nickname="Pelican State" />
    <state name="Maine" nickname="Pine Tree State" />
    <state name="Maryland" nickname="Free State" />
    <state name="Massachusetts" nickname="Bay State" />
    <state name="Michigan" nickname="Wolverine State" />
    <state name="Minnesota" nickname="North Star State" />
    <state name="Mississippi" nickname="Magnolia State" />
    <state name="Missouri" nickname="Show-me State" />
    <state name="Montana" nickname="Treasure State" />
    <state name="Nebraska" nickname="Cornhusker State" />
    <state name="Nevada" nickname="Sagebrush State" />
    <state name="New Hampshire" nickname="Granite State" />
```

```
            <state name="New Jersey" nickname="Garden State" />
            <state name="New Mexico" nickname="Land of Enchantment" />
            <state name="New York" nickname="Empire State" />
            <state name="North Carolina" nickname="Tar Heel State" />
            <state name="North Dakota" nickname="Sioux State" />
            <state name="Ohio" nickname="Buckeye State" />
            <state name="Oklahoma" nickname="Sooner State" />
            <state name="Oregon" nickname="Beaver State" />
            <state name="Pennsylvania" nickname="Keystone State" />
            <state name="Rhode Island" nickname="The Ocean State" />
            <state name="South Carolina" nickname="Palmetto State" />
            <state name="South Dakota" nickname="Mount Rushmore State" />
            <state name="Tennessee" nickname="Volunteer State" />
            <state name="Texas" nickname="Lone Star State" />
            <state name="Utah" nickname="Beehive State" />
            <state name="Vermont" nickname="Green Mountain State" />
            <state name="Virginia" nickname="The Old Dominion" />
            <state name="Washington" nickname="Evergreen State" />
            <state name="West Virginia" nickname="Mountain State" />
            <state name="Wisconsin" nickname="Badger State" />
            <state name="Wyoming" nickname="Equality State" />
        </country>
    </region>
```

And now for something really odd—I can change the hierarchical structure of the output by rearranging the sequence of the fields in the selected list of fields:

```
SELECT country.country AS name, country.currency,
    state.state AS name, state.nickname,
    region.region AS name, region.population, region.area
FROM region JOIN country ON country.region_id = region.region_id
JOIN state ON state.country_id = country.country_id
ORDER BY region.region, country.country, state.state
FOR XML AUTO
GO
```

The partial result is nonsensical but it shows what can be done with AUTO mode:

```
<country name="Canada" currency="Dollars">
  <state name="Alberta" nickname="">
    <region name="North America" population="331599508" area="18729272" />
  </state>
  <state name="British Columbia" nickname="">
    <region name="North America" population="331599508" area="18729272" />
  </state>
  <state name="Nova Scotia" nickname="">
    <region name="North America" population="331599508" area="18729272" />
  </state>
  <state name="Ontario" nickname="">
    <region name="North America" population="331599508" area="18729272" />
  </state>
  <state name="Quebec" nickname="">
```

```
        <region name="North America" population="331599508" area="18729272" />
    </state>
</country>
<country name="United States" currency="">
    <state name="Alabama" nickname="">
        <region name="North America" population="331599508" area="18729272" />
    </state>
    <state name="Alaska" nickname="">
        <region name="North America" population="331599508" area="18729272" />
    </state>
...
    <state name="Wyoming" nickname="Equality State">
        <region name="North America" population="331599508" area="18729272" />
    </state>
</country>
```

The AUTO clause works better when using subqueries. In the following query the TYPE clause is effectively used to typecast a subquery into the class of the calling (parent) query. Additionally, the ELEMENTS clause is used in this query to push all attributes into child elements, and the ROOT clause is used to add a root element as a wrapper for the entire XML document:

```
SELECT region.region AS name, region.population, region.area,
    (SELECT country.country AS name, country.currency,
        (SELECT state.state AS name, state.nickname
          FROM state WHERE state.country_id = country.country_id FOR XML AUTO, TYPE)
     FROM country WHERE country.region_id = region.region_id FOR XML AUTO, TYPE)
FROM region FOR XML AUTO, ROOT, ELEMENTS
GO
```

Here is another partial result:

```
<root>
  <region>
    <name>Africa</name>
    <population>789548670</population>
    <area>26780325</area>
    <country name="Algeria" currency="Algeria Dinars" />
    <country name="Angola" currency="Kwanza" />
...
  <region>
    <name>Near East</name>
    <population>1499157105</population>
    <area>4721322</area>
    <country name="Bangladesh" currency="Taka" />
    <country name="India" currency="Rupees" />
    <country name="Pakistan" currency="Rupees" />
    <country name="Sri Lanka" currency="Rupees" />
    <country name="Turkey" currency="New Lira" />
  </region>
  <region>
    <name>North America</name>
    <population>331599508</population>
```

```
      <area>18729272</area>
      <country name="Canada" currency="Dollars">
        <state name="British Columbia" nickname="" />
        <state name="Nova Scotia" nickname="" />
        <state name="Ontario" nickname="" />
        <state name="Quebec" nickname="" />
        <state name="Alberta" nickname="" />
      </country>
      <country name="Greenland" currency="" />
      <country name="United States" currency="">
        <state name="Alaska" nickname="" />
        <state name="Alabama" nickname="" />
        <state name="Arkansas" nickname="The Natural State" />
...
        <state name="Vermont" nickname="Green Mountain State" />
      </country>
    </region>
    <region>
      <name>Oceania</name>
      <population>9133256</population>
      <area>536238</area>
...
      <country name="Guyana" currency="Dollars" />
      <country name="Paraguay" currency="Guarani" />
      <country name="Peru" currency="Nuevos Soles" />
      <country name="Surinam" currency="" />
      <country name="Uruguay" currency="Pesos" />
      <country name="Venezuela" currency="Bolivares" />
    </region>
  </root>
```

That's enough about AUTO mode. EXPLICIT mode allows for more precise XML document output.

FOR XML EXPLICIT Mode

As stated previously, EXPLICIT mode provides the most flexibility in creation of XML documents but with more complexity when building queries. The EXPLICIT clause allows for complete control of XML document structure and content. The EXPLICIT clause has very specific syntax in that the first field in the selected list is called TAG and the second field is called PARENT. This applies to the primary calling query, and all subqueries that use the EXPLICIT clause.

The TAG and PARENT fields are used to determine the level of each query in the hierarchy. The TAG field is a positive number determining the level of a query in the hierarchy. The PARENT field is also a positive number but is the tag number of the field under which the current element will be placed into the hierarchy. The PARENT of the first element can also be NULL or 0 because the topmost element does not effectively have a parent in the resulting query. Data fields appear after the TAG and PARENT fields.

Every data field retrieved must be aliased using the following syntax notation:

```
[<element>]!<tag#>[!<attribute>][!<directive>]
```

179

This is a simple example query finding records in a single table:

```
SELECT 1 AS TAG, 0 AS PARENT,
   region AS [region!1!name]
FROM region
FOR XML EXPLICIT
GO
```

This is the result:

```
<region name="Africa" />
<region name="Asia" />
<region name="Australasia" />
<region name="Caribbean" />
<region name="Central America" />
<region name="Europe" />
<region name="Far East" />
<region name="Middle East" />
<region name="Near East" />
<region name="North America" />
<region name="Oceania" />
<region name="Russian Federation" />
<region name="South America" />
```

Now let's build a hierarchy. Each layer in the hierarchy is constructed as a separate query. The individual queries for each level are merged together using a UNION clause:

```
SELECT 1 AS TAG, 0 AS PARENT,
    region AS [region!1!name],
    NULL AS [region!2!population], NULL AS [region!2!area]
FROM region
UNION ALL
SELECT 2 AS TAG, 1 AS PARENT,
    region AS [region!1!name],
    population AS [region!2!population], area AS [region!2!area]
FROM region
ORDER BY [region!1!name]
FOR XML EXPLICIT
GO
```

This is the result:

```
<region name="Africa">
  <region population="789548670" area="26780325" />
  <region population="47382633" area="657741" />
</region>
<region name="Asia" />
<region name="Australasia">
  <region population="24340222" area="7886602" />
```

```
    <region population="40417697" area="268857" />
</region>
...
<region name="Russian Federation" />
<region name="South America">
  <region population="375489788" area="17545171" />
</region>
```

Doing the same thing with a multiple table join would look something like this:

```
SELECT 1 AS TAG, 0 AS PARENT,
    region AS [region!1!name],
    population AS [region!1!population], area AS [region!1!area],
    NULL AS [country!2!name], NULL AS [country!2!currency],
    NULL AS [state!3!name], NULL AS [state!3!nickname]
FROM region
UNION ALL
SELECT 2 AS TAG, 1 AS PARENT,
    NULL AS [region!1!name],
    NULL AS [region!1!population], NULL AS [region!1!area],
    country AS [country!2!name], currency AS [country!2!currency],
    NULL AS [state!3!name], NULL AS [state!3!nickname]
FROM region JOIN country ON country.region_id = region.region_id
UNION ALL
SELECT 3 AS TAG, 2 AS PARENT,
    NULL AS [region!1!name],
    NULL AS [region!1!population], NULL AS [region!1!area],
    NULL AS [country!2!name], NULL AS [country!2!currency],
    state AS [state!3!name], nickname AS [state!3!nickname]
FROM country JOIN state ON state.country_id = country.country_id
ORDER BY [region!1!name], [country!2!name], [state!3!name]
FOR XML EXPLICIT
GO
```

The preceding query is ugly and complicated. The better way is by using the PATH clause.

FOR XML PATH Mode

The PATH clause is a better option than the EXPLICIT clause because queries are just as powerful, but much easier to code, and much more efficient.

This example reads a single table, allowing specification of both attributes and elements:

```
SELECT region_id AS "@region_id", region AS "name",
    population AS "population", area AS "area"
FROM region
FOR XML PATH('region'), ROOT
GO
```

This is a partial result:

```
<root>
  <region region_id="1">
    <name>Africa</name>
    <population>789548670</population>
    <area>26780325</area>
  </region>
  <region region_id="2">
    <name>Asia</name>
    <population>47382633</population>
    <area>657741</area>
  </region>
...
  <region region_id="13">
    <name>South America</name>
    <population>375489788</population>
    <area>17545171</area>
  </region>
</root>
```

The next example uses nesting subqueries within the selected fields list in order to create a hierarchical structure. As you can see, using the PATH clause makes the query look a lot more like simple SQL, as opposed to the horrendous complexity of using the EXPLICIT clause:

```
SELECT region_id AS "@region_id", region AS "name",
    population AS "population", area AS "area",
(
    SELECT country_id AS "@country_id", country.country AS name, country.currency,
    (
        SELECT state_id AS "@state_id", state.state AS name, state.nickname
        FROM state
        WHERE state.country_id = country.country_id
        FOR XML PATH('state'), TYPE
    )
    FROM country
    WHERE country.region_id = region.region_id
    FOR XML PATH('country'), TYPE
)
FROM region
FOR XML PATH('region'), ROOT
GO
```

This is a partial result:

```
<root>
  <region region_id="1">
    <name>Africa</name>
    <population>789548670</population>
```

```
      <area>26780325</area>
      <country country_id="1">
        <name>Algeria</name>
        <currency>Algeria Dinars</currency>
      </country>
  ...
    </region>
  ...
    <region region_id="10">
      <name>North America</name>
      <population>331599508</population>
      <area>18729272</area>
      <country country_id="125">
        <name>Canada</name>
        <currency>Dollars</currency>
        <state state_id="1">
          <name>British Columbia</name>
          <nickname />
        </state>
        <state state_id="2">
          <name>Nova Scotia</name>
          <nickname />
        </state>
        <state state_id="3">
          <name>Ontario</name>
          <nickname />
        </state>
  ...
      </country>
    </region>
</root>
```

Overall, the FOR XML clause is quite an effective and simplistic method of producing XML documents data from relational database tables.

Generating Tuples from XML: OPENXML

A special function is available in SQL Server called OPENXML. The OPENXML function can be used to access an XML data type as if it were a set of relational tables. The OPENXML function has to be specifically coded, and is a little complex, but it could perhaps be useful.

This query uses the FOR XML clause to find all regions:

```
SELECT * FROM region FOR XML AUTO, ELEMENTS
GO
```

This is a partial result showing an XML structure for regions:

```
<region>
  <region_id>1</region_id>
  <region>Africa</region>
  <population>789548670</population>
  <area>26780325</area>
</region>
<region>
  <region_id>2</region_id>
  <region>Asia</region>
  <population>47382633</population>
  <area>657741</area>
</region>
...
<region>
  <region_id>13</region_id>
  <region>South America</region>
  <population>375489788</population>
  <area>17545171</area>
</region>
```

The OPENXML function can be used to map from an XML structure back to a relational table structure. In other words, you can convert from an XML hierarchy to a flat relational structure. The following is some example code using the OPENXML function:

```
DECLARE @handle int
DECLARE @xmlstr varchar(5000)
SET @xmlstr =(SELECT region_id, region, population, area FROM region
   FOR XML AUTO, ROOT, ELEMENTS)
SELECT @xmlstr
EXEC sp_xml_preparedocument @handle OUTPUT, @xmlstr
SELECT region_id, region, population, area FROM
   OPENXML(@handle, '/root/region', 2)
WITH Region
GO
```

Figure 6-5 shows the result. Essentially the data is output in records, as shown here:

```
REGION_ID REGION               POPULATION       AREA
--------- ------------------   ----------   --------
        1 Africa                789548670   26780325
        2 Asia                   47382633     657741
        3 Australasia            24340222    7886602
        4 Caribbean              40417697     268857
        5 Central America       142653392    2360325
        6 Europe                488674441    4583335
        7 Far East             2100636517   15357441
        8 Middle East           294625718    6798768
        9 Near East            1499157105    4721322
       10 North America         331599508   18729272
       11 Oceania                 9133256     536238
       12 Russian Federation    258037209   21237500
       13 South America         375489788   17545171
```

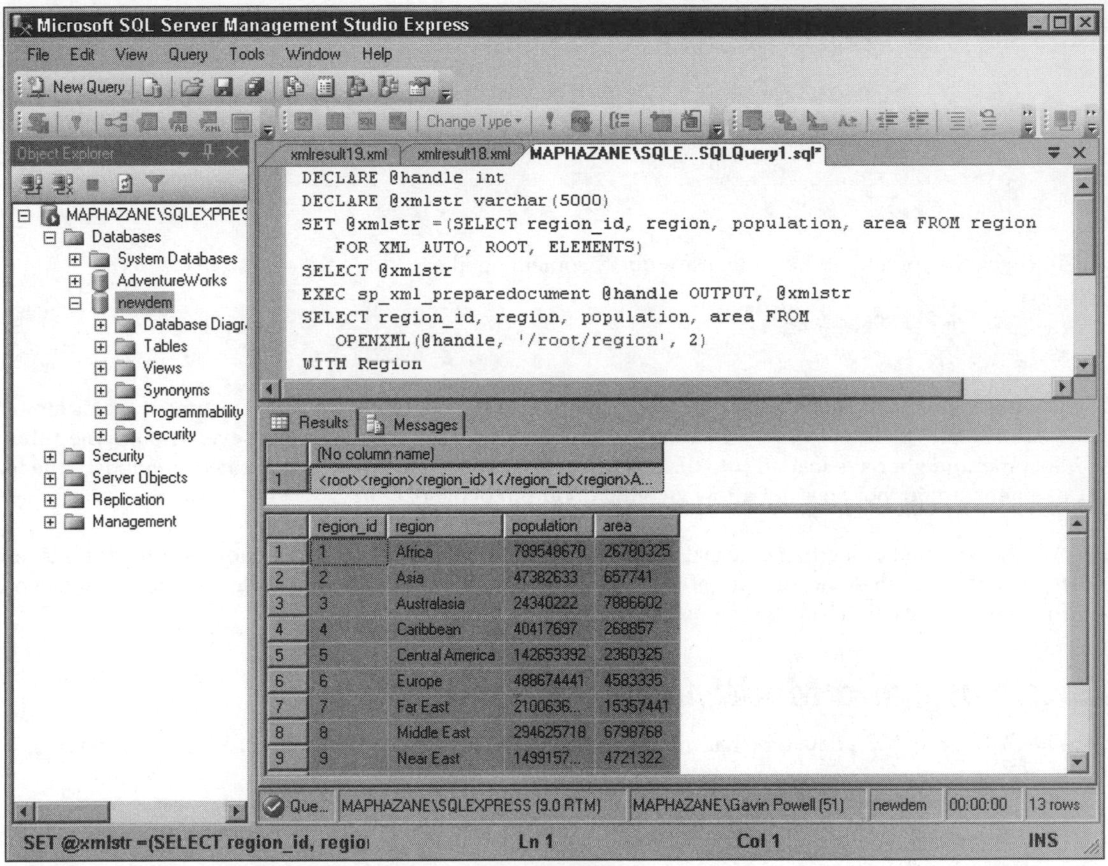

```
DECLARE @handle int
DECLARE @xmlstr varchar(5000)
SET @xmlstr =(SELECT region_id, region, population, area FROM region
     FOR XML AUTO, ROOT, ELEMENTS)
SELECT @xmlstr
EXEC sp_xml_preparedocument @handle OUTPUT, @xmlstr
SELECT region_id, region, population, area FROM
     OPENXML(@handle, '/root/region', 2)
WITH Region
```

Figure 6-5: OPENXML converts from XML to relational tuples

Working with XML Data Types

SQL Server XML data types allow storage of XML document data into tables in a SQL Server database. There are various methods of manipulating the content of XML data types.

Adding XML Documents to SQL Server

The easiest method of loading XML document data into a SQL Server database is to create a table containing an XML data type field, and then load that table using an external data import function called OPENROWSET.

Begin by creating a table:

```
CREATE TABLE demXML (xml XML)
GO
```

Now simply use an INSERT statement to add an XML document directly from an external source into the table containing the XML data type field:

```
INSERT INTO demXML (xml)
SELECT * FROM OPENROWSET (BULK
'C:\Manuscripts\Wiley\BeginningXMLDatabases\app\databa
se\oracle\XMLDB\demographicsCLOB.xml', SINGLE_BLOB) AS TEMP
GO
```

To check the content of the table, use a query something like this:

```
SELECT * FROM demXML
GO
```

The demographics database used for this book (see Appendix B) has an XML document that is almost 4GB in size. SQL Server has a limitation on XML data type storage of 2GB. So, even though the entire document might have loaded into the XML data type in the table demXML created previously, the management studio tool does not allow viewing of output of over 2GB.

Another method of loading external data is to use the SQLXML XML Bulk Loader utility. There is not really any point in demonstrating it as the method described so far is simplistic and more than adequate for the purposes of this book.

Retrieving and Modifying XML Data Types

The SQL Server XML data type has methods called query(), value(), exist(), nodes(), and modify().

> *The case of the methods when executing each one is important in SQL Server. In other words,* xml.Query() *or* xml.QUERY() *returns an error.* xml.query() *will not return an error.*

Using the various XML data type methods could not be easier. The query() method (often mistakenly called a function) allows use of an expression search string. The expression is a pattern match search (searching for a string pattern) through the hierarchical structure of an XML document. The query method can be used to return a set of nodes from an XML data type, which is stored in a SQL Server database.

The following example searches from the root node (demographics.xml) into the regions; until it finds the region containing Australia. Then it looks for the city of Brisbane inside the country node of Australia:

```
SELECT
xml.query('/demographics/region/country[name="Australia"]/city[name="Brisbane"]')
AS node
FROM demXML
GO
```

The query method returns the city node containing the city of Brisbane, in Australia:

```
<city id="176">
   <name>Brisbane</name>
   <population>1775000</population>
</city>
```

Using an attribute the same node can be found:

```
SELECT xml.query('/demographics/region/country[name="Australia"]/city[@id="176"]')
AS node
FROM demXML
GO
```

The result is the same as before but this time an attribute value, rather than an element name, was used to find the same city node. As you can see in the previous example, Brisbane in Australia has an integer identifier value of 176.

There are various methods of building expressions. Different character combinations are used as pattern matching or expression directives, persuading a search pattern to behave in a specific manner. All of these specific pattern matching character sequences are common to both XQuery and XPath, both of which are discussed later on in this book. Explaining the nitty-gritty details for each relational database is pointless for the purposes of this book. In general you should already know from previous chapters that expression rules, as shown in Table 6-1, apply when reading through an XML document.

Table 6-1: Standard XML Document Pattern Matching Expressions

Expression	Function	Example
`element="value"`	Search for a value.	`name="Brisbane"`
`@attribute="value"`	Search for an attribute value.	`@id="176"`
`//`	Search through child nodes.	`/demographics//country [name="Brisbane"]`
`..`	Search for parent nodes.	`/demographics//city [name="Brisbane"]/..`
`.`	Search the current node.	`/name[.="Brisbane"]`
`text()`	Find text value of an element.	`country/name.text()` finds a country like Australia

Expanding on Table 6-1, the following example will again find the node for the city of Brisbane. The difference when using the `//` character sequence is the amount of searching. The following query searches through all child nodes of the demographics node ignoring parent country and region. This example will execute slower than previous, more precise expressions:

```
SELECT xml.query('/demographics//city[name="Brisbane"]') AS node
FROM demXML
GO
```

This next example finds the entire parent node of the country of Australia because Australia contains the city of Brisbane:

```
SELECT xml.query('/demographics//city[name="Brisbane"]/..') AS node
FROM demXML
GO
```

This is a partial result:

```
<country id="46" code="AS">
  <name>Australia</name>
  <population>
...
  </population>
  <area>7617931</area>
  <currency fxcode="AUD" rate="1.30141">Dollars</currency>
  <city id="175">
    <name>Adelaide</name>
    <population>1125000</population>
  </city>
  <city id="176">
    <name>Brisbane</name>
    <population>1775000</population>
  </city>
...
</country>
```

The . character sequence returns only the node searched for, and no child nodes:

```
SELECT xml.query('/demographics//name[.="Brisbane"]') AS node
FROM demXML
GO
```

This is the result:

```
<name>Brisbane</name>
```

This query finds all city <name> nodes in the country of Australia:

```
SELECT xml.query('/demographics//country[name="Australia"]//name') AS node
FROM demXML
GO
```

This is the result:

```
<name>Australia</name>
<name>Adelaide</name>
<name>Brisbane</name>
<name>Canberra</name>
<name>Darwin</name>
<name>Hobart</name>
<name>Melbourne</name>
<name>Perth</name>
<name>Sydney</name>
```

Now, if you use the text() function, all the values within the nodes are returned, as opposed to all the nodes:

```
SELECT xml.query('/demographics//country[name="Australia"]//name/text()') AS node
FROM demXML
GO
```

This is the result:

```
AustraliaAdelaideBrisbaneCanberraDarwinHobartMelbournePerthSydney
```

The `query()` method can be used to return individual element and attribute values. An easier method of returning specific value items is the `value()` method. The following query finds a single node, and the value of the node is supposed to be extracted. This query does not seem to function as it returns an error in the management studio. The problem is typecasting issues for XML data returned from an XML data type so it has to be coded. The following query, as shown before, returns an XML node:

```
SELECT xml.query('/demographics//city[name="Brisbane"]') AS node
FROM demXML
GO
```

This is the node returned:

```
<city id="176">
   <name>Brisbane</name>
   <population>1775000</population>
</city>
```

Next, the `value()` method is used to extract a single value from the result of the `query()` method:

```
DECLARE @xmldoc xml
SET @xmldoc = (SELECT xml.query('/demographics//city[name="Brisbane"]') AS node
FROM demXML)
SELECT @xmldoc.value('/city[1]','nvarchar(64)') AS node
SELECT @xmldoc
GO
```

The result contains all the text contents (excluding attributes) of the node returned by the `query()` method:

```
Brisbane 1775000
```

The `exist()` method simply returns a Boolean response for the existence of a node. This query returns a 1, indicating the node exists:

```
SELECT xml.exist('/demographics//name[.="Brisbane"]') AS node
FROM demXML
GO
```

This query returns a 0, indicating the node does not exist:

```
SELECT xml.exist('/demographics//name[.="Brisban"]') AS node
FROM demXML
GO
```

189

The `modify()` method allows for changes to be made to data in XML documents. More specifically, the `modify()` method allows insertions of new data, updates to existing data, and deletions of existing data. The following query inserts a new node within the node for the city of Brisbane:

```
DECLARE @xmldoc xml
SET @xmldoc = (SELECT xml.query('/demographics//city[name="Brisbane"]')
FROM demXML)
SET @xmldoc.modify('insert <area>100000</area> into (/city)[1]')
SELECT @xmldoc
GO
```

This is the result with the `area` element added as the last child of the `city` element:

```
<city id="176">
  <name>Brisbane</name>
  <population>1775000</population>
  <area>100000</area>
</city>
```

The previous insertion example was executed by simply adding the new element into the specified point. Insertions can also be performed as first, as last, before, and after—all relative to the current element.

Now let's try updating. This query changes the value of the newly added `area` element:

```
DECLARE @xmldoc xml
SET @xmldoc = (SELECT xml.query('/demographics//city[name="Brisbane"]')
FROM demXML)
SET @xmldoc.modify('insert <area>100000</area> into (/city)[1]')
SET @xmldoc.modify('replace value of (/city/area/text())[1] with "200000"')
SELECT @xmldoc
GO
```

The result shows the `area` element value has been changed:

```
<city id="176">
  <name>Brisbane</name>
  <population>1775000</population>
  <area>200000</area>
</city>
```

And now you can remove the newly added `area` element:

```
DECLARE @xmldoc xml
SET @xmldoc = (SELECT xml.query('/demographics//city[name="Brisbane"]')
FROM demXML)
SET @xmldoc.modify('insert <area>100000</area> into (/city)[1]')
SET @xmldoc.modify('delete /city/area')
SELECT @xmldoc
GO
```

The result shows the `area` element now removed:

```
<city id="176">
  <name>Brisbane</name>
  <population>1775000</population>
</city>
```

Defining XML Content with XSD Schemas

XSD can be used to link a set of relational database tables in a schema to an XML document. XSD allows strong typing to be applied to XML data. The result is a typed XML data type where restrictive format and structure is applied to XML data. In other words, the XML document has a certain form and structure, restricted by the content of a schema — the table and field structure of a schema.

Strongly Typing XML Documents with XSD

The definition or structure of a table in a relational database will describe data in that database. Similarly, XSD can be used to explicitly describe the structure of an XML document. The following XSD script defines a pseudocode XSD schema for regions in the demographics database:

```
<xsd:schema xmlns:xsd="http://www.w3.org/2001/XMLSchema">
    <xsd:element name="RegionRecord" >
        <xsd:complexType>
            <xsd:sequence>
                <xsd:element name="region_id" type="xsd:integer" />
                <xsd:element name="region" type="xsd:string" />
                <xsd:element name="population" type="xsd:integer" />
                <xsd:element name="area" type="xsd:integer" />
            </xsd:sequence>
        </xsd:complexType>
    </xsd:element>
</xsd:schema>
```

To continue on with the preceding example, a hierarchical relational database table structure can be built. In the following pseudocode example, the REGION and COUNTRY tables are used. Countries are contained within each of their respective parent regions as a collection of countries, within each region:

```
<?xml version="1.0"?>
<xsd:schema xmlns:xsd="http://www.w3.org/2001/XMLSchema">

    <xsd:element name="RegionRecord">
        <xsd:complexType>
            <xsd:sequence>
                <xsd:element name="region_id" type="xsd:integer" />
                <xsd:element name="region" type="xsd:string" />
                <xsd:element name="population" type="xsd:integer" />
                <xsd:element name="area" type="xsd:integer" />
                <xsd:element name="CountryCollection" type="CountryRecord" />
```

```
        </xsd:sequence>
      </xsd:complexType>
   </xsd:element>

   <xsd:element name="CountryRecord">
      <xsd:complexType>
         <xsd:sequence>
            <xsd:element name="region_id" />
            <xsd:element name="country_id" type="xsd:integer" />
            <xsd:element name="country" type="xsd:string" />
            <xsd:element name="code" type="xsd:string" />
            <xsd:element name="population" type="xsd:integer" />
            <xsd:element name="area" type="xsd:integer" />
            <xsd:element name="fxcode" type="xsd:string" />
            <xsd:element name="currency" type="xsd:string" />
            <xsd:element name="rate" type="xsd:float" />
         </xsd:sequence>
      </xsd:complexType>
   </xsd:element>

</xsd:schema>
```

Mapping an XSD Schema to a Table

The objective of using XSD is to allow generation of XML that is validated against a schema (set of related tables). Instead of writing queries to generate XML documents XSD can be used to map XML to tables in a schema. You can annotate XSD with special elements, allowing a direct mapping process to occur between XML and relational tables. By default, an element represents a table, and element attributes represent fields in tables. The result is a direct correlation between XSD annotations and relational tables (and their inter-relationships):

```
<?xml version="1.0"?>
<xsd:schema xmlns:xsd="http://www.w3.org/2001/XMLSchema"
   xmlns:sql="http://schemas.microsoft.com/sqlserver/2004/sqltypes">

 <xsd:element name="RegionRecord" sql:relation="REGION">
  <xsd:complexType>
   <xsd:sequence>
    <xsd:element name="region_id" sql:field="REGION_ID" type="xsd:integer" />
    <xsd:element name="region" sql:field="REGION" type="xsd:string" />
    <xsd:element name="population" sql:field="POPULATION" type="xsd:integer" />
    <xsd:element name="area" sql:field="AREA" type="xsd:integer" />
    <xsd:element name="CountryCollection" sql:relationship="CountryRecord" />
   </xsd:sequence>
  </xsd:complexType>
 </xsd:element>

 <xsd:element name="CountryRecord" sql:relation="COUNTRY">
  <xsd:complexType>
   <xsd:sequence>
    <xsd:element name="region_id" sql:field="REGION_ID" type="xsd:integer" />
    <xsd:element name="country_id" sql:field="COUNTRY_ID" type="xsd:integer" />
    <xsd:element name="country" sql:field="COUNTRY" type="xsd:string" />
    <xsd:element name="code" sql:field="CODE" type="xsd:string" />
```

```
    <xsd:element name="population" sql:field="POPULATION" type="xsd:integer" />
    <xsd:element name="area" sql:field="AREA" type="xsd:integer" />
    <xsd:element name="fxcode" sql:field="FXCODE" type="xsd:string" />
    <xsd:element name="currency" sql:field="CURRENCY" type="xsd:string" />
    <xsd:element name="rate" sql:field="RATE" type="xsd:float" />
   </xsd:sequence>
  </xsd:complexType>
 </xsd:element>

</xsd:schema>
```

Annotating the XSD Script to Enforce Relationships

Now annotations are added to both specify and enforce the hierarchical relationships between the tables:

```
<?xml version="1.0"?>
<xsd:schema xmlns:xsd="http://www.w3.org/2001/XMLSchema"
   xmlns:sql="http://schemas.microsoft.com/sqlserver/2004/sqltypes">

 <xsd:element name="RegionRecord" sql:relation="REGION">
  <xsd:complexType>
   <xsd:sequence>
    <xsd:element name="region_id" sql:field="REGION_ID" type="xsd:integer" />
    <xsd:element name="region" sql:field="REGION" type="xsd:string" />
    <xsd:element name="population" sql:field="POPULATION" type="xsd:integer" />
    <xsd:element name="area" sql:field="AREA" type="xsd:integer" />
    <xsd:element name="CountryCollection" sql:relationship="CountryRecord" />
   </xsd:sequence>
  </xsd:complexType>
 </xsd:element>

 <xsd:element name="CountryRecord" sql:relation="COUNTRY">
  <xsd:complexType>
   <xsd:sequence>
    <xsd:element name="region_id" sql:field="REGION_ID" type="xsd:integer" />
    <xsd:element name="country_id" sql:field="COUNTRY_ID" type="xsd:integer" />
    <xsd:element name="country" sql:field="COUNTRY" type="xsd:string" />
    <xsd:element name="code" sql:field="CODE" type="xsd:string" />
    <xsd:element name="population" sql:field="POPULATION" type="xsd:integer" />
    <xsd:element name="area" sql:field="AREA" type="xsd:integer" />
    <xsd:element name="fxcode" sql:field="FXCODE" type="xsd:string" />
    <xsd:element name="currency" sql:field="CURRENCY" type="xsd:string" />
    <xsd:element name="rate" sql:field="RATE" type="xsd:float" />
   </xsd:sequence>
  </xsd:complexType>
 </xsd:element>

 <xsd:annotation>
  <xsd:appinfo>
   <sql:relationship name="CountryRecord" parent="RegionRecord" parent-
key="region_id" />
  </xsd:appinfo>
 </xsd:annotation>

</xsd:schema>
```

Now let's add the STATE and CITY tables in the following XSD document:

```
<?xml version="1.0"?>
<xsd:schema xmlns:xsd="http://www.w3.org/2001/XMLSchema"
   xmlns:sql="http://schemas.microsoft.com/sqlserver/2004/sqltypes">

 <xsd:element name="RegionRecord" sql:relation="REGION">
  <xsd:complexType>
   <xsd:sequence>
    <xsd:element name="region_id" sql:field="REGION_ID" type="xsd:integer" />
    <xsd:element name="region" sql:field="REGION" type="xsd:string" />
    <xsd:element name="population" sql:field="POPULATION" type="xsd:integer" />
    <xsd:element name="area" sql:field="AREA" type="xsd:integer" />
    <xsd:element name="CountryCollection" sql:relationship="CountryRecord" />
   </xsd:sequence>
  </xsd:complexType>
 </xsd:element>

 <xsd:element name="CountryRecord" sql:relation="COUNTRY">
  <xsd:complexType>
   <xsd:sequence>
    <xsd:element name="region_id" sql:field="REGION_ID" type="xsd:integer" />
    <xsd:element name="country_id" sql:field="COUNTRY_ID" type="xsd:integer" />
    <xsd:element name="country" sql:field="COUNTRY" type="xsd:string" />
    <xsd:element name="code" sql:field="CODE" type="xsd:string" />
    <xsd:element name="population" sql:field="POPULATION" type="xsd:integer" />
    <xsd:element name="area" sql:field="AREA" type="xsd:integer" />
    <xsd:element name="fxcode" sql:field="FXCODE" type="xsd:string" />
    <xsd:element name="currency" sql:field="CURRENCY" type="xsd:string" />
    <xsd:element name="rate" sql:field="RATE" type="xsd:float" />
    <xsd:element name="StateCollection" sql:relationship="StateRecord" />
    <xsd:element name="CityCollection" sql:relationship="CityRecord" />
   </xsd:sequence>
  </xsd:complexType>
 </xsd:element>

 <xsd:element name="StateRecord" sql:relation="STATE">
  <xsd:complexType>
   <xsd:sequence>
    <xsd:element name="state_id" sql:field="STATE_ID" type="xsd:integer" />
    <xsd:element name="country_id" sql:field="COUNTRY_ID" type="xsd:integer" />
    <xsd:element name="state" sql:field="STATE" type="xsd:string" />
    <xsd:element name="code" sql:field="CODE" type="xsd:string" />
    <xsd:element name="population" sql:field="POPULATION" type="xsd:integer" />
    <xsd:element name="area" sql:field="AREA" type="xsd:integer" />
    <xsd:element name="nickname" sql:field="NICKNAME" type="xsd:string" />
    <xsd:element name="CityCollection" sql:relationship="CityRecord" />
   </xsd:sequence>
  </xsd:complexType>
 </xsd:element>

 <xsd:element name="CityRecord" sql:relation="CITY">
  <xsd:complexType>
```

```
    <xsd:sequence>
     <xsd:element name="city_id" sql:field="CITY_ID" type="xsd:integer" />
     <xsd:element name="country_id" sql:field="COUNTRY_ID" type="xsd:integer" />
     <xsd:element name="city_id" sql:field="CITY_ID" type="xsd:integer" />
     <xsd:element name="city" sql:field="CITY" type="xsd:string" />
     <xsd:element name="population" sql:field="POPULATION" type="xsd:integer" />
     <xsd:element name="area" sql:field="AREA" type="xsd:integer" />
    </xsd:sequence>
   </xsd:complexType>
  </xsd:element>

  <xsd:annotation>
   <xsd:appinfo>
    <sql:relationship name="CountryRecord" parent="RegionRecord" parent-
key="region_id"
       child= "CountryRecord" child-key="country_id" />
    <sql:relationship name="StateRecord" parent="CountryRecord" parent-
key="country_id"
       child= "StateRecord" child-key="state_id" />
    <sql:relationship name="CityRecord" parent="CountryRecord" parent-
key="country_id"
       child= "CityRecord" child-key="city_id" />
   </xsd:appinfo>
  </xsd:annotation>

 </xsd:schema>
```

What an XSD script provides is an XML to relational table mapping. This is also sometimes known as an XML View such that relational table data can be directly mapped into an XML hierarchical structure, and viewed as an XML document.

Storing XSD as a Schema Collection

A SQL Server 2005 schema collection is a collection of definitions, of relational tables and fields, stored as an XSD script. In other words, a schema collection is an XSD script, stored as a definition in a SQL Server 2005 database:

```
CREATE XML SCHEMA COLLECTION RegionalCollection AS
'<?xml version="1.0"?>
<xsd:schema xmlns:xsd="http://www.w3.org/2001/XMLSchema"
   xmlns:sql="http://schemas.microsoft.com/sqlserver/2004/sqltypes">

<xsd:element name="RegionRecord" sql:relation="REGION">
  <xsd:complexType>
   <xsd:sequence>
    <xsd:element name="region_id" sql:field="REGION_ID" type="xsd:integer" />
    <xsd:element name="region" sql:field="REGION" type="xsd:string" />
    <xsd:element name="population" sql:field="POPULATION" type="xsd:integer" />
    <xsd:element name="area" sql:field="AREA" type="xsd:integer" />
    <xsd:element name="CountryCollection" sql:relationship="CountryRecord" />
   </xsd:sequence>
```

```
   </xsd:complexType>
  </xsd:element>
  <xsd:element name="CountryRecord" sql:relation="COUNTRY">
   <xsd:complexType>
    <xsd:sequence>
     <xsd:element name="region_id" sql:field="REGION_ID" type="xsd:integer" />
     <xsd:element name="country_id" sql:field="COUNTRY_ID" type="xsd:integer" />
     <xsd:element name="country" sql:field="COUNTRY" type="xsd:string" />
     <xsd:element name="code" sql:field="CODE" type="xsd:string" />
     <xsd:element name="population" sql:field="POPULATION" type="xsd:integer" />
     <xsd:element name="area" sql:field="AREA" type="xsd:integer" />
     <xsd:element name="fxcode" sql:field="FXCODE" type="xsd:string" />
     <xsd:element name="currency" sql:field="CURRENCY" type="xsd:string" />
     <xsd:element name="rate" sql:field="RATE" type="xsd:float" />
     <xsd:element name="StateCollection" sql:relationship="StateRecord" />
     <xsd:element name="CityCollection" sql:relationship="CityRecord" />
    </xsd:sequence>
   </xsd:complexType>
  </xsd:element>
  <xsd:element name="StateRecord" sql:relation="STATE">
   <xsd:complexType>
    <xsd:sequence>
     <xsd:element name="state_id" sql:field="STATE_ID" type="xsd:integer" />
     <xsd:element name="country_id" sql:field="COUNTRY_ID" type="xsd:integer" />
     <xsd:element name="state" sql:field="STATE" type="xsd:string" />
     <xsd:element name="code" sql:field="CODE" type="xsd:string" />
     <xsd:element name="population" sql:field="POPULATION" type="xsd:integer" />
     <xsd:element name="area" sql:field="AREA" type="xsd:integer" />
     <xsd:element name="nickname" sql:field="NICKNAME" type="xsd:string" />
     <xsd:element name="CityCollection" sql:relationship="CityRecord" />
    </xsd:sequence>
   </xsd:complexType>
  </xsd:element>
  <xsd:element name="CityRecord" sql:relation="CITY">
   <xsd:complexType>
    <xsd:sequence>
     <xsd:element name="city_id" sql:field="CITY_ID" type="xsd:integer" />
     <xsd:element name="country_id" sql:field="COUNTRY_ID" type="xsd:integer" />
     <xsd:element name="city_id" sql:field="CITY_ID" type="xsd:integer" />
     <xsd:element name="city" sql:field="CITY" type="xsd:string" />
     <xsd:element name="population" sql:field="POPULATION" type="xsd:integer" />
     <xsd:element name="area" sql:field="AREA" type="xsd:integer" />
    </xsd:sequence>
   </xsd:complexType>
  </xsd:element>
  <xsd:annotation>
   <xsd:appinfo>
    <sql:relationship name="CountryRecord" parent="RegionRecord"
       parent-key="region_id"
       child= "CountryRecord" child-key="country_id" />
    <sql:relationship name="StateRecord" parent="CountryRecord"
       parent-key="country_id"
       child= "StateRecord" child-key="state_id" />
```

```
      <sql:relationship name="CityRecord" parent="CountryRecord"
          parent-key="country_id"
          child= "CityRecord" child-key="city_id" />
    </xsd:appinfo>
   </xsd:annotation>
  </xsd:schema>'
GO
```

Without applying the schema collection created previously, the following query uses its inherent query structure to determine the structure of the XML output:

```
SELECT region.region AS name, region.population, region.area,
    country.country AS name, country.currency,
    state.state AS name, state.nickname,
    city.city AS name
FROM region JOIN country ON country.region_id = region.region_id
    JOIN state ON state.country_id = country.country_id
        JOIN city ON (city.country_id = country.country_id
                        OR city.state_id = state.state_id)
WHERE country.country = 'Canada'
ORDER BY region.region, country.country, state.state, city.city
FOR XML AUTO, ROOT, ELEMENTS
GO
```

This is a partial result:

```
<root>
  <region>
    <name>North America</name>
    <population>331599508</population>
    <area>18729272</area>
    <country>
      <name>Canada</name>
      <currency>Dollars</currency>
      <state>
        <name>Alberta</name>
        <nickname></nickname>
        <city>
          <name>Burlington</name>
        </city>
        <city>
          <name>Calgary</name>
        </city>
        <city>
          <name>Edmonton</name>
        </city>
...
      </state>
    </country>
  </region>
</root>
```

Now apply the schema collection, and the schema collection called RegionalCollection determines the structure of the returned XML data:

```
SELECT region.region AS name, region.population, region.area,
    country.country AS name, country.currency,
    state.state AS name, state.nickname,
    city.city AS name
FROM region JOIN country ON country.region_id = region.region_id
    JOIN state ON state.country_id = country.country_id
        JOIN city ON (city.country_id = country.country_id
                        OR city.state_id = state.state_id)
WHERE country.country = 'Canada'
ORDER BY region.region, country.country, state.state, city.city
FOR XML AUTO, XMLSCHEMA('RegionalCollection')
GO
```

The result is shown here. At the top, the XSD definition of the schema collection is output (only a partial result of the XSD definition is shown). Following the XSD schema collection definition is the actual XML output, whose structure is determined by the XSD document, stored in the database as a schema collection. Effectively, a direct mapping has been created between relational tables and XML hierarchical structure using the XSD and schema collection definitions. Neat huh?

```
<xsd:schema targetNamespace="RegionalCollection" xmlns:schema="RegionalCollection"
xmlns:xsd="http://www.w3.org/2001/XMLSchema"
xmlns:sqltypes="http://schemas.microsoft.com/sqlserver/2004/sqltypes"
elementFormDefault="qualified">
  <xsd:import namespace="http://schemas.microsoft.com/sqlserver/2004/sqltypes"
schemaLocation="http://schemas.microsoft.com/sqlserver/2004/sqltypes/sqltypes.xsd"
/>
  <xsd:element name="region">
    <xsd:complexType>
      <xsd:sequence>
...
</xsd:schema>
<region xmlns="RegionalCollection" name="North America" population="331599508"
area="18729272">
  <country name="Canada" currency="Dollars">
    <state name="Alberta" nickname="">
      <city name="Burlington" />
      <city name="Calgary" />
      <city name="Edmonton" />
      <city name="Halifax" />
      <city name="Montreal" />
      <city name="Ottawa" />
      <city name="Quebec City" />
      <city name="Toronto" />
      <city name="Vancouver" />
    </state>
    <state name="British Columbia" nickname="">
      <city name="Burlington" />
      <city name="Calgary" />
      <city name="Edmonton" />
```

```
            <city name="Halifax" />
            <city name="Montreal" />
            <city name="Ottawa" />
            <city name="Quebec City" />
            <city name="Toronto" />
            <city name="Vancouver" />
        </state>
        <state name="Nova Scotia" nickname="">
            <city name="Burlington" />
            <city name="Calgary" />
            <city name="Edmonton" />
            <city name="Halifax" />
            <city name="Montreal" />
            <city name="Ottawa" />
            <city name="Quebec City" />
            <city name="Toronto" />
            <city name="Vancouver" />
        </state>
        <state name="Ontario" nickname="">
            <city name="Burlington" />
            <city name="Calgary" />
            <city name="Edmonton" />
            <city name="Halifax" />
            <city name="Montreal" />
            <city name="Ottawa" />
            <city name="Quebec City" />
            <city name="Toronto" />
            <city name="Vancouver" />
        </state>
        <state name="Quebec" nickname="">
            <city name="Burlington" />
            <city name="Calgary" />
            <city name="Edmonton" />
            <city name="Halifax" />
            <city name="Montreal" />
            <city name="Ottawa" />
            <city name="Quebec City" />
            <city name="Toronto" />
            <city name="Vancouver" />
        </state>
    </country>
</region>
```

Creating Indexes on XML Data Types

XML data types can contain very large XML documents and store them inside an SQL Server database. The result is a large chunk of data stored into a binary object data type. Any searches through that XML document involve scanning the entire XML document data space. In many cases, queries can perform better by reading smaller portions of a data space in order to facilitate more efficient scans through large chunks of data. One method of improving performance of data reads is by using indexes.

SQL Server 2005 allows creation of indexes on XML data types. This book really needs to discuss only these indexes, what they are, and how they are created. Demonstrating their use is more of a performance tuning topic and is beyond the scope of this book. SQL Server also uses XML indexes in such a way that queries executed against XML data types use the same SQL query engine process that SQL queries do, including all query planning, query optimization, and query execution processing. So there is additionally no overhead to using a query processing engine specific to XML, and thus not as far advanced as the SQL Server processing query engine.

A query against an XML data type, regardless of the existence of XML indexes or not, uses something called XQuery. XQuery comprises special methods executable directly against XML data types as self-contained object methods. These methods are discussed specifically for SQL Server in the first section of this chapter. XQuery is a standard established as a basis for queries against XML documents. XQuery is discussed later on in this book from a more generic perspective.

The most basic reasons for the existence of an index against a set of data are as follows:

❑ **Index size:** Generally an index will be much smaller than a relational table because an index is created against a small physical portion of a table. If a few rows are selected from the table then reading the index and table in tandem can be faster than reading the entire table.

❑ **Index algorithms:** Indexes use specialized algorithms that allow for rapid selective searching for specific values. These specialized algorithms are not available when reading table data correctly.

❑ **Index order:** Indexes are sorted in the order by which records are selected. For example, using an index on the phone number would help in reading a table of customers in phone number order, when the table was created in customer name order.

SQL Server allows four different types of indexes, which can be created against XML data types:

❑ **Primary XML index:** Contains a single row (like a table) for each node, built into a clustered BTree index structure. Essentially it's a flat relational structure of an XML hierarchy.

❑ **Secondary XML indexes:** These indexes are actually created on the node table produced by the primary index:

    ❑ **PATH index:** An index on the node paths plus values in an XML document. Helps with searching through the paths (hierarchical node structure) of an XML document when using value comparisons.

    ❑ **PROPERTY index:** An index on the primary key of the XML table, plus the path and the values (as for the path index above). A property index is better for searching directly for values in an XML document, as opposed to a path searching through a hierarchical node structure.

    ❑ **VALUE index:** Similar to a path index but in the opposite order where values are indexed before path values. Useful for searching for values across an entire XML document structure, regardless of the node path hierarchy.

The following commands create a primary XML index on the XML field, in the XML table, for the demographics database used for this book. First create a table containing two fields where one is an integer primary key and the other an XML data type field:

```
CREATE TABLE XML(
    ID INT PRIMARY KEY,
    XML XML)
GO
```

Next create the primary key on the XML data type in the XML table:

```
CREATE PRIMARY XML INDEX XMLIDX ON XML(XML)
GO
```

Now let's add some data to the table, copying a single region from the DEMXML table into the new XML table created previously:

```
DECLARE @xmldoc xml
SET @xmldoc = (SELECT xml.query('/demographics/region[name="North America"]')
    FROM demXML)
INSERT INTO XML(ID,XML) VALUES(10,@xmldoc)
SELECT ID, XML FROM XML
GO
```

The disadvantage of creating a primary index on an XML data type is that the primary key index flattens out (or decomposes) the XML hierarchy. This tends to introduce duplication such that the primary index can actually become larger in physical size than the XML document (or fragment in this case). However, the index is constructed using a special algorithm, resulting in a BTree index. Reading a BTree index allows for scans through a tree structure, which is nearly always much faster than reading the entire physical space of an XML document. Exceptions to this rule are when deliberately reading the entire XML document, or reading a large percentage of the XML structure, or when the dataset is very small.

Secondary indexes can assist in XQuery processing by effectively creating a BTree index on all the path routes through an XML document:

```
CREATE XML INDEX XMLIDXPATH ON XML(XML) USING XML INDEX XMLIDX FOR PATH
GO
```

Or all the attribute values through an XML document:

```
CREATE XML INDEX XMLIDXPATH ON XML(XML) USING XML INDEX XMLIDX FOR PROPERTY
GO
```

Or all textual values for nodes through an XML document:

```
CREATE XML INDEX XMLIDXPATH ON XML(XML) USING XML INDEX XMLIDX FOR VALUE
GO
```

This chapter has attempted to introduce the use of XML directly from within SQL Server database. As in the previous chapter, which covered Oracle and XML, XML is vastly more complex and detailed than presented in this chapter.

Summary

In this chapter you learned that:

❑ The XML data type is a specialized data type, used for storing XML documents within an SQL Server database.

❑ SQL Server XML data methods include query(), value(), exist(), and modify() methods; which are executed directly against XML data types.

❑ The query() method retrieves nodes, including all child elements from an XML data type.

❑ The value() method retrieves a single value from an XML data type.

❑ The exist() method validates the existence of items in an XML data type.

❑ The modify() method allows for changes to XML data.

❑ The FOR XML clause enhances the SQL Server SELECT statement, allowing for queries to convert directly to XML output.

❑ The FOR XML clause can be executed in RAW, AUTO, EXPLICIT, or PATH mode.

❑ The FOR XML RAW mode returns a single XML element for each record returned by a query.

❑ The FOR XML AUTO mode is more sophisticated than RAW mode, returning a single layer of nested elements for each table in a join query.

❑ The FOR XML EXPLICIT mode allows for complete control over how XML is displayed, allowing for return of properly structured XML document hierarchical data.

❑ The FOR XML PATH mode is a more sophisticated and easier-to-use option than the FOR XML EXPLICIT mode.

❑ The OPENXML function can be used to access an XML data type as if it were a set of relational tables.

❑ The OPENROWSET function can be used to bulk-load entire XML documents (stored on disk outside of an SQL Server database), directly into an XML data type inside a table.

❑ XML Schema Definition schemas (XSD schemas) can be used to generically impose schema structure onto an XML data type, using a SQL Server schema collection.

❑ XSD can be used to enforce table structure onto XML documents, and even the relationships between those relational database tables.

Exercises

1. What is the document maximum size of an SQL Server XML data type?

    a. 1GB

    b. 3GB

    c. 4GB

    d. Unlimited

    e. None of the above

2. Which of these is a method allowing changes to data within an XML data type?

    a.   `exist()`

    b.   `exists()`

    c.   `change()`

    d.   `modify()`

    e.   `update()`

3. Which of these are valid XML data type methods?

    a.   `exist()`

    b.   `exists()`

    c.   `change()`

    d.   `query()`

    e.   `update()`

4. Which are valid modes for the FOR XML clause?

    a.   RAW

    b.   AUTO

    c.   PATH

    d.   EXPLICIT

    e.   All of the above

5. What does XSD stand for?

    a.   X-ray Definitional Schema

    b.   XML Definitional Schema

    c.   XML Schema Definition

    d.   None of the above

    e.   All of the above

XML in Heterogeneous Environments

From what you have seen of XML and different database engines so far, it should be clear that XML is not just data. The added benefit of XML is that it also provides structure for that data. Thus it contains metadata, which is data about the data. One of the reasons this book includes specifics for different database engines is to show some of the different ways that databases operate with XML. This includes databases such as Oracle and SQL Server.

The beauty of XML is that the data and general structure of XML documents is an established and widely accepted standard. XML is also very easy to use and understand. Therefore passing XML documents, which are just data with some structure, between different database engines and even different operating systems and hardware is easy. The easy part of this process tends to break down a little when trying to push data into and out of the various different databases. There are various ways to solve these problems. One solution is to use the tools available to the different database engines. Another solution is to try to apply standards not only to XML, but also to the different databases. Additionally, standards can even be applied to the ways in which XML is transferred between different computers.

We've really only touched the surface of Oracle and SQL Server databases. For example, there are many other XML capabilities in Oracle Database. Additionally, numerous other database engines include XML capabilities—for example, DB2 from IBM, MySQL, and others. There are even capabilities for managing XML documents in tools such as Microsoft Excel. The primary purpose of the previous two chapters was to present a very brief picture of what different database engines, and different software, can do independently when you're working with XML documents.

This chapter shows you how to transfer XML data between different platforms and databases, regardless of which specific database is used at either end point of an XML data transfer. One of the ideas behind the existence of XML is to allow for sharing of data, without regard for whatever is at either end of a transfer.

Appendix E covers more on different database engines and their XML capabilities.

In this chapter you learn about:

❑   Simple XML document transfer

❑   Sharing of XML documents using Web Services

❑   What a Web Service is

❑   What SOAP is

❑   Applying context semantics to XML documents using SOAP

Basic XML Document Transfer

Basic transfer of XML documents refers to the transferring of an XML document from one point to another. For example, in the two previous chapters, which cover Oracle and SQL Server databases, an XML document was generated from an Oracle database. That XML document was then used to add an XML document into both the Oracle database and the SQL Server database, stored as XML data types. The stored XML document is now fully accessible by all XML capabilities that are available to both the Oracle and the SQL Server databases. The two previous chapters have already demonstrated a basic XML document transfer.

At the end of Chapter 6, a section describing XML Schema Definition (XSD) coding showed that a transformation could be applied to XML data. XML documents can be transferred as XML between two disparate platforms (in this case Oracle and SQL Server). However, one can even apply a transformation (a change) to the XML data at the source or target computers—or even both the source and the target computers. So, XML data can be adapted by each of the two databases if you use something like XSD. The result is XML data conforming to both databases. Additionally, XSD can be used to apply a specific table structure to an XML document. Thus, not only is XML data transferred and transformed between two different platforms, it can even be transformed between two relational table structures. Obviously, there has to be common data content but the Oracle and SQL Server databases could actually contain two different sets of metadata. This is the power of XML.

Once again, the metadata is the data about the data. So, metadata consists of the tables, fields, and inter-table relationships in each different database.

Basic XML document transfer between incompatible systems, such as two different databases, is really very primitive. In fact, the need to write custom code at either end of the transfer to convert between the two systems can be enormously time consuming. On the contrary, XML is actually an intelligent form of communication because XML contains both data and the semantics (the meaning) of that data. Continually mapping XML documents between two different points in a transfer, where those transfer points could be two completely different companies, can cause all sorts of problems. For example, even if two source and target companies dealt with similar types of data, their data structures could be completely different logically. And this is in addition to using different operating systems, different hardware platforms, or even database engines. There has to be a way to organize these data transfers so that they can be more universally understood—and thus limit or completely remove the need for expensive and time-consuming custom coding.

The answer is sharing of XML data, not as just XML, but using software standards common to all platforms. The ideal result would be automated transfer of data between all kinds of computer systems without the need for any custom coding at either end. Part of this solution is realized by the inclusion of

XML data types into relational databases. XML data types have been examined in both Oracle and SQL Server databases in the previous two chapters. The result is that XML documents can be stored at the end points of communication transfers, into a database, into a common format. That common format is the XML data type, which stores XML documents in their entirety. This includes all the bells and whistles such as the XML DOM. An XML document is universal in enforcement of its standardization.

Inclusion of XML data types into relational databases is a big piece of the puzzle along the path to the universal applicability of XML document communication transfers. Any type of computer system applies. How individual databases implement operations on an XML document once they are stored in a database, such as implementing SQL/XML standards, is localized to each database server. And this is also somewhat irrelevant to the topic of repetitive transfer of XML document data between two computers.

So what's next?

Sharing XML with Web Services

A Web Service is essentially a service provider of information as a service, over a local area network (LAN), wide area network (WAN), or even the Internet at large. Many applications are written for the Internet. An internal company application running on a LAN or WAN (internal company intranet site) is essentially a small-scale, secure version of a globally available Internet application. When you log into your bank account over the Internet you are using an Internet application. But your bank account website could also be pictured as a WAN usable by the customers of the bank. Behind the banking application are web servers and databases running in the background. You can't see all that stuff. All those server computers are transparent to you as you reconcile your bank statement online with your checkbook in your hand. The result is that you are running an application to a company's computers using a Web Service. Additionally, the information transfers that occur when you click buttons, and even pay bills online, could cause all sorts of things to happen. For instance, the transfer of information between your computer in your home, and to and from your bank's web servers, could all be handled using XML data.

Essentially, a Web Service is, by definition, a service that provides information over the Internet. So, a Web Service provides a service to the Internet. The application you use to reconcile your bank statement, running in your browser at home, is therefore a Web Service. What needs to be discussed here is what this Web Service comprises:

❑ **Network Transfer Protocol:** HTTP protocol is the most widely used.

❑ **Transformation processing:** Change data from one format to another.

❑ **Web Services protocol:** Allows for semantic interpretation of XML documents.

The HTTP Protocol

There needs to be some kind of network transfer protocol that is used to manage the physical sending of data along cables. By definition, a protocol is a procedure or method of regulating transfers between computers across some type of network (including the Internet). In other words, all computers can understand messages sent and received because they are all sending and receiving messages using the same format and structure (the protocol).

The HTTP protocol is used to open connections, send and receive messages between computers, and finally close the connection. HTTP is the most commonly used component for transfer of information over the Internet. It makes perfect sense for XML data transfers to stick with HTTP. The philosophy behind using HTTP is that it makes XML more acceptable because HTTP largely already exists. Also there won't be any issues with essential security hoops such as firewalls.

Transformation Processing

When transferring XML data, it is not absolutely essential to change the structure of an XML document, as it is transferred between different nodes in a network. For example, transferring an XML document from an Oracle to a SQL Server database could involve writing out from an XML data type on one database, transferring it, and then inserting that same XML document into another XML data type on the second database server. It is more likely that transformations will occur when attempting to map XML data to local database table structures, or locally running applications. Locally running applications and localized transformations are specific to a particular server environment, such as a company. Thus, localized functions have little to do with the physical transfer of data.

Web Services Protocol

A Web Services protocol is a specialized protocol (it could even be called a language) that can be universally interpreted by any computer. And this applies to any computer that understands XML data. An application or web server serves up information to end users, looking at the results of queries in their browsers. There is a slight difference between a web server and a Web Service. The intention of a Web Service is that of serving information to other computers, as opposed to end users. Thus, the purpose of a Web Service protocol is to send data in the form of messages between computers. There is no human interface. There are no people involved.

A very simple example of a Web Service protocol is a spoken language translation protocol, often sent to a specialized service dedicated specifically as a translation service. A protocol would apply a really simple structure to a text message sent in one language, and returned in a different language. The response could also be served up to a browser on the Internet. The syntax for an example protocol sent could be something like this:

```
TranslateThisPlease { text string, source string, target string }
```

The actual translation request could be something like this:

```
TranslateThisPlease { "Hello", "English", "French" }
```

The response would be:

```
"Bonjour"
```

Which, if you don't know, is "Hello" in French.

Obviously if the protocol is improperly coded, the message is not understood. This is because it does not fit in with the Web Service protocol requirements for the translation service. For the following example, an error would be returned:

```
TranslateThisPlease { "Hello", "English" }
```

The preceding error would be caused because the translation service does not know what language to translate the response into.

In the next example, the content will not be understood because there is no such language as Gobbledegook:

```
TranslateThisPlease { "Hello", "English", "Gobbledegook" }
```

A Web Services protocol is a format applied to messages sent between computers. In the preceding example, that format is exclusive to a translation service. There are obviously many other similar Web Services on the Internet that function in the same way. However, other services do different things — for example, a newsfeed that sends information to a browser. A newsfeed contains completely different information and structure to that of a translation service. An example of a newsfeed is the scrolling text that runs across the screen on the Cable News Network news channel (CNN). How can a standard be applied to these examples, such as translation service and a newsfeed? Both Web Services have different content and structure. The answer is a protocol language or standard.

A browser understands XML. Your browser may be Internet Explorer, Netscape, or something else, depending on your operating system and preference. Once again, one of the primary purposes of XML is standardization of data. Therefore, why not try to introduce a standard method of interpreting the semantics of that data. One of the most effective of these protocols is called Simple Object Access Protocol (SOAP).

This leads to the next section, which covers application of semantics (meaning) of XML data being transferred between any computers.

Applying Semantics to XML Transfers

You already know that XML documents contain data, which is the content. The contents of an XML document are the textual items contained between the element tags. So, in the following XML fragment, the name of the country (England) is the content:

```
<country>England</country>
```

You also know that XML documents contain metadata. Metadata is the data describing the content. In the case of XML, metadata can implement or impose structure onto the content. In the following XML fragment, the hierarchical structure is the metadata describing the hierarchy of the regions, countries, and cities:

```
<region name="Europe">
   <country name="England">
      <city>London</city>
      <city>Manchester</city>
   </country>
   <country name="Germany">
      <city>Hamburg</city>
      <city>Frankfurt</city>
   </country>
</region>
```

The XML fragment contains inherent metadata, which determines the following facts based on the hierarchical structure of the XML elements and their respective attributes:

❑   London and Manchester are both cities in England.

❑   Hamburg and Frankfurt are cities in Germany.

❑   England and Germany are part of Europe.

❑   All cities and both countries are all in Europe.

Once again, retrogressing to the language translation and newsfeed examples, the preceding example is completely different from those two aforementioned examples. In other words, sending straightforward XML content and metadata between computers is somewhat meaningless in relation to the context or overall meaning of the XML document. So, what is needed is something on both ends of a transfer that can interpret the context of the XML data. The context in the preceding examples would be the general topic of the XML document: language translation, a newsfeed, and cities in countries in Europe.

How can all this information be drawn together and transferred between different computers, such that the different computers can also interpret the context of these different types of data? The answer to this question is that you would have to send a message to another computer, essentially telling it what you are sending.

How can the context of an XML document transfer be determined at both end points of a transfer?

Simple Object Access Protocol

Simple Object Access Protocol (SOAP) allows for the specification of the context of data sent as messages between different computers. The different computers sending and receiving data all understand both XML and the SOAP specification you are using, and thus the context can be understood as well. Now isn't that clever!

Essentially a SOAP message or document consists of a number of things:

❑   **Envelope:** This is the root node wrapper for the SOAP XML document that allows inclusion of a namespace for interpreting the SOAP namespace tags. SOAP namespace tags are contained within the XML message document.

❑   **Header:** This section is optional and allows for further description of the XML data, which is contained within the SOAP body element. The SOAP header section describes the SOAP body section.

❑   **Body:** This section contains the XML document data. For the previous examples, the body section would contain language translation, a newsfeed, or cities in countries in Europe.

It gets even better. SOAP is also written in XML. XML happens to be universally understood as a standard. And therefore SOAP also becomes a universally understood standard by the computers involved in a transfer of data. How does this work? The envelope of a SOAP message allows for a namespace. That namespace can contain all the definitions of the SOAP tags including the envelope, header, and body tags. So, the interpretation of the XML metadata specific for SOAP is retrieved directly over the Internet, from the World Wide Web Consortium (W3C). The SOAP specification and information about how SOAP tags are interpreted are found at www.w3.org. That's what a namespace does. It's puts interpretation of specialized XML tags onto the Internet, and the interpretation is thus available to anyone, anywhere in the world, with any computer, and any Internet browser.

A namespace provides a set of definitions for the interpretation of specific XML tags. In other words, there is no programming needed for client or server computers in order to interpret the SOAP XML tags. That interpretation is already done for you. No complex programming is required other than the SOAP scripting, of course.

Put all these parts and pieces together and you should see that this is all very clever indeed. It's almost like the computer world's answer to a complete theory of cosmology, melding together all of classical physics, relativity, and quantum physics. That's quite a stretch but there might just be something to get excited about here.

Examine the region of Europe. The SOAP equivalent might look something like this:

```xml
<?xml version="1.0"?>
<SOAP:Envelope xmlns:SOAP="http://www.w3.org/2003/05/soap-envelope">
<SOAP:Header></SOAP:Header>
<SOAP:Body>
    <region name="Europe">
        <country name="England">
            <city>London</city>
            <city>Manchester</city>
        </country>
        <country name="Germany">
            <city>Hamburg</city>
            <city>Frankfurt</city>
        </country>
    </region>
</SOAP:Body>
</SOAP:Envelope>
```

Figure 7-1 shows a browser-executed version of the preceding example.

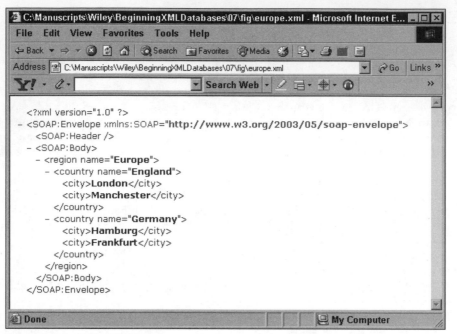

Figure 7-1: Including SOAP namespace commands in an XML document

As you can see in the preceding examples, SOAP element definitions can be found at the following URL:

```
http://www.w3.org/2003/05/soap-envelope
```

Figure 7-2 shows a partial picture of the content contained in the preceding URL.

If we now examine the language translation example again, an equivalent SOAP message might look something like this:

```
<?xml version="1.0"?>
<SOAP:Envelope xmlns:SOAP="http://www.w3.org/2003/05/soap-envelope">
<SOAP:Header></SOAP:Header>
<SOAP:Body>
   TranslateThisPlease { "Hello", "English", "French" }
</SOAP:Body>
</SOAP:Envelope>
```

Figure 7-3 shows a browser-executed version of the preceding example.

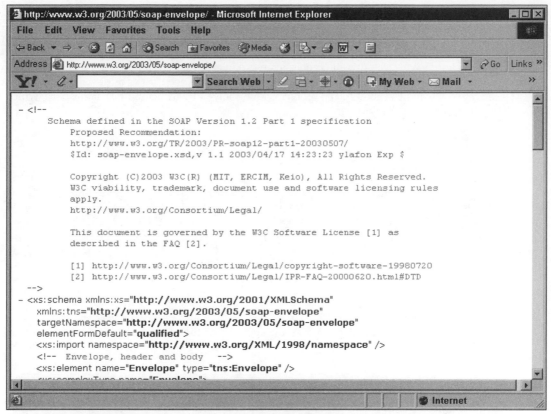

Figure 7-2: The W3C website soap-envelope namespace definition

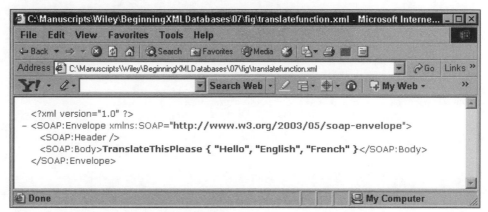

Figure 7-3: Calling a function in a SOAP script

The difference between the countries and cities example in relation to the language translation example, is that the former is just data, and the latter contains a function. Data is static information and a function performs some processing. Technically speaking, the preceding language translation example is incorrect as specified using SOAP because the translation function is not part of the SOAP specification on the W3C website. Here is where all this stuff gets even more interesting. What needs to be done is to provide an interpretation of the function. In other words, the function code needs to be retrieved from somewhere so that the function can be executed. The problem can be solved by using another namespace, which is specific to the function concerned:

```xml
<?xml version="1.0"?>
<SOAP:Envelope xmlns:SOAP="http://www.w3.org/2003/05/soap-envelope">
<SOAP:Header></SOAP:Header>
<SOAP:Body>
   <trans:TranslateThisPlease xmlns="http://www.translationstuff.com/soap-stuff">
      <trans:text>Hello</trans:text>
      <trans:source>English</trans:source>
      <trans:target>French</trans:target>
   </trans:TranslateThisPlease>
</SOAP:Body>
</SOAP:Envelope>
```

Figure 7-4 shows a browser-executed version of the preceding example. Figure 7-4 actually shows an error because the namespace declared at the URL http://www.translationstuff.com/soap-stuff doesn't exist. In fact the URL itself does not exist and neither does the website. This is just for demonstration purposes.

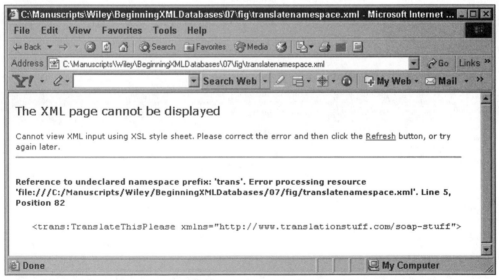

Figure 7-4: Calling a function from a namespace

As you can see in the preceding example, the translation function is contained within a namespace other than the W3C SOAP specification namespace, at a URL that could be owned by a language translation service company. And even that can be written using XML (or at least an XML wrapper) and made and easily available over the Internet.

As you can clearly see, each and every web server can specifically define the context of data contained within an XML document from a web server. This completely eliminates the need for any type of interpretive coding on any computer. The interpretation of the coding is contained on the web server of the company providing the Web Service. No local coding to interpret the context of an XML document is required because it can all be made available over the Internet. Obviously a translation service is not free but the actual translation is coded and implemented by the company performing language translation, as a Web Service to any other Internet site that requires it.

Let's use SOAP by example to create a simple tool that sends a message to a server and returns the same message in reply. The first thing to do is to build a form in an HTML page:

```
<HTML><HEAD><TITLE>Create a Message</TITLE>
<SCRIPT LANGUAGE="JavaScript">
function getCountry(pCountry) { alert(pCountry.value); }
</SCRIPT>
</HEAD>

<BODY>

<FORM NAME="fCountry" ID="fCountry">
   <INPUT TYPE="text" NAME="myCountry" SIZE="16" VALUE="Canada">
   <INPUT TYPE="submit" VALUE="Country" onClick="getCountry(this.form.myCountry);">
</FORM>
</BODY></HTML>
```

Figure 7-5 shows the three stages in the preceding script:

1. Load the page into a browser.

2. Click the button and get the popup (alert) window.

3. The URL is altered as a result of the value of the country in the form.

So now you know how to create a simple message. The fact is, SOAP is actually just a wrapper used to wrap messages. Those SOAP messages are sent to another computer, which simply knows how to interpret the SOAP XML structure. This script generates a SOAP structured XML document inside an HTML page through the use of JavaScript:

```
<HTML><HEAD><TITLE>Create a SOAP Message</TITLE>

<SCRIPT LANGUAGE="JavaScript">
function getCountry(pCountry)
{
    var lSOAP;

    lSOAP = '<?xml version="1.0"?>\n';
```

```
    lSOAP += '<SOAP:Envelope';
    lSOAP += ' xmlns:SOAP="http://www.w3.org/2003/05/soap-envelope">\n';
    lSOAP += '<SOAP:Header></SOAP:Header>\n';
    lSOAP += '<SOAP:Body>\n';
    lSOAP += '   <c:country xmlns="http://www.somewebsite.com/soap-stuff">\n';
    lSOAP += '      <c:text>' + pCountry.value + '</c:text>\n';
    lSOAP += '   </c:country>\n';
    lSOAP += '</SOAP:Body>\n';
    lSOAP += '</SOAP:Envelope>\n';
    alert(lSOAP);
}
</SCRIPT>
</HEAD>
<BODY>
<FORM NAME="fCountry" ID="fCountry">
    <INPUT TYPE="text" NAME="myCountry" SIZE="16" VALUE="Canada">
    <INPUT TYPE="submit" VALUE="Country" onClick="getCountry(this.form.myCountry);">
</FORM>
</BODY></HTML>
```

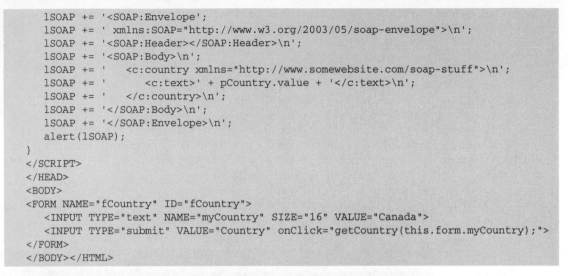

Figure 7-5: Create a simple message in an HTML page.

The result of the preceding code is as shown in Figure 7-6, again demonstrating that SOAP is simply a message, sent somewhere, in this case to a popup in the browser on the current machine.

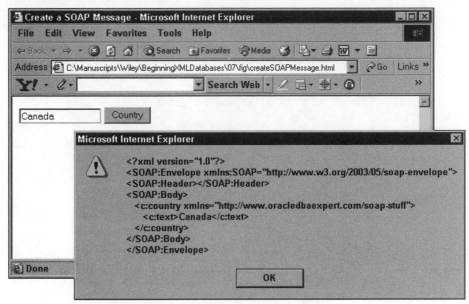

Figure 7-6: Create a simple SOAP message in an HTML page.

And next is something equally as simple except that now rather than being sent to the popup in the current HTML page, the SOAP message is sent to an ASP server running on another computer. Also, the ASP server returns the SOAP message and it gets popped up on the screen in the HTML page. The script simply sends the SOAP message to the ASP server and back again:

```
<HTML><HEAD><TITLE>Send a SOAP Message</TITLE>

<SCRIPT LANGUAGE="JavaScript">
function getError(obj)
{
    var lstr = "Error " + obj.errorCode + " on line " + obj.line
    lstr += ", position " + obj.linepos + "\n\n";
    lstr += obj.reason + "\n\n";
    lstr += obj.srcText + "\n\n";
    alert(lstr);
}

function sendCountry(pCountry)
{
    var lSOAP = '<?xml version="1.0"?>\n';
```

```
        lSOAP += '<SOAP:Envelope';
        lSOAP += ' xmlns:SOAP="http://www.w3.org/2003/05/soap-envelope">\n';
        lSOAP += '<SOAP:Header></SOAP:Header>\n';
        lSOAP += '<SOAP:Body>\n';
        lSOAP += '   <c:country xmlns:c="http://www.oracledbaexpert.com/soap-stuff">\n';
        lSOAP += '       <c:text>' + pCountry.value + '</c:text>\n';
        lSOAP += '   </c:country>\n';
        lSOAP += '</SOAP:Body>\n';
        lSOAP += '</SOAP:Envelope>\n';

        var xmlDoc = new ActiveXObject("Microsoft.XMLDOM");
        xmlDoc.async = false;
        xmlDoc.loadXML(lSOAP);

        if (xmlDoc.parseError.errorCode != 0) { getError(xmlDoc.parseError); }

        var xmlHTTP = new ActiveXObject("Microsoft.XMLHTTP");
        xmlHTTP.open("POST", "http://p1301/getSOAP.asp", false);
        xmlHTTP.send(xmlDoc);

        alert(xmlHTTP.responseXML.xml);

}
</SCRIPT>
</HEAD>

<BODY>
<FORM NAME="fCountry" ID="fCountry">
   <INPUT TYPE="text" NAME="myCountry" SIZE="16" VALUE="Canada">
   <INPUT TYPE="submit" VALUE="Country"
      onClick="sendCountry(this.form.myCountry);">
</FORM>
</BODY></HTML>
```

The result, as shown in Figure 7-7, is exactly the same as in Figure 7-6 except for some slightly different formatting.

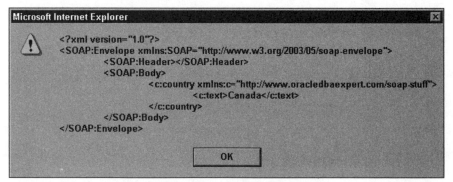

Figure 7-7: Send a simple SOAP message to ASP and back.

The ASP script for the preceding example is as follows, reading and returning the same SOAP XML message back to the calling HTML page:

```
<%
Response.ContentType = "text/xml"
Set xmlDoc = Server.CreateObject ("Microsoft.XMLDOM")
xmlDoc.load Request
Response.Write xmlDoc.xml
%>
```

The critical point to understand here is that SOAP is simply used to send messages. The formatting is understood on both ends, but still, it's just a message.

What would be more useful and applicable to this particular book is using SOAP to send a message from one server to another, interpreting the SOAP structure on both ends, and returning a useful result. A number of questions could be asked at this point:

❑ Can this technology be applied to sending XML documents between two databases? It can but the two databases used in this book both contain XML data types that helps.

❑ Why would one need to transfer XML documents from Oracle to SQL Server, or vice versa, and send them as a SOAP message? This obviously makes this software somewhat irrelevant in the case of this book. Of course if you want to restructure the XML documents between the databases it might make sense to use SOAP. However, there are plenty of other utilities for scanning XML documents and rebuilding that XML into a different structure—particularly within the XML capabilities of the databases themselves.

❑ Is this technology actually useful in relation to database-to-database transfers of XML documents? No. Not when both databases contain XML data types. However, if you want to update one of the databases, either in relational tables or with an XML data type, you can use something like the translation function to pull something off a feed namespace. Feeds contain information such as stock quotes, weather reports, and in the case of this book—population and currency exchange rate figures. This type of service is provided by passing SOAP messages to the service, which the service understands. Additionally, the feed Web Service needs something applying further meaning and structure to the message, using something like Web Service Description Language (WSDL).

External Data and XML

An external data source, even one written using XML, can have a different XML document structure than you may want your XML document to have. When dealing with external data and XML, something like SOAP can be used to interpret the context and contents of an XML document. How can this be achieved? This is where SOAP messages and WSDL structural imposition onto those SOAP messages, come into play. The result is XML implemented across a heterogeneous environment. Obviously there are plenty of companies that use databases other than Oracle and SQL Server. Many of these databases do not have easy-to-use XML data types. So, SOAP and WSDL apply when not using Oracle or SQL server.

Essentially, WSDL uses XML Schema Definition (XSD) schema scripts in order to apply schema (relational table) structures onto SOAP message XML documents. In Chapter 6, you saw an example of using XSD scripting to store schemas, and what can even be called namespace collections, into a SQL Server database.

A heterogeneous environment is where two servers are essentially producing data that cannot be simply pushed in and out of two databases, using something like XML data types. There has to be some kind of transformation of XML data between the two HTTP end points. One method of solving the transformation issue is through the use of SOAP messages and WSDL XSD schemas. SOAP is covered in this chapter and XSD schemas are covered in Chapter 6.

B2B Data Transfer

Business-2-Business, or B2B data transfers, can utilize XML data and XSL style sheets to transfer data between two disparate data sources, such as two completely different companies. XSL can be used to transform the XML data between the two data structural requirements of the two different companies.

Two companies, both having different XML document data structures, can pass the same XML data backwards and forwards. The data structure can be changed very easily simply by using a style sheet. Chapter 3 covers the use of XSL (eXtensible Style Sheets).

Using XSL to reformat XML data is probably the easiest method of transferring XML data across heterogeneous environments. This assumes that you can utilize XML documents at either end. However, even if both ends contain relational databases, with different table structures, there is no reason why XSL should not be used to perform an initial restructuring of XML data — prior to reinsertion into relational databases tables.

Figure 7-1 contains an XML document, wrapped up in a SOAP message. That XML document looks like this:

```
<region name="Europe">
   <country name="England">
      <city>London</city>
      <city>Manchester</city>
   </country>
   <country name="Germany">
      <city>Hamburg</city>
      <city>Frankfurt</city>
   </country>
</region>
```

Now you can use something like this XSL style sheet to rearrange the structure of the XML data:

```
<?xml version="1.0"?>
<xsl:stylesheet version="1.0" xmlns:xsl="http://www.w3.org/1999/XSL/Transform">
   <xsl:template match="/">
      <HTML><BODY>
         <xsl:for-each select="region">
            &lt;<xsl:value-of select="name()"/>&gt;
            &lt;name&gt;<xsl:value-of select="@name"/>&lt;/name&gt;
            <xsl:for-each select="country">
               &lt;<xsl:value-of select="name()"/>&gt;
               &lt;name&gt;<xsl:value-of select="@name"/>&lt;/name&gt;
               <xsl:for-each select="city">
                  &lt;<xsl:value-of select="name()"/>&gt;
```

```
                  <xsl:value-of select="text()"/>
                  &lt;/<xsl:value-of select="name()"/>&gt;
            </xsl:for-each>
            &lt;/<xsl:value-of select="name()"/>&gt;
         </xsl:for-each>
         &lt;/<xsl:value-of select="name()"/>&gt;
      </xsl:for-each>
   </BODY></HTML>
   </xsl:template>
</xsl:stylesheet>
```

There are better methods of resolving the preceding transformation using templates but this seemed like a good way to explain it in a programmatic, rather than a declarative, fashion. The result of the transformation looks like this:

```
<region>
   <name>Europe</name>
   <country>
      <name>England</name>
      <city>London</city>
      <city>Manchester</city>
   </country>
   <country>
      <name>Germany</name>
      <city>Hamburg</city>
      <city>Frankfurt</city>
   </country>
</region>
```

As opposed to the structure shown in Figure 7-1, the output of the transformed XML data looks like that shown in Figure 7-8.

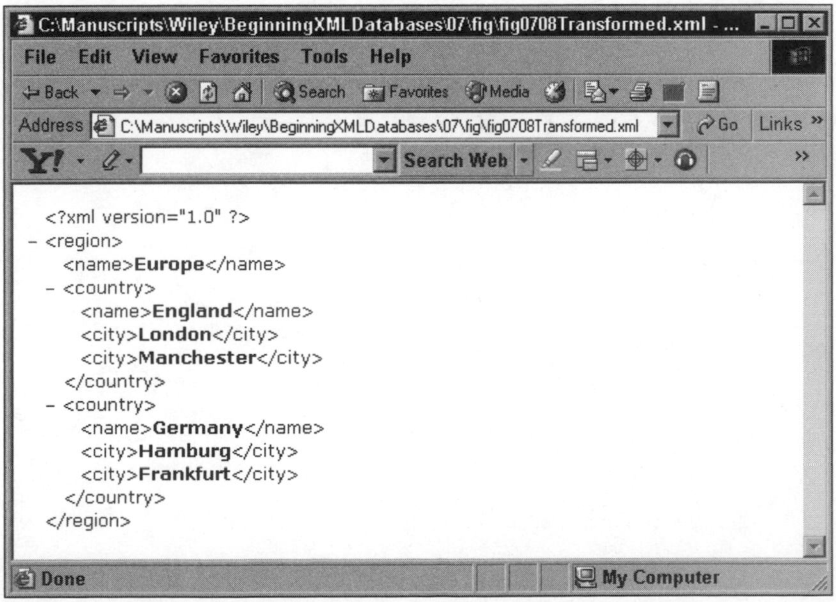

Figure 7-8: Transferring data using XSL transformations

This chapter has covered the use of XML in heterogeneous environments. A heterogeneous environment is one in which there is more than one database, quite often more than two databases. Additionally, there might be multiple operating systems and various different hardware platforms. It is essential to have some method of passing messages between the various environments. SOAP can help to accomplish this by wrapping XML documents into specialized XML wrappers. SOAP XML wrapper elements are as universally understood as XML is itself.

Summary

In this chapter you learned the following:

❑   Copying XML documents can be as simple as copying them from one server to another.

❑   Not only is XML universally understood by computers, but SOAP can be used to apply meaning to the context of an XML document.

❑   SOAP is used to send messages between computers using the HTTP protocol.

❑   A Web Service exists on the Internet as a namespace from which you can extract functional data, when given an appropriate expression, contained with a SOAP XML message.

Exercises

1.   Which is the best answer?

   a.   SOAP is used to wash in the shower.

   b.   SOAP is used to apply schema structure to tables in a database.

   c.   SOAP is used to send messages.

   d.   SOAP is used to send context-rich messages between computers.

   e.   None of the above.

2.   Which elements are allowed in a SOAP XML document?

   a.   A body section

   b.   A tail section

   c.   A header section

   d.   An envelope section

   e.   A letter section

3. What does XSD stand for?

    a. XML Standard Definition

    b. XML Surrogate Definition

    c. XML Story Definition

    d. eXtra Stovetop Derailer

    e. None of the above

4. Which of these is the best answer?

    a. SOAP sends messages and a Web Service provides information.

    b. SOAP is used to send text messages and a Web Service can provide answers to functional expressions.

    c. SOAP wraps XML documents into specialized XML tags and a Web Service can provide answers to functional expressions.

    d. All of the above.

    e. None of the above.

5. Which of the following statements best describes what will cause an error with this SOAP message?

```xml
<?xml version="1.0"?>
<SOAP:Envelope xmlns:SOAP="http://www.w3.org/2003/05/soap-envelope">
<Body>
    <region name="Europe">
        <country name="England">
            <city>London</city>
            <city>Manchester</city>
        </country>
        <country name="Germany">
            <city>Hamburg</city>
            <city>Frankfurt</city>
        </country>
    </region>
<Body>
</SOAP:Envelope>
```

    a. It has no header section.

    b. The envelope tag is incorrect and the body tag is correct.

    c. It has no header section, the body tag is incorrect, and the envelope tag is incorrect.

    d. The body tag is incorrect and the envelope tag is incorrect.

    e. All of the above.

Understanding XML
Documents as Objects

This book has examined XML, XSL, relational tables, and even specifics in both the Oracle and SQL Server relational databases. You should already know that XML documents are generally hierarchically structured, but they can be flat-structured as well. However, a hierarchical structure is most often appropriate to XML data and it can give better access and structure to data.

Therefore, because the object data model is hierarchical in nature, it makes perfect sense to attempt to describe XML document structure as being similar to object data model structure. And thus this chapter attempts to very briefly describe what exactly the object data model is.

In this chapter you learn about:

❑   The object data model

❑   The relational data model in comparison to the object data model

❑   How the object data model can help to support the most effective structure for XML data

❑   A flat-structured XML document

❑   A hierarchically structured XML document

❑   The differences between using flat and hierarchical structure for XML

Why Explain the Object Model Here?

Why examine the object model when reading about XML? The answer is that XML document structure is very similar to the object model for data. XML structure can easily be misconstrued as being more akin to a hierarchical data structure, rather than an object data structure. However, in a hierarchical data model one must always begin at the root of a data structure and search the entire structure for what is being selected from the database. With an XML document this is not the case. When parsing through an XML document, the human eye does not pass through the structure of the document, but rather searches for patterns in strings in a left to right, and top to bottom fashion. In other words, you don't build a hierarchical structure in your mind as you glance at an XML document. I don't anyway. Some may do that kind of thing because it interests them. That kind of mental gymnastics doesn't interest me unless I think it is necessary to the task at hand.

Why explain all this by discussing the scanning of an XML document by eye? Because that is how a parsing expression, such as a simple Perl script, would probably search an XML document for a specific value. Therefore, it could be said that scanning for a specific value in an XML document does not necessarily involve building the data hierarchy and then mathematically traversing that hierarchy.

Why explain the object model for a database? It will help you to understand the basic structure of an XML document. An XML document allows the containment of entire structures (subtrees) within a single node (parent node). This containment aspect is true for any of the nodes in an XML document. The only exceptions are the root node, which has no parent node, and the leaf nodes, which have no child nodes. A relational database structure, when built using something like a text file, such as an XML document, results in a flattened or two-dimensional structure. In a two-dimensional structure one cannot contain subtree nodes in a single parent tree. That type of structure is completely contrary to a normalized relational database structure.

> A normalized structure attempts to establish complex (not contained), inter-relationships between objects for the purpose of removing duplication from data.

XML document structure does not necessarily remove duplication from data. At least it is not quite as fussy as a relational table structure. By examining the object model as applied to data in this chapter, you will gain a better understanding of XML documents, how they can be used and how they can be accessed. So, let's take a look at a very simple conversion of relational data into an XML structure.

XML Data as a Relational Structure

In Chapters 5 and 6, I examined various aspects of both Oracle and SQL Server databases for handling XML data generation from relational tables. For the purposes of this argument, let's assume you have none of any of the tricks and tools demonstrated in those two chapters. In other words, to build XML data from relational tables, you have to write the XML structure from scratch.

So, the only way to read relational tables and convert them into XML document data would be to read the tables, and manually code in the XML structure, such as elements and values. This is not a problem as long as the relationships between the tables remain one-to-many in nature. A one-to-many relationship can technically be described as one of containment. A collection of many records (in a table) is contained in (or related to) a single record in the related parent table. The parent table is on the one side of the one-to-many relationship. This is all fine and good for XML, until a many-to-many relationship appears. An XML document hierarchical structure means that many (child nodes) are contained within one (parent node). And thus many cannot be contained within many because it contradicts the collection containment hierarchy.

So already the relational model falls short of the hierarchical requirement of an XML document. As a result, the conversion of relational table data to that of the XML document equivalent has to be drastically simplified. As already mentioned, let's assume that we don't have access to any of the types of

XML functionality described in Chapters 5 and 6. The only way to resolve relational table data in XML documents is to flatten out the structure. This flattening is much like a data warehouse or a join query, denormalizing a normalized relational table structure.

The following query retrieves three fields from the REGION table in the demographics database (see Appendix B):

```
SELECT REGION, POPULATION, AREA FROM REGION;
```

The result of the preceding query is shown here:

```
REGION                     POPULATION      AREA
------------------------   ----------   ----------
Africa                      789548670     26780325
Asia                         47382633       657741
Australasia                  24340222      7886602
Caribbean                    40417697       268857
Central America             142653392      2360325
Europe                      488674441      4583335
Far East                   2100636517     15357441
Middle East                 294625718      6798768
Near East                  1499157105      4721322
North America               331599508     18729272
Oceania                       9133256       536238
Russian Federation          258037209     21237500
South America               375489788     17545171
```

Now let's create some simple XML using only simple SQL functionality. The following single table query does not produce a root element containing records within that root node. Without using anything but simple SQL functionality, I can't add in the opening and closing root elements:

```
SELECT '<record region="'||REGION||'" population="'
    ||POPULATION||'" area="'||AREA||'"></record>'
FROM REGION;
```

This is the result:

```
<record region="Africa" population="789548670" area="26780325"></record>
<record region="Asia" population="47382633" area="657741"></record>
<record region="Australasia" population="24340222" area="7886602"></record>
<record region="Caribbean" population="40417697" area="268857"></record>
<record region="Central America" population="142653392" area="2360325"></record>
<record region="Europe" population="488674441" area="4583335"></record>
<record region="Far East" population="2100636517" area="15357441"></record>
<record region="Middle East" population="294625718" area="6798768"></record>
<record region="Near East" population="1499157105" area="4721322"></record>
<record region="North America" population="331599508" area="18729272"></record>
<record region="Oceania" population="9133256" area="536238"></record>
<record region="Russian Federation" population="258037209" area="21237500"></record
>
<record region="South America" population="375489788" area="17545171"></record>
```

The preceding query and all queries in this chapter, together with the rest of this book, are tested using an Oracle Database. There is no use of SQL Server Database outside of Chapter 6.

I actually cannot get the root element tags into the preceding query unless I do so manually.

The next query joins multiple tables together, again flattening the result into a report-like, single-layered structure:

```
SELECT R.REGION, R.POPULATION, R.AREA,
    C.COUNTRY, C.CURRENCY
FROM REGION R JOIN COUNTRY C ON(C.REGION_ID = R.REGION_ID)
WHERE C.CURRENCY IS NOT NULL;
```

This is a partial result:

```
REGION        POPULATION        AREA COUNTRY      CURRENCY
-----------   ----------   ---------- ------------ ------------------
Africa        789548670    26780325 Tunisia       Dinars
Africa        789548670    26780325 Uganda        Shillings
Africa        789548670    26780325 Zambia        Kwacha
Africa        789548670    26780325 Zimbabwe      Zimbabwe Dollars
Australasia   24340222      7886602 Australia     Dollars
Australasia   24340222      7886602 New Zealand   Dollars
Caribbean     40417697       268857 Bahamas       Dollars
Caribbean     40417697       268857 Barbados      Dollars
Caribbean     40417697       268857 Bermuda       Dollars
Caribbean     40417697       268857 Costa Rica    Colones
Caribbean     40417697       268857 Cuba          Pesos
```

And now the same join query but including coding to allow for XML tags:

```
SELECT '<record region="'||R.REGION||'" population="'
    ||R.POPULATION||'" area="'||R.AREA||'" country="'||C.COUNTRY
    ||'" currency="'||C.CURRENCY||'"></record>'
FROM REGION R JOIN COUNTRY C ON(C.REGION_ID = R.REGION_ID)
WHERE C.CURRENCY IS NOT NULL;
```

The partial result, which is a single layer containing one record for each country, is shown here. This is exactly the way that a simple SQL-based report would produce join query data, all flattened into a single record for each member of the join:

```
<record region="Africa" population="789548670" area="26780325" country="Tunisia" cu
rrency="Dinars"></record>
<record region="Africa" population="789548670" area="26780325" country="Uganda" cur
rency="Shillings"></record>
<record region="Africa" population="789548670" area="26780325" country="Zambia" cur
rency="Kwacha"></record>
<record region="Africa" population="789548670" area="26780325" country="Zimbabwe" c
urrency="Zimbabwe Dollars"></record>
<record region="Australasia" population="24340222" area="7886602" country="Australi
a" currency="Dollars"></record>
<record region="Australasia" population="24340222" area="7886602" country="New Zeal
and" currency="Dollars"></record>
<record region="Caribbean" population="40417697" area="268857" country="Bahamas" cu
```

```
rrency="Dollars"></record>
<record region="Caribbean" population="40417697" area="268857" country="Barbados" c
urrency="Dollars"></record>
<record region="Caribbean" population="40417697" area="268857" country="Bermuda" cu
rrency="Dollars"></record>
<record region="Caribbean" population="40417697" area="268857" country="Costa Rica"
currency="Colones"></record>
<record region="Caribbean" population="40417697" area="268857" country="Cuba" curre
ncy="Pesos"></record>
```

Again, there is no root element in the query shown in the preceding code. Additionally, there is no hierarchy, which is expected for XML. The hierarchy would contain countries within each region where the result would have two layers (in addition to the root node layer). One layer would be regions where each region contains a collection of countries. That hierarchy would look something like this:

```
<region name="Africa" population="789548670" area="26780325">
   <country name="Tunisia" currency="Dinars"></country>
   <country name="Uganda" currency="Shillings"></country>
   <country name="Zambia" currency="Kwacha"></country>
   <country name="Zimbabwe" currency="Zimbabwe Dollars"></country>
</region>
<region name="Australasia" population="24340222" area="7886602">
   <country name="Australia" currency="Dollars"></country>
   <country name="New Zealand" currency="Dollars"></country>
</region>
<region name="Caribbean" population="40417697" area="268857">
   <country name="Bahamas" currency="Dollars"></country>
   <country name="Barbados" currency="Dollars"></country>
   <country name="Bermuda" currency="Dollars"></country>
   <country name="Costa Rica" currency="Colones"></country>
   <country name="Cuba" currency="Pesos"></country>
</region>
```

Let's go a little further with the partial result shown next. This is a properly formed XML document with four hierarchical layers (including a manually added root node) instead of the two layers in the previous result:

```
<planet>
   <name>earth</name>
   <region>
      <name>Africa</name>
      <population>789548670</population>
      <area>26780325</area>
      <country>
         <name>Tunisia</name>
         <currency>Dinars</currency>
      </country>
      <country>
         <name>Uganda</name>
         <currency>Shillings</currency>
      </country>
...
   </region>
</planet>
```

Figure 8-1 shows the browser representation of the partial XML document shown in the preceding code, with the <xml> tag processing instruction included in the figure to make it function properly.

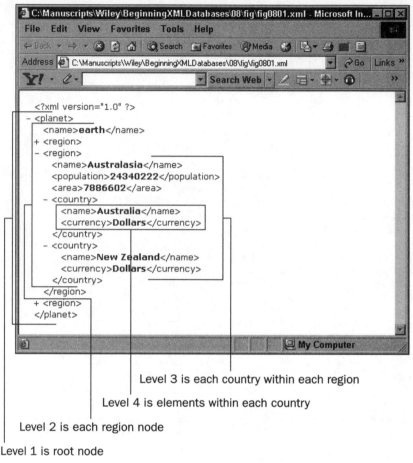

Level 3 is each country within each region

Level 4 is elements within each country

Level 2 is each region node

Level 1 is root node

Figure 8-1: The different hierarchical layers in an XML document

What have these two examples demonstrated? That simple SQL queries executed against tables in a relational database do not suffice for generation of XML documents. Of course, you already know that from previous chapters. However, it should be clear from all those tricks and toys demonstrated in Chapters 5 and 6 that specialized functionality is needed to map between the relational structure of Oracle or SQL Server database and the hierarchical-object structure of an XML document.

The Basics of the Object Data Model

This is where I go off at what might appear to be a tangent, describing the object model for data. From what you've read so far, it might be apparent that the object data model has something to do with XML documents. However, without even a brief explanation of the object data model it is unlikely that XML documents can ever truly be understood as being object structured—and perhaps never properly understood at all. The last thing you want is to create XML documents containing only single-layer hierarchies, as shown in the previous section. Why? Because a single-layer flat structure does not take advantage of the true power of XML hierarchies, where structure is included within the data itself. In other words, some data that is normally data in a relational data model is likely to become metadata in an object model.

The object model is somewhat different from the relational model. The relational model tends to simplify structures (some may say complicate them) by application of normalization. Normalization helps to remove duplication from data by dividing data into related sets. The object data model, much like object methodologies for application programming languages, tends to simplify by reducing information to the smallest possible parts. Each part can operate independently of every other part in the database. Relationships still exist in the object data model but they are different. The relational model makes a very distinct separation between metadata (tables) and data (values in fields in tables). The object model also links information together, but in addition it can apply structure to the values of data, as well as the metadata.

The structures, connections, and specific terms used for the object data model are as follows:

- **Class:** A class defines a structure into which data is stored, and is the equivalent of a relational entity or table. A class contains attributes for storing values in much the same way as a table uses fields for storing values into.

  It is essential to understand that a class is not the same thing as an object. An object is the instantiation or iteration of a class during execution. In other words, objects are created as one or more copies of a class. The class is the structural definitional element. The object is the data copy of the class.

  - **Attribute:** An attribute defines specific slots within classes. Attributes are the equivalent of a relational entity column or field.

  - **Collection:** A collection is a special type of attribute, and is the term applied to a repetition of elements of one class contained within another class. At run-time, that collection becomes a collection of objects. A collection effectively defines a one-to-many relationship between a parent class and a child class. A collection is similar to a relational entity on the many side of a one-to-many relationship.

- **Method:** A method is unique to the object model where a method can contain executable code, applicable to objects instantiated from the class the method is attached to. A method is vaguely equivalent to a relational database stored procedure, except that a method executes on the data contents of an object within the bounds of that object. Methods are far more powerful than relational database stored procedures.

- **Inheritance:** One class can inherit structure (attributes) and even methods from another class. In fact, during execution, an object that inherits structure from a parent class can even inherit attribute values. Again, the object model tends to make the difference between data and metadata more of a gray zone. Inheritance allows the application of any structure (attributes), values (attribute values), and functionality (methods), all the way down through a class hierarchy. A class inheriting from a parent class can use what is defined for a parent class, or can even redefine some or all of what is inherited.

  Retrieving attributes and behavior of a class of objects in a hierarchy is known as type casting, in which the specifics of one particular class are extracted from an object.

❏   **Multiple inheritance:** Some object models allow multiple inheritance. Multiple inheritance allows a class to inherit details from more than one class at the same time. The result is a hierarchy that goes both upward and downward. In fact, a class can be both a parent and a child of another class. Multiple inheritance can create a dual-direction hierarchical structure, which is flexible but can also be exceedingly complicated.

❏   **Specialization and abstraction:** A specialization of a class is an inherited, specific type of a class. Specializations often substitute for what are usually called types in a relational database. For example, an employee and a manager are both employees of a company, but they are different types of employees. So, two specializations for company employees would be employees and managers. The result would be an abstraction of the employees and managers, and that could be a class containing descriptions of all people employed by the company. Specialization and abstraction are effectively the same thing in that they both involve inheritance of one class from another. The difference is semantic rather than syntactical. A specialization is created to divide a class into something like multiple types. An abstraction is created to generalize attributes, values and methods that are common to multiple classes.

Creating an Object Model from a Relational Model

Unlike a relational model, an object model supports relationships between objects through the structure of objects and the classes defining those objects. Classes are defined as containing collections of pointers to other classes, as being inherited from other classes above in a hierarchy, or as being abstractions of other classes below in a hierarchy (*inheritee's*).

The relational model forces dependencies to exist between the different tables; otherwise data in different tables might be meaningless. The object model allows each structure to be autonomous of all other structures (self-contained). There is much less inter-object dependency in the object model than for the relational model. This is because, as already stated, the object model includes relationships within the structure of the model itself.

The diagram shown in Figure 8-2 is an ERD showing an enhanced version of the demographics database, relational data model used in this book (see Appendix B). The only change in Figure 8-2, in addition to what appears in Figure B-1 in Appendix B, is that an ECONOMY table is added. The ECONOMY table can contain values such as 1st World, 2nd World, and 3rd World. This implies that each country is classifiable into one of these three economic categories.

Figure 8-3 shows an object data model for the relational model shown in Figure 8-2. The Occupation class in Figure 8-3 is ignored in this case because the diagram is getting a little too cluttered.

Figures 8-2 and 8-3 enhance the relational and object data models, making it clearer how relational types and relational many-to-many relationships are managed by the object data model.

Data models shown in Figures 8-2 and 8-3 are not implemented in this book. These data models are included here merely to demonstrate the way that the object model can handle relational database issues.

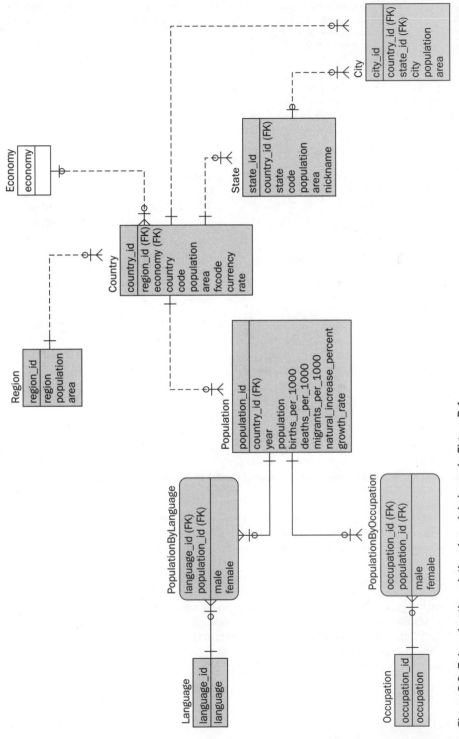

Figure 8-2: Enhancing the relational model shown in Figure B-1

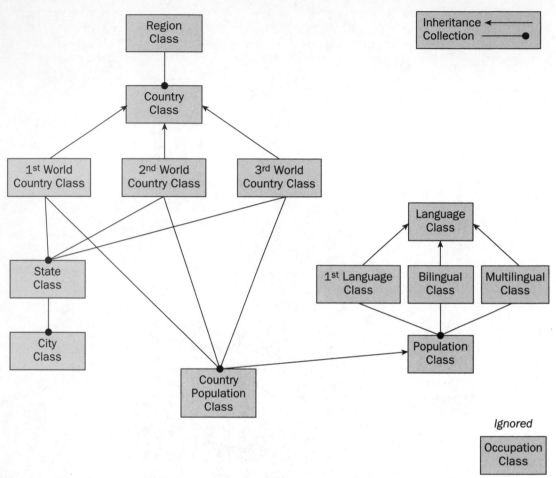

Figure 8-3: Converting the enhanced relational model of Figure 8-2 to an object model

You should be able to see some obvious differences between the two diagrams in Figures 8-2 and 8-3. This is because there are two ways in which the object model can help to reduce the complexity of the relational model. The object model does not need types or many-to-many relationships:

❑   The object model in Figure 8-3 has no types. The ECONOMY table is a type table, as shown in the relational model of Figure 8-2. The object model in Figure 8-3 creates an individual class for each type in the ECONOMY table. This is an example of the object data model beginning to change some relational data into object metadata. Data of economic types of 1st World Class, 2nd World Class, and 3rd World Class are represented in the object model by specializations of the Country Class.

❑ The many-to-many relationship between the POPULATION and LANGUAGE tables in the relational model is catered to in the object model by creating a class for different language groups. In other words, in Figure 8-3 a population in a country can speak one language (1st language), speak two languages (bilingual), or even be multilingual (speak many languages).

The following can be concluded from the example conversion shown between Figures 8-2 and 8-3, in which a relational data model is converted to an object data model:

❑ The relationships between classes in an object model are represented by the class structure, those relationships being both collection inclusion and inheritance. The result is that static data, such as types with few unique values, can sometimes become metadata.

❑ The object model contains objects containing pointers to other contained objects.

❑ An invisible difference is the power of black-box processing using methods in an object database. The object model uses data abstraction to conceptualize both data and encapsulated functionality using methods. Inheritance allows the passing of data definition and functionality onto specialized objects and extensive coding reuse.

❑ The crux and greatest benefit of objects is in their simplicity. The more that objects are broken down into smaller granular pieces, the more powerful and efficient the structure becomes. A relational database cannot be broken down to the level of an object structure. Additionally, a relational structure can only be made more granular using normalization. Too much normalization can hurt performance drastically.

❑ The object model is therefore highly efficient at handling small, precise transactions. However, an object structure is dreadful at handling any kind of reporting because objects can become so very specific. Any kind of reporting using an object data model can require merging of data from an unmanageably large number of different objects, making reporting not viable. A relational structure can handle both reporting and small transaction sizes fairly well. The result is that the practical and commercial uses for object data modeling are in reality very limited.

Another form of a data model mixes both relational and object modeling methodologies. The result is the object-relational data model, which is irrelevant to this book and XML.

XML Data as an Object Structure

A discussion of the relational and object data models, and specifically the object data model, should tell you the following about XML:

❑ An XML document can be flat-structured as a single-layer hierarchy report from a relational database.

❑ Allowing an XML document to become a multiple-layered, hierarchical structure, which is somewhat akin to the object data model, allows much more flexibility.

Let's say for example that you want to find a single country from the XML document shown in Figure 8-4.

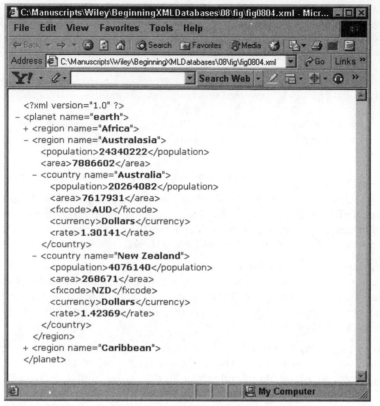

```
<?xml version="1.0" ?>
- <planet name="earth">
  + <region name="Africa">
  - <region name="Australasia">
      <population>24340222</population>
      <area>7886602</area>
    - <country name="Australia">
        <population>20264082</population>
        <area>7617931</area>
        <fxcode>AUD</fxcode>
        <currency>Dollars</currency>
        <rate>1.30141</rate>
      </country>
    - <country name="New Zealand">
        <population>4076140</population>
        <area>268671</area>
        <fxcode>NZD</fxcode>
        <currency>Dollars</currency>
        <rate>1.42369</rate>
      </country>
    </region>
  + <region name="Caribbean">
  </planet>
```

Figure 8-4: A properly structured multiple-layered hierarchical XML document

So what if you want to find New Zealand? Your algorithm can search through the structure of the XML document tree, stopping the search when it has found the country you are looking for. In Figure 8-4, a tree scan or depth-first search would parse the XML document something like this:

1. Start at the root node, which is `<planet name="earth">`.

2. Dismiss the first region at the region level because you know that New Zealand is not in Africa and so the element `<region name="Africa">` is examined but all its subtree nodes (countries) will be ignored.

3. The second region is `<region="Australasia">`, which is the region you are looking for.

4. Then you ignore the first country because it is not New Zealand, but it is `<country="Australia">`.

5. The second country in Australasia is the country you are looking for and thus New Zealand will be retrieved.

> The most important point is that everything else, all countries, are ignored! It's just like searching an index.

The way you can most efficiently perform the preceding steps is to search, or parse, the XML document using an expression that directs the search for the correct country, within the correct region. The @ sign is used to denote use of an attribute value:

```
/planet/region/region[@name=Australasia]/country[@name=New Zealand]
```

The preceding expression is pseudocode. This means it won't work as it is in any particular environment.

So now let's use similar information, as shown in the XML document of Figure 8-4, but this time using a single hierarchical layer, flattened relational structure, as shown in Figure 8-5. The following query reduces the number of fields returned for the XML document shown in Figure 8-4, because there are just as many fields in Figure 8-4:

```
SELECT '   <record region="'||R.REGION
   ||'" r_population="'||R.POPULATION||'" r_area="'||R.AREA
   ||'" country="'||C.COUNTRY
   ||'" c_population="'||C.POPULATION||'" c_area="'||C.AREA||'"></record>'
FROM REGION R JOIN COUNTRY C ON(C.REGION_ID = R.REGION_ID)
WHERE C.CURRENCY IS NOT NULL ORDER BY C.POPULATION;
```

I have also re-sorted the results in the preceding query, essentially mixing up countries and regions into a random order, and Figure 8-4 has the `<xml>` tag processing instruction included.

In actuality, there are two layers in the XML document shown in Figure 8-5. The first layer is the root node. Everything else is in the second layer.

Now imagine a program searching through the XML document shown in Figure 8-5. Let's say you wanted to find information on the two countries of China and Gambia. The XML document is not sorted according to the names of countries. In the extreme cases of China and Gambia, the document must be parsed from start to finish looking for both countries. Not using a tree-like hierarchical structure is extremely inefficient. There is no high-performance tree-searching algorithm for this example because there is no tree. A full scan is required for two reasons:

❑   Records are not necessarily sorted in the order required.

❑   Countries are not necessarily contained within regions. If you want to find a single region you would have to read the entire document, unless of course you knew beforehand exactly how many countries were in a particular region.

The benefit of using a hierarchical structure within XML documents should now be clear. And because an XML document hierarchical structure is somewhat equivalent to an object data model, it is an advantage to have even just a brief understanding of the object data model. Of course, XML does not require a specific structure because it is built to be as flexible as possible. However, because of the efficient nature of building tree structures into XML documents, the benefits should be plain to see.

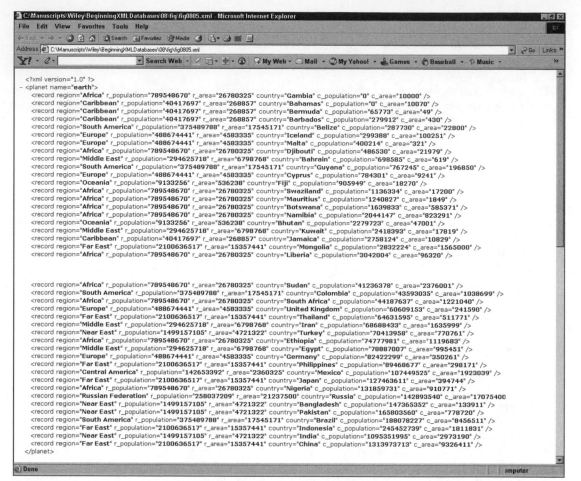

Figure 8-5: A poorly structured, single-layered XML document, sharing starting and editing records only

So how can an XML document be compared with that of an object structure? Consider the following:

❑ Every node in an XML document can contain a collection of other nodes.

❑ Every node can have attributes further describing itself.

❑ There are no methods attached to XML elements although something like eXtensible Style Sheet (XSL) templating could possibly be loosely considered as such.

❑ There is no capacity for inheritance in basic XML documents because XML documents are data not metadata. Classes are very definitely a basic metadata structure, and object modeling inheritance occurs at the class level.

Try It Out   Using Flat and Hierarchical Data

The following query executes against a relational database, producing a flattened structure of records from five tables. Alter the XML data to a hierarchical, properly object-structured XML document, and execute the result as an XML document in a browser:

```
SELECT r.REGION, c.COUNTRY, l.LANGUAGE, p.YEAR,
    SUM(pl.FEMALE) AS Females, SUM(pl.MALE) AS Males
FROM REGION r JOIN COUNTRY c ON (c.REGION_ID = r.REGION_ID)
    JOIN POPULATION p ON (p.COUNTRY_ID = c.COUNTRY_ID)
        JOIN POPULATIONBYLANGUAGE pl ON (pl.POPULATION_ID = p.POPULATION_ID)
            JOIN LANGUAGE l ON (l.LANGUAGE_ID = pl.LANGUAGE_ID)
WHERE pl.FEMALE > pl.MALE AND p.YEAR BETWEEN 1981 AND 1985
GROUP BY r.REGION, c.COUNTRY, p.YEAR, l.LANGUAGE
ORDER BY r.REGION, c.COUNTRY, l.LANGUAGE, p.YEAR;
```

This is the result, which has flattened out regions, countries, population, and languages from the demographics relational database model:

REGION	COUNTRY	LANGUAGE	YEAR	FEMALES	MALES
Africa	Mauritius	Bhojpuri	1983	99467	97609
Africa	Mauritius	French	1983	19330	16888
Europe	Finland	Czech	1985	42	36
Europe	Finland	Estonian	1985	330	102
Europe	Finland	Finnish	1981	2323676	2177310
Europe	Finland	Finnish	1985	2371522	2225386
Europe	Finland	Icelandic	1985	21	16
Europe	Finland	Korean	1985	17	13
Europe	Finland	Norwegian	1985	123	115
Europe	Finland	Polish	1985	274	236
Europe	Finland	Russian	1985	1463	800
Europe	Finland	Siamese	1985	48	7
Europe	Finland	Swedish	1981	156237	143913
Europe	Finland	Swedish	1985	154975	144123
Far East	Nepal	Limbu	1981	65318	63916
Far East	Nepal	Magar	1981	107247	105434
Far East	Nepal	Sunwar	1981	5509	5141
Middle East	Israel	Arabic	1983	334885	332925
Middle East	Israel	Bucharian	1983	2740	2675
Middle East	Israel	Bulgarian	1983	9775	8215
Middle East	Israel	Czech	1983	1475	1175
Middle East	Israel	Dutch	1983	2080	1480
Middle East	Israel	French	1983	60835	46500
Middle East	Israel	Georgian	1983	10545	10065
Middle East	Israel	German	1983	37215	24195
Middle East	Israel	Greek	1983	1550	1425
Middle East	Israel	Hungarian	1983	23710	18055
Middle East	Israel	Indian	1983	7485	6825

Middle East	Israel	Italian	1983	4225	3650
Middle East	Israel	Kurdish	1983	3695	3470
Middle East	Israel	Persian	1983	22420	20575
Middle East	Israel	Polish	1983	23705	15370
Middle East	Israel	Portugese	1983	2340	1930
Middle East	Israel	Rumanian	1983	63730	52960
Middle East	Israel	Russian	1983	56565	44500
Middle East	Israel	Serbian	1983	1640	1335
Middle East	Israel	Spanish	1983	49805	42560
Middle East	Israel	Turkish	1983	5175	5050
Middle East	Israel	Yiddish	1983	101445	87775
North America	Canada	English	1981	7521960	7396495
North America	Canada	French	1981	3178190	3070905
North America	Canada	German	1981	266770	256085
North America	Canada	Ukrainian	1981	148570	143695
South America	Paraguay	Castellano	1982	91431	75010

Use a simple SELECT statement to produce a flat-structured XML document with two levels, including the root node. After that, edit the document manually such that all appropriate layers are included, making the XML document a hierarchical structure of more than two layers. This is how:

1. Edit the preceding SELECT statement and put all fields into a single record, for each row:

```
SELECT '    <record region="'||r.REGION||'" country="'||c.COUNTRY
    ||'" language="'||l.LANGUAGE||'" year="'||p.YEAR
    ||'" females="'||SUM(pl.FEMALE)||'" males="'||SUM(pl.MALE)||'"></record>'
FROM REGION r JOIN COUNTRY c ON (c.REGION_ID = r.REGION_ID)
    JOIN POPULATION p ON (p.COUNTRY_ID = c.COUNTRY_ID)
        JOIN POPULATIONBYLANGUAGE pl ON (pl.POPULATION_ID = p.POPULATION_ID)
            JOIN LANGUAGE l ON (l.LANGUAGE_ID = pl.LANGUAGE_ID)
WHERE pl.FEMALE > pl.MALE AND p.YEAR BETWEEN 1981 AND 1985
GROUP BY r.REGION, c.COUNTRY, p.YEAR, l.LANGUAGE
ORDER BY r.REGION, c.COUNTRY, l.LANGUAGE, p.YEAR;
```

2. Store the output in a file and call it whatever you like. I will call it fig0806.xml.

3. Edit the XML file you just created. Add these two lines to the beginning of the file:

```
<?xml version="1.0"?>
<planet name="earth">
```

4. Add this line to the end of the XML file:

```
</planet>
```

5. In a browser, execute the XML file you just created and edited. The result should look something like that shown in Figure 8-6.

6. The next stage is to restructure the XML file shown in Figure 8-6 into a multiple level hierarchy XML document. The result is shown in Figure 8-7.

```
C:\Manuscripts\Wiley\BeginningXMLDatabases\08\fig\fig0806.xml - Microsoft Internet Explorer

File   Edit   View   Favorites   Tools   Help

Back    →      Search    Favorites    Media       My Web    Mail    My My Yahoo!

Address    C:\Manuscripts\Wiley\BeginningXMLDatabases\08\fig\fig0806.xml

Y!           Search Web

    <?xml version="1.0" ?>
  - <planet name="earth">
      <record region="Africa" country="Mauritius" language="Bhojpuri" year="1983" females="99467" males="97609" />
      <record region="Africa" country="Mauritius" language="French" year="1983" females="19330" males="16888" />
      <record region="Europe" country="Finland" language="Czech" year="1985" females="42" males="36" />
      <record region="Europe" country="Finland" language="Estonian" year="1985" females="330" males="102" />
      <record region="Europe" country="Finland" language="Finnish" year="1981" females="2323676" males="2177310" />
      <record region="Europe" country="Finland" language="Finnish" year="1985" females="2371522" males="2225386" />
      <record region="Europe" country="Finland" language="Icelandic" year="1985" females="21" males="16" />
      <record region="Europe" country="Finland" language="Korean" year="1985" females="17" males="13" />
      <record region="Europe" country="Finland" language="Norwegian" year="1985" females="123" males="115" />
      <record region="Europe" country="Finland" language="Polish" year="1985" females="274" males="236" />
      <record region="Europe" country="Finland" language="Russian" year="1985" females="1463" males="800" />
      <record region="Europe" country="Finland" language="Siamese" year="1985" females="48" males="7" />
      <record region="Europe" country="Finland" language="Swedish" year="1981" females="156237" males="143913" />
      <record region="Europe" country="Finland" language="Swedish" year="1985" females="154975" males="144123" />
      <record region="Far East" country="Nepal" language="Limbu" year="1981" females="65318" males="63916" />
      <record region="Far East" country="Nepal" language="Magar" year="1981" females="107247" males="105434" />
      <record region="Far East" country="Nepal" language="Sunwar" year="1981" females="5509" males="5141" />
      <record region="Middle East" country="Israel" language="Arabic" year="1983" females="224005" males="222225" />

Done                                                               My Computer
```

Figure 8-6: Another poorly structured, single-layered XML document

```
C:\Manuscripts\Wiley\BeginningXMLDatabases\08\fig\fig0807.xml - Microsoft...

File   Edit   View   Favorites   Tools   Help

Back    →      Search    Favorites    Media

Address    C:\Manuscripts\Wiley\BeginningXMLDatabases\08\fig\fig0807.xml

Y!           Search Web

    <?xml version="1.0" ?>
  - <planet name="earth">
    - <region name="Africa">
      - <country name="Mauritius">
        - <language name="Bhojpuri">
            <year>1983</year>
            <female>99467</female>
            <male>97609</male>
          </language>
        </country>
      - <country name="Mauritius">
        - <language name="French">
            <year>1983</year>
            <female>19330</female>
            <male>16888</male>
          </language>
        </country>
      </region>
    - <region name="Europe">
        <country name="Finland">

Done                                                               My Computer
```

Figure 8-7: Another properly structured, multiple-layered XML document

How It Works

You created a complex SELECT statement retrieving a number of fields from five different related tables. You created a flat-structured XML document, and from that manually altered that XML document to a hierarchical structure, similar to that shown in Figure 8-7.

This chapter has attempted to briefly explain the object data model, and then apply some facets of that model to the hierarchical structure of XML documents. I hope this approach has helped to explain both topics and, in particular, the benefits of utilizing a hierarchical structure in XML documents rather than a flat structure.

Summary

In this chapter you learned the following:

❑ The components of the object data model.

❑ The difference between an object and a class.

❑ Classes, attributes, methods, inheritance, and other facets of the object data model.

❑ The relational data model in comparison to the object data model.

❑ The relational data model in its most basic form produces flat data structures.

❑ The object model is the same hierarchical structure as XML documents should be.

❑ Describing the object model helps to explain hierarchical XML data structure.

Exercises

1. A class is the same thing as an object. True or False?

2. An object model contains tree-like hierarchies, and a relational model contains flattened structures. True or False?

3. Between the object and relational data models, which of these are correct?

    a. A class is equivalent to a table.

    b. An object is equivalent to a record.

    c. A field is equivalent to an attribute.

    d. A method is equivalent to a stored procedure.

    e. All of the above.

4. Examine the diagram in Figure 8-3. Which of these are correct?

    a. Country class is an abstraction of 1st World, 2nd World, and 3rd World classes.

    b. 1st World, 2nd World, 3rd World classes are all specializations of `Country` class.

    c. Language class is an abstraction of 1st Language, Bilingual, and Multilingual classes.

    d. 1st Language, Bilingual, and Multilingual classes are all specializations of the `Language` class.

    e. All of the above.

5. Which of these is the best answer and the most applicable to XML?

    a. A relational table is metadata and its rows are data.

    b. An object model class is metadata and object copies of that class are data.

    c. XML documents contain only data.

    d. XML documents contain only metadata.

    e. XML documents contain both metadata and data.

What Is a Native XML Database?

This book has examined XML from various perspectives. The first three chapters covered what are essentially programming basics. Chapter 4 examined basic SQL programming, used for retrieving datasets from relational databases. A basic understanding of SQL is helpful for understanding the basics of data retrieval for any database. Chapters 5 and 6 covered specific implementations of XML functionality contained within Oracle and SQL Server databases, respectively. Then I examined heterogeneous environments, which essentially use XML as a platform-independent method of passing data between different databases — using XML to send messages. The previous chapter examined the object data model, which is very similar to XML document hierarchical structure.

Where Chapter 5 and Chapter 6 covered specifics of Oracle and SQL Server databases, this chapter attempts to conceptually refine some of the details covered in those chapters, and also to expand on much of what is covered in previous chapters. This chapter begins the process of describing native XML databases from a non-vendor–specific database perspective.

There are no Try It Out sections in this chapter as the content of this chapter is primarily concep-tual, but also introductory with respect to native XML database standards.

In this chapter you learn about:

❑   What a native XML database is

❑   How an XML data type is a native XML database

❑   Schema-less native XML databases

❑   How many XML documents become collections of XML fragments in a native XML database

❑   Indexing in a native XML database

❑   The difference between document-centric and data-centric XML

An XML Document Is a Database

Is an XML document a database? Yes, of course. As you already know from previous chapters, an XML document contains both data and metadata. The most basic definition of a database is a repository for data. That repository contains information or data, such as all your company's account information, or in the case of this book, a slew of worldwide demographics data. In addition, the basic database structure describes the data or information contained within that database. What is the structure describing data in a database? The answer, of course, is the database metadata. Database metadata is the data in a database describing the information that is stored in that database. That metadata allows for sensible retrieval of that information, such that when your customer or demographics data is read, you actually know that you are reading the names of customers, or the populations of all countries of a particular region of the world. Without that metadata, the data stored in your database is completely meaningless. Obviously, the semantics of data can be written into programs. Those programs can be instructed where on the disk to read specific items, such as customer names. However, it is much easier to store some semantic metadata into a database itself. The resulting structure is much easier on programmers and applications in general, and thus more efficient and cheaper in that most costly of commodities: time. Time really is money!

One of the terms commonly used to describe XML data is that it is *self-describing*. XML is self-describing because it contains both data and metadata that describes the structure of the data in the XML document. That metadata is contained both in the elements and attributes of the XML document, and also in the hierarchy of the XML document itself. XML metadata can be described as being two-fold in nature:

> **You might be asking something like this: "Isn't the information about the data contained in something like an XML Schema Definition (XSD) instead of the actual XML document itself?" The answer to that question is of course, no! An XML document is a database unto itself — it is what it is. An XSD or Document Type Definition (DTD) is only necessary to interpret XML documents as relational structures.**

1.   XML elements and attributes describe the properties of data. This is the equivalent of tables and fields in a relational database.

2.   A properly structured hierarchical XML document describes relationships between different types of data in a dataset. This is more or less equivalent to relationships between tables in a relational database, but better matched to the structure established between classes in an object model of data.

Again, you might be thinking something like this: "I thought the structure of a relational database table in a database was related to an XML Schema in XML?" Again, that would be incorrect. A schema, is a schema, is a schema. XSD and DTD are for mapping relational tables to objects. Because an XML document is an object structure, XSDs and DTDs are completely superfluous with respect to a native XML database. By definition, any XML document is a native XML database. Metadata in an XML document is inherent with the elements (tables), attributes (fields), and element hierarchy (relationships between tables) of the XML document — they are the metadata. An XML document does not need a relational table structure to define itself because it is already a database in itself. See Chapters 6 and 13 for applications of XSD and DTD. This chapter focuses on an XML document as an independent storage medium (a native XML database). If you have relational tables and schemas in your mind while reading this chapter, then try to mentally shelve those thoughts until you read Chapter 13. An XML document does not need a schema, an XSD, or a DTD — or anything other than itself — to be a database. Only a relational database needs an XSD or DTD in order to map to XML document structure.

So, the advantages of using XML are that an XML document is actually a database structure in itself. XML is self-describing in that it contains both data and metadata. Metadata is also descriptive in both a scalar (as fields and values) and a structural sense (as a hierarchy). XML is portable because it is universally understood (that is the goal at least).

Disadvantages of using XML as a database storage medium are numerous. XML documents can include duplication, and thus become verbose. The result is that access to XML documents, in its most basic form, will involve full scanning and parsing of what could potentially be enormous text files.

Physical size comparison between commercial implementations of native XML databases and that of relational databases is not practical. Typical Oracle or SQL Server database implementations (both data warehouses and OLTP database) are considered as being VLDB (Very Large Database) at terabyte levels. Five years ago relational database sizes were generally considered very large at a few hundred megabytes. I may be incorrect in this assumption but so far I have not found any native XML databases described as being larger than gigabyte-level in size. Thus, comparison is impractical and pointless. XML documents can be stored in Oracle and SQL Server XML data types. What you don't know is that a typical installation stores a collection of XML data types.

In reality, an XML document contains a large amount of information all in on place, and quite often even in a single file. This single-file nature can create tremendous issues with respect to large amounts of data, lots of users, and any general background processing. Native XML databases are therefore usually commercially most appropriate to that. This includes small scale applications, small quantities of data, very few users (low concurrency and multi-user requirements), low security, low data integrity needs, and above all, low performance.

So, how can an XML document be described as a database?

Defining a Native XML Database

By definition, an NXD (native XML database) can be both an XML document and an XML data type. An XML data type is a specialized storage facility containing a relational database. It follows that a native XML database is essentially any method of storing XML data as an XML document. Thus, an XML document, as executed in a browser, is a native XML database. Additionally, using XML data types in relational databases, such as Oracle or SQL Server databases (as described in Chapters 5 and 6) makes some relational databases native XML database–capable as well. Essentially all that is needed to describe a database as being an NXD, or at least NXD-capable, is that an XML document is stored as an XML document. No particular modeling technique applies. Thus relational, object, or even hierarchical databases can be used.

> *A native XML database does not have to be a self-contained, independent database. An NXD can be included in other database engines using XML data types, as used in Oracle and SQL Server databases.*

Creating a Native XML Database

Now let me demonstrate what the term "native XML database" really means. The way to do this is very simple — you can try to create a native XML database, simply by describing how that native XML database might be created using XML.

The term "native XML" essentially means that the database part of that term is an intrinsic part of XML. In other words, as described previously and repeatedly in this book, XML documents describe both data and metadata. Data is the data, and metadata applies structure or at least some meaning to that data. Examine the example XML document shown in Figure 9-1.

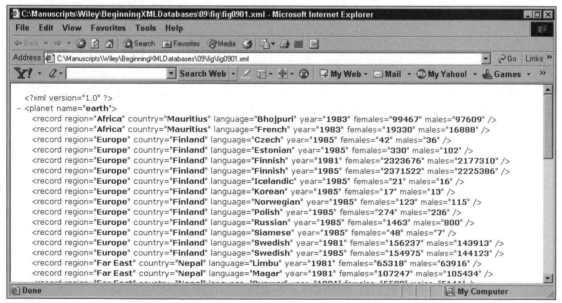

Figure 9-1: A single-layered XML document

The XML document in Figure 9-1 shows a single-layered, poorly structured, XML document. However, those who are familiar with relational database structure will find this particular document easier to interpret as containing both data and metadata. Let's break down the document shown in Figure 9-1. This section of the XML document shown in Figure 9-1 shows data values in boldface:

```
<planet name="earth">
    <record region="Africa" country="Mauritius" language="Bhojpuri" year="1983" fema
les="99467" males="97609"></record>
    <record region="Africa" country="Mauritius" language="French" year="1983" female
s="19330" males="16888"></record>
    <record region="Europe" country="Finland" language="Czech" year="1985" females="
42" males="36"></record>
    ...
</planet>
```

And this section of the XML document in Figure 9-1 shows metadata values in boldface:

```
<planet name="earth">
    <record region="Africa" country="Mauritius" language="Bhojpuri" year="1983" fema
les="99467" males="97609"></record>
    <record region="Africa" country="Mauritius" language="French" year="1983" female
s="19330" males="16888"></record>
    <record region="Europe" country="Finland" language="Czech" year="1985" females="
42" males="36"></record>
    ...
</planet>
```

If you can execute (some may call this rendering) an XML document in Windows Internet Explorer, then the XML document shown in Figure 9-1 should show the metadata and data in two different colors. The metadata will be a reddish-brown color, and the data will be both bold and black. Different browsers may show XML documents differently. The point is that even a browser program delineates between data and metadata in XML documents.

So, if you think in terms of a relational database, the XML document shown in these previous three examples could look something like what is shown in Figure 9-2.

In Figure 9-2 the metadata is on the left in the form of the PLANET table. The data is on the right side of Figure 9-2 shown as rows, or multiple iterations of the table structure (metadata). Each row is divided into specific fields called REGION, COUNTRY, LANGUAGE, YEAR, FEMALES, and MALES.

Now let's use the same information as shown in Figures 9-1 and 9-2, but this time make sure that the XML document has an acceptable hierarchical structure. That document is partially shown in Figure 9-3.

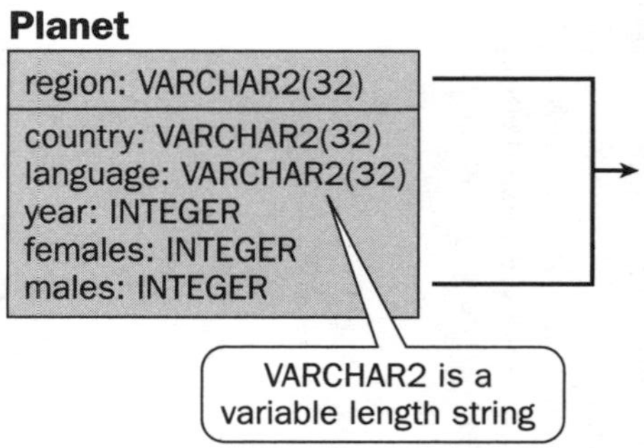

Planet

region: VARCHAR2(32)
country: VARCHAR2(32)
language: VARCHAR2(32)
year: INTEGER
females: INTEGER
males: INTEGER

VARCHAR2 is a variable length string

Planet

REGION	COUNTRY	LANGUAGE	YEAR	FEMALES	MALES
Africa	Mauritius	Bhojpuri	1983	99467	97609
Africa	Mauritius	French	1983	19330	16888
Europe	Finland	Czech	1985	42	36
Europe	Finland	Estonian	1985	330	102
Europe	Finland	Finnish	1981	2323676	2177310
Europe	Finland	Finnish	1985	2371522	2225386
Europe	Finland	Icelandic	1985	21	16
Europe	Finland	Korean	1985	17	13
Europe	Finland	Norwegian	1985	123	115
Europe	Finland	Polish	1985	274	236
Europe	Finland	Russian	1985	1463	800
Europe	Finland	Siamese	1985	48	7
Europe	Finland	Swedish	1981	156237	143913
Europe	Finland	Swedish	1985	154975	144123
Far East	Nepal	Limbu	1981	65318	63916
Far East	Nepal	Magar	1981	107247	105434

Figure 9-2: Converting a single-layered XML document to a single relational table

Figure 9-3: A properly structured, multiple-layered, hierarchical XML document

In Figure 9-3, you now see a completely different picture. The tags in the XML document are now structured within a hierarchy and parent object data is not duplicated. The tree structure shown in Figure 9-3 has a number of advantages over that of the flattened structure shown in Figure 9-1:

❑   There is less repetition.

❑   The structure of the data mimics reality.

❑   Searching the hierarchy in Figure 9-3 can use a specialized tree scanning algorithm allowing for potentially much faster performance.

Additionally, as for the flattened structure, XML divides up its content between metadata and data where data is the values of the elements. The metadata is the actual element names. So, in the case of the XML document in Figure 9-3, the following XML document snippet shows the metadata in boldface:

```
<planet name="earth">
  <region name="Africa">
    <country name="Mauritius">
      <language name="Bhojpuri">
        <year>1983</year>
        <female>99467</female>
        <male>97609</male>
      </language>
    </country>
    <country name="Mauritius">
      <language name="French">
        <year>1983</year>
        <female>19330</female>
        <male>16888</male>
      </language>
    </country>
  </region>
  <region name="Europe">
  ...
  </region>
</planet>
```

So this is all very well and good. An XML document can effectively be mentally pictured as being a database in itself, which is therefore natively XML, or a native XML database. Is there a way to allow some kind of consistent programming access to an XML document, or perhaps even a collection of XML documents, where the sum of those XML documents makes up a native XML database as a whole? The answer is yes.

Schema-Less Native XML Database Collections

Native XML databases often store and manage multiple XML documents as collections of XML fragments. A single native XML database can contain multiple collections of different types of XML documents, where those different XML documents cover different subject matter, and thus unrelated sets of data. For example, one collection could contain customers for a company, and another collection could contain demographics for a specific country in the world. Additionally, within each collection, the structure of individual XML fragments does not have to be consistent across the collection. In fact, every single fragment within a collection can have a different structure in relation to every other fragment within that same collection. The result is XML data that is structurally independent, and thus schema independent or *schema-less*.

Collections can be associated with schemas, as described at the end of Chapter 6, when briefly demonstrating schema collections and XSD (XML Schema Definition) with SQL Server database.

> *There is also the potential for validation of XML data using DTD (Document Type Definition) and XML Schema. All of these are advanced topics and will be covered later in this book.*

Schema-independent XML is extremely flexible, which enables more rapid and easier development. However, flexibility comes at a price in terms of low data integrity and the risk of errors propagating throughout the data in the database.

In reality, there are probably innumerable approaches to making collections of XML documents into a native XML database, capable of useful storage capacity and performance. Let's present one simplistic method, which also happens to tie into much of the information presented throughout the rest of this book.

As already mentioned, you may remember that Chapter 6, which covers XML use in SQL Server database, contained a section at the end of the chapter describing schema collections, using XSD to apply schema structures to XML data type storage in. It also describes a SQL Server database. An XML document, or even a collection of XML documents as a database, does not need any schema definitions to function as a native XML database. Once again, this is because XML contains both data and metadata. This is what is known as a schema-less database. The following example defines a database describing the region of Africa:

```
<?xml version="1.0"?>
<database name="Africa">
   <collections>
     <collection name="Countries">
     </collection>
   </collections>
</database>
```

The preceding example has no data in it but it includes a container for multiple collections, where each collection represents a set of countries. In this example, the set of countries would be in the region of Africa.

We can expand the previous example to allow definition of multiple databases. Each database defines a separate region. In this example, the two databases are the regions of Africa and Europe. Again each region contains collections of countries within their respective regions:

```
<?xml version="1.0"?>
<databases>
   <database name="Africa">
      <collections>
        <collection name="Countries">
        </collection>
      </collections>
   </database>
   <database name="Europe">
      <collections>
        <collection name="Countries">
        </collection>
      </collections>
   </database>
   ...
</databases>
```

And obviously, you can retain a single database and simply create more collections. This is shown in the following example where each region is a collection, and each country within each region is in a separate collection:

```
<?xml version="1.0"?>
<database>
   <collections>
      <collection name="Regions">
         <region name="Africa">
             <population>789548670</population>
```

```
            </region>
            <region name="Europe">
                <population>488674441</population>
            </region>
        </collection>
        <collection name="Countries">
            <country name="Finland" region="Europe">
                <population>5231372</population>
            </country>
            <country name="Germany" region="Europe">
                <population>82422299</population>
            </country>
        </collection>
        ...
    </collections>
</database>
```

You can also embed the countries (as collections) within their respective regions contained within regional collections:

```
<?xml version="1.0"?>
<database>
    <collections>
        <collection name="Regions">
            <region name="Africa">
                <population>789548670</population>
            </region>
            <region name="Europe">
                <population>488674441</population>
                <collection name="Countries">
                    <country name="Finland" region="Europe">
                        <population>5231372</population>
                    </country>
                    <country name="Germany" region="Europe">
                        <population>82422299</population>
                    </country>
                </collection>
            </region>
        </collection>
        ...
    </collections>
</database>
```

The collections within collections can be completely dispensed with in place of a realistic hierarchy of countries within their respective regions:

```
<?xml version="1.0"?>
<database>
    <collections>
        <collection name="Regions">
            <region name="Africa">
```

```
                <population>789548670</population>
            </region>
            <region name="Europe">
                <population>488674441</population>
                <country name="Finland" region="Europe">
                    <population>5231372</population>
                </country>
                <country name="Germany" region="Europe">
                    <population>82422299</population>
                </country>
            </region>
        </collection>
        ...
    </collections>
</database>
```

And you can even duplicate information into separate collections:

```
<?xml version="1.0"?>
<database>
    <collections>
        <collection name="Regions">
            <region name="Africa">
                <population>789548670</population>
            </region>
            <region name="Europe">
                <population>488674441</population>
                <country name="Finland">
                    <population>5231372</population>
                </country>
                <country name="Germany">
                    <population></population>
                </country>
            </region>
        </collection>
        <collection name="Countries">
            <country name="Finland" region="Europe">
                <population>5231372</population>
            </country>
            <country name="Germany" region="Europe">
                <population>82422299</population>
            </country>
        </collection>
        ...
    </collections>
</database>
```

The enormous flexibility of using XML data as a storage medium should be apparent. Obviously, misunderstanding and abusing this flexibility can lead to problems, for example, as too much data through duplication, too much or too little structural complexity, and so on. The list of potential pitfalls is as long as the list of different possible variations on a theme when using something as flexible as XML.

255

What Is Indexing?

What I have not intended to do in this section is to describe a specific native XML database or tool used for accessing XML documents as a database. What I have attempted to do is present you with a description of how a database can be created using XML documents. The result is that XML is incredibly flexible in terms of how it can be constructed. As you can see, creating a basic database storage facility or model using XML is actually very easy. Your options are limited only by what your applications require and your understanding of the data involved with your applications.

Indexing is an entirely different kettle of fish. In a database, an index is a physical copy of a small portion of an entire table. The concept behind the creation of the index that assists performance is, in its simplest form, that the physical size of the index is much less than the table size itself, as demonstrated in Figure 9-4.

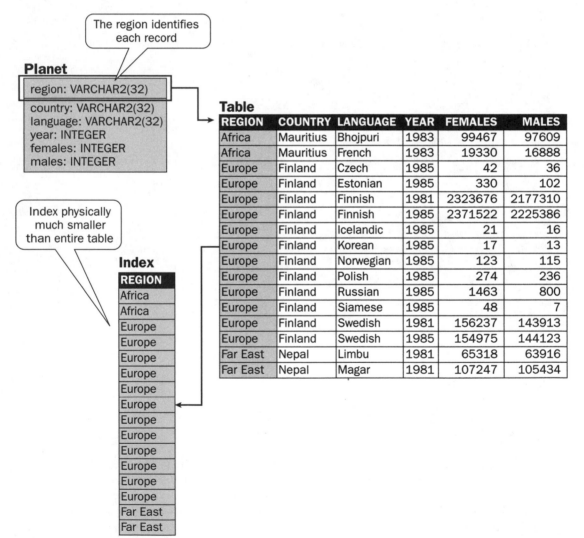

Figure 9-4: Using indexing reduces I/O activity

In Figure 9-4, an index is created for only the region names. When searching for a region with a region name, only the index can be scanned, potentially scanning much less physical disk space. The result is less physical I/O activity and generally less hardware resource usage. The result is improved performance.

Creating indexing for fast access is a little more complex because, technically speaking, an index usually involves a copy of a small portion of data, and it allows for specialized searching algorithms. Figure 9-5 illustrates the physically scanned path through a specially constructed index.

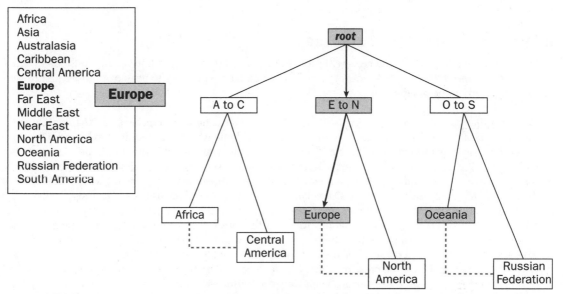

Figure 9-5: Indexing allows fast scanning using specialized index structures and scanning algorithms.

When searching for the region of Europe in Figure 9-5, only the following physical areas of the index are read to find the region of Europe:

- ❑ The physical start of the index (the root), which points to three other areas containing ranges of the first letters in region names.

- ❑ A branch section containing the first letters of all regions between E and N. Each branch section contains references to physical areas on disk containing each region.

- ❑ A leaf section containing the actual region of Europe.

It is important to note that the index shown in Figure 9-5 contains only the name of the region. When the region is found in the index, there will be a pointer (some kind of address reference) into the entire table, and all the fields relevant to the region of Europe.

So the objective of using indexing is to reduce disk I/O activity and to utilize specialized high performance searching algorithms. Commonly used algorithms for indexing relational databases include binary trees, hashing algorithms, and sometimes bitmaps. A binary tree creates a tree structure much like that shown in Figure 9-5. A hashing index creates a number code for each unique string value where subsequent searching scans the hash table of numbers. A bitmap literally creates a map of bits — a 0 indicates a value does not exist, and 1 indicates a value does exist. Even a brief understanding of different indexing algorithms is well beyond the scope of this book. However, you now know that there are numerous different methods.

There is one more thing to remember about indexing. An index imposes a sorted order on itself. Thus, when an index is read the data is read in the sorted order in which the index is created, regardless of the order of data in a table or XML document. However, XML documents do contain an inherent sorting based on the structure of the XML document concerned so index sorting is not always an advantage with respect to native XML database access.

Indexing a Native XML Database

Different native XML database tools will probably use all sorts of different indexing methods in actual implementation. However, the indexing structures created are unlikely to vary from those just presented from an algorithmic perspective.

The most likely method for indexing XML documents in a relational database, even XML data types, is the creation of a separate structure containing the XML elements that are required to be indexed. So, in the case of the index in Figure 9-5, the index would contain a single field copy of all the records in the table. That single field would contain a single region name entry for each region. In addition, the index would contain some kind of pointer, which would allow a direct link between index and table (or XML document), as a disk address at the I/O level. In other words, your database needs to assign a disk address to every item in the XML document (every index item). Then the index contains a copy of that pointer address. The result is that when a region is found in the index, the pointer related to that region in the index object is passed to a procedure that finds the record in the table (or XML document) based on the disk address of the entire record. The disk addresses assigned to elements in the table or XML document will either be assigned on the creation of the full dataset, or perhaps when an index is created. The process and placement of all these various steps depend entirely on the software that is used to access an XML native database, or essentially what is actually a single XML document, or a set of XML documents maintained as a set of collections. And those collections are stored as XML as well.

You might ask yourself some questions here. Perhaps something like this: "Why store XML documents into XML data types when XML data type indexing is suspect, and perhaps inferior to relational database indexing?" Also, "Why not simply store data into relational tables, and convert backwards and forwards between tables and XML documents as needed?" The second question should be answered first, and the answer is that storing as XML removes the need to continually convert. It also gives access to specialized, highly flexible and powerful XML functionality, such as XPath and XQuery. In answer to the first question: An index, is an index, is an index. Some relational databases have more sophisticated indexes than others. There is no reason why XML indexing is not particularly less efficient than all types of indexing, in all relational databases. Of course, XML data can be stored in relational tables. It's an option and a choice. There are advantages and disadvantages to both relational database and XML data type storage of XML data. In general, the larger a database is, the more prudent the option of relational table storage becomes — and not XML storage into XML data types. Unless of course you use XML data type collections.

So that's how indexes might be constructed from a purely technical perspective. How would indexes need to be created with respect to XML document content? It is likely that indexing on an XML document is to be of four different types:

❑ **Structural index:** Indexes of elements and attributes, plus the locations relative to other elements and attributes within a single XML document. These help searches are based on elements. For example, in a demographics database, you could search for all countries in a particular region that have more than one city for a country.

❑ **Value index:** Text and attribute values are often searched for in a single XML document and thus creating indexes on some, all, or combinations of textual and attribute values makes perfect sense. For example, in a demographics database, you might want to find all countries where population exceeds 1,000,000.

❑ **Full-text index:** This applies to searching for specific values across a collection of XML documents to return a subset collection of XML documents. This index is effectively a large value index across many XML documents, or fragments, in a collection.

❑ **Context index:** This is a more generalized form of indexing, perhaps a little antiquated, where many documents are indexed by creating an index containing some value that uniquely identifies subject matter of each XML document. The indexed values are stored in what is sometimes known as a *side table*, and then an index is created on the side table. The result is fast indexed access into a large collection of XML documents, based on whatever indexed values are created for each XML document in the collection. This approach is probably very tedious. It is better to index XML document contents. This is because of the flexible nature of XML. It is more likely that XML documents will be large and disorganized, rather than small fragments that can be easily categorized. Any kind of manual categorization could take forever with the sheer physical size of information stored in modern databases.

What About Using XSL and the XML DOM?

XSL is used to apply consistent templating, or visible results, to repeated data content and context across an XML document. The XML DOM is a generic structure upon which an XML document is built. The result is that the XML DOM can be used to access XML documents programmatically, regardless of the data and metadata content of an XML document. XSL can be used to apply formatting based either on XML document content or even applied to the XML DOM, thus templating generically across an XML document, again regardless of data or metadata content. What does all that mean? It means that you don't have to know what the content, context, subject matter, or topic area of an XML document is in order to apply XML DOM and XSL templating at the programming level. In other words, XSL and the XML DOM simply don't care whether you are dealing with customers, demographics, aircraft parts, or simple wobbly widget things. That's why it's called *programmatically*. You can put something onto a web page in a similar fashion, regardless of what the actual data is. Obviously, generic access to data will result in generic output, depending on how much specific programming is applied.

When using the XML DOM, you can actually store the XML DOM in a native XML database. Thus you can then use the XML DOM structure for future generic programming and processing, when retrieving XML data from the database at a later point in time.

Using the XML DOM boils down to one simple point. The XML DOM, for any particular XML document, is generally much bigger than the document itself — in terms of the amount of code it generates, and ultimately the amount of memory it occupies. As a result, using the XML DOM from within a native XML database, which requires storage of the XML DOM in the database, can cause serious performance issues down the road. This is true for both large and smaller XML documents, and is likely to be relatively exacerbated for the smallest of XML documents. The general consensus of opinion, as far as I can see, is that if you are going to use XSL and the XML DOM, do so at run-time and on a web or application server. Do not persistently store the XML DOM for XML documents into a native XML database. If you think about it, XML data encompasses all of data, metadata, and structure. That's plenty of definition with respect to data and database storage. Why store programming semantics in a database, in the form of XML DOM and XSL programming structures?

Classify Native XML Databases by Content

So, we know that XML documents contain data, metadata (data describing the data), and some semantics in the form of any inherent hierarchical structure. Now I want to describe XML document content just a little further, by describing its nature. In other words, XML documents can be document-centric, which is suitable for human consumption. They can also be data-centric. A data-centric XML document is generally a chunk of data shared between computers. This also implies that data-centric information is more generic and is more likely to be subject to program control using scripting languages such as XSL.

Document-Centric XML

A document-centric XML document, suitable for human consumption, is essentially not really easily understandable for a computer, if at all possible. Document-centric XML is essentially the type of documents that would normally be written by hand, by an author — such as a Word document, a PDF document, or even something like this book. These types of XML documents are generally stored in their entirety and are generally not accessed programmatically, or even by XML element content. Sometimes these types of documents are indexed for index searching such as for libraries of technical papers. On the contrary, there are some databases of technical papers in existence that tend to mix document-centric and data-centric data. For example, in a library database containing technical papers going back years, it would be sensible to categorize those documents based on subject matter, authors, dates written, and any other generic descriptive information. The content of those documents can be indexed to create generic information of indexed subset phrases as well.

> *A specialized type of document-centric native XML database is called a content management system. Content management database systems allow a certain amount of management and control over human-written XML data, stored inside XML data types of native XML databases.*

Data-Centric XML

A data-centric XML document in its purest form uses XML data as a method of transporting data between computers. In reality, XML is often a mixture of data-centric and document-centric. The document-centric part is the human-written and readable part. The data-centric section is that which is generic and program accessible because it is repetitive. Some of the best examples of data-centric documentation is on websites such as Amazon and eBay. These sites contain pages and pages of information — with varying levels of flexibility and different types of content. For example, for a book on Amazon, all the primary details such as title, ISBN, publisher, dates, and otherwise are all data-centric details. On the other hand, many books on Amazon are listed with PDF downloads of the actual book. The PDFs are document-centric, specific to a particular book and only programmable in relation to the PDF document itself, as opposed to the content of the PDF.

Using a Native XML Database

Various aspects of using native XML databases are important to introduce briefly:

❑ **Storage in native XML databases:** XML documents can be stored in a database as a large string, a binary object, or in some kind of XML data type. Some relational databases allow storage of strings as much as 4,000 characters long. For the unpredictable nature of the length of XML documents this is usually inappropriate. Binary objects can either be straightforward binary storage (BLOB data types), or specialized binary-stored, very large text objects, sometimes known as CLOB (Character Large Binary Object). Size for CLOB data types is usually restricted physically, as in 4GB, as opposed to string length. Additionally, unlike long strings or BLOBs, CLOBs usually allow some type of text searching and pattern matching within them. However, any CLOB pattern matching is no match for XML-enabled functionality of XML data types. Some relational databases allow storage of XML documents in their entirety into XML data types, with full XML enablement. Obviously, a purpose-built native XML database should allow full enablement of XML functionality as a part of the storage of XML data.

❑ **Concurrency, locking, and transactional control:** Native XML databases, in the form of XML data types in relational databases, or otherwise, will likely support locks at the XML document-level only. So, the larger your XML documents, the worse your concurrency and multi-user capacity will be. Node level within XML documents is certainly a possibility but just imagine implementing it. Node level locking would certainly need validating and enforced schemas; and there goes your flexibility, right out the window, right off the bat! And it gets even worse because XML documents are by nature hierarchical, and thus any node level locking requires locking of all existing parent nodes at the same time. Node level locking is not really an option with existing technology. How you structure your XML storage essentially depends on application requirements. The larger your XML documents are when stored, the less capable your database will be as a multi-user environment. A single XML document Native XML database is only a single user environment.

❑ **Reading native XML databases:** Reading data from a native XML database, or XML data type, can be performed using specialized tools. These tools include things such as XPath, XQuery, flat text file parsing, and all the goodies presented in Chapters 5 and 6. Some of the functionality presented in Chapters 5 and 6 is, in actuality, an implementation of more generalized functionality such as XPath and XQuery. XPath and XQuery will be covered explicitly in later chapters.

❑ **Changing content in native XML databases:** There are numerous tools and functionality available for changing XML document content. As you saw in Chapters 5 and 6, some of that functionality is more sophisticated in some cases than in others. As far as standards are concerned, XQuery will eventually allow updates (even though it is entitled *Query*). There is also something called DDML. You can also use precise access to XML document content using XML schemas, DTD, and the XML DOM.

This chapter has introduced some very basic concepts and ideas behind the architecture of native XML databases. In fact, it might be surprising to realize that an XML data type, as stored in an Oracle or SQL Server database, is actually a native XML database in itself. In addition, much of what was discussed in Chapters 5 and 6 for Oracle and SQL Server database, respectively, will be covered in later chapters under the guise of topics such as XPath, XQuery, XLink, XPointer, and otherwise.

Summary

In this chapter you learned that:

❑ A native XML database can be a database in itself.

❑ An XML data type is a native XML database all by itself.

❑ A simple native XML database can be constructed using simple XML.

❑ Schema-less native XML databases are schema independent and less restrictive.

❑ A schema-dependent native XML database does not require a schema.

❑ Many XML documents become collections of XML fragments in a native XML database.

❑ Indexing native XML databases involves data (values), metadata (elements and structure), or collections of XML documents.

❑ Using XSL and the XML DOM is bad for performance.

❑ Document-centric XML is not programmable and is stored as is.

❑ Data-centric XML is programmable.

Exercises

1. VLDB stands for _____ _____ _____.
2. OLTP stands for _____ _____ _____.
3. NXD stands for _____ ___ _____.
4. Pick the best answer:

    a. The typical size of a modern-day VLDB is megabytes, and NXD is gigabytes.

    b. The typical size of a modern-day VLDB is gigabytes, and NXD is megabytes.

    c. The typical size of a modern-day VLDB is gigabytes, and NXD is gigabytes.

    d. The typical size of a modern-day VLDB is terabytes, and NXD is megabytes.

    e. None of the above.

5. XML data improves on relational data in which of the following ways?

    a. Flattened XML documents contain data and metadata describing data directly.

    b. Hierarchical XML documents contain data, metadata, and relationships between different data items.

    c. Both of the above.

    d. Neither of the above.

6. Which of these is true?

    a. Schema-dependent XML document collections can be validated and can have good data integrity.

    b. Schema-less XML document collections are extremely flexible but lack data integrity validation.

    c. XML document collection elements can each be complete XML documents or XML fragments.

    d. XML document collections can have varying content and structure within the same collection.

    e. All of the above.

    f. None of the above.

7. Typical XML indexes are of which of the following forms?

    a. Structural indexes based on XML document hierarchical structure and node placement within that structure.

    b. Value indexes comprised of the text values of nodes and the values of attributes.

    c. Concurrency indexes made up of multi-user XML document attributes.

    d. Transactional indexes created when XML data is created and terminated when XML data is destroyed.

    e. None of the above.

Navigating XML Documents Using XPath

What is XPath? XPath is a specialized expression language used to parse through XML node hierarchies and retrieve chunks of data from XML documents. XPath is a major part of the scripting language eXtensible Style Sheet Transformations (XSLT). XSLT is a World Wide Web Consortium (W3C at http://www.w3.org) established standard along with other tools, such as XPointer and XQuery, both of which happen to be based on XPath. Therefore it is important to have a good understanding of XPath technology.

In this chapter you learn about:

- ❑ Building simple expressions using XPath
- ❑ Accessing inter-nodal relationships using XPath axes
- ❑ Using predicates to help filter XPath expression results
- ❑ Using wildcards in XPath expressions
- ❑ Retrieving multiple data sets using multiple XPath expressions
- ❑ Using built-in functions in advanced XPath expressions and XQuery

What Is XPath?

XPath is a language used for finding data in XML documents by parsing (scanning) those XML documents for specific values. XPath performs parsing of XML documents by applying an expression to the text of an XML document. The effective result is that an XPath expression allows navigation through XML document elements and attributes, retrieving items and values that match the expression passed into the XML document by XPath.

XPath performs a number of tasks:

❑ Defines parts of an XML document using XPath syntax.

❑ Utilizes path expressions to navigate through XML documents. The expression allows selection of nodes or sets of nodes from an XML document.

❑ Uses numerous built-in functions to facilitate the processing of the preceding tasks. Built-in functions include functionality covering specific data types, including strings, numbers, dates, and times. Also, node and node sequences can be manipulated, among numerous other functions.

Three logical models have been developed by the W3C for representation of XML documents. These are the XML Document Object Model (XML DOM), XPath, and XML Infoset (XML Information Set). The XML DOM in Chapter 2 is generally relatively slow with respect to performance when compared with XPath. XML Infoset (`http://www.w3.org/TR/xml-infoset`*) will not be covered in this book in favor of the more up-to-date XPath 2.0 and XQuery 1.0.*

Absolute and Relative Paths

In its simplest form, an XPath expression forms an absolute or a relative path. An absolute path has a starting forward slash (/), and a relative path does not. An absolute path searches an XML document from the precise path specified. A relative path searches relatively (possibly within an XML document — not starting at the root node) from wherever specified. So, an absolute path searching from the root node looks something like this:

```
/root/nodeA/nodeB
```

And a relative path looks something like this:

```
nodeA/nodeB
```

XPath Nodes

XPath recognizes numerous different types of nodes in XML documents. These nodes include element nodes, attribute nodes, text value nodes, namespace nodes, processing instruction nodes, comment nodes, and document nodes.

A document node is the equivalent of a root node, and an XML document is a tree of nodes containing a single root node.

Figure 10-1 shows some different node types, as defined by XPath.

In Figure 10-1, <?xml version="1.0"?> is a processing instruction node, <demographics> is the document or root node, <name>Africa</name> is a text value node, and code="AG" is an attribute node.

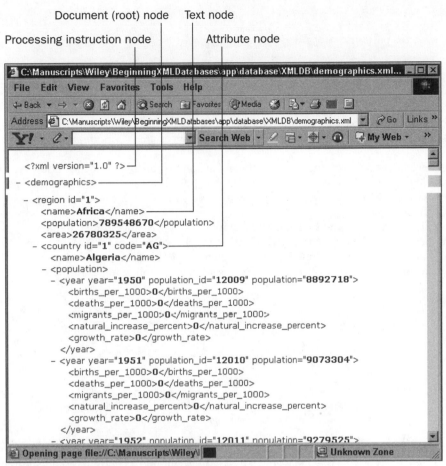

Figure 10-1: XPath syntax defines various different node types.

XPath Node Relationships

XPath node relationships simply define precise and obvious relationships between different nodes within an XML document. An atomic or text value has no relationship with any other nodes, in that it is a value of a text or attribute node. Atomic values are actual data values and not metadata. For example, in Figure 10-1 the following are atomic values:

```
Africa
"AG"
```

A parent node is defined as being the parent of any element or attribute node. In the following example, the year node is the parent of all the nodes births_per_1000, deaths_per_1000, migrants_per_1000, natural_increase_percent, and growth_rate:

```
<year year="1950" population_id="12009" population="8892718">
   <births_per_1000>0</births_per_1000>
   <deaths_per_1000>0</deaths_per_1000>
   <migrants_per_1000>0</migrants_per_1000>
   <natural_increase_percent>0</natural_increase_percent>
   <growth_rate>0</growth_rate>
</year>
```

And similarly, in the preceding example, the nodes births_per_1000, deaths_per_1000, migrants_per_1000, natural_increase_percent, and growth_rate are all children of the year node.

Sibling nodes are nodes with the same parent and are on the same level of the node hierarchy. So once again, in the previous example, the nodes births_per_1000, deaths_per_1000, migrants_per_1000, natural_increase_percent, and growth_rate are all sibling nodes of one another.

Ancestor nodes are any nodes higher in the hierarchy of the tree, including parent node, parent's parent (grandfather), and so on up the tree all the way up to the root node of the XML document. So once again, if you use the XML document from Figure 10-1, then the population, country, region, and demographics nodes are all ancestor nodes of the year node, as shown in the following example:

```
<demographics>
   <region id="1">
      <country id="1" code="AG">
         <population>
            <year year="1950" population_id="12009" population="8892718">
               <births_per_1000>0</births_per_1000>
               <deaths_per_1000>0</deaths_per_1000>
               <migrants_per_1000>0</migrants_per_1000>
               <natural_increase_percent>0</natural_increase_percent>
               <growth_rate>0</growth_rate>
            </year>
```

Obviously, the descendants of a node are all its children, children's children (grandchildren), and so on. So in the previous example, the nodes region, country, population, year, births_per_1000, deaths_per_1000, migrants_per_1000, natural_increase_percent, and growth_rate are all descendants of the document node.

XPath Expression Syntax

XPath utilizes expressions based on paths through an XML document, similar to the paths used to navigate the directories of an operating system like DOS or UNIX. Some simple path expressions are demonstrated shortly.

At this point I will be using the demographics XML database document as described in Appendix B (also available online as a download). Essentially the downloadable XML document is large, and I will use a small portion of that document, accessible from the relational database structure using the following query:

```
select co.country as country, p.year, l.language, o.occupation
from country co join population p on(co.country_id=p.country_id)
    join populationbylanguage pl on(pl.population_id=p.population_id)
       join populationbyoccupation po on (po.population_id=p.population_id)
          join language l on(pl.language_id=l.language_id)
             join occupation o on(po.occupation_id=o.occupation_id)
where co.country in('Bangladesh');
```

I decided which country to use by selecting the country with the smallest number of rows when joining both occupations and languages:

```
select country, count(country) from(
    select co.country as country, p.year, l.language, o.occupation
    from country co join population p on(co.country_id=p.country_id)
       join populationbylanguage pl on(pl.population_id=p.population_id)
          join populationbyoccupation po on (po.population_id=p.population_id)
             join language l on(pl.language_id=l.language_id)
                join occupation o on(po.occupation_id=o.occupation_id)
) group by country order by count(country);
```

This is the result of the preceding query:

COUNTRY	COUNT(COUNTRY)
Bangladesh	**21**
Bulgaria	28
Bolivia	40
Singapore	50
Hungary	63
Malaysia	64
Panama	72
Canada	111
Nepal	152
South Africa	216
Australia	225
Finland	386
Zambia	600

The preceding query result indicates that Bangladesh has the fewest rows, where both multiple languages and multiple occupations are available in the data. A small dataset is required because we don't want examples and graphics in this book printed over multiple pages. That is simply too difficult to follow.

Now you execute the preceding query again to display the actual data:

```
select co.country as country, p.year, l.language, o.occupation
from country co join population p on(co.country_id=p.country_id)
    join populationbylanguage pl on(pl.population_id=p.population_id)
       join populationbyoccupation po on (po.population_id=p.population_id)
          join language l on(pl.language_id=l.language_id)
             join occupation o on(po.occupation_id=o.occupation_id)
where co.country in('Bangladesh');
```

The data is also all in the single year of 1974:

```
COUNTRY             YEAR LANGUAGE          OCCUPATION
----------------    ---------- ----------------  ----------------
Bangladesh          1974 Urdu              Professional
Bangladesh          1974 Bengali           Professional
Bangladesh          1974 Others            Professional
Bangladesh          1974 Urdu              Management
Bangladesh          1974 Bengali           Management
Bangladesh          1974 Others            Management
Bangladesh          1974 Urdu              Clerical
Bangladesh          1974 Bengali           Clerical
Bangladesh          1974 Others            Clerical
Bangladesh          1974 Urdu              Sales
Bangladesh          1974 Bengali           Sales
Bangladesh          1974 Others            Sales
Bangladesh          1974 Urdu              Agriculture
Bangladesh          1974 Bengali           Agriculture
Bangladesh          1974 Others            Agriculture
Bangladesh          1974 Urdu              Labor
Bangladesh          1974 Bengali           Labor
Bangladesh          1974 Others            Labor
Bangladesh          1974 Urdu              Service
Bangladesh          1974 Bengali           Service
Bangladesh          1974 Others            Service
```

Figure 10-2 shows the data from the preceding result, in a browser, in the XML document version of the demographics database.

The following is the XML fragment for the country of Bangladesh, including root node, languages, occupations, and cities. And excluding all years other than 1974 (a manageable fragment):

```
<?xml version="1.0"?>
<demographics>
   <region id="9">
      <name>Near East</name>
      <population>1499157105</population>
      <area>4721322</area>
      <country id="120" code="BG">
         <name>Bangladesh</name>
         <population>
            <year year="1974" population_id="1131" population="74679411">
               <deaths_per_1000>17.68</deaths_per_1000>
               <languages>
                  <language name="Bengali" language_id="231">
                     <male>36646900</male>
                     <female>34006448</female>
                  </language>
                  <language name="Urdu-Ourdou" language_id="490">
                     <male>93094</male>
                     <female>85465</female>
                  </language>
```

```
                    </languages>
                    <occupations>
                        <occupation name="Professional" occupation_id="1">
                            <male>705852</male>
                            <female>44332</female>
                        </occupation>
                        <occupation name="Management" occupation_id="2">
                            <male>60778</male>
                            <female>904</female>
                        </occupation>
                        <occupation name="Clerical" occupation_id="3">
                            <male>412490</male>
                            <female>4500</female>
                        </occupation>
                        <occupation name="Sales" occupation_id="4">
                            <male>1846066</male>
                            <female>22548</female>
                        </occupation>
                        <occupation name="Agriculture" occupation_id="5">
                            <male>30458150</male>
                            <female>1217616</female>
                        </occupation>
                        <occupation name="Labor" occupation_id="6">
                            <male>4281968</male>
                            <female>212378</female>
                        </occupation>
                        <occupation name="Service" occupation_id="7">
                            <male>593566</male>
                            <female>178736</female>
                        </occupation>
                    </occupations>
                </year>
            </population>
            <area>133911</area>
            <currency fxcode="BDT" rate="0">Taka</currency>
            <city id="312">
                <name>Chittagong</name>
                <population>4150000</population>
            </city>
            <city id="313">
                <name>Khulna</name>
                <population>1525000</population>
            </city>
            <city id="270">
                <name>Dacca</name>
                <population>12750000</population>
            </city>
        </country>
    </region>
</demographics>
```

So now let's begin with the XPath demonstration process.

Figure 10-2: Isolating a dataset in the demographics XML document

Simple Expressions to Find Nodes

XPath uses what is called a path expression to pull nodes from an XML document. A path expression is quite literally an expression, expressed as a path, through a hierarchical structure. The term "expression" is appropriate because the path is a pattern that is matched to the structure of an XML document. This finds all paths that match to the expression. The most basic XPath expressions are as shown in Figure 10-3.

Expression	Matching results
node	All child nodes
/	Search from the root node down
//	Search from specified node down
.	Current node
..	Parent node
@	Attributes

Figure 10-3: Basic XPath expressions

The script that follows is an XSL (eXtensible Style Sheet) script. This script is applied to the Bangladesh demographics XML document fragment shown previously:

```
<HTML xmlns:xsl="http://www.w3.org/TR/WD-xsl"><BODY>
<TABLE CELLPADDING="5" CELLSPACING="1" BORDER="1">
<TH BGCOLOR="silver">City</TH>
<xsl:for-each select="demographics/region/country/city">
   <TR>
      <TD><xsl:value-of select="."/></TD>
   </TR>
</xsl:for-each>
</TABLE></BODY></HTML>
```

When executing the preceding script, it must be included into the XML document fragment as follows:

```
<?xml version="1.0"?>
<?xml:stylesheet type="text/xsl" href="fig1004.xsl" ?>
<demographics>
   <region id="9">
      <name>Near East</name>
      <population>1499157105</population>
      <area>4721322</area>
      <country id="120" code="BG">
         <name>Bangladesh</name>
...
         <city id="312">
            <name>Chittagong</name>
            <population>4150000</population>
         </city>
         <city id="313">
            <name>Khulna</name>
            <population>1525000</population>
         </city>
         <city id="270">
            <name>Dacca</name>
            <population>12750000</population>
         </city>
      </country>
   </region>
</demographics>
```

Applying the XSL script to the XML document fragment searches for all city elements within the structure demographics/region/country/city, retrieving all the child elements for all city elements. The result is shown in Figure 10-4.

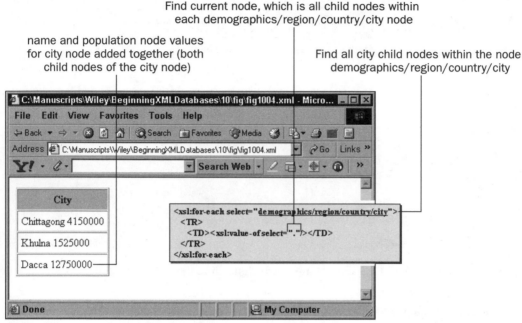

Figure 10-4: Using XPath basic expressions

Figure 10-5 shows slightly different results because different expressions are used. //city/name will find all city/name nodes, anywhere in the XML structure, regardless of country, or otherwise. The @ character is used to find an attribute value, as in 312 extracted from the node <city id="312">. The periods, or ../population expression finds the parent node, this finds the population node in the parent of the node //city/name (or the sibling of the name node, within the city node).

Find Specific Values Using Predicates

So far you have retrieved nodes from XML regardless of the values of nodes or their attributes. Predicates are the equivalent of SQL filters, or WHERE clauses. So, a predicate can be used to qualify which nodes are retrieved based on the values contained within those nodes. Predicate syntax is very simple — applied to a specific node within an XPath expression, and enclosed in square brackets as follows:

```
... [predicate] ...
```

In general, a predicate is a filter, requiring an operator to mathematically filter specific results. Thus the syntax changes slightly to:

```
... [node operator value] ...
```

where operator can be operators such as =, >, and so on.

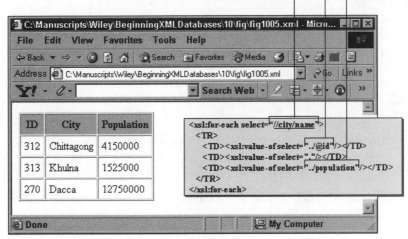

Find any attribute called id, in the parent node of
the //city/name node (the city node id attribute)

//city/name finds all name nodes within
any city node, within the entire structure

Find population node in parent
node (parent node is city node)

Figure 10-5: Using XPath basic expressions

Predicate tests can be performed against text or attribute values:

```
... [text='value'] ...
```

or

```
... [@attribute=value] ...
```

A predicate can also be the collection subscript of a child node. This syntax will find the second node in a collection of two or more child nodes:

```
... [node[2]] ...
```

Next you examine the details of XPath operator syntax.

XPath Operators

The table in Figure 10-6 shows the various operators available to XPath expressions and their meanings and uses.

So if you go back to using XPath predicates, the following example will find the first city node within the country of Bangladesh:

```
demographics/region/country[name='Bangladesh']/city[1]"/>
```

Operator	Description	Example
|	Finds two nodes	//languages | //occupations
+	Addition	3+2
-	Subtraction	3-2'
*	Multiplication	3*2
div	Division	4 div 2
=	Equal to	id=9
!=	Not equal to	id!=9
<	Less than	id<9
<=	Less than or equal to	id<=9
>	Greater than	id>9
>=	Greater than or equal to	id>=2
or	Or (either can be true)	id=2 or id=2
and	And (both must be true)	id>2 and id<2
mod	Modulus (division remainder)	3 mod 2

Figure 10-6: Available XPath operators

This example finds all cities with a population over 10,000,000 people:

```
demographics/region/country/city[population>10000000]"/>
```

And this example finds the second city, in the country of Bangladesh, in the region with `id` attribute of 9:

```
demographics/region[@id=9]/country[name='Bangladesh']/city[2]"/>
```

Figure 10-7 shows the browser results of the preceding three examples.

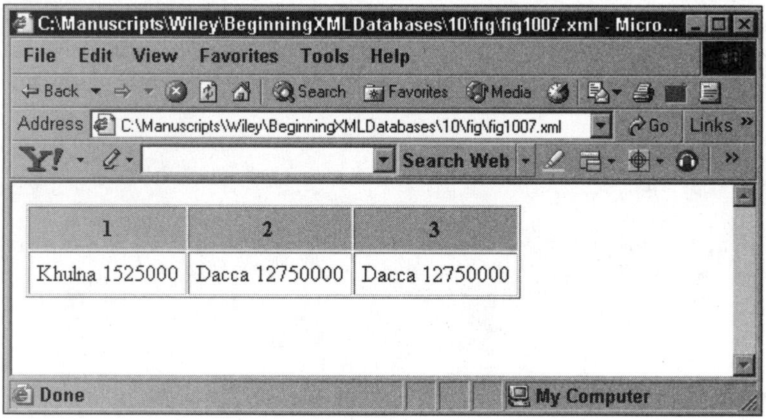

Figure 10-7: Using XPath predicates

Context functions such as `last()` *and* `position()` *can also be used in XPath predicate expressions. Context functions are discussed later on in this chapter.*

Use Wildcards to Find Unknown Nodes

A wildcard is like a wildcard in poker in that it can mean more than one thing. In most programming languages there are two wildcards: one for matching strings and one for matching a single character. In XPath expressions only a string wildcard is allowed. Essentially, a wildcard character is the * (star or asterisk character) and applies to node names or attribute names.

There is also a node() *function that can find nodes of any kind which will be covered later on under functions.*

In Figure 10-8 the for loop finds all language nodes within all languages nodes (language collections), and then specifies a predicate that all language nodes found must have at least 1 attribute indicated by the [@*] predicate part of the XPath expression.

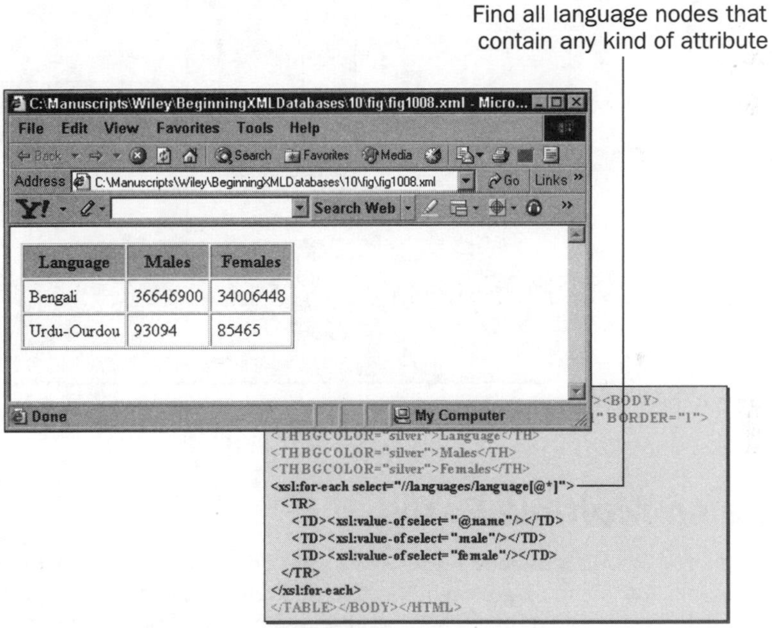

Figure 10-8: Using wildcards in XPath

In Figure 10-9, the for loop finds all nodes that have an id attribute, regardless of the content and type of the node. Thus, all regions, countries, and cities are found.

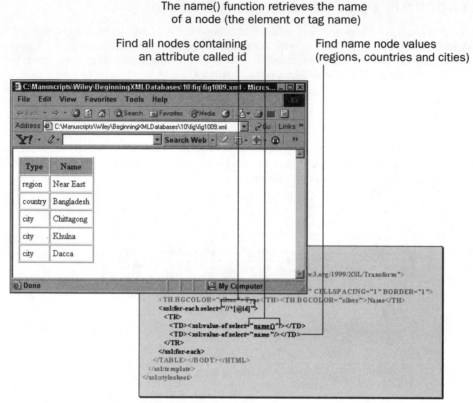

Figure 10-9: Using wildcards in XPath

Expressions on Multiple Paths

A multiple path expression allows you to retrieve two sets of data at once. In other words, it looks for one path, then another, and then merges them together and returns them. The | operator is used to merge multiple XPath expression results. This operator is sometimes known, in various programming languages, as the pipe or concatenation operator. Concatenation is perhaps appropriate in this case because two separate datasets are concatenated (added together). The result shown in Figure 10-10 is a concatenation of two XPath expression searches, returning both the languages and occupations collections node contents.

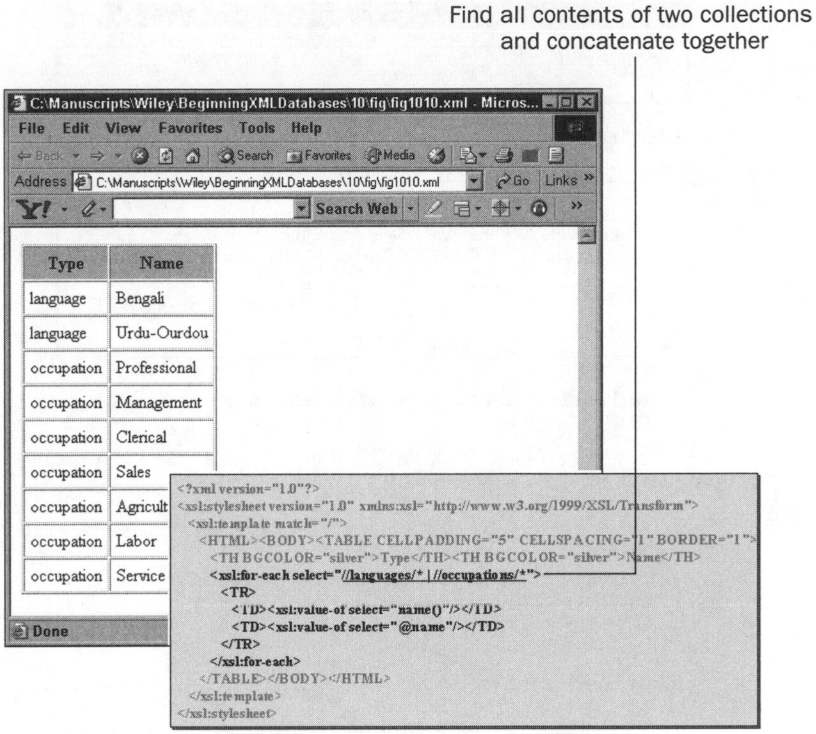

Find all contents of two collections
and concatenate together

Figure 10-10: Concatenating two expression results in XPath

XPath Axes

XPath axes define and allow access to any node within an XML document, from the current node, relative to that current node. XPath axes are a little like giving directions, allowing navigation through an XML document, using the XPath data model for an XML document, as established by XPath. An XPath axis gives directions from whatever the current node is in, in terms of the current node being a current location or context within an XML document, as established by XPath.

The current node is the node currently found by the most recently executed XPath expression. Figure 10-11 shows the various XPath axes that can be used. Technically, one can find any node, from any node, using the XPath axes.

Axis	Output
ancestor	Find all ancestor nodes (parents, grandparents, ...)
ancestor-or-self	Find all ancestor nodes plus the current node
attribute	Find all attributes
child	Find all direct child nodes (not the same as descendants)
descendant	Find all descendants (children, grandchildren, ...)
descendant-or-self	Find all descendant nodes plus the current node
following	Find all nodes and text after the closing tag of the current node (after </node>)
following-sibling	Find all siblings (nodes on the same level), before the current node
namespace	Find all namespace nodes applying to the current node
parent	Find the parent node
preceding	Find all nodes and text before the opening tag of the current node (before <node>)
preceding-sibling	Find all siblings (nodes on the same level), after the current node
self	Find the current node

All axes operate on the current node

Figure 10-11: XPath axes on the current node

The syntax for applying an XPath axis is as follows:

```
axis::test-on-node[predicate]
```

Figure 10-12 shows some example uses of XPath axes.

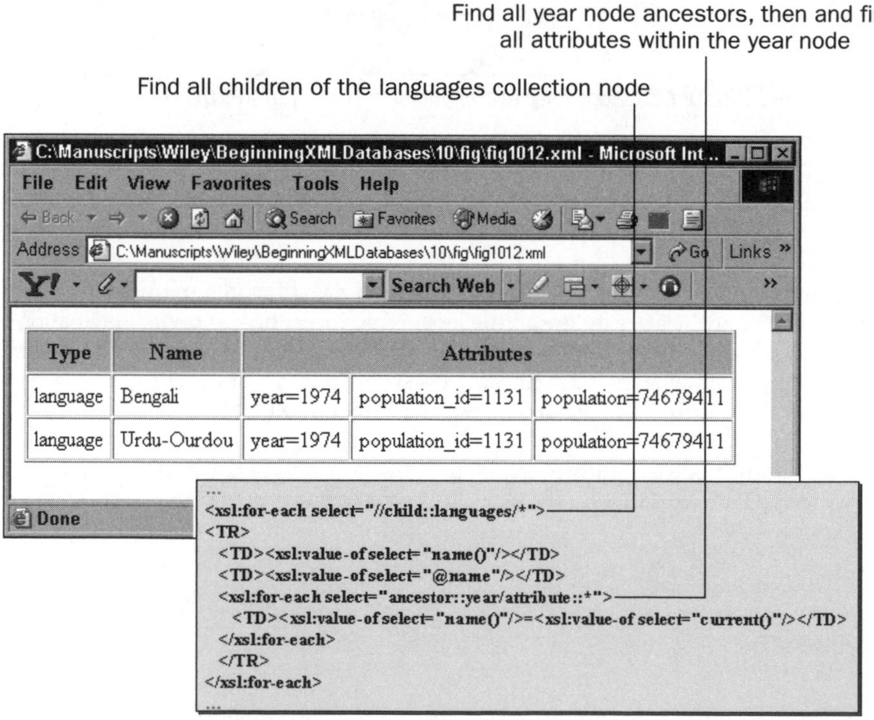

Find all year node ancestors, then and find all attributes within the year node

Find all children of the languages collection node

Type	Name		Attributes	
language	Bengali	year=1974	population_id=1131	population=746794411
language	Urdu-Ourdou	year=1974	population_id=1131	population=746794411

```
...
<xsl:for-each select="//child::languages/*">
<TR>
  <TD><xsl:value-of select="name()"/></TD>
  <TD><xsl:value-of select="@name"/></TD>
  <xsl:for-each select="ancestor::year/attribute::*">
    <TD><xsl:value-of select="name()"/>=<xsl:value-of select="current()"/></TD>
  </xsl:for-each>
  </TR>
</xsl:for-each>
...
```

Figure 10-12: Applying XPath axes

XPath Functions

There are a plethora of functions that can be used with XPath 2.0, XQuery 1.0, and XSLT 2.0.

XQuery is covered in the next chapter.

XPath functions actually apply to both XQuery (XQuery 1.0 data model) and XPath (XPath 2.0 data model) but since they are included in both, it is appropriate to describe all of these functions in the explanation of XPath expressions.

The sheer quantity and variety of functionality provided by XPath built-in functions are enormous. All the functions are included and usable by including the fn namespace at the W3C URL:

```
xmlns:fn="http://www.w3.org/2005/02/xpath-functions"
```

At the time of this writing, there is a problem with demonstrating XPath functionality. According to W3C documentation, if a namespace XML document cannot be found from within something like an XSL style sheet, then that specific namespace is not yet released for general use. I have found various other namespace files for including XPath 2.0 functionality, none of which function at the time of writing this book:

```
xmlns:fn="http://www.w3.org/2003/11/xpath-functions"
xmlns:fn="http://www.w3.org/TR/xpath-functions"
xmlns:fn="http://www.w3.org/2005/xpath-functions"
```

The other option is to demonstrate XPath 1.0, which with the introduction of XPath 2.0, is out-of-date. I don't see the point in describing software that is out-of-date.

XPath 2.0 functions are conveniently divided into various categories:

❑ **Accessor functions:** These provide access to privately held data, privately held by other objects in other words, a function allowing access to setting and retrieving values of a property, without allowing direct access to the object containing the property. A read-only property has only one accessor function, and that allows retrieval of the property value. This is because a read-only property cannot be set.

❑ **Errors and tracing:** Raise errors and debug using tracing during processing.

❑ **Constructor functions:** These create an object instance from a class, or in really simplistic terms, they define a type. In other words, when declaring a variable as being of a simple data type such as a string or a number, in any programming language, one is constructing a variable. The mere definition of the variable as being of a specific type is actually a simple form of a constructor function. A constructor function constructs an iteration or copy of a variable from a definition.

❑ **Numeric functions:** As in any programming language, a numeric function performs some kind of conversion or calculation such that a number value is returned.

❑ **String functions:** As for number functions, but in this case a string is returned. Operations are usually performed on strings and return strings, rather than numbers, but not always.

❑ **URI function:** A URI function operates on a URI. What is a URI? A URI is a Uniform Resource Identifier. A URI is also a type of a URL (Universal Resource Locator).

❑ **Boolean function:** These functions produce a Boolean result, which programmatically allows for specific types of coding that result in either true or false.

❑ **Functions on durations, dates, and times:** These functions operate on return dates, times, and durations of time.

❑ **QName functions:** A QName is a qualified name. A QName contains a namespace URI. A QName is an optional prefix and a colon followed by a local name, or a URI plus a local element or attribute name.

❑ **Node functions:** These functions are applied specifically to XML document nodes.

❑ **Sequence functions:** A sequence is effectively a list of zero or more potentially repetitive items contained within a parent node. A sequence is therefore a collection. Sequence functions can be applied to a single collection as a whole, applying the same execution of a function to all elements in a collection at once.

❑ **Context functions:** These functions apply to the meanings and thus the metadata within an XML document.

❑ **Other types of functions:** These will not be demonstrated in this book as they are too obscure but are included at this stage so that you are aware of their existence:

    ❑ **Operators on base64Binary and hexBinary:** Used for comparison of values where values do not have a decimal base (they are not decimal numbers).

    ❑ **Functions and operators on NOTATION:** XML notation is a form of XML that is dialect-specific, and established for very specific applications in XML, such as MathXML and CML (chemistry). Specific XML dialect notations establish standards to, and apply topic regional semantics to otherwise generic XML data.

Now let's look at some of the details of XPath functions. The problem with demonstrating XPath functions at this point in this book is that these XPath functions are used in XQuery 75 percent of the time. Therefore, any examples will be delayed until the next chapter, which covers XQuery.

Accessor Functions

Accessor functions provide access to privately held data, privately held by other objects. In other words, a function allowing access to setting and retrieving values of a property, without allowing direct access to the object containing the property. A read-only property has only one accessor function, and that allows retrieval of the property value. This is because a read-only property cannot be set. Accessor functions are shown in Figure 10-13.

Function	Returns
fn:node-name(node)	The name of a node
fn:string	Returns the string form of a value
fn:nilled(node)	True if node is nilled, where a nilled node is an empty node (<node/> or <node></node>)
fn:data(item [, item, ...])	Converts a list of items into a sequence of values
fn:base-uri([| node])	URI of a specirfied node, or the current node if no node specified

Figure 10-13: XPath accessor functions

Errors and Tracing

Error and tracing functions (see Figure 10-14) allow raising of errors and debugging using tracing.

Function	Returns
fn:error(error, description, object)	Raises an error. The error parameter is QName
fn:trace(value, label)	XQuery query debugging

Figure 10-14: XPath error and trace functions

Constructor Functions

Constructor functions (see Figure 10-15) are used to create an object instance from a class; constructor functions define a type. In other words, when declaring a variable as being of a simple data type, such as a string or a number in any programming language, one is constructing a variable. As already stated, the mere definition of the variable as being of a specific type is actually a simple form of a constructor function. A constructor function constructs an iteration or copy of a variable from a definition. Therefore a constructor function is actually a variable definition as well.

Datatype	Description
xs:string()	
xs:integer()	Other numeric datatypes: xs:int(), xs:long(), xs:negativeInteger(), xs:nonNegativeInteger(), xs:nonPositiveInteger(), xs:positiveInteger(), xs:short(), xs:unsignedInt(), xs:unsignedInt(), xs:unsignedLong(), xs:unsignedShort(), xs:decimal(), xs:double(), xs:float()
xs:date()	Other date and time datatypes: xs:time(), xs:dateTime(), xs:duration(), xs:gDay(), xs:gMonth(), xs:gMonthDay(), xs:gYear(), xs:gYearMonth(), xdt:dayTimeDuration(), xdt:yearMonthDuration()
fn:dateTime(xs:date, xs:time)	Function to create a data and time timestamp from a date and a time value
prefix:TYPE()	User defined type constructor function (creates a user defined datatype). For example, dem:population(xdt:anyAtomicType?) as dem:population?
xs:anyURI()	
xs:boolean()	
xs:ENTITY()	
xs:ID()	
xs:IDREF()	
xs:language()	
xs:Name()	
xs:NCName()	
xs:NMTOKEN()	
xs:normalizedString()	
xs:QName()	
xs:token()	
xdt:untypedAtomic()	

Figure 10-15: XPath constructor functions (data type definitions)

Some of the more obscure functions are omitted from Figure 10-15, and subsequent similar figures in this chapter, in order to maintain focus on the topic of XML and databases.

An XML Schema defines most of these data types. Most essentially create specific data types from atomic types. An atomic data type or TYPE is essentially a very simple value, which when converted to a specific data type gives it the specific qualities of the data type to which it is converted.

Numeric Functions

Numeric functions in XPath (see Figure 10-16) are as in any programming language — numeric functions used to perform some kind of conversion or calculation, such that a number value is returned.

Name	Description
fn:number(arg)	Converts an appropriate string to a number
fn:abs(num)	An absolute value where all negative values are returned as positives
fn:ceiling(num)	Returns the next integer upwards, regardless of decimal value. For example, ceiling(5.1) becomes 6 and not 5
fn:floor(num)	The opposite of ceiling where the result is truncated downwards to the nearest integer
fn:round(num)	Rounds a number to the nearest integer. 0.5 is rounded up and < 0.5 is rounded down
fn:round-half-to-even()	Rounds a number to the nearest even numbered integer

Figure 10-16: XPath numeric functions

Numeric Operators

There are various numeric operators (see Figure 10-17) available for use with XPath. Many of these operators, such as numeric-add, act as options to their more commonly used symbolic representations (the plus sign: +).

Operators	Meaning
op:numeric-add	Addition
op:numeric-subtract	Subtraction
op:numeric-multiply	Multiplication
op:numeric-divide	Division
op:numeric-integer-divide	Integer division
op:numeric-mod	Modulus (remainder)
op:numeric-unary-plus	Unary plus
op:numeric-unary-minus	Unary minus or negation
op:numeric-equal	Equality
op:numeric-less-than	Less-than
op:numeric-greater-than	Greater-than

Figure 10-17: XPath numeric operators

String Functions

String functions (see Figure 10-18) are similar to number functions. However, operations are usually performed on strings and return strings rather than numbers, but not always.

Name	Description
fn:string(arg)	Converts a number, boolean, or node-set to a string
fn:codepoints-to-string(int [, int ...]) and fn:codepoint-equal(arg1, arg2)	Convert between strings and a sequence of code points
	Returns true if the two arguments are equal in Unicode
fn:compare(arg1, arg2, collation)	Returns -1 if arg1 < arg2, 0 if arg1 = arg2, 1 if arg1 > arg2 (according to collation rules in use)
fn:concat(string [, string ...])	Concatenates two strings
fn:string-join((string [, string ...]), separator)	Concatenates multiple strings using a specified separator
fn:substring(string, start, len)	Substring, from start, for length
fn:string-length([| string])	Length of a string (or the current node when blank)
fn:normalize-space([| string])	Removes leading and trailing spaces from a string (or the current node when blank)
fn:upper-case(string), fn:lower-case(string)	Changes case
fn:translate(string1,string2,string3)	Converts string1 by replacing the characters in string2 with the characters in string3
fn:escape-uri(stringURI,esc-res)	Generate escape sequence characters in URI addresses such as replacing space characters with their hexdecimal equivalent, and ignored by a browser
fn:contains(string1,string2)	Checks for the instance of a string in another string
fn:starts-with(string1,string2)	Checks for the instance of a string at the start of a string
fn:ends-with(string1,string2)	Checks for the instance of a string at the end of a string
fn:substring-before(string1,string2)	Substring before another
fn:substring-after(string1,string2)	Substring after another
fn:matches(string,pattern)	Matches a pattern to a string
fn:replace(string,pattern,replace)	String replacement function
fn:tokenize(string,pattern)	Breaks a delimited list into tokens (single items)

Figure 10-18: XPath string functions

URI Functions

A URI function operates on a URI. (A URI is a Uniform Resource Identifier.) A URI is also a type of a URL (Universal Resource Locator). In other words, `http://www.yahoo.com` is a DNS (Directory Names Service), and 216.109.112.135 is its IP address. Effectively the two make up a URL. A URL is an Internet address. So, a URI is a subset type of a URL. The difference is subtle in that a URL always refers to a remote resource on the Internet, whereas a URI can refer to a remote resource or a local resource. A local resource is not on the Internet and is locally located (on your LAN). A URI is thus not publicly accessible. For example, `file:/// c:/tmp/MyFile.txt` is a URI because it is located locally on my computer. Additionally, a URI does not necessarily refer to a specific network protocol because it may not be on a network, and a URL does refer to a specific network protocol.

The only function in this section is as follows:

```
fn:resolve-uri (relative, base)
```

The preceding function resolves a relative URI to an absolute URI.

Boolean Functions

Boolean functions produce a Boolean result, which programmatically allows for specific types of coding in that the result produced by a Boolean function is either true or false. Figure 10-19 shows Boolean functions.

Name	Description
fn:boolean(arg)	A boolean for a number, string, or node-set. So,
fn:not(arg)	Known as an inverted boolean in that the argument is first reduced to a boolean value by applying the boolean() function. Returns true if the boolean value is false, and false if the boolean value is true
fn:true()	Returns true
fn:false()	Returns false

Figure 10-19: XPath Boolean functions

Boolean Operators

Specialized Boolean operators allow for testing of Boolean values, as shown in Figure 10-20.

Operator	Meaning
op:boolean-equal	Are two booleans equal?
op:boolean-less-than	False is less than true, which results in true
op:boolean-greater-than	True is greater than false, which results in true

Figure 10-20: XPath Boolean operators

Functions on Durations, Dates, and Times

These functions operate on date values of one form or another, and they usually return dates, times, and durations of time. These functions are shown in Figure 10-21.

Name	Description
fn:dateTime(date, time)	Produce a timestamp
fn:years-from-duration(duration)	Returns years from a duration, where a duration represents a period of time, rather than a date which is a static point in time. Other similar functions are fn:months-from-duration(datetimedur), fn:days-from-duration(datetimedur), fn:hours-from-duration(datetimedur), fn:minutes-from-duration(datetimedur) and fn:seconds-from-duration(datetimedur)
fn:year-from-dateTime(datetime)	Returns years from a timestamp, static point in time. Other similar functions are fn:month-from-dateTime(datetime), fn:day-from-dateTime(datetime), fn:hours-from-dateTime(datetime), fn:minutes-from-dateTime(datetime), fn:seconds-from-dateTime(datetime) and fn:timezone-from-dateTime(datetime)
fn:year-from-date(date)	Returns years from a date, static point in time. Other similar functions are fn:month-from-date(date), fn:day-from-date(date) and fn:timezone-from-date(date)
fn:hours-from-time(time)	Returns hours from a time value. Other simiarl functions are fn:minutes-from-time(time), fn:seconds-from-time(time) and fn:timezone-from-time(time)
fn:adjust-dateTime-to-timezone(datetime,timezone)	Converts a timestamp to a time zone adjusted timsestamp. Other similar functions are fn:adjust-date-to-timezone(date,timezone) and fn:adjust-time-to-timezone(time,timezone)

Figure 10-21: XPath duration, date, and time functions

Date, Time, and Duration Operators

There are specialized operators that operate on data, time, and duration values, as shown in Figure 10-22.

Operator	Meaning
op:yearMonthDuration-equal	Equality comparison. Similar functions are op:dayTimeDuration-equal, op:duration-equal, op:dateTime-equal, op:date-equal, op:time-equal, op:gYearMonth-equal, op:gYear-equal, op:gMonthDay-equal, op:gMonth-equal, op:gDay-equal
op:yearMonthDuration-less-than	Less-than comparison. Similar functions are op:dayTimeDuration-less-than, op:dateTime-less-than, op:date-less-than, op:time-less-than
op:yearMonthDuration-greater-than	Greater-than comparison. Similar functions are op:dayTimeDuration-greater-than, op:dateTime-greater-than, op:date-greater-than, op:time-greater-than

Figure 10-22: XPath duration, date, and time operators

And there are also numerous arithmetic functions that can be applied to durations, as shown in Figure 10-23.

Function	Meaning
op:add-yearMonthDurations	xdt:yearMonthDuration arithmetic. Similar functions are op:subtract-yearMonthDurations and op:multiply-yearMonthDuration, op:divide-yearMonthDuration, op:divide-yearMonthDuration-by-yearMonthDuration
op:add-dayTimeDurations	xdt:dayTimeDuration arithmetic. Similar functions are op:subtract-dayTimeDurations, op:multiply-dayTimeDuration, op:divide-dayTimeDuration, op:divide-dayTimeDuration-by-dayTimeDuration

Figure 10-23: XPath duration arithmetic functions

And then arithmetic functions can be applied to dates, times, and durations, as shown in Figure 10-24.

Function	Meaning
op:subtract-<datatype>	op:subtract-dateTimes, op:subtract-dates, op:subtract-times, op:subtract-yearMonthDuration-from-dateTime, op:subtract-dayTimeDuration-from-dateTime, op:subtract-yearMonthDuration-from-date, op:subtract-dayTimeDuration-from-date, op:subtract-dayTimeDuration-from-time
op:add-<datatype>	op:add-dateTimes, op:add-dates, op:add-times, op:add-yearMonthDuration-from-dateTime, op:add-dayTimeDuration-from-dateTime, op:add-yearMonthDuration-from-date, op:add-dayTimeDuration-from-date, op:add-dayTimeDuration-from-time

Figure 10-24: XPath duration, date, and time arithmetic functions

QName Functions

A QName is a qualified name that contains a namespace URI. A QName is an optional prefix and a colon followed by a local name, or a URI plus a local element or attribute name. QName functions are shown in Figure 10-25.

Function	Description
fn:QName()	Returns a QName
fn:local-name-from-QName()	Local name from QName
fn:namespace-uri-from-QName()	Namespace and URI from QName
fn:namespace-uri-for-prefix()	Returns all currently active namespaces
fn:in-scope-prefixes()	Returns all namespace prefixes, which are currently in scope

Figure 10-25: XPath qualified name (QName) functions

Node Functions

Node functions are applied specifically to XML document nodes.

Name	Description
fn:name([nodeset])	Current node, or first node of set
fn:local-name([nodeset])	Same as above but with no naemspace prefixes
fn:namespace-uri([nodeset])	Namepace URI for current node, or first node of set
fn:lang(lang)	Check for language match of current node
fn:number	Current context item value returned as a number
fn:root([node])	Returns the root of the tree to which the current node or the specified belongs. This will usually be a
op:is-same-node	True if the two nodes are the same
op:node-before and op:node_after	Indicates whether one node appears before (or after) another node in document order

Figure 10-26: XPath node functions

Sequence Functions

A sequence is a list of zero or more potentially repetitive items, contained within a parent node. A sequence is therefore a collection. Sequence functions can be applied to a single collection as a whole, which means applying the same execution of a function to all elements in a collection at once. Figure 10-27 shows sequence functions.

The following XSL script uses the XML document shown in Figure 10-2 to apply two XPath functions:

```
<xsl:stylesheet version="2.0"
 xmlns:xsl="http://www.w3.org/1999/XSL/Transform"
 xmlns:xs="http://www.w3.org/2001/XMLSchema"
 xmlns:fn="http://www.w3.org/2005/xpath-functions"
 xmlns:xdt="http://www.w3.org/2005/xpath-datatypes">
   <xsl:template match="/">
      <HTML><BODY>
         Sum of all male entries =<xsl:value-of select=
            "sum(//year[@year=1974]/occupations/occupation/male)"/>
         <BR/>
         Count of male entries = <xsl:value-of select=
            "count(//year[@year=1974]/occupations/occupation/male)"/>
      </BODY></HTML>
   </xsl:template>
</xsl:stylesheet>
```

Name	Description
General Sequence Functions ... (a sequence is a collection, which in this case is a comma delimited list of items of one or more values: item [, item ...])	
fn:index-of((collection), pattern)	Collection positions (or subscripts), of items matching pattern
fn:remove((collection), position)	Creates a new collection less the removed items. Does not delete items from existing colelction
fn:empty(collection)	Empty collection returns true
fn:exists(collection)	Non-empty collection returns true
fn:distinct-values((collection), collation)	Finds unique items only
fn:insert-before((collection), position, inserts)	Creates a new collection from the existing collection, plus inserted items
fn:reverse(collection)	Creates a reverse ordered collection
fn:subsequence((collection), start, length)	Creates a subset collection from position at start, for length (number of items). The first item is in the first
fn:unordered(collection)	Creates an unsorted collection
op:concatenate	An operator concatenating two collections together
Cardinality ... (a measure of unique or distinct items in a collection containing duplicated items)	
fn:zero-or-one(collection)	Gets the specified subset collection if zero or more items, otherwise raises an error
fn:one-or-more(collection)	Gets the specified subset collection if one or more items, otherwise raises an error
fn:exactly-one(collection)	Gets the specified subset collection if one item, otherwise raises an error
Sets	
fn:deep-equal(item1, item2, collation)	True if two items, in corresponding positions, are the same
op:union, op:intersect and op:except	Three operators returning (excluding duplicates), the union, intersection and the anti-intersection of two
Aggregates	
fn:count(collection)	Counts all nodes
fn:avg(collection)	Average across a collection
fn:max(collection)	Maximum across a collection
fn:min(collection)	Minimum across a collection
fn:sum(collection)	Sum across a collection
Sequence Generators	
fn:id(collection, node)	Return a subset collection of nodes, with ID values in the collection specified
fn:idref(collection, node)	Return a subset collection of nodes, with IDREF values in the collection specified
fn:doc(URI)	Gets a document node
fn:doc-available(URI)	Set to true if the doc() function returns a document node, in other words it is an XML document
fn:collection(string)	Convert a string to a collection (a sequence of nodes)

Figure 10-27: XPath sequence functions

The result of the preceding script is shown in Figure 10-28.

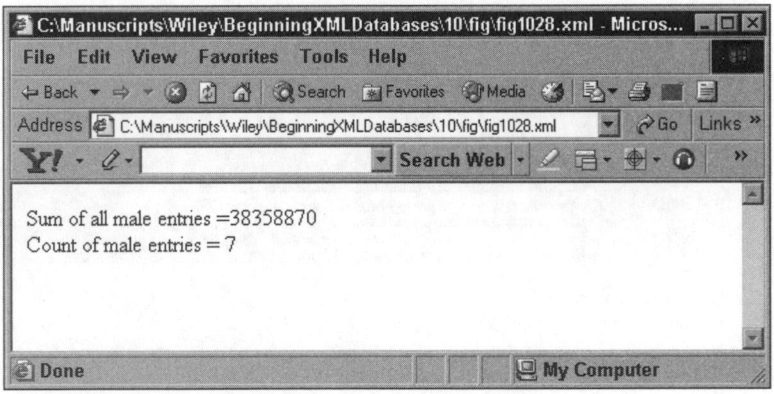

Figure 10-28: XPath sequence functions by example

Context Functions

These functions apply to the meanings, and thus the metadata within an XML document. Figure 10-29 shows context functions.

Name	Description
fn:position()	Finds the position or iteration of an element within a collection
fn:last()	Finds the last element in a collection
fn:current-dateTime()	Finds current date and time, in its time zone
fn:current-date()	Finds current date in its time zone
fn:current-time()	Finds current time, in its time zone
fn:implicit-timezone()	Finds time zone value
fn:default-collation()	Finds default collation
fn:static-base-uri()	Finds the base URI

Figure 10-29: XPath context functions

Once again, using the same small dataset, as shown in Figure 10-2, the following XSL script is applied to the XML data, including use of the `last()` and `position()` XPath context functions:

```
<?xml version="1.0"?>
<xsl:stylesheet version="1.0" xmlns:xsl="http://www.w3.org/1999/XSL/Transform">
   <xsl:template match="/">
      <HTML><BODY>
         Last male entry = <xsl:value-of select="//year[@year=1974]/occupations/occ
upation[last()]/male"/>
         <BR/>
         First female entry = <xsl:value-of select="//year[@year=1974]/occupations/
occupation[position()=1]/female"/>
      </BODY></HTML>
   </xsl:template>
</xsl:stylesheet>
```

Figure 10-30 shows the result of applying the preceding XSL script to the data shown in Figure 10-2.

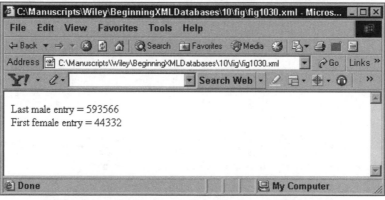

Figure 10-30: Using some simple XPath context functions

Try It Out   Using Simple XPath Expression Syntax

The following query executes against the demographics relational database used in this book (see Appendix B). This query finds cities with all their populations, regardless of where the cities are located in the world:

```
SELECT r.REGION, co.COUNTRY, ci.CITY, ci.POPULATION
FROM REGION r JOIN COUNTRY co ON (co.REGION_ID = r.REGION_ID)
   JOIN CITY ci ON (ci.COUNTRY_ID = co.COUNTRY_ID)
ORDER BY ci.CITY;
```

This is a partial result of the preceding query (you will use the demographics.xml XML document for this example):

```
REGION            COUNTRY          CITY             POPULATION
----------------  ---------------- ---------------- ----------
Africa            Ivory Coast      Abidjan          4000000
Central America   Mexico           Acapulco         0
Africa            Ghana            Accra            2550000
Near East         Turkey           Adana            1300000
Africa            Ethiopia         Addis Ababa      0
Africa            Ethiopia         Addis Abeba      3000000
...
```

Using the query and the data shown as a guide, create an XPath expression in an XSL style sheet, parsed against the XML document form of the demographics database. Produce the same result using the XML data, XSL, and a browser. This is how:

1. This is a very simple task. Create an HTML framework as follows:

```
<HTML xmlns:xsl="http://www.w3.org/TR/WD-xsl">
<BODY>
<TABLE CELLPADDING="5" CELLSPACING="1" BORDER="1">
<TH BGCOLOR="silver">City</TH>
...
</TABLE></BODY></HTML>
```

2. Now add in a for loop containing an XPath expression to find cities:

```
<HTML xmlns:xsl="http://www.w3.org/TR/WD-xsl"><BODY>
<TABLE CELLPADDING="5" CELLSPACING="1" BORDER="1">
<TH BGCOLOR="silver">City</TH>
<xsl:for-each select="demographics/region/country/city">
...
</xsl:for-each>
</TABLE></BODY></HTML>
```

3. Perhaps sort the results based on the name of the city:

```
<HTML xmlns:xsl="http://www.w3.org/TR/WD-xsl"><BODY>
<TABLE CELLPADDING="5" CELLSPACING="1" BORDER="1">
<TH BGCOLOR="silver">City</TH>
<xsl:for-each select="demographics/region/country/city" order-by="name">
...
</xsl:for-each>
</TABLE></BODY></HTML>
```

4. And now add in the simple detail to get the actual values:

```
<HTML xmlns:xsl="http://www.w3.org/TR/WD-xsl"><BODY>
<TABLE CELLPADDING="5" CELLSPACING="1" BORDER="1">
<TH BGCOLOR="silver">City</TH>
<xsl:for-each select="demographics/region/country/city" order-by="name">
   <TR>
      <TD><xsl:value-of select="."/></TD>
   </TR>
</xsl:for-each>
</TABLE></BODY></HTML>
```

5. The result looks like that shown in Figure 10-31.

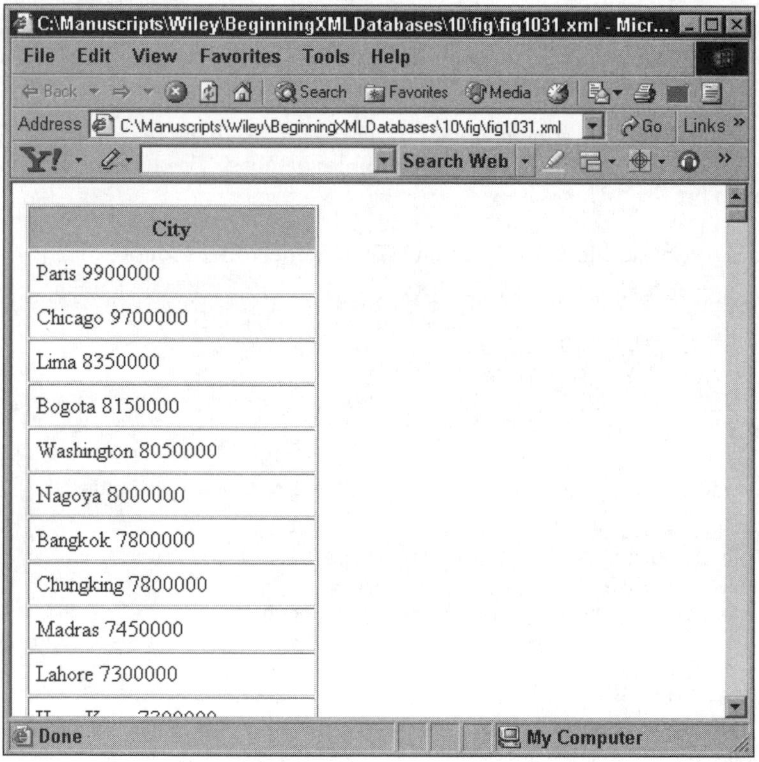

Figure 10-31: Try It Out simple XPath expression syntax

How It Works

You created a simple XPath expression to selectively read data from an XML document. That same reading of data was accomplished as a simple relational database SQL statement, executed against tables in a database. This demonstrates that XPath expression syntax allows you to pull data from an XML data source as you would pull data from an XML document. In other words, the two different methods perform the same function.

This chapter has addressed the XML expression language XPath, which is used to parse and extract information from XML documents. Other tools such as XQuery and XPointer are based on XPath, and so XPath is fundamental to understanding information presented in the next few chapters.

Summary

In this chapter you learned that:

❑   XPath can be used to pull specific data items and substructures from XML data.

❑   XPath can use both simple and complex expressions.

❑   XPath inter-nodal relationships can be accessed using XPath axes.

❑   Numerous forms of predicates can help to filter XPath expression results.

❑   XPath expressions can use wildcards to retrieve data regardless of values and names.

❑   Multiple datasets can be merged by using multiple XPath expressions.

❑   Built-in functions are used in advanced XPath expressions and XQuery.

❑   Built-in functions are numerous and extremely complex.

❑   Built-in functions can be classified in many different categories.

Exercises

1.   What is the difference between the following two XPath expressions?

```
/root/nodeA/nodeB
```

and:

```
nodeA/nodeB
```

2.   Which of the following statements is the best answer for the following XPath expression:

```
//country/../@name
```

a.   Find all countries whose name node is not empty.

b.   Find parent nodes for all countries.

c.   Find all parents of all countries where the country node has a name attribute.

d.   Find nothing because no root node is specified.

e.   None of the above.

3. What is the best answer for what this XPath expression will find?

```
demographics/region/country/city[last()-1]"/>
```

    a. The first city for every country

    b. The last city for every country

    c. The second city for every country

    d. The second last city for every country

    e. None of the above

4. What will this XPath expression find?

```
demographics/region/country[@*]
```

    a. The entire contents of an XML document

    b. Only regions with a region id attribute of between 1 and 10

    c. Countries with a name beginning with the letter A

    d. All countries with at least 1 attribute

    e. None of the above.

5. Which of the following are possible answers, with respect to this XPath expression?

```
//child::collectionofthings/../parentofcollectionofthings/bigthings/attribute::*
```

    a. Get all attributes of a node called bigthings.

    b. Get all attributes of the parent node, of a node called collectionofthings.

    c. Get the node parentofcollectionofthings.

    d. Get the parent node of parentofcollectionofthings.

    e. Get zip!

Reading XML Documents Using XQuery

XPath is used to navigate through XML documents, based on the absolute and relative position of a node in that XML document. Now that you know a thing or two about XPath, the next thing to examine is XQuery.

There are further steps beyond XPath and XQuery, such as XLink and XPointer, which will be covered in later chapters.

XQuery is to XML as SQL (Structured Query Language) is to relational databases. Simply put, XQuery is used to read XML documents. XQuery is designed to query anything appearing as XML data, even XML data type structures (or otherwise) stored in a database.

There are no Try It Out sections in this chapter as the content here is primarily conceptual, but also introductory with respect to native XML database standards.

In this chapter you learn about:

❑ XQuery not written in XML

❑ Querying XML data using XQuery

❑ XPath and XQuery sharing a lot, including XPath functions

❑ Executing XQuery commands using Saxon

❑ Embedding of XQuery commands, HTML, and XML

❑ The FLWOR XQuery `for` loop

❑ Some specialized XQuery capabilities in Oracle Database as a part of Oracle XML DB

What Is XQuery?

XQuery is a standardized language that can be used to query XML documents much as SQL is used to query relational database tables. Essentially, XQuery consists of a data model and a set of query operators that operate on that data model.

XQuery is implemented in industry. However, it is not yet completely finalized by the W3C.

Like SQL, XQuery is a declarative rather than a procedural programming language. A procedural programming language uses a step-by-step process to solve problems, where different lines of code (or groups of lines of code) can pass values back and forth between each other. A declarative programming language simply defines a set of things such as boundaries, conditions, and constraints. The computer is then left to figure out an answer that meets those specified restrictions. A declarative language is much higher level (less detailed) than a procedural language in that it is used to describe a problem, as opposed to problem solving.

So, XQuery scans through an XML document (or a portion thereof), applies restrictions to the query (such as filtering predicates), and returns whichever data matches the boundaries, conditions, and constraints set by a specific query. The result is a subset copy of the originally scanned XML document in XML form.

The current version of XQuery cannot be used to change XML data. However, this is coming in the future.

Technically, XQuery can be used anywhere that XML is used. That's the idea at least. The intention of XML is to make for a universally understood platform-independent source of data. Thus, XQuery follows in the same mold by attempting to provide a universally usable XML document query tool.

Shared Components

XPath 2.0 and XQuery 1.0 support all of the same functions and operators, and they share the same data model. In fact, XQuery queries of XML data are built using XPath expressions. Documentation states that approximately 75 percent of the functionality of XQuery 1.0 is provided by XPath 2.0 — a large part of which would be the XPath functions and operators as presented in the previous chapter.

The Basics of XQuery

There are a number of syntax options to discuss here. The most significant factor to remember about XQuery is that it is not written in XML. However, XQuery queries can be embedded with XSL style sheets.

Executing XQuery Queries

This is an example XQuery coded command:

```
for $i in doc("demographics.xml")/demographics/region/country/city
where $i/population>10000000
order by $i/name
return $i/name
```

Now you might ask questions like this: How does the preceding code work? What tool does it run in? How does one execute it? The answer is not in your browser. Remember XQuery is not written in XML. XQuery is written as a W3C specification, which implies a guideline. Thus, any vendor can use the specification to construct a program to execute XQuery queries, such as the `for` loop shown in the preceding code. Your Internet Explorer browser (or otherwise) will not simply execute the preceding XQuery code example. The preceding example is not XML code and thus not universally interpreted by a standard issue Internet browser program such as Internet Explorer or Netscape.

So, before you go any further with describing XQuery, you can download and install a piece of software called Saxon. You can do this if you wish to follow along with examples as you read through this chapter. It is not essential that you perform the download. I will also be using an Oracle Database proprietary product called XML DB and various other Oracle Database tools and commands. All of these Oracle tools will allow execution of XQuery coded commands, along with a lot of other functions within the Oracle XML DB software.

Using Saxon

Saxon is a program that allows you to execute XQuery queries like the one shown in the previous section. You can download Saxon software from the following URL:

```
http://saxon.sourceforge.net
```

The best option is probably the latest version. However, the version you find when reading this book might not be the version I found when writing it. So be aware that there might be differences. Saxon version 8.7.1 was used to write this book.

In order to use Saxon you need to have a Java virtual machine (JVM) installed on your computer to install the Java version. Execute the following command in a shell to check which version of Java you have installed, if any:

```
java -version
```

If nothing appears, you need to download an appropriate version of Java. Java can be downloaded at the following URL:

```
http://www.java.sun.com
```

When Java is installed, typing a command such as the following will give an indication as to Saxon status. This depends on where the Saxon JAR files are installed:

```
java -jar "c:\program files\saxon\saxon8.jar"
```

You should get a list of options for Saxon, something like that shown in Figure 11-1.

Now you can execute a query using a command something like the following, assuming all appropriate PATH and CLASSPATH settings are appropriate:

```
java -jar "c:\program files\saxon\saxon8.jar" test.xml test.xsl
```

```
Command Prompt (2)                                                    _ □ X
C:\>java -jar "c:\program files\saxon\saxon8.jar"
No source file name
Saxon 8.7.1J from Saxonica
Usage: java net.sf.saxon.Transform [options] source-doc style-doc {param=value}.

Options:
  -a                    Use xml-stylesheet PI, not style-doc argument
  -c                    Indicates that style-doc is a compiled stylesheet
  -cr classname         Use specified collection URI resolver class
  -ds                   Use linked tree data structure
  -dt                   Use tiny tree data structure (default)
  -im modename          Start transformation in specified mode
  -it template          Start transformation by calling named template
  -l                    Retain line numbers in source document tree
  -o filename           Send output to named file or directory
  -m classname          Use specified Emitter class for xsl:message output
  -novw                 Suppress warning when running with an XSLT 1.0 stylesheet
  -r classname          Use specified URIResolver class
  -p                    Recognize Saxon file extensions and query parameters
  -sa                   Schema-aware transformation
  -sall                 Strip all whitespace text nodes
  -signorable           Strip ignorable whitespace text nodes (default)
  -snone                Strip no whitespace text nodes
  -t                    Display version and timing information
  -T                    Set standard TraceListener
  -TJ                   Trace calls to external Java functions
  -TL classname         Set a specific TraceListener
  -u                    Names are URLs not filenames
  -v                    Validate source documents using DTD
  -val                  Validate source documents using schema
  -vlax                 Lax validation of source documents using schema
  -vw                   Treat validation errors on result document as warnings
  -w0                   Recover silently from recoverable errors
  -w1                   Report recoverable errors and continue (default)
  -w2                   Treat recoverable errors as fatal
  -x classname          Use specified SAX parser for source file
  -y classname          Use specified SAX parser for stylesheet
  -1.1                  Allow XML 1.1 documents
  -?                    Display this message
  param=value           Set stylesheet string parameter
  +param=file           Set stylesheet document parameter
  !option=value         Set serialization option

C:\>
```

Figure 11-1: Executing the Saxon XQuery command processor

I opted to use the .NET version of Saxon. You will need the .NET Framework version 1.1 to accomplish this. .NET can be downloaded from Microsoft at the following URL (you will have to search for .NET Framework version 1.1):

```
http://www.microsoft.com
```

Now go to the sourceforge website and download the .NET version of Saxon found at the following URL:

```
http://saxon.sourceforge.net/
```

Then download the latest .NET version of Saxon software. You will find instructions for installation in the documentation included with the download. The easiest method is as follows. Download the Zip file, in my case called saxonb8-7-1n.zip, and unzip the file's contents into a directory called c:\saxon (on a Windows computer). Then set the SAXON_HOME variable to c:\saxon and add the c:\saxon\bin directory to your path (the PATH environment variable).

The documentation for Saxon 8.7 (the version I downloaded) is included in a file called saxon-resources8-7-1.zip. Included in that Zip file is a large quantity of samples. The easiest way to make sure you have installed the software properly is to use the examples suggested in the installation documentation. Saxon is a command-line tool. In other words, it is executed in a DOS shell window on a Windows computer.

In my case, I navigate to the c:\saxon directory and execute these two examples, as included in the documentation. This first example gives a rather long-winded result for a graphic but it does function:

```
bin\Transform -t samples\data\books.xml samples\styles\books.xsl
```

This second example gives a nice short example, as shown in Figure 11-2:

```
bin\Query -t -s samples\data\books.xml samples\query\books-to-html.xq
```

```
C:\saxon>bin\Query -t -s samples\data\books.xml samples\query\books-to-html.xq
Saxon 8.7.1N from Saxonica
.NET 1.1.4322.573 on Microsoft Windows NT 5.0.2195.0
Compiling query from samples\query\books-to-html.xq
Compilation time: 187 milliseconds
Processing file:/C:/saxon/samples/data/books.xml
<?xml version="1.0" encoding="UTF-8"?>
<html>
   <head>
      <title>A list of books</title>
   </head>
   <body>
      <h1>A list of books</h1>
      <p>Here are some interesting books:</p>
      <ul>
         <li>
            <i>Jude the Obscure</i> by Thomas Hardy</li>
         <li>
            <1>Pride and Prejudice</i> by Jane Austen</li>
         <li>
            <i>Tess of the d'Urbervilles</i> by Thomas Hardy</li>
         <li>
            <i>The Big Over Easy</i> by Jasper Fforde</li>
         <li>
            <i>The Eyre Affair</i> by Jasper Fforde</li>
         <li>
            <i>Wuthering Heights</i> by Charlotte Bront½</li>
      </ul>
   </body>
</html>Execution time: 141 milliseconds

C:\saxon>_
```

Figure 11-2: Executing the Saxon .NET post-installation samples

Embedding XQuery Code into HTML

As demonstrated by Figure 11-2, the direct output in the shell contains HTML commands. How is this? XQuery commands can be embedded into HTML files. So let's demonstrate this by using an example not found in XQuery documentation. The following XQuery will find all cities in my entire demographics.xml file and then reorder them in reverse order of population so that the largest cities are returned first:

```
xquery version "1.0";
<HTML>
<HEAD><TITLE>Demographics</TITLE></HEAD>
<BODY>
<OL>
{
   for $n in //city[population>0]
   order by $n/population descending
   return <LI><I>{ string($n/name) }</I> has { string($n/population) } people</LI>
}
</OL>
</BODY></HTML>
```

Note in the preceding script how the XQuery code is embedded into HTML code by using the curly braces—for example, `<I>{ string($n/name) }</I>`. There is also the `xquery version` command at the beginning of the script. Also be aware of the multiple layers of embedding using the curly braces, which is actually a little confusing, particularly on the line containing the return clause: The HTML tags `<LI><I>` change back to HTML such that the following XQuery `string($n/name)` command must once again be enclosed in curly braces. That's the way it works.

Execute the preceding XQuery using the following Saxon command:

```
Query -s demographics.xml fig1103.xquery > fig1103.html
```

The HTML file is produced from the Saxon processing of the XQuery command by redirecting the Saxon output to an HTML file, rather than the shell display. I have also removed the –t (timing) option, which was in the Saxon examples.

This is a partial result of the preceding XQuery:

```
<?xml version="1.0" encoding="UTF-8"?>
<HTML>
    <HEAD>
        <TITLE>Demographics</TITLE>
    </HEAD>
    <BODY>
        <OL>
            <LI>
                <I>Tokyo</I> has 34000000 people</LI>
            <LI>
                <I>Mexico City</I> has 22350000 people</LI>
            <LI>
                <I>Seoul</I> has 22050000 people</LI>
            <LI>
                <I>New York</I> has 21800000 people</LI>
            <LI>
                <I>Sao Paulo</I> has 20000000 people</LI>
            ...
        </OL>
    </BODY>
</HTML>
```

Figure 11-3 shows the same result but as an HTML page executed in a browser.

Another way to get a numbered list into the output of a `for` loop is by using the `at` keyword as shown in this script:

```
for $n at $m in //city[population>0]
order by $n/population descending
return <city>{$m}. { string($n/name) } has { string($n/population) } people</city>
```

The result of the preceding script is shown in Figure 11-4.

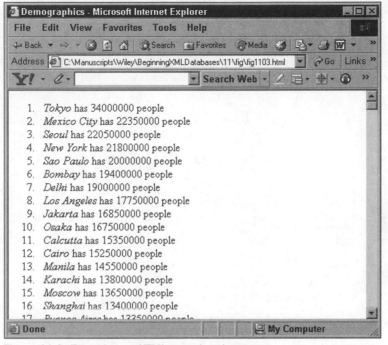

Figure 11-3: Executing an HTML page in a browser

```
C:\Manuscripts\Wiley\BeginningXMLDatabases\11\fig>Query -s demographics.xml fig1
104.xquery|more
<?xml version="1.0" encoding="UTF-8"?>
<city>79. Paris has 9900000 people</city>
<city>318. Chicago has 9700000 people</city>
<city>409. Lima has 8350000 people</city>
<city>405. Bogota has 8150000 people</city>
<city>312. Washington has 8050000 people</city>
<city>182. Nagoya has 8000000 people</city>
<city>127. Chungking has 7800000 people</city>
<city>204. Bangkok has 7800000 people</city>
<city>268. Madras has 7450000 people</city>
<city>167. Hong Kong has 7300000 people</city>
<city>286. Lahore has 7300000 people</city>
<city>309. San Francisco has 7200000 people</city>
<city>33. Johannesburg has 7150000 people</city>
<city>203. Taipei has 6900000 people</city>
<city>248. Bangalore has 6900000 people</city>
<city>38. Kinshasa has 6800000 people</city>
<city>338. Philadelphia has 6000000 people</city>
<city>158. Tientsin has 5950000 people</city>
<city>345. Dallas has 5850000 people</city>
<city>88. Ruhr has 5800000 people</city>
<city>324. Detroit has 5750000 people</city>
-- More --
```

Figure 11-4: Adding a list iterator to a for loop

Now let's go into some of the details and syntax of XQuery.

XQuery Terminology

XQuery has seven different types of nodes: element, attribute, text, namespace, processing-instruction, comment, and document. A document node is actually an XML document root node. Having read all the previous chapters in this book, it should be very clear what all these nodes are. Figure 11-5 shows a brief picture of some of the different types of nodes and atomic values that XQuery can read from an XML document.

XQuery is not constructed in XML but it is used to parse through XML documents.

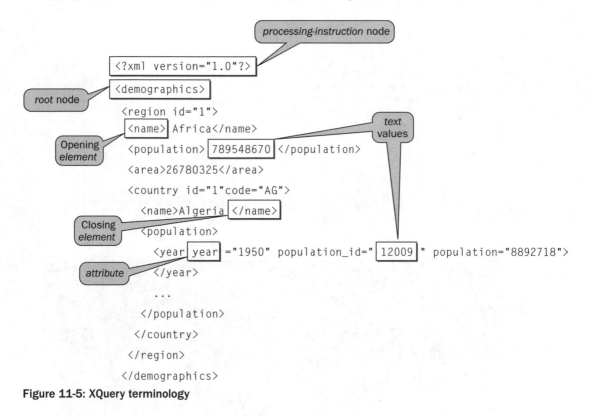

Figure 11-5: XQuery terminology

Other commonly used terms are as follows:

❑ **Atomic value:** A text value, having no children or parent node.

❑ **Item value:** This can be an atomic value or a node.

❑ **Parent:** Refers to the parent node of a node, generally referring to nodes and not atomic values.

❑ **Child:** Opposite of parent where a node can have zero or more nodes. A node that can have a child node, but does not, is referred to as an empty node.

❑ **Sibling:** A sibling is a node in the same collection that has the same parent node.

❑ **Ancestor:** Any node above the current node in a tree. For example, the parent, grandparent, great-grandparent, or the root node.

❑ **Descendant:** Any node below the current node. For example, child, grandchild, and so on.

All this terminology has been introduced in previous chapters.

XQuery Syntax

There are a number of general rules for XQuery syntax:

❑ XQuery commands and coding in general are all case sensitive, just as XML is.

❑ All nodes — as in elements, attributes, and variables — must be valid as XML names.

❑ Define variables using a $ character, as in $var.

❑ Include comments into XQuery scripts by enclosing as follows:

❑ If-then-else statements are permitted in XQuery as follows, where the if statement expression is enclosed in round brackets (parentheses):

```
if ( ...)
then ...
else ...
```

❑ Compare multiple values using standard arithmetic operators, such as =, !=, >, and <=.

❑ Compare individual values using eq, ne, gt, lt, ge, and le.

Functions in XQuery

As you have seen in the numerous examples already shown in this chapter, XPath 1.0 and XPath 2.0 functions, as presented in the previous chapters, can be used easily in XQuery. You can even custom build your own functions to use within an XQuery query using the following syntax, which is fairly consistent syntactically with many other programming languages, both declarative and procedural:

```
declare function prefix:function_name($parameter AS datatype) AS returnDatatype
{
   {(: ... :)}
};
```

A custom-built function can be called as any other function would. If the function is defined as having a prefix then the prefix must be included in the function call.

XQuery FLWOR

The XQuery FLWOR statement is a form of a `for` loop. In programming parlance, a `for` loop allows repetitive processing of all the items in a collection of items. In other words, a `for` loop allows the same processing to be executed against every item in a collection.

FLWOR stands for "For, Let, Where, Order By, and Return." What this means is that the `for` loop allows you to loop through multiple collection elements from one element to another. The `where` clause allows filtering of items to be used in the collection. So, you don't have to process all items in the collection. The `Order By` clause sorts the resulting collection of items sent back by the `return` clause. The `return` clause dictates specific data items that should be returned from a `for` loop.

This is a `doc` function in XPath 2.0, which finds all cities with a population of over 10 million people:

```
doc("demographics.xml")/demographics/region/country/city[population>10000000]
```

An XQuery equivalent of the preceding `doc` function would be as follows (you have seen this command previously):

```
for $i in doc("demographics.xml")/demographics/region/country/city
where $i/population>10000000
order by $i/name
return $i/name
```

FLWOR: The Basic for Loop and Return Clause

That's a bit of a complex `for` loop to begin with so let's retrogress somewhat and go through each part of a FLWOR expression in detail. Here's a very simple FLWOR expression comprising just a loop, an expression determining values in the collection looped through, and the collection returned:

```
xquery version "1.0";
<HTML><HEAD><TITLE>Demographics</TITLE></HEAD><BODY>
<OL>{
    for $n in //language[@name='Swazi']
    return <LI>Population is { string($n/male) } males</LI>
}</OL></BODY></HTML>
```

The boldfaced parts in the preceding script are XQuery code; everything else is HTML code used for beautification. The result is shown in Figure 11-6.

At this point I will stop using XQuery commands embedded into HTML scripts for the sake of simplicity with Saxon. Any subsequent use of HTML embedding later in this chapter is merely to beautify, and is not for any specific technical reason. This following script removes the HTML tags:

```
for $n in //language[@name='Swazi'] return $n/male
```

Figure 11-7 shows the Saxon shell with the result of executing the preceding script.

The `return` clause is used to return either whatever the `for` loop has found in its entirety, or a subset part of the `for` loop results. In the following example, the `for` loop finds all country nodes (including all child elements) within all regions. The `return` clause filters out the `for` loop results, returning only language nodes within all countries found by the `for` loop:

```
for $n in //region/country return $n//year/languages/language
```

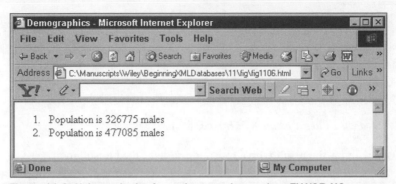

Figure 11-6: Using only the for and return clauses in a FLWOR XQuery statement

Figure 11-7: An FLWOR XQuery statement without using HTML

Figure 11-8 shows a partial result, containing language nodes, including child elements within each language element.

Figure 11-8: An FLWOR XQuery statement without using HTML

I can even add a root node and other nodes to the result shown in Figure 11-8, both within and outside of the `return` clause:

```
<lotsoflanguages>
{
    for $n in //region/country
    return <country> { $n//year/languages/language } </country>
}
</lotsoflanguages>
```

Curly braces are used to embed the XQuery code within XML tags.

Figure 11-9 shows a partial result with a root node added called lotsoflanguages.

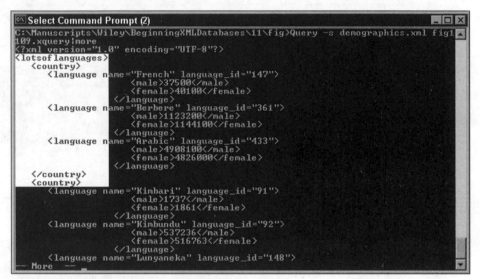

Figure 11-9: Adding XML tags using the return clause

FLWOR: Adding a where Clause

Now I will add the `where` clause to the previous `for` loop. As you see in the text that follows, all I do is move the predicate from the XPath expression to the `where` clause. The script that follows is the same example used in Figure 11-6, except in this case the `for` clause predicate has been shifted into a `where` clause:

```
xquery version "1.0";
<HTML><HEAD><TITLE>Demographics</TITLE></HEAD><BODY>
<OL>{
    for $n in //language
    where $n/@name='Swazi'
    return <LI>Population is { string($n/male) } males</LI>
}</OL></BODY></HTML>
```

As you can see in Figure 11-10, using the where clause does not change the result from that of Figure 11-6.

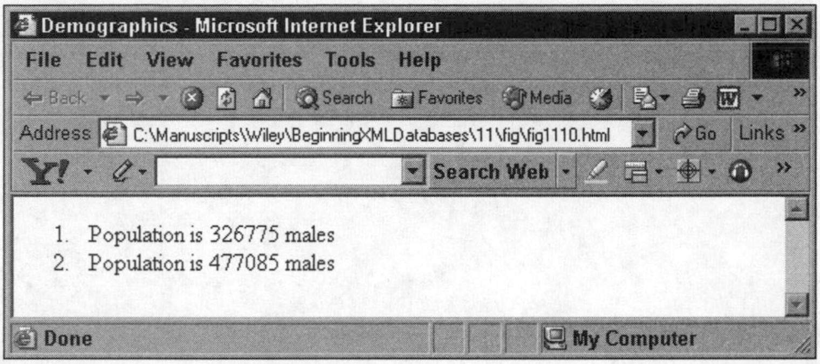

Figure 11-10: Substituting a where clause for a for clause predicate

Embedded HTML has been used for Figure 11-10 because the result is identical to that of Figure 11-6, which is an HTML-coded example.

As a final note, the where clause can use operators such as and and or in order to test multiple conditions, as in the following pseudocode examples:

```
where $x=1 and $y=2
```

and:

```
where $x=1 or $y=2
```

FLWOR: Adding an Order By Clause

The order by clause will sort the resulting collection of items sent back by the return clause. The order by will sort after the completion of the read performed by the for loop, not during the read I/O process. In other words, the order by clause resorts the result, but does not change the order in which the for loop accesses collection items.

Let's use a previously used example from Figure 11-3, which already has an order by clause:

```
for $n in //city[population>0]
order by $n/number(population) descending
return <city> { concat(string($n/name), string($n/population)) } </city>
```

The preceding order by clause is descending from the highest population to the lowest. If nothing is specified then the default will be an ascending sort, but ascending can be specified if you want. Then execute the preceding script using this command:

```
Query -s demographics.xml fig1111.xquery
```

The result appears in Figure 11-11, which shows the result sorted in order of language, unlike Figure 11-9, which was not sorted at all.

Figure 11-11: Using an FLWOR order by clause

You can also sort on multiple values. The following cities are sorted in ascending alphabetical order with decreasing populations:

```
for $n in //region/country/city
order by round(number($n/population div 1000000)) descending, $n/name ascending
return <city> {
   concat(
       string(round(number($n/population div 1000000)))
      ,string(' ')
      ,string($n/name)
   )
} </city>
```

In this example, city populations are divided into millions. As you can see in Figure 11-12, dividing populations into millions ensures that population values are repeated, thus showing sorting of city names within those repeated population numbers.

FLWOR: Declaring Variables with the Let Clause

The let clause will allow you to create a variable and assign a value to it:

```
let $maxLimit := 20000000
let $highDensity := //city[population > $maxLimit]
return $highDensity/name
```

Obviously a variable can be used later on in the XQuery FLWOR command but the result shown in Figure 11-13 describes all cities with a population of over 20,000,000 inhabitants.

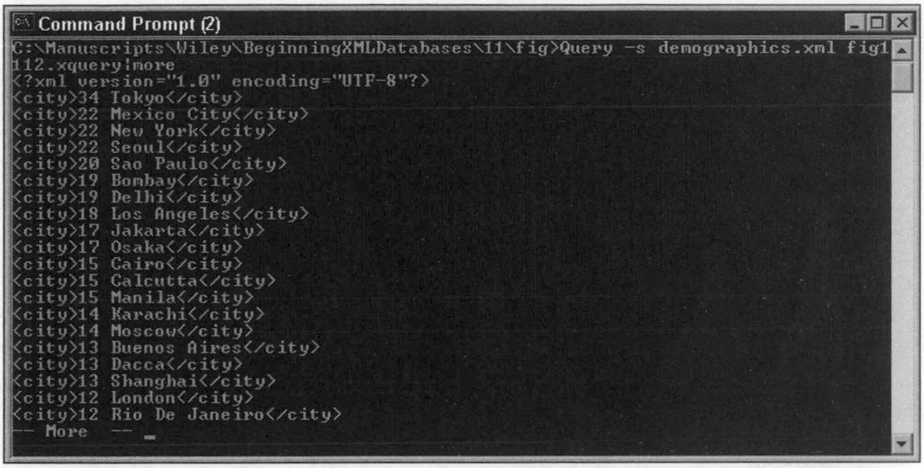

Figure 11-12: Sorting with multiple values in an FLWOR for loop

Figure 11-13: The `let` clause sets variables for subsequent use in a query.

FLWOR: Embedded for Loops and Communication

Multiple `for` loops can be embedded, one within another, simply by returning the result of one `for` loop, up into a calling `for` loop. Obviously, the result returned by an embedded `for` loop must be a properly formatted XML tree (including a root node). One important point to note is that you can pass the current value of the calling `for` loop into any child `for` loops, effectively allowing a one-to-many join. The following example finds all countries within each respective region:

```
<regions>
{
   for $n in //region
   return <region name="{$n/name}">
   {
      for $m in $n/country
      return <country name="{$m/name}"></country>
   }
   </region>
}
</regions>
```

The result of the preceding script is shown in Figure 11-14.

Figure 11-14: For loops can be embedded and values can be passed between the loops

The following example is an ugly kind of cross-join that I have seen mentioned in many places. Cross-joins are not really efficient, and are rarely used except in data warehouses for very large reports on even bigger amounts of data. XML document sizes are unlikely to get to data warehouse sizes any time soon. However, you can follow one `for` loop by another (without embedding), as follows:

```
for $n in ("A", "B")
for $m in ("i", "ii", "iii", "iv")
return concat($n, $m)
```

Syntactically you can achieve the same thing with the following XQuery code:

```
for $n in ("A", "B", "C"),
    $m in ("i", "ii", "iii", "iv")
return concat($n, $m)
```

A `for` loop does not have to read a collection from an XML document; it can also read literal values, as shown in the preceding code.

Figure 11-15 shows the result returned by the preceding two queries.

Figure 11-15: Cross-joins with multiple for loops

A `let` clause can also use literal values as a `for` loop can. In the following example, the `let` clause iterates between two values:

```
let $n := (1 to 3)
return <counter> { $n } </counter>
```

The result looks like this:

```
<?xml version="1.0" encoding="UTF-8"?>
<counter>1 2 3</counter>
```

XQuery in Oracle XML DB

Oracle XML DB is the Oracle XML Database software suite. Essentially, Oracle XML DB is a fancy name for all of the XML technology included with Oracle Database software. This includes all the tools and gadgets introduced in Chapter 5, plus a few other things such as handling of XQuery and XML Schemas. Chapter 5 covered the basics of XMLType data types in Oracle Database, plus basic coverage of XML data access coding standards, such as SQL/XML and changes to XML documents. Now you can expand on Oracle Database implementation of XML coverage and include some specific tools and functions, which can help execute XQuery queries in an Oracle database.

Oracle XML DB supports XQuery using two SQL/XML functions: `XMLQuery` and `XMLTable`. There is also a very simple-to-use SQL*Plus command called `XQUERY`, which allows SQL*Plus to be used in a very similar fashion to that of Saxon. `XQUERY` allows SQL*Plus to be used as an Oracle built-in shell tool (or command-line interpreter). The objective of SQL/XML is a combination of the best of both worlds of SQL and XML. The `XMLQuery` and `XMLTable` commands allow building of XML from relations, building of relations from XML, and querying of relational data as if it were XML data.

Oracle XML DB approaches XML data in two ways:

❑ **Unstructured XML:** There is no schema and XPath expressions evaluate XML data functionally (based on an XPath expression). An XML DOM structure is created for parsing, and any changes involve writing the entire XMLType data type structure back to disk (after in-memory changes).

❑ **Structured XML:** This is XML data with an Oracle relational table schema to back it up through an XML Schema definition (or XML Schema collections). This allows for translation between XML and SQL queries plus potentially partial updates. I will ignore this method for now, as being too Oracle Database–specific with respect to this part of this book. Additionally, XML Schemas are covered later on in this book.

Oracle database software uses various SQL coding tools—most are one form or another of a shell tool called SQL*Plus. SQL*Plus has a command called `XQUERY`, which accepts an expression that is a little of XPath and a little of SQL put together.

The following example selects all rows from the REGION table:

```
SET LONG 2000 WRAP ON LINESIZE 5000
xquery for $n in ora:view("REGION") return $n
/
```

The result of the preceding query is shown in Figure 11-16.

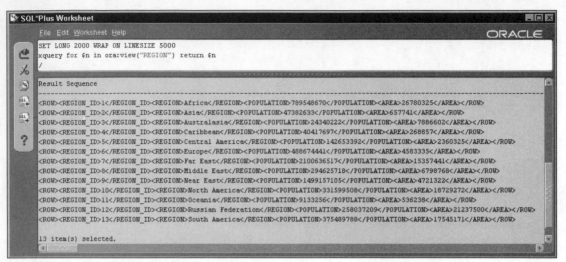

Figure 11-16: Using the SQL*Plus XQUERY command

The query shown in Figure 11-16 will not function in SQL*Plus in Oracle Database 10.2.

The XMLQuery and XMLTable functions allow for a powerful combination of SQL and XML capabilities. Using the XMLQuery and XML Table functions you can essentially pass data backward and forward between relational and XML data structures. These two functions are a little too complex for a book of this nature, and a lot of XML functionality for Oracle Database is covered in Chapter 5.

What Is XQueryX?

XQueryX is a variation on the XQuery XML document querying tool that is written in XML. The trouble is that all the complexity programmed into tools such as Saxon and Oracle XML DB has to be contained within the XML document structure of an XQueryX query. It can get very nasty. The coding of XQueryX queries is not complicated but when compared with the simplicity of XQuery, using XQueryX is not really worth the aggravation.

Without an example XQueryX query, XQueryX XML document construction requires explicit definition for all data, metadata, and programming constructs. So when including a for loop, as for an XQuery for loop, you have to code the for loop, the variable definitions, and the parameters passed in and out of the for loop. In this respect, XQueryX almost goes into the realm of tokenized programming — perhaps a little like writing a C programming language syntax compiler. That's too much for XML, and asking too much of developers. It is nice to do everything in one language (in this case), but in the case of queries, XQueryX appears impractical and perhaps even a little overzealous in its application of ensuring the globalized use of XML.

The downside to XQuery is that it is not written in XML. This is not really a problem in itself, except that in tandem with all other XML bits and pieces you have looked at in this book (excepting Oracle and SQL Server), everything else is written in XML. The beauty of a lot of the XML specifications from the W3C is that they are all written in the same language (XML). That XML coding is platform independent and vendor independent. And XML is very easy to code. My perspective is that if an XML project is beginning to look like it is getting too complex, then you may be overextending the capabilities of XML.

Why is XQuery not written in XML? Probably because XQueryX (the XML-constructed version of XQuery) is far too complex and thus unwieldy and awkward to use. Why use the something that is overcomplicated when there are easy-to-use, intuitive tools such as Saxon and Oracle XML DB available?

This chapter has expanded on XPath from the previous chapter, examining use of XPath expressions in XQuery commands. XQuery commands are used to submit data queries to XML documents, and sometimes XMLType data types in relational databases. The next chapter examines more specific areas of XML functionality including XLink, XPointer, XForms, and XML-FO.

Summary

In this chapter you learned that:

- ❑   XQuery commands are not written in XML.

- ❑   XQuery can be used to query XML data.

- ❑   XQuery has capabilities similar to a primitive form of SQL.

- ❑   XPath and XQuery share many components, especially functions and axes.

- ❑   Saxon is a very simple-to-use shell tool for executing XQueries.

- ❑   XQuery commands can be embedded with HTML text and tags.

- ❑   XQuery commands can be embedded with XML tags.

- ❑   XQuery terminology and syntax is common to much of XML.

- ❑   XQuery has a `for` loop called FLWOR.

- ❑   FLWOR represents "For, Let, Where, Order By, and Return."

- ❑   A `for` loop iterates through a collection (sequence) of sibling nodes.

- ❑   The FLWOR `where` clause filters out data.

- ❑   The FLWOR `order by` clause resorts data.

- ❑   The FLWOR `return` clause restricts what is returned from a `for` loop collection.

- ❑   XQuery and XPath allow construction of user-defined functions.

- ❑   Oracle Database has a specialized suite of capabilities it calls Oracle XML DB (Oracle XML Database).

- ❑   Oracle XML DB includes various functions allowing transformation between XML and relational data.

Exercises

1. What does FLWOR represent?

    a. For, Loop, When, Order, Replace

    b. For, Loop, Where, Order, Return

    c. For, Let, Where, Order, Replace

    d. For, Let, Where, Order By, Return

    e. None of the above

2. XQuery is written in XML. True or False?

3. Saxon allows for execution of XQuery queries. True or False?

Some Advanced XML Standards

Many of the advanced standards of XML are not essentially database-specific, but more front-end application coding-specific. Whereas your database stores your data, your front-end application is made up of the screens you use to communicate with that database.

So, topics such as XLink, XPointer, and XForms may not at first seem quite relevant to this text. However, in order to do XML justice, we have to at least touch on both database and application XML capabilities. And as you shall see in this chapter, front-end applications can sometimes be very closely related to database content. This is especially true in the case of XML documents, where an XML document can be both database and application driver. An XML document can be a database in itself (a native XML database). Additionally, application coding using tools such as XLink, XPointer, and XForms can generate front-end application display screens using XML document content. That XML document content is, of course, the very same native XML database.

There are no Try It Out sections in this chapter as the content of this chapter is primarily conceptual, but also introductory with respect to native XML database standards.

In this chapter you learn about:

- ❏ Generating links between XML documents using XLink
- ❏ Generating links between XML document fragments using XPointer
- ❏ How simple type XLinks link one XML document to another
- ❏ How extended type XLinks link many XML documents to many other XML documents
- ❏ The XForms model and how it generates entry screens
- ❏ All the aspects and capabilities of XForms
- ❏ How XForms binds display objects directly to the content of XML documents
- ❏ How XInclude merges multiple XML documents together

XLink and XPointer

XML varies in the meaning it applies to the results of output, such as transformation through XSL, or something like reading from a database using XQuery. One of the primary reasons for the enormous success of the Internet is the ability for web pages to link to one another all over the Internet. So, XML must provide that linking ability as well. This is because XML documents provide not only data, but also metadata, which adds meaning to data. Thus, links created using XML document data are likely to be flexible, if perhaps less predictable. Predictability is not a requirement. XLink and XPointer are XML standards established by the World Wide Web Consortium, intended to standardize the way in which hyperlinks between Internet pages are linked.

Web page hyperlinks (linking) are created and managed in XML using two parts: XLink (XML Linking Language) and XPointer (XML Pointing Language). XLink defines the standard by which web page hyperlinks are created. Those XLink hyperlink standards are thus universally understandable. XPointer refines XLink, allowing for pointing of hyperlinks to XML fragments within larger XML documents.

So, why is this stuff included in this book on XML and databases? The answer is simple. XML data can be stored in various databases, in various ways. Additionally, an XML document (or collection thereof), can exist as a native XML database in itself. Therefore, the building of HTML <A HREF . . . > (hyperlinks) in web pages, which are built from XML data, is dependent on XML content. Ultimately, those hyperlinks are very much dependent on the content of XML document data and metadata content.

What Is XLink?

In short, XLink lets you define links in a web page whose source is XML data, of one form or another. Essentially XLink enforces, or perhaps provides, a standard by which links can be generated from XML data. HTML uses the <A HREF ...> ... </A> tags to create links, linking from one web page to another. XLink allows creation of links similar to that of HTML pages. However, XLink is much more capable in that any XML document element can be created as a hyperlink. Additionally, XLink allows creation of links, which join multiple resources together, as opposed to just one page linking to another page for HTML.

The result is that any XML element in an XML document can be a link to another web page on the Internet. HTML is restricted to specific elements including <A> and <IMG> tags. Creating links in HTML documents requires that links be preconstructed as the HTML page is created (manually or automatically). XLinks are generated based on the content of an XML document, and require no human or programming intervention.

The problem with XML is that it can't provide links by itself and must rely on HTML to implement <A> tags for creating links. XLinks resolves this issue.

Simple XLinks

Why are XML links different from HTML links? HTML links are created using the <A> tag. XML elements are flexible and the tag name can be anything. So, an XML link tag name can be anything. As a result, a browser cannot decide on what is and is not a link in XML, as it can when parsing an <A> tag element in an HTML page. The obvious solution is to indicate somehow which elements in an XML document will become links.

The following example shows the syntax for creating hyperlinks (XLinks) in XML documents:

```
<?xml version="1.0"?>
<websites xmlns:xlink="http://www.w3.org/TR/xlink/">
    <website xlink:type="simple" xlink:href="http://www.yahoo.com">Yahoo</website>
    <website xlink:type="simple" xlink:href="http://www.google.com">Google</website>
    <website xlink:type="simple" xlink:href="http://www.ebay.com">EBay</website>
    <website xlink:type="simple" xlink:href="http://www.etrade.com">ETrade</website>
</websites>
```

Figure 12-1 shows what the preceding sample XML script looks like in a browser. Currently, this is just XML code. I am not as of yet actually doing anything useful—just demonstrating syntax.

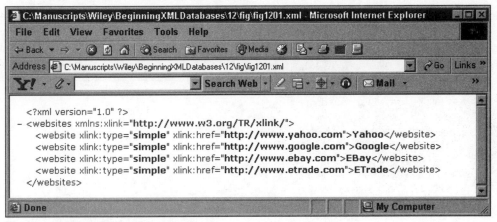

Figure 12-1: Simple XLinks in a browser

In Figure 12-1, attributes of the website element define that these elements are part of the XLink namespace (xlink), that the XLink is a simple type of XLink, and that the XLink linked URL is defined by the href attribute value.

Basic XLink attribute syntax allows for a number of attributes for an XLink value, as shown in Figure 12-2.

Attribute	Value	Description
xlink:type	simple, extended, locator, arc, resource, title, none	The type of link
xlink:href	The linked URL	A URL
xlink:show	Embed, new, replace, other, none	Where is the link opened
xlink:actuate	OnLoad, OnRequest, other, none	When is the link activated (read and shown)

Figure 12-2: The basics of XLink attributes

Figure 12-3 shows the previous example from Figure 12-1, including some new attribute settings.

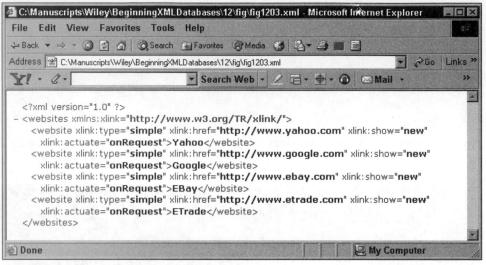

Figure 12-3: Adding more XLink attributes

You can now add an XSL script such as this one:

```
<HTML xmlns:xsl="http://www.w3.org/TR/WD-xsl"><BODY>
<TABLE CELLPADDING="5" CELLSPACING="1" BORDER="1">
<TH BGCOLOR="silver">Website</TH>
<xsl:for-each select="websites/website">
    <TR>
        <TD><xsl:value-of select="."/></TD>
    </TR>
</xsl:for-each>
</TABLE></BODY></HTML>
```

Next, you can add in the XSL script reference into the XML file:

```
<?xml version="1.0"?>
<?xml:stylesheet type="text/xsl" href="fig1204.xsl" ?>
<websites xmlns:xlink=" http://www.w3.org/TR/xlink/">
    <website xlink:type="simple" xlink:href="http://www.yahoo.com" xlink:show="new"
xlink:actuate="onRequest">Yahoo</website>
    <website xlink:type="simple" xlink:href="http://www.google.com" xlink:show="new"
xlink:actuate="onRequest">Google</website>
    <website xlink:type="simple" xlink:href="http://www.ebay.com" xlink:show="new" x
link:actuate="onRequest">EBay</website>
    <website xlink:type="simple" xlink:href="http://www.etrade.com" xlink:show="new"
xlink:actuate="onRequest">ETrade</website>
</websites>
```

The result looks as shown in Figure 12-4, and if my browser were XLink enabled, it would contain links to the websites, not just the text names of those websites.

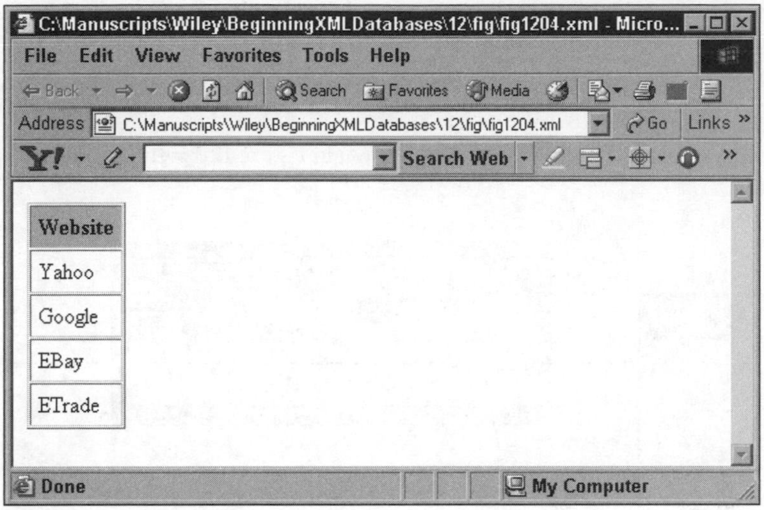

Figure 12-4: Adding links with XLink

You can make the example shown in Figure 12-4 function properly in Internet Explorer by substituting the `xlink:actuate` attribute with an `onClick` event by using an XML link element, and by setting link display attributes using a cascading style sheet (CSS).

XLink is not yet in production (recommended standard only) and does not actually work for my version of Internet Explorer (version 6). It is unlikely to work in version 7 either. XLink has not been implemented in industry to a point where it is an accepted industry standard. The onClick event is neither XML nor XLink; it is Dynamic HTML (DHTML). DHTML is a combination of HTML, JavaScript, and perhaps CSS. CSS is to HTML what XSL is to XML.

The following example demonstrates the preceding information:

```xml
<?xml version="1.0"?>
<?xml-stylesheet type="text/css" href="fig1205.css"?>
<websites>
    <link xmlns:xlink = "http://www.w3.org/TR/xlink/" xlink:type="simple" xlink:sho
w="new" xlink:href="http://www.yahoo.com" onClick="location.href='http://www.yahoo.
com'">Yahoo</link>
    <link xmlns:xlink = "http://www.w3.org/TR/xlink/" xlink:type="simple" xlink:sho
w="new" xlink:href="http://www.google.com" onClick="location.href='http://www.googl
e.com'">Google</link>
    <link xmlns:xlink = "http://www.w3.org/TR/xlink/" xlink:type="simple" xlink:sho
w="new" xlink:href="http://www.ebay.com" onClick="location.href='http://www.ebay.co
m'">EBay</link>
    <link xmlns:xlink = "http://www.w3.org/TR/xlink/" xlink:type="simple" xlink:sho
w="new" xlink:href="http://www.etrade.com" onClick="location.href='http://www.etrad
e.com'">ETrade</link>
</websites>
```

The CSS script looks like this when the link tag is defined as having the color blue, the link is underlined, and the mouse cursor changes to a hand when rolling over the link:

```
link { color: #0000FF; text-decoration: underline; cursor: hand }
```

The result of executing the preceding code is shown in Figure 12-5, which demonstrates the functioning XLink links.

Figure 12-5: Getting XLink links to function in Internet Explorer 6

Some More Advanced XLink Attributes

More detailed XLink attribute syntax is shown in Figure 12-6, which is in addition to that shown in Figure 12-2.

Attribute	Description	Value	Purpose
xlink:type	The type of the link. Minimum required attribute for an XLink. Requires href setting as well.	simple	
		extended	A linking element
		locator	The location of a remote resource
		arc	Traversal rules definition between different links
		resource	A link to a specific resource
		title	Readable title for a remote resource
		none	Don't link to anything
xlink:href	The linked URL	A URL	Equivalent of an HTML <A HREF ... > tag
xlink:show	Where is the link opened	Embed	Embed within existing content
		new	Add new content
		replace	Replace existing content
		other	Some other method other than the show function
		none	Don't show anything
xlink:actuate	When is the link activated (read and shown)	OnLoad	When XML document loaded
		OnRequest	Resource shown only when link clicked
		other	Leave to other software
		none	Don't activate (actuate)

Figure 12-6: More advanced XLink attribute details

There are of course even more attributes. Many of the other attributes, not shown in Figures 12-2 and 12-6, are applicable to specific types of XLink (xlink:type). This is why additional attributes have not as yet been displayed. Let's briefly summarize different XLink types once again:

- ❏ **simple:** Quite literally a simple link from one resource to another.

- ❏ **extended:** A more complex link where multiple links can be joined together based on a number of other attributes.

- ❏ **locator:** The exact location of a remote resource.

- ❏ **arc:** Rules that define how, or the path by which links are traversed.

- ❏ **resource:** A link to a specific resource link.

This leads us to various other XLink attributes, based on the meanings of the preceding noted XLink types, where the different attributes are applicable to different XLink types:

- ❏ **from and to:** The `xlink:from` and `xlink:to` attributes are specific to an arc XLink type because an arc defines a link between two resources.

- ❏ **arcrole:** This describes the role of a link in an arc between two links.

- ❏ **label:** An `xlink:title` gives an easily readable form to a resource. An `xlink:label` gives an easily readable form to a link (the underlined text things you see in the diagram in Figure 12-5).

- ❏ **role:** As opposed to `xlink:title`, which describes a resource in easily readable form, an `xlink:role` describes a resource in a form readable by a computer, not a person.

In the example shown in Figure 12-7, the `xlink:role` and `xlink:title` attributes are used to describe the remote resource that is linked to by the XLink.

Figure 12-7: More advanced XLink attribute details

Extended XLinks

The only XLink hyperlinks examined so far have been simple links. Extended links are also available but not widely supported. An extended XLink allows definition of multiple resources (targets of links) and many paths between all of those resources, plus paths between resources that can go in both directions.

Unlike simple XLink types, extended XLink types establish multiple connections between multiple resources, similar to the way that multiple inheritance can be constructed in an object application of an object database. Thus, extended XLinks can have child types, including locator, arc, resource, and title types. Locators are remote resources (website URLs). An arc has two child elements of `xlink:from` and `xlink:to`, defining the source and target resources of the arc link.

Extended XLink types essentially allow the linking of multiple XML documents with each other and others. The easiest way to demonstrate this is by example. Figure 12-8 shows a logical split for the demographics database (see Appendix B). Also in Appendix B is a reference to a URL on my website, which contains code for building an XML document equivalent to the relational database, entity relationship diagram (ERD), shown in Figure 12-8. What I have done in Figure 12-8 is to show a logical split in the demographics data by placing regional data on the right and more personal data on the left of the diagram. Thus, the personal information becomes language and occupation groupings, and regional data is represented by regions, countries, states, and cities.

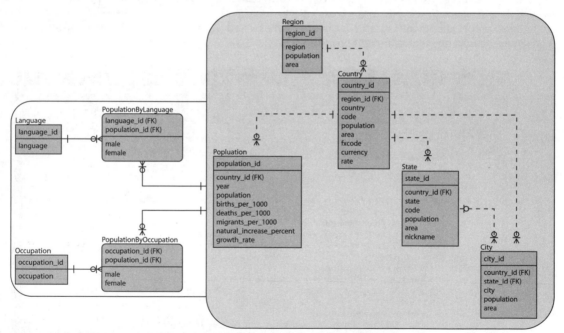

Figure 12-8: Splitting a database by metadata structure is logically visible.

What is the purpose of splitting the metadata, as shown in Figure 12-8? The idea is to create two separate demographics databases—this would create two separate XML documents—and then link those two documents together using XLink. However, I am not actually going to split data logically because it is extra effort, it messes up that nicely organized relational data structure, and there is an easier way. Figure 12-8 does demonstrate that something like this can be done.

An easier way to split demographic data is to split the data rather than the metadata. The easiest solution to splitting data is to split the entity at the highest level of the hierarchy. This assumes it does not have a huge number of records. This is unlikely in any sensibly designed relational database as that entity will likely be small and static in nature. In the case of the demographics database, the simplest split is separating all the data into regions, of which there are few. At a later stage, you can link the data across different regions using data items that are common to different regions, such as years, as demonstrated in the XML documents displayed in Figure 12-9.

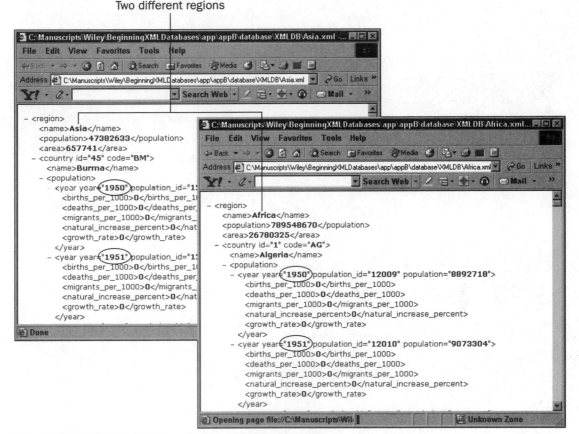

Figure 12-9: Splitting a database by data is physically visible.

So in Figure 12-9, I split demographics data based on regions, given that years are common to child elements of different regions. Then, you can form links between multiple regional XML documents for regions containing data based on common years. Those years are, in actuality, population figures for various countries, for various different years. Not all countries have data for all years, and some countries not even for any year at all. Additionally, all regions contain the same XML element structure in general so they all have common elements such as `<country>`, `<city>`, `<languages>`, or `<occupations>` for example. As shown in Figure 12-10, the parts of the XML document very clearly show that the year attribute of the `<year>` element, plus language and occupation names, are both common as data elements. Other factors such as country and city `<name>` elements could be construed as being linkable items but are unlikely to be useful.

```
<?xml version="1.0" ?>
- <demographics>
  - <region id="1">
      <name>Africa</name>
      <population>789548670</population>
      <area>26780325</area>
    + <country id="1" code="AG">


    - <country id="35" code="SF">
        <name>South Africa</name>
      - <population>
          <year year="1950" population_id="14547" population="13595840" />


        - <year year="1980" population_id="10186" population="29251588">
            <births_per_1000>33.2</births_per_1000>
            <deaths_per_1000>10.6</deaths_per_1000>
            <migrants_per_1000>.62</migrants_per_1000>
            <natural_increase_percent>2.26</natural_increase_percent>
            <growth_rate>2.322</growth_rate>
          - <languages>
            - <language name="Italian" language_id="27">
                <male>7438</male>
                <female>6920</female>
              </language>
            - <language name="Gujarati" language_id="45">
                <male>7568</male>
                <female>10189</female>
              </language>
            + <language name="Afrikaans" language_id="110">


            + <language name="Tamil Only" language_id="511">
            </languages>
          - <occupations>
            - <occupation name="Professional" occupation_id="1">
                <male>349040</male>
                <female>273240</female>
              </occupation>
            - <occupation name="Management" occupation_id="2">
                <male>123580</male>
                <female>13560</female>
              </occupation>


              </occupation>
            </occupations>
          </year>


      - <city id="164">
          <name>Johannesburg</name>
          <population>7150000</population>
        </city>
      </country>
    - <country id="36" code="SU">
        <name>Sudan</name>


      </country>
    </region>
</demographics>
```

Figure 12-10: Demographics data shows multiple links for both data and metadata.

So, when creating the demographics XML database in previous chapters (see Appendix B), I also created some separate documents for each region. An example region is shown in Figure 12-11.

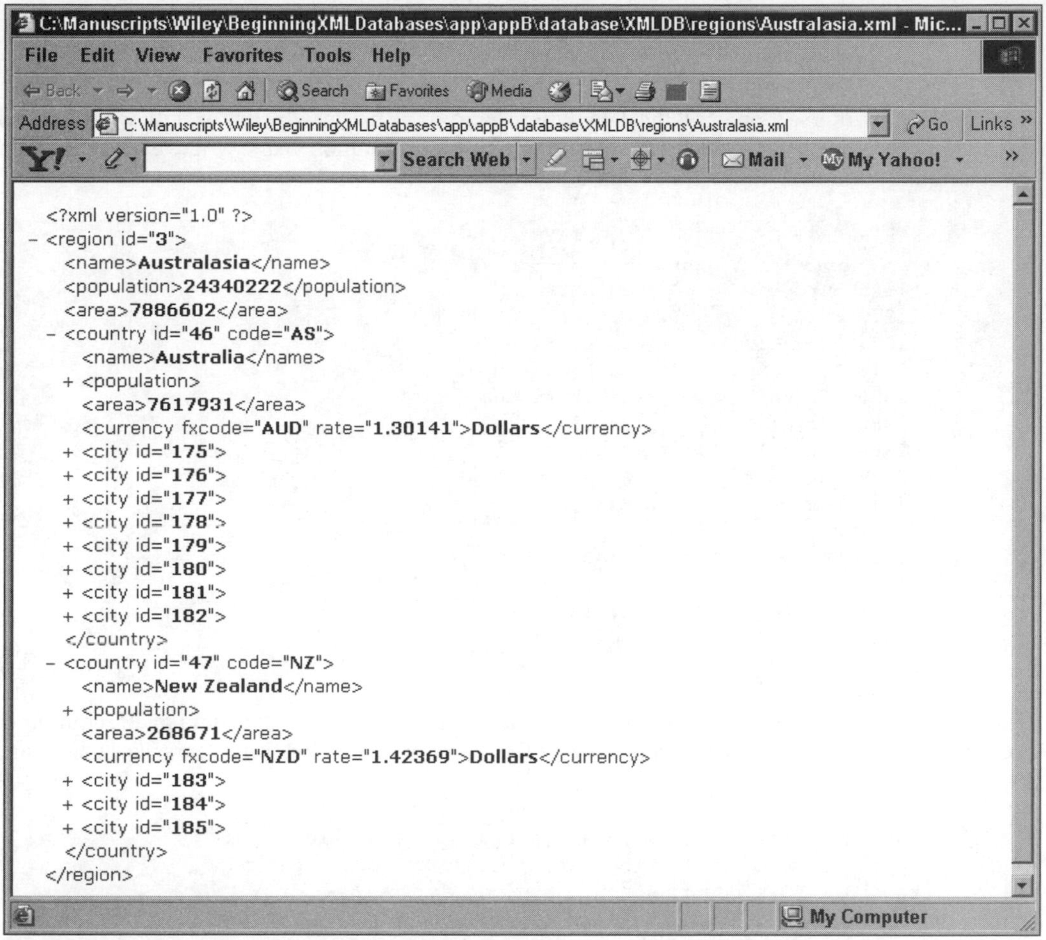

```
<?xml version="1.0" ?>
- <region id="3">
    <name>Australasia</name>
    <population>24340222</population>
    <area>7886602</area>
  - <country id="46" code="AS">
      <name>Australia</name>
    + <population>
      <area>7617931</area>
      <currency fxcode="AUD" rate="1.30141">Dollars</currency>
    + <city id="175">
    + <city id="176">
    + <city id="177">
    + <city id="178">
    + <city id="179">
    + <city id="180">
    + <city id="181">
    + <city id="182">
    </country>
  - <country id="47" code="NZ">
      <name>New Zealand</name>
    + <population>
      <area>268671</area>
      <currency fxcode="NZD" rate="1.42369">Dollars</currency>
    + <city id="183">
    + <city id="184">
    + <city id="185">
    </country>
  </region>
```

Figure 12-11: Demographics data is split into separate XML documents for each region.

The result of splitting regions from a single demographics XML document into one XML document for each region is a collection of regional XML documents. You can use this collection of multiple region XML documents to create sensible XLink connections across that collection.

Before creating XLink code, I query one of the relational databases, from which the XML demographics documents were created in the first place. I want to isolate some data that has year, language, and occupation values that are common to more than one region. The first step is to join all the tables in the database, with all the information I need:

```
select distinct year, region, country from (
select r.region, c.country, p.year, l.language, o.occupation
from region r join country c on(c.region_id=r.region_id)
   join population p on(p.country_id=c.country_id)
```

```
         join populationbylanguage pl on(pl.population_id=p.population_id)
            join populationbyoccupation po on(po.population_id=p.population_id)
               join language l on(l.language_id=pl.language_id)
                  join occupation o on(o.occupation_id=po.occupation_id)
   order by r.region, c.country, p.year, l.language, o.occupation
   ) order by 1,2,3;
```

The result is an intersection of all the data, where everything exists, which is exactly what I am looking for. In the preceding query I am trying to find regions with common years, where each year contains both language and occupation data. This is the result:

```
   YEAR  REGION              COUNTRY
   ----------  ----------------    ----------------
   1965  Europe              Bulgaria
   1970  Europe              Finland
   1974  Near East           Bangladesh
   1976  Australasia         Australia
   1980  Africa              South Africa
   1980  Africa              Zambia
   1980  Central America     Panama
   1980  Europe              Hungary
   1980  Far East            Malaysia
   1981  Far East            Nepal
   1981  North America       Canada
   1985  Europe              Finland
   1986  North America       Canada
   1988  South America       Bolivia
   1990  Far East            Singapore
```

The obvious conclusion from the preceding result is that 1980 has extensive data in all requirements for multiple regions. Now I am going to refine the query to find the regions, years, languages, and occupations:

```
select distinct region, year, language, occupation from (
select r.region, c.country, p.year, l.language, o.occupation
from region r join country c on(c.region_id=r.region_id)
   join population p on(p.country_id=c.country_id)
      join populationbylanguage pl on(pl.population_id=p.population_id)
         join populationbyoccupation po on(po.population_id=p.population_id)
            join language l on(l.language_id=pl.language_id)
               join occupation o on(o.occupation_id=po.occupation_id)
where r.region in('Africa','Central America','Far East')
and l.language in('English','French','Spanish','Espanol')
order by r.region, c.country, p.year, l.language, o.occupation
) order by 1,2,3;
```

This is the result of the preceding query, with records containing common values in one common group highlighted (1980, English, Agriculture):

REGION	YEAR	LANGUAGE	OCCUPATION
Africa	**1980**	**English**	**Agriculture**
Africa	1980	English	Clerical
Africa	1980	English	Labor
Africa	1980	English	Management
Africa	1980	English	Professional
Africa	1980	English	Sales
Africa	1980	English	Service
Africa	1980	English	Unknown
Africa	1980	French	Agriculture
Africa	1980	French	Clerical
Africa	1980	French	Labor
Africa	1980	French	Management
Africa	1980	French	Professional
Africa	1980	French	Sales
Africa	1980	French	Service
Africa	1980	French	Unknown
Central America	1980	Espanol	Agriculture
Central America	1980	Espanol	Clerical
Central America	1980	Espanol	Labor
Central America	1980	Espanol	Management
Central America	1980	Espanol	Professional
Central America	1980	Espanol	Sales
Central America	1980	Espanol	Service
Central America	1980	Espanol	Unknown
Far East	**1980**	**English**	**Agriculture**
Far East	1980	English	Clerical
Far East	1980	English	Labor
Far East	1980	English	Management
Far East	1980	English	Professional
Far East	1980	English	Sales
Far East	1980	English	Service
Far East	1980	English	Unknown
Far East	1990	English	Agriculture
Far East	1990	English	Clerical
Far East	1990	English	Labor
Far East	1990	English	Management
Far East	1990	English	Professional
Far East	1990	English	Sales
Far East	1990	English	Unknown

One interesting point about the preceding query is that I am searching for the Spanish language as being either Spanish or Espanol. Obviously, demographics data is reliable but often sparse, haphazard, and variant. However, this is another factor that can be used to demonstrate how well generic URL linking can function with XLink, which you will examine shortly. Ultimately, it makes sense to link the preceding language data with the region of Europe, which is of course the original source of the English, French, and Spanish (or Espanol) languages.

So, now let's try to link some of the regions together using XLink, based on common data values between the different regions. Those common data values are quite clearly the years, languages, and occupations. Let's use just Africa and Europe as an example in this case. Because both are regional XML fragments, both begin as regions:

```xml
<?xml version="1.0"?>
<regions>
   <link xmlns:xlink = "http://www.w3.org/TR/xlink/" xlink:type="extended">
      <region xlink:type="locator" xlink:label="region" xlink:href="Africa.xml"/>
      <region xlink:type="locator" xlink:label="region" xlink:href="Europe.xml"/>
   </link>
</regions>
```

The result of the preceding script is shown in Figure 12-12.

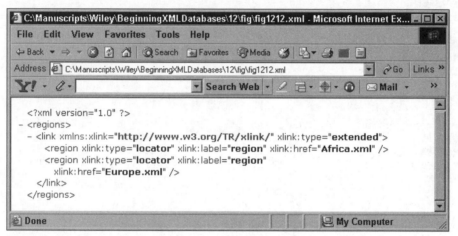

Figure 12-12: Basic XML interpretation of XLink

Now I can define both regions as containers for regions, years, languages, and occupations:

```xml
<?xml version="1.0"?>
<regions>
   <link xmlns:xlink = "http://www.w3.org/TR/xlink/" xlink:type="extended">
      <region xlink:type="locator" xlink:label="africa" xlink:href="Africa.xml"/>
      <region xlink:type="locator" xlink:label="europe" xlink:href="Europe.xml"/>
      <year xlink:type="locator" xlink:label="1980" xlink:href="Africa.xml"/>
      <year xlink:type="locator" xlink:label="1980" xlink:href="Europe.xml"/>
      <language xlink:type="locator" xlink:label="english"
         xlink:href="Africa.xml"/>
      <language xlink:type="locator" xlink:label="english"
         xlink:href="Europe.xml"/>
      <occupation xlink:type="locator" xlink:label="agriculture"
         xlink:href="Europe.xml"/>
      <occupation xlink:type="locator" xlink:label="agriculture"
         xlink:href="Europe.xml"/>
   </link>
</regions>
```

The result of the preceding script is shown in Figure 12-13.

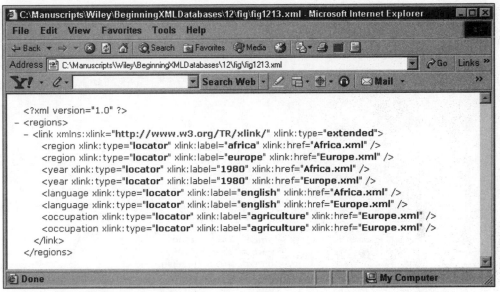

Figure 12-13: Adding labels within labels using XLink

Now I need to refine the preceding script, adding arcs to connect common data elements between the two different XML documents. You do this using arcs:

```xml
<?xml version="1.0"?>
<regions>
   <link xmlns:xlink = "http://www.w3.org/TR/xlink/" xlink:type="extended">
      <region xlink:type="locator" xlink:role="africa" xlink:href="Africa.xml"/>
      <region xlink:type="locator" xlink:role="europe" xlink:href="Europe.xml"/>
      <year xlink:type="locator" xlink:label="1980" xlink:href="Africa.xml"/>
      <year xlink:type="locator" xlink:label="1980" xlink:href="Europe.xml"/>
      <language xlink:type="locator" xlink:label="english"
         xlink:href="Africa.xml"/>
      <language xlink:type="locator" xlink:label="english"
         xlink:href="Europe.xml"/>
      <occupation xlink:type="locator" xlink:label="agriculture"
         xlink:href="Europe.xml"/>
      <occupation xlink:type="locator" xlink:label="agriculture"
         xlink:href="Europe.xml"/>
      <bind xlink:type="arc" xlink:from="africa" xlink:to="1980"/>
      <bind xlink:type="arc" xlink:from="europe" xlink:to="1980"/>
      <bind xlink:type="arc" xlink:from="africa" xlink:to="english"/>
      <bind xlink:type="arc" xlink:from="europe" xlink:to="english"/>
      <bind xlink:type="arc" xlink:from="africa" xlink:to="agriculture"/>
      <bind xlink:type="arc" xlink:from="europe" xlink:to="agriculture"/>
   </link>
</regions>
```

The result of the preceding script is shown in Figure 12-14.

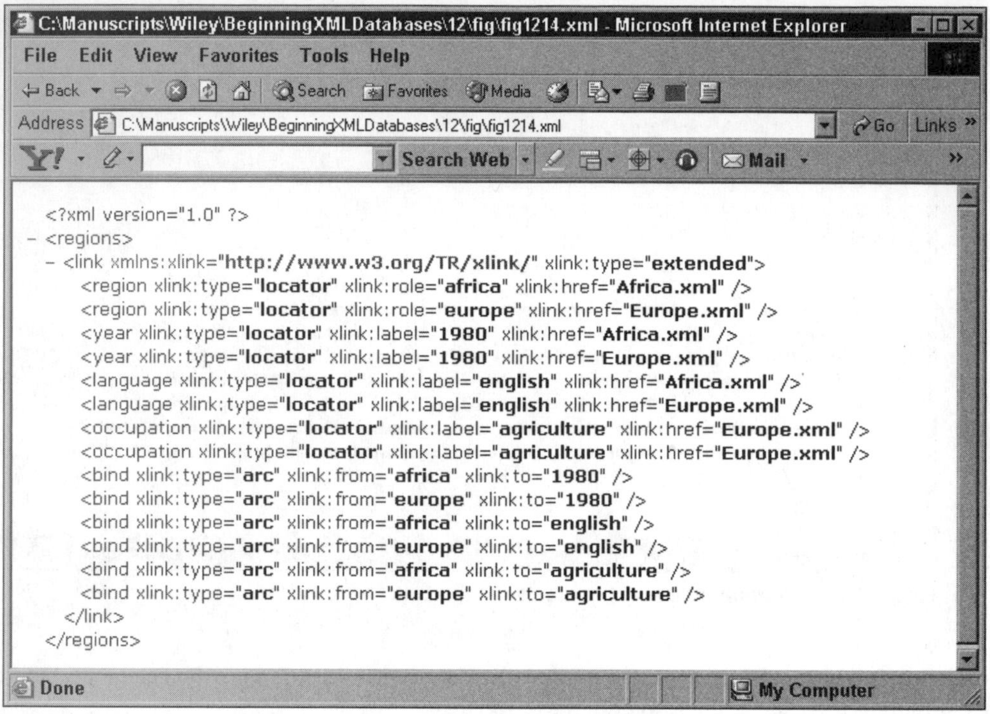

Figure 12-14: Connect data elements in XLink using arcs.

What I have done in the preceding script is change the `<region>` element XLinks to roles and added arcs connecting all defined regions to the year of 1980, the English language, and the occupation of Agriculture. This seems a little convoluted but what has actually been done is that the two regional XML documents (Africa.xml and Europe.xml) have been connected based on years, languages, and occupations. Yes, this implementation will cause conflict because the same labels are used for different things. A solution is to create three separate XLink XML documents, as opposed to splitting up the data into its nice and neat little boxes. In other words, don't fix the data to suit XLink; change XLink definitions to suit the data. Otherwise, why link both with XLink. So, each region needs to link to years, occupations, and languages, both within itself and to all other regions. However, there is no reason to place the years, occupations, and languages within the same definition. This script defines years:

```
<?xml version="1.0"?>
<regions>
   <link xmlns:xlink = "http://www.w3.org/TR/xlink/" xlink:type="extended">
      <region xlink:type="locator" xlink:role="africa" xlink:href="Africa.xml"/>
      <region xlink:type="locator" xlink:role="europe" xlink:href="Europe.xml"/>
      <year xlink:type="locator" xlink:label="africa1980" xlink:href="Africa.xml"/>
      <year xlink:type="locator" xlink:label="europe1980" xlink:href="Europe.xml"/>
```

```
            <bind xlink:type="arc" xlink:from="africa" xlink:to="africa1980"/>
            <bind xlink:type="arc" xlink:from="africa" xlink:to="europe1980"/>
            <bind xlink:type="arc" xlink:from="europe" xlink:to="africa1980"/>
            <bind xlink:type="arc" xlink:from="europe" xlink:to="europe1980"/>
        </link>
    </regions>
```

The result of the preceding script is shown in Figure 12-15.

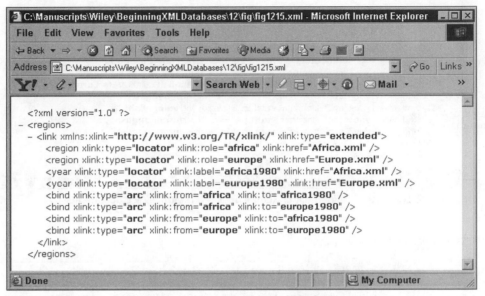

Figure 12-15: XLink can refine links between multiple XML documents.

This script defines languages:

```
<?xml version="1.0"?>
<regions>
    <link xmlns:xlink = "http://www.w3.org/TR/xlink/" xlink:type="extended">
        <region xlink:type="locator" xlink:role="africa" xlink:href="Africa.xml"/>
        <region xlink:type="locator" xlink:role="europe" xlink:href="Europe.xml"/>
        <language xlink:type="locator" xlink:label="africaenglish"
           xlink:href="Africa.xml"/>
        <language xlink:type="locator" xlink:label="europeenglish"
           xlink:href="Europe.xml"/>
        <bind xlink:type="arc" xlink:from="africa" xlink:to="africaenglish"/>
        <bind xlink:type="arc" xlink:from="africa" xlink:to="africaenglish"/>
        <bind xlink:type="arc" xlink:from="europe" xlink:to="europeenglish"/>
        <bind xlink:type="arc" xlink:from="europe" xlink:to="europeenglish"/>
    </link>
</regions>
```

The result of the preceding script is shown in Figure 12-16.

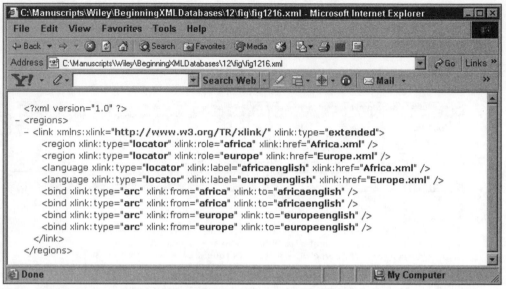

Figure 12-16: Further refinement of XLinks between multiple XML documents

This script defines occupations:

```xml
<?xml version="1.0"?>
<regions>
    <link xmlns:xlink = "http://www.w3.org/TR/xlink/" xlink:type="extended">
        <region xlink:type="locator" xlink:role="africa" xlink:href="Africa.xml"/>
        <region xlink:type="locator" xlink:role="europe" xlink:href="Europe.xml"/>
        <language xlink:type="locator" xlink:label="africaagriculture"
            xlink:href="Africa.xml"/>
      <language xlink:type="locator" xlink:label="europeagriculture"
            xlink:href="Europe.xml"/>
        <bind xlink:type="arc" xlink:from="africa" xlink:to="africaagriculture"/>
        <bind xlink:type="arc" xlink:from="africa" xlink:to="africaagriculture"/>
        <bind xlink:type="arc" xlink:from="europe" xlink:to="europeagriculture"/>
        <bind xlink:type="arc" xlink:from="europe" xlink:to="europeagriculture"/>
    </link>
</regions>
```

The result of the preceding script is shown in Figure 12-17.

Now imagine the following scenario. You use all the possible regions, years, languages, and occupations—from the entire demographics set of data (see Appendix B). The result is a lot of complexity and a lot of *XLinking*. Too much perhaps. The real question could be something different. How much complexity can be introduced using something like XLink? And still you need to retain the desired flexibility. There may be better methods of resolving generic linking between XML data, which may of course be why XLink does not have a reputation for being widely implemented. Application level coding can also resolve these types of issues. So, perhaps much like Native XML databases and their practicality in relation to well-established and industry-tested relational databases (with XMLType data types added in), too much of a good thing (XML and XLink) may not always be quite as good a thing as you might think.

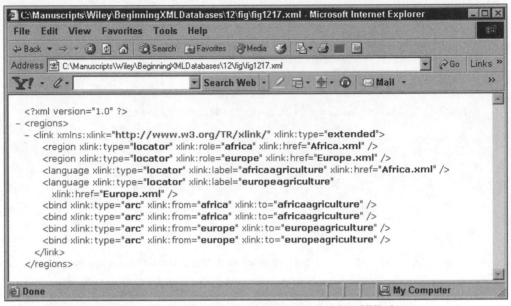

Figure 12-17: And yet further refinement of XLinks between multiple XML documents

What Is XPointer?

For the demographics XML document (database), it might be best to leave the data all in a single document. Then you can link across that document, connecting things such as common valued years, languages, and occupations, using XPointer definitions. XPointer allows connecting of XLink definitions between different points within the same XML document. It is still probable that the result could be unwanted and unmanageable complexity. Additionally, the simplification of data into a single demographics XML document might introduce excessive cross linking both between and within different regions.

So, what is XPointer and what does it do? Let's begin this explanation by using simple HTML. Examine the HTML script that follows. Note how the <A NAME> and <A HREF> tags are highlighted:

```
<HTML>
<HEAD><TITLE>Links Within a Page in HTML - An Alphabetical Index</TITLE></HEAD>
<BODY>

<A NAME="top"><B><FONT size="3" COLOR="red">Index</FONT></B></A>
<A HREF="#A">A</A> <A HREF="#B">B</A> <A HREF="#C">C</A>
<A HREF="#D">D</A> <A HREF="#E">E</A> <A HREF="#F">F</A>
<A HREF="#G">G</A> <A HREF="#H">H</A> <A HREF="#I">I</A>
<A HREF="#J">J</A> <A HREF="#K">K</A> <A HREF="#L">L</A>
<A HREF="#M">M</A> <A HREF="#N">N</A> <A HREF="#O">O</A>
```

```
<A HREF="#P">P</A> <A HREF="#Q">Q</A> <A HREF="#R">R</A>
<A HREF="#S">S</A> <A HREF="#T">T</A> <A HREF="#U">U</A>
<A HREF="#V">V</A> <A HREF="#W">W</A> <A HREF="#X">X</A>
<A HREF="#Y">Y</A> <A HREF="#Z">Z</A><HR>

<A NAME="A"><B><FONT size="3" COLOR="red">A</FONT></B></A>
<UL>
 <LI>Aardvaark
 <LI>Able
</UL>
<A HREF="#top">Index</A><HR>

<A NAME="B"><B><FONT size="3" COLOR="red">B</FONT></B></A>
<UL>
 <LI>Beer
 <LI>Beer Belly
 <LI>Bat
 <LI>Ball
</UL>
<A HREF="#top">Index</A><HR>
...
</BODY></HTML>
```

As shown in Figure 12-18, `<A HREF>` defines a link and `<A NAME>` defines a link target within the same document.

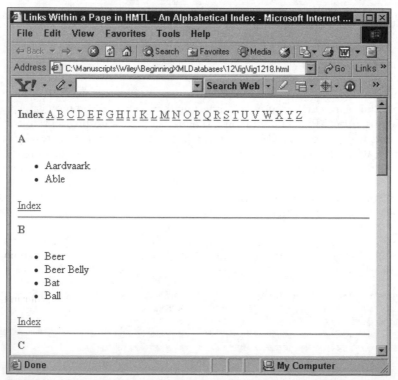

Figure 12-18: Demographics is split into separate regional XML documents for each region.

The objective of using XPointer is to prove the same function as shown in Figure 12-18, allowing pointing within a document. However, XPointer goes a little further, allowing pointing to a point within the same document or another document. In other words, XLink provides a link to the same, or another, XML document. XPointer enhances (or extends) the functionality of XLink by allowing a link to a specific point within the same or another XML document.

So, you can use XPointer to link to an XML fragment (part of an XML document). Let's use our various regional XML documents — both source and target documents. As with HTML, you use the # (or hash) character in order to define an XPointer source and target within an XML document. The difference between HTML and XML/XLink/XPointer, when pointing into documents using XML, is that the points are flexible. In HTML, the points are not flexible. This flexibility is based on the fact that XML is not only flexible in itself, but also that the XML document is a database as well. A database is a database because its content (its data) is flexible.

This is a previous example that uses XLink to join multiple regional documents to one another:

```xml
<?xml version="1.0"?>
<regions>
   <link xmlns:xlink = "http://www.w3.org/TR/xlink/" xlink:type="extended">
      <region xlink:type="locator" xlink:role="africa" xlink:href="Africa.xml"/>
      <region xlink:type="locator" xlink:role="europe" xlink:href="Europe.xml"/>
      <year xlink:type="locator" xlink:label="1980" xlink:href="Africa.xml"/>
      <year xlink:type="locator" xlink:label="1980" xlink:href="Europe.xml"/>
      <language xlink:type="locator" xlink:label="english"
         xlink:href="Africa.xml"/>
      <language xlink:type="locator" xlink:label="english"
         xlink:href="Europe.xml"/>
      <occupation xlink:type="locator" xlink:label="agriculture"
         xlink:href="Europe.xml"/>
      <occupation xlink:type="locator" xlink:label="agriculture"
         xlink:href="Europe.xml"/>
      <bind xlink:type="arc" xlink:from="africa" xlink:to="1980"/>
      <bind xlink:type="arc" xlink:from="europe" xlink:to="1980"/>
      <bind xlink:type="arc" xlink:from="africa" xlink:to="english"/>
      <bind xlink:type="arc" xlink:from="europe" xlink:to="english"/>
      <bind xlink:type="arc" xlink:from="africa" xlink:to="agriculture"/>
      <bind xlink:type="arc" xlink:from="europe" xlink:to="agriculture"/>
   </link>
</regions>
```

What you really want to do is to allow the various regions to be connected by their years, languages, and occupations. For example, the current XLink connections, shown in the preceding script, link the document of Africa.xml directly to the entire document of Europe.xml. What you want to do is to link the year of 1980 (in Africa.xml) to the year of 1980 (in Europe.xml). You need to point from fragment to fragment. Why? It's much more efficient.

So, how do you point to XML fragments? Consider the SQL query output earlier in this chapter, showing various countries with data in the year of 1980:

```
1980  Africa            South Africa
1980  Africa            Zambia
1980  Central America   Panama
1980  Europe            Hungary
1980  Far East          Malaysia
```

You know already from previous SQL query executions that the preceding countries have common languages and occupations in the year of 1980. You also know that the different countries are stored in different regional XML documents covering Africa, Central America, Europe, and the Far East. You create XPointer fragment links with the following syntax:

```
#xpointer(id("<value>"))
```

So, if I change the preceding syntax to this:

```
#xpointer(id("35"))
```

or this:

```
#xpointer(code("SF"))
```

you will find the country of South Africa, as shown in Figure 12-19.

```
    </country>
 -  <country id="35" code="SF">
      <name>South Africa</name>
    - <population>
        <year year="1950" population_id="14547" population="13595840" />
```

```
 -  <year year="1980" population_id="10186" population="29251588">
      <births_per_1000>33.2</births_per_1000>
      <deaths_per_1000>10.6</deaths_per_1000>
      <migrants_per_1000>.62</migrants_per_1000>
      <natural_increase_percent>2.26</natural_increase_percent>
      <growth_rate>2.322</growth_rate>
    - <languages>
```

```
 +  <language name="English" language_id"299">
 -  <language name="German" language_id="366">
      <male>20849</male>
      <female>20208</female>
    </language>
```

Figure 12-19: A snapshot of different parts of the Africa.xml document

An XLink link can be built as follows:

```
xlink:href="Europe.xml#xpointer(id('35'))"
```

So, you can alter the previous example as follows:

```
<?xml version="1.0"?>
<regions>
   <link xmlns:xlink = "http://www.w3.org/TR/xlink/" xlink:type="extended">
      <year xlink:type="simple" xlink:href="Africa.xml#xpointer(year('1980'))"/>
```

```
          <year xlink:type="simple" xlink:href="Europe.xml#xpointer(year('1980'))"/>
          <language xlink:type="simple"
              xlink:href="Africa.xml#xpointer(name('English'))"/>
          <language xlink:type="simple"
              xlink:href="Europe.xml#xpointer(name('English'))"/>
          <occupation xlink:type="simple"
              xlink:href="Africa.xml#xpointer(name('Agriculture'))"/>
          <occupation xlink:type="simple"
              xlink:href="Europe.xml#xpointer(name('Agriculture'))"/>
      </link>
  </regions>
```

The result of the preceding script is shown in Figure 12-20.

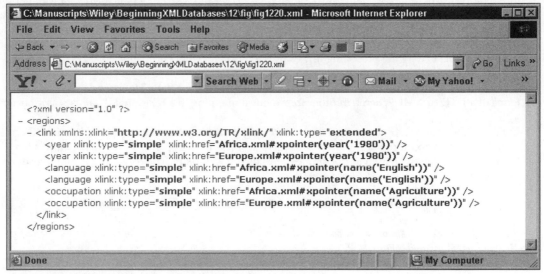

Figure 12-20: Using XPointer in Internet Explorer

As a side issue, there is a benefit to using an attribute called id in that XPointer doesn't need the syntax to be specific about the code id or even the term xpointer:

```
xlink:href="Europe.xml#35"
```

The only problem I find with the preceding example is that of conflicting instructions and methods of resolving these issues. For example, in contrast to the preceding example, the following example points to the element with the name country, i.e. <country>:

```
link:href="Europe.xml#country"
```

Also, I can find examples such as the following, which allow you to find an element based on the value of an attribute where that attribute is called id:

```
link:href="Europe.xml#country(id)"
```

And there are things like this where you can also find child sequences (collection elements) based on their sequential positions in the collection:

```
link:href="Europe.xml#country(id/2/3)"
```

Or even this to find a child element in a collection:

```
link:href="Europe.xml#id('35').child(4, item)"
```

The preceding examples contradict the initial example using the id attribute name and are all essentially dependent upon a DTD (Document Type Definition), which can underlie an XML document with a relational database structure. So far in this book I have avoided DTDs and XML Schemas and will continue to do so until the next chapter. Why? Because Chapters 5 and 6 described changing a relational database into a native XML database, using XML data types. DTDs and XML Schemas form a logical mapping between XML and relational database structure. With the advent of XML data types, this method is somewhat out-of-date. Additionally, XPath 2.0 and XQuery 1.0 do not rely on DTDs and XML Schemas, but more or less use XML data as a database (the equivalent of XML data type storage into a relational database). This is why the preceding few examples are somewhat confusing.

You can use XPath functionality and expressions with XPointer. XPath 2.0 is not dependent on the existence of a DTD or XML Schema in order to provide a mapping to a relational database table structure.

In reality, the original XPointer specification was highly complex and unpopular. Utilizing XPath expressions to define XPointer makes perfect sense. The result is utilizing already learned XPath syntax, rather than introducing a further layer of complexity to define XPointers. The following example uses an XPath expression to point to a particular country:

```
link:href="Europe.xml#xpointer(//country[name="France"])
```

The xpointer() *syntax must be used, obviously to distinguish XPointer and other syntax definitions such as XLink and XPath itself.*

This example finds the name of the city, in the first country, listed under the region of Africa:

```
link:href="Europe.xml#xpointer
    (/demographics/region[name="Africa"]/country[position()=1]/city/name)
```

My objective here was not to utilize simple XML document examples in order to demonstrate XLink and XPointer, perhaps too vaguely. The demographics data is semi–real world data but it is fairly large. In general, demographics data is relatively static (meaning it changes perhaps on an annual rather than daily basis). In fact, commercial applications performing transactions for customer-facing systems could likely perform hundreds, if not millions, of transactions per second. eBay and eTrade are good examples of database requirements with millions of transactions per second. So my demographics data is not real world on that scale, but compared to XLink and XPointer examples I find online (XML documents with ten lines each), my demographics XML document of 4GB will suffice.

How useful are XLink and XPointer in a real-world scenario?

As with XLink, XPointer is not yet in production (a recommended standard only). XPointer does not work for my version of Internet Explorer (version 6). It is unlikely to work in version 7 either.

XForms and HTML Form Generation

XForms is a generic (generate from XML content), the XML equivalent of creating static forms using HTML. Like HTML forms, XForms is used to create the ability for end users to input information into an application, ultimately changing data in a database. So, XForms performs the same function as HTML forms does, except that it is XML driven. Thus it can be easily data driven, allowing for more specific input screens, such as unique input screens for individual users, or groups of users.

The XForms Model

XForms utilizes what it calls the XForms Model, defining a template for data that will be collected using a form. An XForms model defines what a form is, the data it contains, and what its function is. Then there are the form input fields, which define input fields and the way they are displayed. So, let's examine the basic structure of the XForms model step-by-step. The XForms model conformant script is wrapped by the <model> tag:

```
<xforms>
    <model>
        <instance>
            <region>
                <name></name>
                <population></population>
                <area></area>
            </region>
        </instance>
        <submission id="form1" action="submitted.asp" method="get"/>
    </model>
</xforms>
```

Additionally, the <instance> tag defines the template for how data is gathered. In actuality, the <instance> tag defines the structure of the resulting XML data document. And the <submission> tag tells how data is submitted. Notice the form identifier, action, and method attributes — just as for HTML.

Details of HTML are not included in this book but can be found in innumerate books available in bookstores.

Now back to the <instance> tag. If you know anything about applications, you will realize that XForms is a front-end applications screen generator. So, an SLE form is a Single Line Entry screen. In a relational database, an SLE form essentially adds a single object, usually a single row to a single table. This depends on the granularity of the relational database model. So, to add a city using the model detailed by the preceding example, the resulting XML data might look something like this:

```
<region>
    <name>Africa</name>
    <population>789548670</population>
    <area>26780325</area>
</region>
```

Now to get the data into the XML dataset, you need to add what are called XForms controls into the `<submission>` tag. So, you can expand on the previous example as follows:

```xml
<?xml version="1.0"?>
<xforms>
    <model>
        <instance>
            <region>
                <name></name>
                <population></population>
                <area></area>
            </region>
        </instance>
        <submission id="form1" action="submitted.asp" method="get">
            <input ref="name"><label>Region</label></input>
            <input ref="population"><label>Population</label></input>
            <input ref="area"><label>Area</label></input>
            <submit submission="form1"><label>Submit</label></submit>
        </submission>
    </model>
</xforms>
```

Figure 12-21 shows the preceding script in Internet Explorer.

XForms Namespaces

Processing of XForms is accessible from the XForms namespace and may be built into the browser you are using. The XForms processing namespace is as shown in the adaptation to the following script, which assigns the XForms namespace to the HTML page and thus, also all XForms elements to that namespace so that they are not interpreted as HTML commands:

```html
<html xmlns:xf="http://www.w3.org/2002/xforms">
<head>
    <xf:model>
        <xf:instance>
            <region>
                <name/>
                <population/>
                <area/>
            </region>
        </xf:instance>
        <xf:submission id="form1" action="submitted.asp" method="get"/>
    </xf:model>
</head>
<body>
    <xf:input ref="name">
        <xf:label>Region</xf:label>
    </xf:input><br/>
```

```
    <xf:input ref="population">
       <xf:label>Population</xf:label>
    </xf:input><br/>
    <xf:input ref="area">
       <xf:label>Area</xf:label>
    </xf:input><br/><br/>
    <xf:submit submission="form1">
       <xf:label>Submit</xf:label>
    </xf:submit>
</body></html>
```

It does appear that Internet Explorer 5.0 and beyond can interpret some XForms commands directly, without reference to a namespace, but not all of them.

Figure 12-21: Executing XForms in Internet Explorer

Other XForms Input Types

Some tag types are sometimes similar in function to HTML tags, but some are additional in XForms. The `<secret>` tag can be used to hide the input of a password with * characters:

```
<secret ref="name/password"><label>Password:</label></secret>
```

The `<trigger>` tag is used to execute an action, perhaps another function, when an event occurs:

```
<trigger ref="GoDoThis"><label>Go Do This:</label></trigger>
```

The `<output>` tag can be used to display data from within XForms:

```
Country: <output ref="region/name"/>
```

The `<upload>` tag allows uploading of files to a server:

```
<upload bind="name">
    <label>Filename: </label>
    <filename bind="thisisthefilename"/>
    <mediatype bind="media"/>
</upload>
```

You can also use multiple selection items, which are much the same as in HTML. However, in addition to HTML, XForms provides a range tag, which allows selection of a value of range of literal values:

```
<range ref="length" start="1" end="10" step="1">
    <label>Range of values: </label>
</range>
```

Data Types in XForms

XForms can utilize XML Schema data types (see the next chapter). Use of Data types attached to input fields allows enforcement of restrictions on what is added as an entry field value. So, to make sure that certain input fields accept only specific values and types of values, you can change the previous XForms HTML page example like this:

```
<html xmlns:xf="http://www.w3.org/2002/xforms"
 xmlns:xsd="http://www.w3.org/2001/XMLSchema"
 xmlns:xsi="http://www.w3.org/2002/XMLSchema-instance">
<head>
  <xf:model>
    <xf:instance>
      <region>
        <name xsi:type="xsd:string"/>
        <population xsi:type="xsd:integer"/>
        <area xsi:type="xsd:integer"/>
        <dateofmeasure xsi:type="xsd:date"/>
```

```
        </xf:instance>
        <xf:submission id="form1" action="submitted.asp" method="get"/>
    </xf:model>
</head>
<body>
    <xf:input ref="name">
        <xf:label>Region</xf:label>
    </xf:input><br/>
    <xf:input ref="population">
        <xf:label>Population</xf:label>
    </xf:input><br/>
    <xf:input ref="area">
        <xf:label>Area</xf:label>
    </xf:input><br/><br/>
    <xf:submit submission="form1">
        <xf:label>Submit</xf:label>
    </xf:submit>
</body></html>
```

Restricting Values with XForms Properties

XForms can allow restriction to value inputs, such as forcing a value to be entered with the following property setting:

```
required="true()"
```

To instantiate the functioning of an XForms property to an input field, the property must be bound to data values. The following example reverts back to purely XForms (no HTML), where the nodeset attribute of the <bind> tag applies (binds) the given property to the instance of the <name> tag in the region:

```
<xforms>
    <model>
        <instance>
            <region>
                <name></name>
                <population></population>
                <area></area>
            </region>
        </instance>
        <submission id="form1" action="submitted.asp" method="get">
            <input ref="name"><label>Region</label></input>
            <input ref="population"><label>Population</label></input>
            <input ref="area"><label>Area</label></input>
            <submit submission="form1"><label>Submit</label></submit>
        </submission>
    </model>
</xforms>
```

Other XForms properties apply to the data item they are bound to (applied to), as follows:

❑ constraint: A constraint is a restriction such as allowing only specific values.

❑ required: A required value cannot be left as blank. This restriction can be a form of a constraint.

❑ type: A value must be of a specific data type, which effectively applies a form of a constraint and defines the data type for the item.

❑ calculate: Perform a calculation.

❑ readonly: A value can only be viewed, not changed.

❑ relevant: Relevance applies to display or submission.

XForms Object Actions

Various actions can be taken, based on specific events. For example, when rolling over an object, a tooltip can be displayed, much like the ALT attribute on an HTML <IMG> tag. The following script demonstrates:

```
<xforms>
    <model>
        <instance>
            <region>
                <name></name>
                <population></population>
                <area></area>
            </region>
        </instance>
        <submission id="form1" action="submitted.asp" method="get">
            <input ref="name">
                <label>Region</label>
                <message level="ephemeral" event="DOMFocusIn">
                    Add the name of the region
                </message>
            </input>
            <input ref="population"><label>Population</label></input>
            <input ref="area"><label>Area</label></input>
            <submit submission="form1"><label>Submit</label></submit>
        </submission>
    </model>
</xforms>
```

In the preceding script, the event is set to DOMFocusIn. This means that when the input field takes the focus on the screen, the message pops up briefly on the display. The ephemeral setting displays a tooltip, which can also be set in other ways as well.

Focus is placed on an input screen when the user tabs to the entry field, clicks the mouse on the entry field, or the entry field is selected automatically by the applications program.

The dictionary definition of "ephemeral" is lasting for a markedly brief time. *It's like an HTML button or ALT attribute rollover.*

Another example object-induced action is the setting of a value using the `setvalue` action, as shown in the example script value:

```xml
<xforms>
   <model>
      <instance>
         <region>
            <name></name>
            <population></population>
            <area></area>
         </region>
      </instance>
      <submission id="form1" action="submitted.asp" method="get">
         <input ref="name">
            <label>Region</label>
               <message level="ephemeral" event="DOMFocusIn">
                  Add the name of the region
               </message>
         </input>
         <input ref="population">
            <label>Population</label>
            <setvalue value="0" event="xforms-ready"/>
         </input>
         <input ref="area">
            <label>Area</label>
            <setvalue value="1" event="xforms-ready"/>
         </input>
         <submit submission="form1"><label>Submit</label></submit>
      </submission>
   </model>
</xforms>
```

In the preceding script, the population defaults to 0, and area to 1, because `xforms-ready` refers to when XForms is first loaded to the display. These are again just some examples. Much more is possible, but this is application- and not database-level functionality so it is covered only briefly.

Built-in and User-Defined Functions

Just like many other aspects and tools of XML, such as XQuery, XForms has direct access to XPath built-in functions (see Chapter 10). XForms does have a few additional functions, specifically for use with XForms. For example:

❑ `property(<string>)`: This returns the current value of a property. For example, `property("version")` returns the version number of the XForms model implemented in your browser.

❑ `instance(<string>)`: An XForms instance is an instantiation (or copy) of an XForms model. So, obviously, each XForms model can contain more than one instance (or `<instance>` tag). This function simply returns the XML fragment (node plus children), containing the specified instance.

And as with XPath, user-defined functions can also be created for use with XForms models.

Binding Data Using XPath

In computer lingo, the term "binding" means to cause some type of programming language or model, and data, to be stuck together somehow (to be bound). XForms can use XPath to address data in XML documents. And thus, XForms can be bound using XPath. This following example was shown previously in this chapter, where the `<upload>` tag allows uploading of files to a server by binding the `<upload>` tag to a filename and media type:

```
<upload bind="name">
   <label>Filename: </label>
   <filename bind="thisisthefilename"/>
   <mediatype bind="media"/>
</upload>
```

In fact, so far in this chapter, you have seen multiple references to the `ref` attribute. Let's examine the `ref` attribute in detail. Again, another previous example is shown here. In this case, the `<input>` tags (the entry fields on display) are bound to the `<instance>` of the XForms model using the `ref` attribute. In other words, the display fields are directly linked to the XML document data values of name, population, and area — for each of the regions in any XML document in use. And also, region/name, region/population, and region/area are all XPath expressions:

```
<xforms>
   <model>
      <instance>
         <region>
            <name></name>
            <population></population>
            <area></area>
         </region>
      </instance>
      <submission id="form1" action="submitted.asp" method="get">
         <input ref="/region/name"><label>Region</label></input>
         <input ref="/region/population"><label>Population</label></input>
         <input ref="/region/area"><label>Area</label></input>
         <submit submission="form1"><label>Submit</label></submit>
      </submission>
   </model>
</xforms>
```

So, XPath expressions can be changed to do the same thing in another manner, in the following case, not searching from the root of the XML document:

```
<xforms>
   <model>
      <instance>
         <region>
```

```
            <name></name>
            <population></population>
            <area></area>
        </region>
    </instance>
    <submission id="form1" action="submitted.asp" method="get">
        <input ref="//name"><label>Region</label></input>
        <input ref="//population"><label>Population</label></input>
        <input ref="//area"><label>Area</label></input>
        <submit submission="form1"><label>Submit</label></submit>
    </submission>
  </model>
</xforms>
```

Once again, variables and values have been bound (linked) together using the ref attribute of an XForms <input> tag.

You can also use the XForms bind keyword to bind variables and values together, as shown in the following repeated adaptation of this now familiar example. The name established in the <bind> tag can be referred to later on in the <input> tag by the name assigned to its id attribute:

```
<xforms>
    <model>
        <instance>
            <region>
                <name></name>
                <population></population>
                <area></area>
            </region>
        </instance>
        <bind nodeset="/region/name" id="region">
        <bind nodeset="/region/population" id="regionalPopulation">
        <bind nodeset="/region/area" id="squareMiles">
        <submission id="form1" action="submitted.asp" method="get">
            <input bind="region"><label>Region</label></input>
            <input bind="regionalPopulation"><label>Population</label></input>
            <input bind="squareMiles"><label>Area</label></input>
            <submit submission="form1"><label>Submit</label></submit>
        </submission>
    </model>
</xforms>
```

Most of what is involved in XForms coding is really like any front-end application programming language. This book is about XML and databases, and covering application details too deeply is beyond the scope of this book.

As with XLink and XPointer, XForms is not yet in production (a recommended standard only). XPointer does not work for my version of Internet Explorer (version 6). It is unlikely to work in version 7 either.

Embedding XML Documents with XInclude

The W3C definition of XInclude is available at `http://www.w3.org/TR/xinclude`. Essentially, you can include one script within another. The following script should merge two included XML regional documents into a single demographics document containing a collection of regions (this does not function in Internet Explorer 6):

```
<?xml version="1.0"?>
<demographics xmlns:xi="http://www.w3.org/2001/XInclude">
   <xi:include href="./Africa.xml"/>
   <xi:include href="./Asia.xml"/>
</demographics>
```

Formatting XML Output Using XML-FO

XML-FO or XML Format is used to format and beautify the output of XML for output display to the user. In reality, XML-FO is the formatting part of XSL (as opposed to XSLT). Both of these have already been covered extensively in this book.

This chapter has expanded more into the realm of front-end applications rather than specific database activity. Still, XLink, XPointer, and XForms are important XML technologies, even if only partially database-driven in nature. The next chapter examines Document Type Definitions (DTD) and XML Schemas — both of which are used to form a direct mapping between XML document data and relational database table structures.

This chapter has no Try It Out sections because a large majority of this functionality is not released for general use and may depend on browser type and version.

Summary

In this chapter you learned that:

❏   XLink allows for generation of generic links into web pages, based on XML document content.

❏   XLink links to entire XML documents and XPointer links to fragments within XML documents.

❏   Simple type XLinks link one XML document to another.

❏   Extended type XLinks can link many XML documents to many other XML documents.

❏   XForms is a model used to generate entry screens based on XML document content.

❏   XForms allows anything and more than HTML does.

❏   XForms includes a basic model, namespaces, input fields, data types, actions, and constraints.

❏   XForms can bind form objects directly to the content of an XML document.

An XML document is a native XML database.

❑   XInclude can be used to merge multiple XML documents into one XML document.

❑   XML-FO is the formatting part of eXtensible Style Sheets (XSL).

Exercises

1.   How many XML documents are linked to this XML document sample?

```
<?xml version="1.0"?>
<websites xmlns:xlink="http://www.w3.org/TR/xlink/">
    <website xlink:type="simple" xlink:href="http://www.ws1.com">Yahoo</website>
    <website xlink:type="simple" xlink:href="http://www.ws2.com">Google</website>
    <website xlink:type="simple" xlink:href="http://www.ws3">EBay</website>
</websites>
```

a.   None

b.   1

c.   2

d.   3

e.   4

f.   5

2.   Attribute `xlink:from` and `xlink:to` apply to what type of an XLink?

a.   simple

b.   extended

c.   resource

d.   locator

e.   arc

f.   None of the above

3.   XLink links to entire XML documents and XPointer links to fragments within individual XML documents. True or False?

4.   How is XForms more powerful than HTML?

a.   XForms has greater functionality.

b.   XForms has more flexibility based on its generation from XML document content.

c.   XForms has all the capabilities of HTML.

d.   XForms is far more complex to use than HTML.

e.   All of the above.

f.   None of the above.

Data Modeling and XML

This chapter is left until the end of this book because it ties together the conceptual application and database aspects of XML. Document Type Definition (DTD) is an older form of XML Schema Definition (XSD). However, it is important to cover both DTD and XSD, partially because DTD is less complex than XSD. Less complexity can help to demonstrate concepts gradually. Additionally, DTDs are still in use so it cannot really be avoided.

It is assumed throughout this book that you are at least familiar with relational database modeling, in terms of tables, fields, and relationships between tables. As you read through this chapter, you should see the distinct similarity between relational database tables and fields, when compared to that of DTD and XSD. One of the primary reasons for the existence of DTD and XSD is for validation of XML data against an existing table structure in a relational database model. If you remember, Chapter 6 included an extensive section about using XSD to map between XML and relational tables. So, another purpose of the existence of DTD and XSD is for an automated mapping process between XML and relational database data. Of course, this type of processing can be performed using XSL, as already shown in this book. However, it is essential to understand that DTD and XSD can be used to achieve the same result.

There are no Try It Out sections in this chapter as the content of this chapter is primarily conceptual, but also introductory with respect to native XML database standards.

In this chapter you learn about:

❑ The Document Type Definition (DTD)

❑ Using non-standard XML syntax in DTD scripts

❑ DTD elements, attributes, and entities

❑ Using entities to allow for substitution in DTD scripting

❑ The XML Schema Definition (XSD)

❑ Using standard XML structure and syntax in XSD

❑ The more advanced capabilities of XSD in comparison to DTD

The Document Type Definition

The Document Type Definition (DTD) allows the definition for the building blocks of an XML document. In other words, you create a DTD document. That DTD document contains the structural definition for the data in an XML document. That DTD definition can be used as a mapping structure, mapping between the metadata; plus it can be used as a data mix in an XML document, and the metadata table structure of a relational database model. The result is a DTD document, which can be used to validate the structure of an XML document. Errors in XML data, XML metadata, or XML document structure can be detected and thus repaired. For example, passing data between two relational databases can be managed nicely using DTDs. Each relational database can have different table structures, perhaps even be different vendor database engines. DTD documents can be used at both ends to validate XML document structure before attempting to add newly transferred XML data into a relational database. This can help to avoid data errors in the relational databases.

A DTD document begins with a document type declaration in its simplest form, as shown here:

```
<!DOCTYPE root [ <all the elements in the document> ]>
```

Other parts of a DTD declaration are elements, attributes, entities, PCDATA, and CDATA:

❑ **Elements:** Defines XML document elements.

❑ **Attributes:** Attribute and attribute values, as part of elements.

❑ **Entities:** An entity is essentially a reference, including an escape sequence such as &amp or an included DTD definition, which has been given a name and is referenced elsewhere by that name, as in &entity.

❑ **PCDATA:** XML document, element text values of an XML document, which has already been successfully parsed.

❑ **CDATA:** Character data, which is not to be parsed by an XML parser.

For example, regions containing countries, which in turn contain cities, might look something like this:

```
<?xml version="1.0"?>
<!DOCTYPE demographics [
<!ELEMENT demographics (region*)>
   <!ELEMENT region (name, area, country*)>
   <!ELEMENT name (#PCDATA)>
   <!ELEMENT area (#PCDATA)>
   <!ELEMENT country (name, population, area, city*)>
      <!ELEMENT name (#PCDATA)>
      <!ELEMENT population (#PCDATA)>
      <!ELEMENT area (#PCDATA)>
      <!ELEMENT city (name, population)>
         <!ELEMENT name (#PCDATA)>
         <!ELEMENT population (#PCDATA)>
]>
<demographics>
   <region>
      <name>Europe</name>
```

```
            <area>4583335</area>
            ...
            <country>
                <name>Belgium</name>
                <population>10000000</population>
                <area>30230</area>
                <city>
                    <name>Antwerp</name>
                    <population>1125000</population>
                </city>
                <city>
                    <name>Brussels</name>
                    <population>1875000</population>
                </city>
            </country>
            ...
        <region>
            ...
        </region>
        ...
    </demographics>
```

The preceding example is easy to understand. All that is being done is that the DTD definition is creating a formal structure for the XML demographics data. The only new factor in the preceding script is the use of the asterisk (*) character. The * character indicates that there are zero or more of the indicated elements included within the parent element. For example, this indicates that the `<demographics>` element contains multiple `<region>` elements:

```
<!ELEMENT demographics (region*)>
```

Do not omit the space character between element name and content, as in `demographics (region...`

Similarly, the same applies to regions, countries, and cities as well:

```
<!ELEMENT region (name, population, area, country*)>
<!ELEMENT country (name, population, area, city*)>
```

One more thing that can be done with the DTD DOCTYPE declaration is that the DTD definition can be stored into a separate file. So the externally stored DTD file would be like this, and would be called something like demographics.dtd:

```
<!ELEMENT demographics (region*)>
    <!ELEMENT region (name, area, country*)>
    <!ELEMENT name (#PCDATA)>
    <!ELEMENT area (#PCDATA)>
    <!ELEMENT country (name, population, area, city*)>
        <!ELEMENT name (#PCDATA)>
        <!ELEMENT population (#PCDATA)>
        <!ELEMENT area (#PCDATA)>
        <!ELEMENT city (name, population)>
            <!ELEMENT name (#PCDATA)>
            <!ELEMENT population (#PCDATA)>
```

And the XML document, including the DTD definition from the file called demographics.dtd would look like this:

```
<?xml version="1.0"?>
<!DOCTYPE demographics SYSTEM "demographics.dtd">
<demographics>
   <region>
      <name>Europe</name>
      <area>4583335</area>
      ...
      <country>
         <name>Belgium</name>
         <population>10000000</population>
         <area>30230</area>
         <city>
            <name>Antwerp</name>
            <population>1125000</population>
         </city>
         <city>
            <name>Brussels</name>
            <population>1875000</population>
         </city>
      </country>
      ...
   <region>
      ...
   </region>
      ...
</demographics>
```

Executing the XML document in a browser does not really show you much other than that shown in Figure 13-1.

DTD Elements

The basic syntax for declaring a DTD element is as follows:

```
<!ELEMENT element { <category> | (content [, ...]) }>
```

DTD Element Categories

An element can contain a category of data, such as EMPTY, or a subset of other elements. A completely empty element can be defined as follows:

```
<!ELEMENT element EMPTY>
```

The EMPTY keyword is applicable to something such as an HTML tag not requiring both opening and closing tags:

```
<!ELEMENT <HR/> EMPTY>
```

or an XML tag containing no data content:

```
<!ELEMENT <year/> EMPTY>
```

354

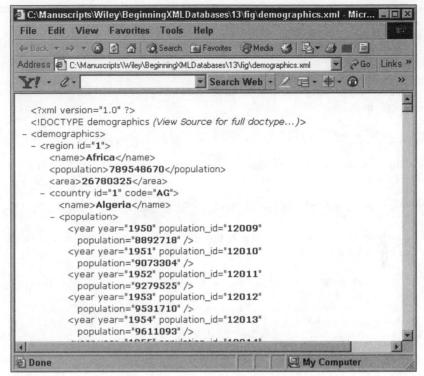

Figure 13-1: Validating an XML document with a DTD

Any combination of anything that is parseable by XML can be defined using the ANY keyword:

```
<!ELEMENT element ANY>
```

DTD Element Content

So, that's the basic syntax for DTD element definitions. Elements can also contain what is called content, as opposed to just a category item. That content can be a single item, such as a single string value as defined by PCDATA:

```
<!ELEMENT element (#PCDATA)>
```

Content can also be a sequence of subset elements where an element contains a subset tree of subset elements. The syntax is as follows:

```
<!ELEMENT element (child [, ... ])>
```

For example, this <country> element contains a list of three subset elements (name, population, and area):

```
<!ELEMENT country (name, population, area)>
```

The child elements must be defined in the same sequence, immediately after the parent element definition:

```
<!ELEMENT name (#PCDATA)>
<!ELEMENT population (#PCDATA)>
<!ELEMENT area (#PCDATA)>
```

Content can also be a set of choices, which are separated by a | character (sometimes called a pipe command or an OR operator):

```
<!ELEMENT element (child1 | child2)>
```

The preceding code means the parent element can contain either of the child elements. This even applies to sequences, as in the following syntax example:

```
<!ELEMENT element (childA, childB, (child1 | child2))>
```

In the following example, the country can optionally contain a collection of languages, or a list of occupations, but in this case not both:

```
<!ELEMENT country (name, population, area, (languages | occupations))>
<!ELEMENT name (#PCDATA)>
<!ELEMENT population (#PCDATA)>
<!ELEMENT area (#PCDATA)>
<!ELEMENT languages (name, male, female)>
<!ELEMENT name (#PCDATA)>
<!ELEMENT male (#PCDATA)>
<!ELEMENT female (#PCDATA)>
<!ELEMENT occupations (name, male, female)>
<!ELEMENT name (#PCDATA)>
<!ELEMENT male (#PCDATA)>
<!ELEMENT female (#PCDATA)>
```

Content can even be of mixed content. However, mixed content in DTD is severely restricted to a single item, which contains a repetition of one or more elements. The mixed context part of that *one or more elements* is that each of those elements can be a text item or an element. So the following example causes an error because it includes three separate subelements:

```
<?xml version="1.0"?>
<!DOCTYPE demographics [
<!ELEMENT demographics (region)>
<!ELEMENT region (#PCDATA, population, area)>
]>
<?xml version="1.0"?>
<demographics>
   <region>Africa
      <population>789548670</population>
      <area>26780325</area>
   </region>
</demographics>
```

The only way that mixed content can be defined with DTD is by mixing multiple items into the same optional context, as in the following example including text, <B>, <I>, and <P> tags within the description string text value:

```
<?xml version="1.0"?>
<!DOCTYPE demographics [
<!ELEMENT demographics (region)>
<!ELEMENT region (name, population, area, description)>
<!ELEMENT description (#PCDATA | B | I | P)*>
]>
<demographics>
   <region>
      <name>Africa</name>
      <population>789548670</population>
      <area>26780325</area>
      <description>
         <P>This region has a dense population in <B>high</B> rainfall areas and is
sparsely populated in very <I>low</I> rainfall areas.</P><P>Africa is one of the
largest regions of the world, when measured in <B><I>square miles</I></B>.</P>
      </description>
   </region>
</demographics>
```

Note the use of the asterisk (*) character in the preceding script. This is required as it denotes there can be zero or more of one or more of the listed options (i.e. #PCDATA, B, I, P). This is called cardinality, which I will deal with in the next section.

The result is shown in Figure 13-2.

DTD Element Cardinality

Cardinality determines how many times an item or element can occur within a specific content layer. There are four DTD cardinality syntax specifiers:

❏   *: Zero or more times.

❏   +: One or more times (not zero). Thus a minimum of once.

❏   ?: Once and only once, or not at all.

❏   [none]: Must be included once and only once.

In the following example, there can be zero or more <language> elements contained within each <languages> element:

```
<?xml version="1.0"?>
<!DOCTYPE demographics [
<!ELEMENT demographics (region)>
<!ELEMENT region (name, population, area, country)>
<!ELEMENT country (name, languages)>
<!ELEMENT languages (language*)>
<!ELEMENT language (name, male, female)>
]>
<demographics>
   <region>
      <name>Africa</name>
      <population>789548670</population>
      <area>26780325</area>
      <country>
```

357

```
            <name>Algeria</name>
            <languages>
                <language>
                    <name>French</name>
                    <male>37500</male>
                    <female>40100</female>
                </language>
                <language>
                    <name>Berbere</name>
                    <male>1123200</male>
                    <female>1144100</female>
                </language>
                <language>
                    <name>Arabic</name>
                    <male>4908100</male>
                    <female>4826000</female>
                </language>
            </languages>
        </country>
    </region>
</demographics>
```

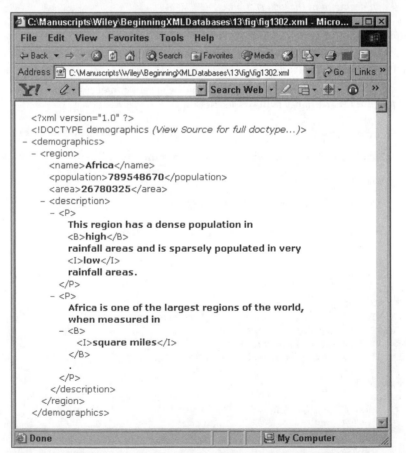

Figure 13-2: Mixed content can contain both text values (PCDATA) and subset elements.

The result is shown in Figure 13-3.

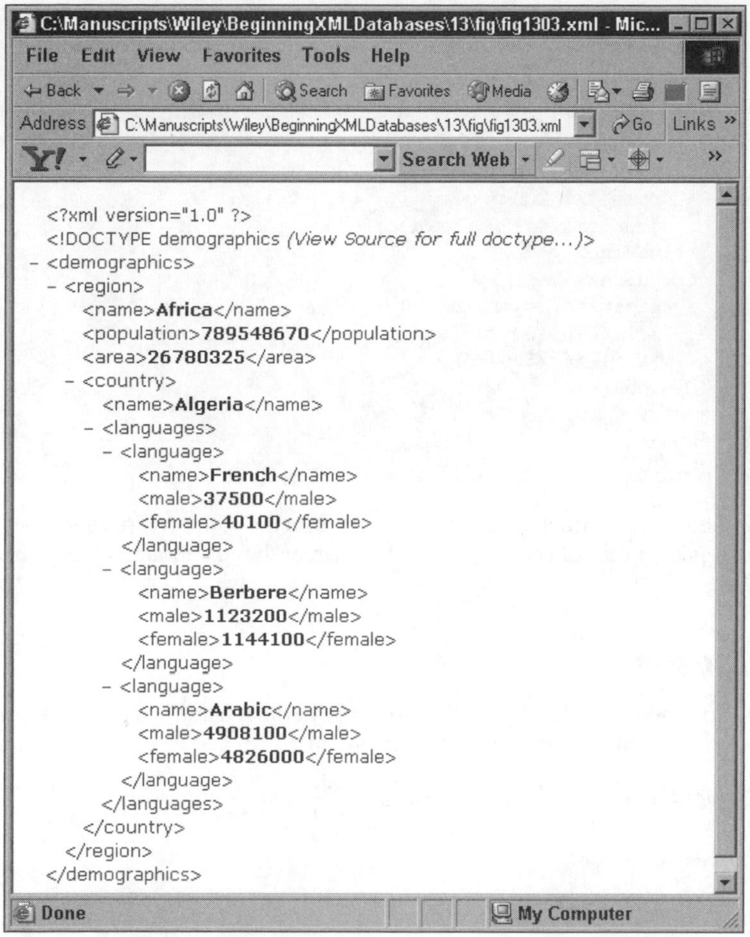

Figure 13-3: Zero or more elements on a single parent element

Now you can change the preceding example, removing the `<languages>` elements from the XML document altogether:

```
<?xml version="1.0"?>
<!DOCTYPE demographics [
<!ELEMENT demographics (region)>
<!ELEMENT region (name, population, area, country)>
<!ELEMENT country (name, languages)>
<!ELEMENT language (name, male, female)*>
]>
<demographics>
    <region>
        <name>Africa</name>
        <population>789548670</population>
        <area>26780325</area>
```

```
        <country>
           <name>Algeria</name>
           <language>
              <name>French</name>
              <male>37500</male>
              <female>40100</female>
           </language>
           <language>
              <name>Berbere</name>
              <male>1123200</male>
              <female>1144100</female>
           </language>
           <language>
              <name>Arabic</name>
              <male>4908100</male>
              <female>4826000</female>
           </language>
        </country>
     </region>
</demographics>
```

See how the asterisk (*) character has been moved from the collection parent `<languages>` (now no longer in existence) to the collection itself in the form of the `<language>` elements. The result is shown in Figure 13-4.

DTD Attributes

Attributes are defined in DTDs, for an XML document data, using what is called an ATTLIST declaration. Attributes are defined using the following syntax:

```
<!ATTLIST element attribute type default>
```

For example, this definition:

```
<!ATTLIST region id CDATA "1">
```

represents this piece of XML:

```
<region id="1">
```

And similarly, this definition containing multiple attributes:

```
<!ATTLIST year year CDATA "1950">
<!ATTLIST year population_id CDATA "12009">
<!ATTLIST year population CDATA "8892718">
```

represents this piece of XML:

```
<year year="1950" population_id="12009" population="8892718">
```

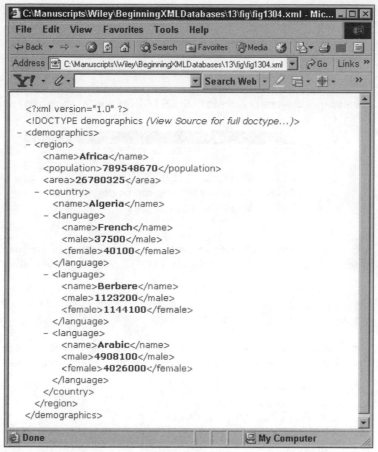

Figure 13-4: Zero or more elements on a collection of elements

Attribute Types

Attributes can be defined as being of various different types, as shown in Figure 13-5.

Default	Description
CDATA	Characters
(p, q [, ...])	Originates from a list of values
ID	Unique identifier
IDREF[S]	Identifier of a different element (a reference). Plural is a list of
NMTOKEN[S]	XML name. Plural is a list of
ENTIT[Y|IES]	An entity. Plural is a list of
NOTATION	Notational name
xml:	A predefined XML value

Figure 13-5: DTD attributes can be defined as various different types.

The following example shows an enumerated list of various different values. So, the year attribute in the following example can be set to any year between 2003 and 2006, even though initially defaulted to 2006:

```
<!ATTLIST year year (2003|2004|2005|2006) "2006">
```

Attribute Defaults

Attributes can be assigned default values in their DTD definition, as shown in Figure 13-6.

Default	Description
value	The initial setting for an attribute
#REQUIRED	An attribute must have a default value
#IMPLIED	An attribute does not have to have a default value
#FIXED value	An attribute value is predetermined

Figure 13-6: DTD attributes can be defaulted to various different settings.

Let's use the previous example once again: In the following definition, of the three attributes defined, all have default values of year set to 1950, population_id set to 12009, and population set to 8892718:

```
<!ATTLIST year year CDATA "1950">
<!ATTLIST year population_id CDATA "12009">
<!ATTLIST year population CDATA "8892718">
```

A setting of #IMPLIED dictates that the XML data does not require that an element actually must always have an attribute. Thus, the preceding example can be changed as shown below:

```
<!ATTLIST year year CDATA #IMPLIED>
<!ATTLIST year population_id CDATA #IMPLIED>
<!ATTLIST year population CDATA #IMPLIED>
```

The preceding DTD definition implies that attributes are not necessarily required for a specific element, and so this is valid XML:

```
<year year="1950" population_id="12009" population="8892718">
```

And this is valid:

```
<year year="1950" population="8892718">
```

And even this is valid, too:

```
<year>
```

Now if you change the default value to #REQUIRED, as shown here:

```
<!ATTLIST year year CDATA #REQUIRED>
<!ATTLIST year population_id CDATA #REQUIRED>
<!ATTLIST year population CDATA #REQUIRED>
```

Then this:

```
<year year="1950" population="8892718">
```

and the example that follows, are now both illegal for this XML document because none of the attributes can be omitted:

```
<year>
```

Now if you change the default values again as follows, the year must always be 2006, the population_id value is required, and the population number is not absolutely required:

```
<!ATTLIST year year CDATA #FIXED "2006">
<!ATTLIST year population_id CDATA #REQUIRED>
<!ATTLIST year population CDATA #IMPLIED>
```

So this is valid where the population_id is required but can be anything, and the year must be 2006:

```
<year year="2006" population_id="12009">
```

In the preceding example, the population figure is optional.

Now you can enhance the definition for a small section of the demographics.xml database, adding some attributes:

```
<?xml version-"1.0"?>
<!DOCTYPE demographics [
<!ELEMENT demographics (region*)>
<!ELEMENT region (name, population, area, country*)>
<!ATTLIST region id CDATA #REQUIRED>
<!ELEMENT name (#PCDATA)>
<!ELEMENT population (#PCDATA)>
<!ELEMENT area (#PCDATA)>
<!ELEMENT country (name, population)>
<!ATTLIST country id CDATA #REQUIRED>
<!ATTLIST country code CDATA #IMPLIED>
<!ELEMENT name (#PCDATA)>
<!ELEMENT population (year*)>
<!ATTLIST year year (2003|2004|2005|2006|2010|2020) "2006">
<!ATTLIST year population_id CDATA #REQUIRED>
<!ATTLIST year population CDATA #IMPLIED>
<!ELEMENT year (births_per_1000?, deaths_per_1000?, growth_rate?)>
<!ELEMENT births_per_1000 (#PCDATA)>
<!ELEMENT deaths_per_1000 (#PCDATA)>
<!ELEMENT growth_rate (#PCDATA)>
]>
<demographics>
    <region id="1">
        <name>Africa</name>
```

```
        <population>789548670</population>
        <area>26780325</area>
        <country id="1" code="AG">
            <name>Algeria</name>
            <population>
                <year year="2003" population_id="410" population="31713719">
                    <births_per_1000>18.34</births_per_1000>
                    <deaths_per_1000>4.63</deaths_per_1000>
                    <natural_increase_percent>1.371</natural_increase_percent>
                    <growth_rate>1.329</growth_rate>
                </year>
                <year year="2004" population_id="411" population="32129324">
                    <births_per_1000>17.76</births_per_1000>
                    <deaths_per_1000>4.61</deaths_per_1000>
                    <natural_increase_percent>1.315</natural_increase_percent>
                    <growth_rate>1.275</growth_rate>
                </year>
                <year year="2005" population_id="412" population="32531853">
                    <births_per_1000>17.13</births_per_1000>
                    <deaths_per_1000>4.6</deaths_per_1000>
                    <natural_increase_percent>1.253</natural_increase_percent>
                    <growth_rate>1.216</growth_rate>
                </year>
                <year year="2006" population_id="413"/>
                <year year="2010" population_id="417"/>
                <year year="2020" population_id="427"/>
            </population>
        </country>
    </region>
</demographics>
```

The result of the preceding DTD definition and XML data is shown in Figure 13-7.

The only oddity about Figure 13-7 is that I removed the <natural_increase_percent> element from the DTD definition, but not from the XML data. Internet Explorer 6.0 did not produce an error.

DTD Entities

An entity is used to define a variable, and can be built-in or custom made. The syntax for declaring an entity is as follows:

```
<!ENTITY entity "value">
```

Built-In Entities and ASCII Code Character Entities

Built-in entities are essentially any reference entities usable in XML, which are escape sequence commands outputting a single character that is otherwise interpreted as something else by XML. The built-in entities are as follows:

❏   &: Display an & character.

❏   <: Display a < character.

❑ >: Display a > character.

❑ ': Display a single quotation character.

❑ ": Display a double quotation character.

```
C:\Manuscripts\Wiley\BeginningXMLDatabases\13\fig\fig1307.xml - Microsoft Internet E...

File   Edit   View   Favorites   Tools   Help

Back  →     Search   Favorites   Media

Address  C:\Manuscripts\Wiley\BeginningXMLDatabases\13\fig\fig1307.xml        Go   Links »

Y!  -  -                        Search Web  -       -    -   Mail  -   »

<?xml version="1.0" ?>
<!DOCTYPE demographics (View Source for full doctype...)>
- <demographics>
  - <region id="1">
      <name>Africa</name>
      <population>789548670</population>
      <area>26780325</area>
    - <country id="1" code="AG">
        <name>Algeria</name>
      - <population>
        + <year year="2003" population_id="410" population="31713719">
        + <year year="2004" population_id="411" population="32129324">
        - <year year="2005" population_id="412" population="32531853">
            <births_per_1000>17.13</births_per_1000>
            <deaths_per_1000>4.6</deaths_per_1000>
            <natural_increase_percent>1.253</natural_increase_percent>
            <growth_rate>1.216</growth_rate>
          </year>
          <year year="2006" population_id="413" />
          <year year="2010" population_id="417" />
          <year year="2020" population_id="427" />
        </population>
      </country>
    </region>
  </demographics>

My Computer
```

Figure 13-7: Elements and attributes can be verified using DTD definitions.

An ASCII code character entity, as with XML and HTML, allows you to utilize an ASCII numeric code to display any character in the ASCII character set. For example, &#32 will display a space character, or a &#156 will display the currency symbol for British Pounds (£).

Custom and Parameter Entities

A custom created entity is one created to allow repeated inclusion of a piece of text. So, in the example that follows, some unknown values occur for some of the elements: births_per_1000, growth_rate, and deaths_per_1000. The result is that an unknown value will be replaced by the entity string value for the *unknown* entity:

```
<?xml version="1.0"?>
<!DOCTYPE demographics [
<!ELEMENT demographics (region*)>
<!ELEMENT region (name, population, area, country*)>
<!ATTLIST region id CDATA #REQUIRED>
<!ELEMENT name (#PCDATA)>
<!ELEMENT population (#PCDATA)>
<!ELEMENT area (#PCDATA)>
<!ELEMENT country (name, population)>
<!ATTLIST country id CDATA #REQUIRED>
<!ATTLIST country code CDATA #IMPLIED>
<!ELEMENT name (#PCDATA)>
<!ELEMENT population (year*)>
<!ATTLIST year year (2003|2004|2005|2006|2010|2020) "2006">
<!ATTLIST year population_id CDATA #REQUIRED>
<!ATTLIST year population CDATA #IMPLIED>
<!ELEMENT year (births_per_1000?, deaths_per_1000?, growth_rate?)>
<!ELEMENT births_per_1000 (#PCDATA)>
<!ELEMENT deaths_per_1000 (#PCDATA)>
<!ELEMENT growth_rate (#PCDATA)>
<!ENTITY unknown "No value available">
]>
<demographics>
    <region id="1">
        <name>Africa</name>
        <population>789548670</population>
        <area>26780325</area>
        <country id="1" code="AG">
            <name>Algeria</name>
            <population>
                <year year="2003" population_id="410" population="31713719">
                    <births_per_1000>&unknown;</births_per_1000>
                    <deaths_per_1000>4.63</deaths_per_1000>
                    <natural_increase_percent>1.371</natural_increase_percent>
                    <growth_rate>&unknown;</growth_rate>
                </year>
                <year year="2004" population_id="411" population="32129324">
                    <births_per_1000>17.76</births_per_1000>
                    <deaths_per_1000>&unknown;</deaths_per_1000>
                    <natural_increase_percent>1.315</natural_increase_percent>
                    <growth_rate>1.275</growth_rate>
                </year>
                <year year="2005" population_id="412" population="32531853">
                    <births_per_1000>17.13</births_per_1000>
                    <deaths_per_1000>4.6</deaths_per_1000>
                    <natural_increase_percent>1.253</natural_increase_percent>
                    <growth_rate>1.216</growth_rate>
                </year>
            </population>
        </country>
    </region>
</demographics>
```

The result is shown in Figure 13-8.

Figure 13-8: Adding and referencing custom entity values

While custom entities can be placed within XML data, parameter entities are placed only within DTD definitional structure. Parameters allow removal of repetition in DTD declarative scripting. For example, you can change the XML data and then adapt the DTD as shown in the script that follows. This script presents you with a lot of duplication:

```
<?xml version="1.0"?>
<!DOCTYPE demographics [
<!ELEMENT demographics (region*)>
<!ELEMENT region (country*)>
<!ATTLIST region id CDATA #REQUIRED>
```

```
<!ATTLIST region name CDATA #REQUIRED>
<!ATTLIST region population CDATA #IMPLIED>
<!ATTLIST region area CDATA #IMPLIED>
<!ELEMENT country (city*)>
<!ATTLIST country id CDATA #REQUIRED>
<!ATTLIST country name CDATA #REQUIRED>
<!ATTLIST country population CDATA #IMPLIED>
<!ATTLIST country area CDATA #IMPLIED>
<!ELEMENT city EMPTY>
<!ATTLIST city id CDATA #REQUIRED>
<!ATTLIST city name CDATA #REQUIRED>
<!ATTLIST city population CDATA #IMPLIED>
<!ATTLIST city area CDATA #IMPLIED>
]>
<demographics>
   <region id="1" name="Africa" population="789548670" area="26780325">
      <country id="1" name="Algeria" population="" area="2381741" code="AG">
         <city id="307" name="Oran" population="1200000" area=""/>
         <city id="130" name="Algiers" population="4100000" area=""/>
      </country>
   </region>
   <region id="6" name="Europe" population="488674441" area="4583335">
      <country id="65" name="Austria" population="" area="82730" code="AU">
         <city id="205" name="Vienna" population="1875000" area=""/>
      </country>
      <country id="66" name="Belgium" population="" area="30230" code="BE">
         <city id="315" name="Antwerp" population="1125000" area=""/>
         <city id="206" name="Brussels" population="1875000" area=""/>
      </country>
   </region>
</demographics>
```

You can use parameters to remove DTD definitional duplication in the example that follows:

```
<?xml version="1.0"?>
<!DOCTYPE demographics SYSTEM "fig1309.dtd">
<demographics>
   <region id="1" name="Africa" population="789548670" area="26780325">
      <country id="1" name="Algeria" population="" area="2381741" code="AG">
         <city id="307" name="Oran" population="1200000" area=""/>
         <city id="130" name="Algiers" population="4100000" area=""/>
      </country>
   </region>
   <region id="6" name="Europe" population="488674441" area="4583335">
      <country id="65" name="Austria" population="" area="82730" code="AU">
         <city id="205" name="Vienna" population="1875000" area=""/>
      </country>
      <country id="66" name="Belgium" population="" area="30230" code="BE">
         <city id="315" name="Antwerp" population="1125000" area=""/>
         <city id="206" name="Brussels" population="1875000" area=""/>
      </country>
   </region>
</demographics>
```

Additionally, an externally stored DTD file must be used because parameters cannot be interpreted when placed within the same file as the XML data. Otherwise, I get an error in Internet Explorer 6. The DTD file is shown here:

```
<!ENTITY % locationAttributes "id CDATA #REQUIRED
                               name CDATA #REQUIRED
                               population CDATA #IMPLIED
                               area CDATA #IMPLIED">
<!ELEMENT demographics (region*)>
<!ELEMENT region (country*)>
<!ATTLIST region %locationAttributes;>
<!ELEMENT country (city*)>
<!ATTLIST country %locationAttributes;>
<!ELEMENT city EMPTY>
<!ATTLIST city %locationAttributes;>
```

The entity declaration must appear within the DTD file before it is actually referenced, as shown in the preceding example. The result of the preceding XML document and DTD file is shown in Figure 13-9.

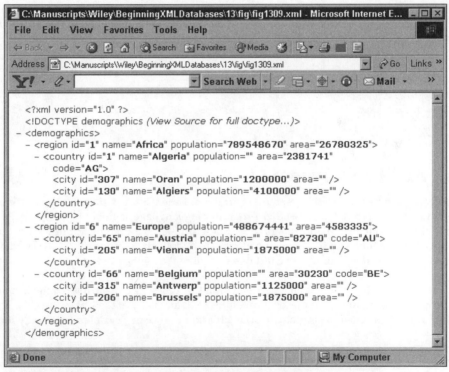

Figure 13-9: Using entity parameters to remove DTD scripting duplication

That is how you create Document Type Definitions, or DTDs, in order to attempt to impose some restrictive structural requirements onto XML document data. A more advanced solution to this type of issue is that of XML Schemas.

The XML Schema Definition

XML Schemas are used to define logical structure onto XML data, much like defining a mapping between XML data and relational table structures in a relational database. In addition, XML Schemas are also used in hand with other XML technologies, including XPath 2.0, XQuery, and even things such as SOAP.

You might have noticed that DTD definitions are not exactly XML coding. XSD is written in XML. Again, XML is universally understood regardless of platform and environment; at least that is the intention for XML. So, XSD is capable of deeper structural description of XML data, but DTDs allow embedding of DTD definitions into an XML document; DTDs also allow entity functionality. XSDs must be in a file separate to that of XML data. DTD entity functionality can be useful but it's not that much to write home about. XSDs also enforce strict typing, which allows for more accurate constraint value mapping of data.

If you remember, Chapter 6 included a brief introduction to small parts of the XML Schema and creating XSD scripts, when I covered SQL Server Database. In Chapter 6, you saw how an XSD script can be used to create a mapping between XML data and one or more related tables, in a relational database model of tables. The intention in Chapter 6 is a purely relational database-centric approach, and particularly for the SQL Server database. This chapter takes a more generic and perhaps native XML database approach to XSD. Any repetition between this chapter and Chapter 6 is intentional and necessary to facilitate explanation to all levels of expertise.

So, the most basic tag is the schema tag, demonstrated in this example script snippet:

```
<?xml version="1.0">
<xsd:schema xmlns:xsd="http://www.w3.org/2001/XMLSchema">
   ...
</xsd:schema>
```

Global and Local Types

Before you examine the various parameters for the `<element>` tag in detail, let's examine the definition of global and local types. Like any other programming language, a global type is globally accessible (in this case throughout an XML document, the XSD script file). A local type applies to the contents of the element (the elements with the element concerned). A global type is one that is declared as a child of the `<schema>` tag, and not a non-direct child descendant of the `<schema>` tag.

A global type essentially allows later access within the XSD script, regardless of the location within the XSD script, or the point within the location of the XML hierarchy of the XSD script file. The `<region>` element in this XSD example is globally accessible and the `<country>` element is only locally accessible:

```
<?xml version="1.0"?>
<xsd:schema xmlns:xsd="http://www.w3.org/2001/XMLSchema">
   <xsd:element name="region">
      <xsd:element name="country">
         ...
      </xsd:element>
   </xsd:element>
</xsd:schema>
```

Basic XSD Structures

The basic XSD structures are the `<element>` and the `<attribute>` tags. As shown in the previous example, you can define elements using the `<element>` tag. The XSD syntax for the `<element>` tag is as follows:

```
<element name="" type="" ref="" form="" minOccurs="" maxOccurs="" default="" fixed=
"">
```

The `name` attribute is obviously the name of the tag. The `type` attribute is the data type of the element (data types are discussed shortly). The `ref` attribute is a reference to another XSD definition (again to be discussed later on in this chapter). The `minOccurs` and `maxOccurs` attributes determine cardinality (how many occurrences of). The `default` attribute sets a default value when nothing is entered. The `fixed` attribute requires a fixed value regardless of what is entered.

The XSD syntax for defining an attribute is as follows:

```
<attribute name="" type="" ref="" form="" use="" default="" fixed="">
```

As you can see, there are some differences between element and attribute syntax definitions. The `use=""` attribute of an attribute definition is either optional, required, or prohibited. The default value is optional as most attributes are generally optional in nature. A required attribute must be present and a prohibited attribute is not allowed to be included.

There is nothing difficult to understand with respect to the definitions of XSD elements and attributes. However, a few of the details (some of their attributes) will be covered as you read through this chapter, at appropriate points on the learning curve. For example, basic data types apply to elements and attributes.

XML Schema Data Types

XPath, XQuery, XForms, and XML Schemas all share the same basic data types. Because of this, coverage of these data types has been left until this chapter, where it makes the most sense. Additionally, at this point in this chapter, basic data types are essentially applicable to each element in an XSD script file. These data types are very similar to the data types applied to the fields of tables in a relational database.

There are numerous other basic data types in addition to those mentioned in this section, used to implement an innumerate quantity of specialized capabilities. These data types include those shown in Figure 10-15, back in Chapter 10. Going into the nitty-gritty details of all the different variations of each data type is a little too detailed and advanced for this book. In this case, I will stick to the basic strings, numbers, dates, times, and miscellaneously categorized basic data types.

XML Schema String Data Types

Obviously, string data types can contain string values. You can define a value to be a string data type, as in the following example:

```
<xsd:element name="region" type="xsd:string"/>
```

A string data type (xsd:string) preserves white space characters in the string value, including characters such as new lines, tabs, and space characters. So, the following element will look as it stands here:

```
<region>      North America      </region>
```

A normalized string data type removes white space characters:

```
<xsd:element name="region" type="xsd:normalizedString"/>
```

And thus the preceding example region element would look like this in the output even if space characters are included in the XML document:

```
<region>North America</region>
```

XML Schema Numeric Data Types

Standard numeric data types in XSD are more or less the same as in any strictly typed programming language or database engine. Figure 10-15 shows numeric data types of int, long, negativeInteger, nonNegativeInteger, nonPositiveInteger, positiveInteger(), short(), unsignedInt(), unsignedInt(), unsignedLong(), unsignedShort(), decimal(), double(), and float(). Mathematically speaking, and from the perspective of computer programming, these data types are all self-explanatory.

For example, the following declares a number to be an integer. An integer is a whole number:

```
<xsd:element name="population" type="xsd:integer"/>
```

This would be a valid entry for an integer:

```
<population>2000000</population>
```

And this would be an invalid entry for an integer because a whole number does not have decimals:

```
<population>2000000.54</population>
```

A more fitting definition for the preceding real number (a number containing a decimal value) is as follows:

```
<xsd:element name="population" type="xsd:decimal"/>
```

XML Schema Date and Time Data Types

Date and time data types can be used to restrict values to contain easily understandable date and time values. A simple date data type can be defined as follows:

```
<xsd:element name="entryDate" type="xsd:date"/>
```

The default format for a date is of the form YYYY-MM-DD, indicating a four-digit year, a month, and a day. So, the following is a valid date entry:

```
<entryDate>2006-06-10</entryDate>
```

You can also specify that dates have times zones, times, dates including times and durations of time in all sorts of forms such as years, months, and so on. For example, a datetime value can be specified as follows:

```
<xsd:element name="entryDateTime" type="xsd:dateTime"/>
```

The default format for datetime values is YYYY-MM-DDThh:mm:ss, indicating years, months, days, hours, minutes, and seconds. For example, this value indicates 10:41 a.m. and 1 second, on the morning of June 10, 2006:

```
<entryDateTime>2006-06-10T10:41:01</entryDateTime>
```

XML Schema Miscellaneous Data Types

A miscellaneous data type in any computer technical text is often a method of lumping in things that don't really fit too well anywhere else. For example, consider a Boolean data type, which can be true (or 1), or false (or 0):

```
<xsd:element name="country" type="xsd:string"/>
<xsd:attribute name="languages" type="xsd:boolean"/>
<xsd:attribute name="occupations" type="xsd:boolean"/>
```

So, a country in the demographics database containing at least one `<languages>` element and no `<occupations>` elements within its `<population>` element subtree can be represented by the following `<country>` element:

```
<country id-"1" code="AG" name="Algeria" languages-"true" occupations="false">
```

Another miscellaneous data type is the anyURI data type, representing a Universal Resource Indicator (URI), or a web page address on the Internet. So, you can add a URI to the previous country definition like this:

```
<xsd:attribute name="webpage" type="xsd:anyURI"/>
```

And then change the country of Algeria, as follows:

```
<country id="1" code="AG" name="Algeria" webpage="http://www.algeria.com" languages
="true" occupations="false"/>
```

Cardinality

You may remember the minOccurs and maxOccurs attributes of the XSD `<element>` tag from the beginning of this section. These attributes determine cardinality. Cardinality determines how many times a specific item can occur, in this case an element or attribute.

Cardinality cannot be defined for global declarations because global declarations define a type (in the relational world), or a class (in the object world). A type is instantiated as a variable and a class as an object. In other words, there is no such thing as multiple iterations of a type of a class, but there are multiple iterations of a variable (declare many variables of the same data type), or an object (create many objects of the same class). So, in the case of an XSD definition, you can iterate the referenced object, but not the definition of that reference.

The possible values for cardinality are as follows:

❑ minOccurs: A positive integer only, which is a value from 0 upward. 0 is a positive integer. The default value is 1.

❑ maxOccurs: A positive integer or unbounded (implies an infinite integer). The default value is 1. maxOccurs must be greater than or equal to minOccurs.

In the following example, between 1 and 20 regions are allowed in a single demographics native XML database document (it can get large). And countries within each region can be none, or any number:

```
<xsd:element name="region" minOccurs="1" maxOccurs="20"/>
<xsd:element name="country" minOccurs="0" maxOccurs="unbounded"/>
```

That is what cardinality means!

Element Ordering Sequence and Choice

Sequencing and choices implies a number of elements, contained within some other collection definition, must appear in a specific order (a sequence). Or there is a choice of various elements.

The syntax of the <sequence> element is as follows, implying that sequences have cardinality and that they can be repeated:

```
<sequence minOccurs="" maxOccurs"">
```

Here is an example sequence definition:

```
<xsd:element name="region" minOccurs="1" maxOccurs="20">
    <xsd:sequence>
        <xsd:element name="name" type="xsd:string"/>
        <xsd:element name="population" type="xsd:integer"/>
        <xsd:element name="area" type="xsd:integer"/>
        <xsd:element name="country" minOccurs="0" maxOccurs="unbounded">
            <xsd:sequence>
                <xsd:element name="name" type="xsd:string"/>
                <xsd:element name="population" type="xsd:integer"/>
                <xsd:element name="area" type="xsd:integer"/>
            </xsd:sequence>
        </xsd:element>
    </xsd:sequence>
</xsd:element>
```

If you use the preceding definition, both regions and countries can contain all of the name, population, and area values; but they must occur in the sequence of name, population, and area. Additionally, the region has one final element for countries within regions. In other words, this is a valid <region> tag:

```
<region>
    <name>Africa</name>
    <population>789548670</population>
    <area>26780325</area>
    <country>
        ...
    </country>
</region>
```

And this is not a valid `<country>` tag because the `<area>` and `<population>` tags are in the wrong sequence:

```
<region>
    <name>Africa</name>
    <area>26780325</area>
    <population>789548670</population>
    <country>
       ...
    </country>
</region>
```

There is an `<all>` sequencing element definition, allowing any order of elements. This is the same as not using a `<sequence>` element.

Where the `<sequence>` element enforces element order, the `<choice>` element allows a selection from a list of elements. Again, the syntax is similar to that of the `<sequence>` element for the same reason, cardinality:

```
<choice minOccurs="" maxOccurs"">
```

Here is an example choice definition, sensibly allowing a single population entry in various different formats (including all would be a little pointless because they can all be recalculated):

```
<xsd:element name="region" minOccurs="1" maxOccurs="20">
    <xsd:sequence>
        <xsd:element name="name" type="xsd:string"/>
        <xsd:element name="population" type="xsd:integer"/>
        <xsd:choice>
            <xsd:element name="populationInHundreds" type="xsd:integer"/>
            <xsd:element name="populationInThousands" type="xsd:integer"/>
            <xsd:element name="populationInMillions" type="xsd:integer"/>
        </xsd:choice>
        <xsd:element name="area" type="xsd:integer"/>
        <xsd:element name="country" minOccurs="0" maxOccurs="unbounded">
            <xsd:sequence>
                <xsd:element name="name" type="xsd:string"/>
                <xsd:element name="population" type="xsd:integer"/>
                <xsd:element name="area" type="xsd:integer"/>
            </xsd:sequence>
        </xsd:element>
    </xsd:sequence>
</xsd:element>
```

Custom Data Types

A custom data type allows a programmer to create user-defined data types. Both simple and complex data types in XSD allow for the creation of custom data types. A simple data type is a predefined data type, such as a string or an integer, but with some refinement. A complex data type is a custom-built data type consisting of multiple elements, much like a C programming struct command, defining a new table in a relational database, or even creating a new class in an object development environment.

Let's begin with simple data types.

Simple Data Types

A simple data type is a predefined data type, such as a string or an integer, but with some added refinement. The syntax for a simple data type is as follows:

```
<simpleType name="" final="">
```

A `simpleType` declaration is always based on a data type that already exists (a built-in XSD data type or another user-defined type). There are three types of refinements that can be made to an existing data type using `simpleType`: a restriction, a list, or a union.

Restricting Simple Types

Restriction `simpleType` definitions use the `<restriction>` element. This option restricts a data type to have a more restrictive definition such as a more restrictive range of values. Restrictions use what are called *simple type facets*. A facet is essentially a restriction. You can also create user-defined facets to apply to a `simpleType`. Let's begin with this XML fragment from the demographics XML document database:

```
<population>
    <year year="2003" population_id="410" population="31713719"/>
    <year year="2004" population_id="411" population="32129324"/>
    <year year="2005" population_id="412" population="32531853"/>
    <year year="2006" population_id="413" population="32930091"/>
    <year year="2010" population_id="417" population="34554588"/>
    <year year="2020" population_id="427" population="38555436"/>
</population>
```

The basic syntax for a `simpleType` restriction is as follows:

```
<simpleType>
    <restriction base="<datatype | type>">
       ... application of facets ...
    </restriction>
</simpleType>
```

> *The* `base` *attribute is the* `simpleType` *being derived from, which can be a basic data type, or even another user-defined type. For example,* `<xsd:restriction base="xsd:string">`.

Facets as applied to a `simpleType`, as a restriction, are what make up the refinement or redefinition of a `simpleType` definition. The various facets available for use are shown in Figure 13-10. A *facet* is what in a relational database would be called a constraint.

Facet (Constraint)	Purpose of Constraint
minInclusive & minExclusive	Restrict a value to a minumum, allowing the minimum value (inclusive), or not (exclusive)
maxInclusive & maxExlclusive	As above but a maximum value
minLength & maxLength	String length or number of items in a collection
length	Fixed number of items in a collection
totalDigits & fractionDigits	Numeric type restriction of a number of digits, and fractional digits (to the right of the decimal point)
enumeration	One value in a a restricted list of values
pattern	Restrict string datatypes, restricting a string by pattern matching with a regular expression
whitespace	Whitespace interpretation instruction

Figure 13-10: simpleType declaration restriction facets (constraints)

In the following example, an attribute called `year` is restricted to integer values of anywhere between the years 2003 and 2020, such that the year 2002 is excluded from the permissible range of values. Also, the `year` value must be exactly four digits long (a valid Y2K year representation):

```
<xsd:attribute name="year">
   <xsd:simpleType>
      <xsd:restriction base="xsd:integer">
         <xsd:minExlcusive value=2002/>
         <xsd:maxInclusive value=2020/>
         <xsd:totalDigits value=4/>
      </xsd:restriction>
   </xsd:simpleType>
</xsd:attribute>
```

An enumerated list is a list of permissible values. For example, you can further restrict the years by changing the code as shown in the example that follows, where years are restricted to 2003, 2004, 2005, 2006, 2010, and 2020:

```
<xsd:attribute name="year">
   <xsd:simpleType>
      <xsd:restriction base="xsd:integer">
         <xsd:enumeration value=2003/>
         <xsd:enumeration value=2004/>
         <xsd:enumeration value=2005/>
         <xsd:enumeration value=2006/>
         <xsd:enumeration value=2010/>
         <xsd:enumeration value=2020/>
         <xsd:totalDigits value=4/>
      </xsd:restriction>
   </xsd:simpleType>
</xsd:attribute>
```

Here is another interesting example that can be used to restrict the entry value for a telephone number, restricting a string to a telephone number format, as in (123) 456-7890:

```
<xsd:element name="region" type="xs:string">
   <restriction base="string">
      <length value="10"/>
      <minLength value="1"/>
      <maxLength value="10"/>
      <pattern value=" ([0-9]{3}) [0-9]{3}-[0-9]{4}"/>
   </restriction>
</xsd:element>
```

Simple Type List Declarations

The `<list>` element is used to create a whitespace-separated list of items. In effect, this approach can be used to create a list of multiple value, or perhaps a list of multiple options. Let's say you wanted to change the demographics data to include a new `<yearSummary>` element, which summed up all the years of 2003, 2004, 2005, 2006, 2010, and 2020:

```
<xsd:attribute name="yearSummary">
   <xsd:simpleType>
      <xsd:list itemType="xsd:nonNegativeInteger"/>
   </xsd:simpleType>
</xsd:attribute>
```

377

The result would be something like the following:

```
<population>
   <yearSummary>2003 2004 2005 2006 2010 2020</yearSummary>
   <year year="2003" population_id="410" population="31713719"/>
   <year year="2004" population_id="411" population="32129324"/>
   <year year="2005" population_id="412" population="32531853"/>
   <year year="2006" population_id="413" population="32930091"/>
   <year year="2010" population_id="417" population="34554588"/>
   <year year="2020" population_id="427" population="38555436"/>
</population>
```

Union List Declarations

A `<union>` element can be used to create two or more types, allowing verification against the contents of two type definitions at the same time. So, let's say hypothetically that the previous examples were created a little differently, where restrictions were created in two different `simpleType` definitions:

```
<xsd:attribute name="yearRange">
   <xsd:simpleType>
      <xsd:restriction base="xsd:integer">
         <xsd:minExlcusive value=2002/>
         <xsd:maxInclusive value=2020/>
      </xsd:restriction>
   </xsd:simpleType>
</xsd:attribute>
```

And here is the second definition:

```
<xsd:attribute name="yearLength">
   <xsd:simpleType>
      <xsd:restriction base="xsd:integer">
         <xsd:totalDigits value=4/>
      </xsd:restriction>
   </xsd:simpleType>
</xsd:attribute>
```

So, you can merge the preceding two definitions something like this:

```
<xsd:attribute name="yearRestricted">
   <xsd:simpleType>
      <xsd:union memberTypes="yearRange yearLength"/>
   </xsd:simpleType>
</xsd:attribute>
```

The result would be a validation of a combination of the years, ensuring that any years in the data had four digits in them.

Complex Data Types

A complex data type typically involves a structure, consisting of more than one element. Subsequently, that `complexType` can be accessed as a single item that contains subset elements. Here is a simple example, combining elements for each region into a single type structure:

```
<xsd:element name="region">
   <xsd:complexType>
      <xsd:sequence>
         <xsd:element name="name" type="xsd:string"/>
         <xsd:element name="population" type="xsd:integer"/>
         <xsd:element name="area" type="xsd:integer"/>
      </xsd:sequence>
   </xsd:complexType>
</xsd:element>
```

Substitution

The <group> element can be used to create a structure, which can then be referred to later on as a reference. The result is a form of a substitution, as shown in the following example. This is the grouping:

```
<xsd:group name="regionGroup">
   <xsd:sequence>
      <xsd:element name="name" type="xsd:string"/>
      <xsd:element name="population" type="xsd:integer"/>
      <xsd:element name="area" type="xsd:integer"/>
   </xsd:sequence>
</xsd:group>
```

And this script snippet refers to the declaration of the <group> element:

```
<xsd:element name="region">
   <xsd:complexType>
      <xsd:group ref="regionGroup"/>
      <xsd:element name="malePopulation" type="xsd:integer"/>
      <xsd:element name="femalePopulation" type="xsd:integer"/>
   </xsd:complexType>
</xsd:element>
```

The <group> element allows specification and later reference to groups of elements. The <attributeGroup> element does the same but for attributes. So, I can create an attribute group something like this:

```
<xsd:attributeGroup name="regionAttributes">
   <xsd:attribute name="region" type="xsd:string"/>
   <xsd:attribute name="population" type="xsd:string"/>
   <xsd:attribute name="area" type="xsd:string"/>
</xsd:attributeGroup>
```

And this is how the group of attributes can be referenced later on:

```
<xsd:element name="region">
   <xsd:complexType>
      <xsd:element name="region"/>
      <xsd:attributeGroup ref="regionAttributes"/>
   </xsd:complexType>
</xsd:element>
```

This chapter has attempted to demonstrate how a mapping between XML document data and a relational database can be achieved. Document Type Definition (DTD) is a little less up-to-date than XML Schema (XSD).

Summary

In this chapter you learned that:

❏ DTD stands for the Document Type Definition.

❏ DTD can be used to model an XML document using non-XML command structures.

❏ DTD allows for definition of elements, attributes, and entities.

❏ DTD elements and attributes are the conceptual equivalent of XML entities.

❏ DTD entities allow for substitution of previously constructed DTD scripting elements.

❏ XSD stands for XML Schema Definition.

❏ XSD is a more advanced form of DTD.

❏ XSD is constructed using standard XML structure.

❏ XSD allows for the same capabilities as DTD, except in much more detail.

Exercises

1. What is DTD?

2. What is XSD?

3. DTD uses XML syntax and XSD does not. True or False?

4. Which of the following are accurate statements:

    a. XSD does not have the capabilities of DTD entities.

    b. XSD can reference previously constructed script sections.

    c. DTD is more advanced than XSD.

    d. None of the above.

    e. All of the above.

Applying XML Databases in Industry

The purpose of this chapter is to give you, the reader, a brief picture of how and for what XML is used in industry today. In other words: What is being used, what is it being used for, and how is it being used?

There are no Try It Out sections in this chapter as the content of this chapter is primarily conceptual, but also introductory with respect to native XML database standards.

In this chapter you learn about:

❑   What XML is capable of

❑   XML and its relationship with complexity, that of physical database size, and schema flexibility

❑   Some native XML database products

❑   Specific XML vocabularies

❑   XML implementations in industry

❑   When to use a native XML database

What Can XML Do?

XML can do all sorts of things and can be used for all sorts of things. Mostly, it can manage complexity and it can help make data transfers easier. It is also far more readily human readable than the contents of a relational database. In fact, it is more computer readable as well because it is universally understandable by being platform independent. That's the idea anyway.

One of the problems with XML and database storage is its probable inability to compete with the sheer incredible database sizes and volume processing capabilities of modern relational databases. Another factor often mentioned is that schema changes are easier in XML. You can decide that one for yourself but I would suggest looking at it from a database perspective. Your conclusion might be quite different when considering the same concepts from an application development perspective.

Managing Complex Data with XML

XML is sometimes touted as a revolutionary method for management of highly complex data structures. This is something that is sometimes true, and also sometimes not true. Why both?

❏ XML is object structured and theoretically capable of being used to build what is effectively an object database. Obviously, a fully capable object database includes all object-oriented techniques, including capabilities such as inheritance. Going further into the realms of encapsulation of coding within an object-built XML database, you would have to expand on XML with specialized tools, such as DTDs and XSDs. Object databases are much more capable than relational databases at managing highly complex data structures. The real reasoning behind these comments is that as an object design breaks things down into smaller parts, that object design becomes more efficient, and more amenable to applications. The opposite is often true of relational databases. This is because as a relational database is normalized to extremes, it becomes less efficient and more difficult to write applications for. In commercial environments, denormalization of relational database models is common in order to increase performance.

❏ XML is also not good at dealing with huge amounts of data, even when that data is complicated. Relational databases can do everything, even if management complexity is mediocre. The reasons for this are two-fold:

  ❏ XML and object structures are far too complex for large quantities of information.

  ❏ Relational databases are better industry tested than any other database modeling approach.

Does Database Size Matter?

So, XML can be useful for handling complex data structures, but generally only when the database content size is small. Small is a relative term. Ten years ago *small* could have been 1 megabyte. Present day *small* could be 100 megabytes. In fact, measuring a database as being small is probably pointless. A better method might be to measure a database as being large, or not. Very large databases (VLDB) are presently in the terabyte range. On the contrary, a few years ago a VLDB might have been a few hundred gigabytes. The issue is that using XML documents to store even a few hundred megabytes is probably very brave to say the least. A few megabytes, or under 100 megabytes, might be realistically within the capabilities of XML document storage.

Storing large quantities of data into XML documents can cause serious performance issues. Even collections of XML documents will ultimately make the individual XML fragments in the collection too large for efficient searching. Of course, some modern native XML database engines do allow some forms of indexing, which might help performance.

From a purely I/O disk-reading physical perspective, reading an XML document requires the XML document to read from beginning of file to end of file, unless effective indexing can be used. Large files equate to heavy I/O activity. Reading all of a large file is incredibly inefficient, especially when you don't want to read the entire file. A relational database, on the other hand, is built to point at different isolated parts of a database using indexes. Additionally, even the indexes can be read selectively because indexes have specialized algorithms to search indexes algorithmically.

Selective disk I/O means that only a very small portion of a database must be read to satisfy database queries. Unless of course the intention is to read all the data, which is of course counterproductive when reading terabytes of data on disk.

Once again, some native XML databases do incorporate indexing. How effective those XML indexes are is unknown as this technology is very new, and comparisons with Oracle or SQL Server indexing is also unknown. I wouldn't write home about it without extensive commercial implementation. And if anyone tells you that XML can handle data warehouse storage and activities, then you might want to experiment even more before implementing.

Are Schema Changes Easier with XML?

There is also much talk about schema changes between XML data storage and relational databases. Yes, it is quite possible that some older relational databases do not allow easy changes to schemas. Most up-to-date relational databases do allow profligate and relatively simple schema changes, using built-in commands. For example, change a table with an ALTER TABLE command. And some relational databases even allow dynamic changes to metadata objects, and even cater to concurrency during the processing of those changes. So, even multiple user and concurrency aspects are automatically handled by a relational database when changing a schema.

The issue with XML is that XML is so flexible that it more or less expects structural changes to its schemas. Part of the reason for its flexibility is it accessibility, which is of course its intention, and a sensible intention it certainly is. One case for flexibility in schema structure is this: Do you really want flexibility in metadata? Yes, perhaps for B2B data transfers but perhaps not in database environments requiring high levels of security from prying eyes.

The fact of the matter is that XML documents store both data and metadata. And program code can access and manipulate both data and metadata within the same XML document. Access to relational database data and metadata is a little more complex, in that data must be accessed separately from metadata. Additionally, in a relational database, changing any metadata, such as a table, does force data changes. This may not always be a requirement when changing XML metadata because some XML metadata changes alter structure only, not the data itself (easily transformed using XSLT). However, changing the hierarchical structure of XML data will still involve disk I/O activity, and probably heavier than that for a relational database. This is because more of the XML document will likely be read to accomplish any specific task.

The result is that schema changes are perhaps easier in XML for two reasons:

❑ When the size of a database is small enough, it is more efficiently read in its entirety, rather than reading a small part of it.

❑ Accessing XML is visibly much more appealing and requires use of low complexity, highly available tools (Internet Explorer is a good example).

In XML you can see the data and the metadata simply by popping it up in a browser. Retrieving the same data and metadata, on the same page, from a relational database might require complex coding and sometimes even more than one tool.

All this leads you back to using the size of a database to determine if XML is a better option. Try this as an experiment:

1. Load a very small XML document, maybe a few kilobytes in size, into a browser such as Internet Explorer. How long does it take?

2. Now do the same thing with a larger XML document, such as the demographics.xml document file mentioned throughout this book. It takes a lot longer because even though you see the top part of the XML document, the little load time bar at the bottom of the Internet Explorer sits around for while. If you open or close one of the subtrees you might have to wait for a response. And this demographics XML document is only 4 megabytes. Just imagine the same thing, in a browser, with an XML document of a 1 gigabyte, or even 1 terabyte.

Don't do this at home! You might wind up watching your browser load up the document for a week or so.

After 20 years of building databases and writing software, I find that an appropriate mix of development environments (this includes the database you use) is the most prudent option. An object approach is often the most efficient modern approach to building applications code. However, as little as ten years ago, this was not the case because computers were simply not fast enough. Now they are. CPU processing speed and front side bus speed (the thing between the processor and the RAM on the motherboard of your home computer) have caught up with software tools such as Java.

Then again, I also worked on financial applications more than ten years ago. This was back when computers could not cope with object-oriented application processing requirements. Those financial applications were so incredibly complicated that implementation in a relational database and a procedural programming language would have resulted in bankrupt software development companies.

I have also worked extensively with purely object-oriented databases, with tools such as Java as front-end. Object databases enable you to create classes, and allow multiple inheritance and encapsulation of procedural code, all black-boxed within the database itself. I concluded from my work with object databases that they have their niche. Object modeling can handle complexity as long as the data remains small (a few megabytes). Anything larger than that needs enormous hardware computing power. Perhaps as computers become more powerful and cheaper, the use of XML as a database storage device will become increasingly cost effective and practical. In fact, this is highly likely. Then again, the established relational database vendors have in the past become very proficient at simply including new technologies within their databases (see Chapters 5 and 6). And some of those vendors perform this inclusion process quite successfully. As quite an odd comparison, one of the most successful civilizations in history was the Roman Empire. They were savage, brutal, and quite undemocratic. But when it came to the religions of conquered nations, they assimilated into their own. And sometimes even vice versa, assimilating themselves. Relational database vendors have been quite adept at assimilating new technologies. History can often repeat itself.

Use whatever solves your problems. Don't dig yourself into a hole by not keeping an open mind about other options and products. And other options and products include both older technologies (relational databases) as well as newer leading edge technologies (native XML databases). Then again, beware of rushing in and being overzealous with the use of bleeding edge technologies. It is always best to test, verify, and make sure something works before sinking precious time and money into it.

Native XML Databases

Chapter 9 gave a generic introduction to what exactly a native XML database is. Essentially, a native XML database is an XML document. Every XML document is a form of a database, all by itself. Why? Because every XML document contains both metadata and data. The data lies in the textual values between the opening and closing tags, and in the values of attributes in elements. In the following example, Algeria is data, and 1 is also data because it is the value of the id attribute:

```
<country id="1">Algeria</country>
```

Metadata in an XML document is dictated by the elements, the attributes describing those elements (relating attributes to parent elements), and the relationships between all the elements in the entire XML document (the hierarchy). In the following example, a hierarchy can be clearly seen between the various types of locations. Also, attributes describe aspects of each location:

```
<?xml version="1.0"?>
<demographics>
   <region id="1" name="Africa">
      <population>"Lots and lots"</population>
      <area>"More than most would think"</area>
      <country id="1" name="Egypt">
         <population>"20 million"</population>
         <area>"A big country"</area>
         <city id="1" name="Cairo">
            <population>"Could be 12 million"</population>
            <area>"Kinda big"</area>
         </city>
         <city id="2" name="Alexandria">
            <population>"Lets say 5 million"</population>
            <area>"Not as big as Cairo"</area>
         </city>
      </country>
      <country id="2" name="South Africa"/>
   </region>
   <region id="2" name="Europe">
      <population>"Probably close to  1 billion"</population>
      <area>"Less than you might think"</area>
   </region>
   <region id="3" name="North America"/>
</demographics>
```

There are numerous well-known, widely used, and also well-supported native XML databases:

❑ **Tamino:** This is a suite of products including a native XML database. The data storage can consist of multiple data sources, including both native XML and relational database storage. Tamino is a heterogeneous storage environment.

❑ **eXist:** This native XML database uses a specialized indexing mechanism with BTrees pointing at page divided files, which might make it more efficient.

❑ **TigerLogic:** This native XML database can be used to store both structured (XML) documents, and unstructured data (multimedia). This database might be edging a little closer to object database technology, as compared to other competing native XML databases.

❑ **XHive:** This native XML database supports anything and everything that is XML. It also allows for extensive indexing. Indexing is important to large data stores because it enables you to search into those large data stores for specific data items. Indexing saves you from having to scan large areas of disk every time something small is required. Even when large sets of data are searched, indexes help to scan information in pre-constructed, sorted order. Indexing can help to improve overall performance drastically, also enabling a native XML database to be far more scalable than, perhaps, other competing native XML databases.

❑ **XIndice:** This native XML database engine is built with the specific task of storing and managing large collections of small-sized XML documents. It also allows for indexing and compression.

❑ **DBPrism:** This tool is not actually a native XML database but a tool that's interesting enough that it's worth mentioning here. DBPrism allows for dynamic generation of XML documents directly from a database. That generated data can be transformed directly from a relational database into an XML document. That XML document is, in reality, a native XML database in itself. However, Chapters 5 and 6 show that relational databases that include native XML data types allow this type of functionality within industry-tested and accepted bounds of a relational database anyway.

Many native XML databases support tools such as XPath 2.0, XQuery, XLink, and XPointer — as do some relational databases, to a lesser and greater degree. If not, then relational database vendors are likely working on these issues, if they are in demand.

Specific XML Vocabularies

XML is flexible and technically can have subset vocabularies built on top of standard XML syntax and structure. What this allows is for standard practices to be set for a particular industry, discipline, or application. And these different vocabularies are all based on XML syntax, which as you already know is more or less platform independent and universally usable, by anyone. Building of these vocabularies is very similar to the way in which specialized classes are built from more abstracted classes, in an object modeling environment.

In general, vocabularies can be divided into two main groups:

❑ Application-specific XML vocabularies, which are shared across multiple industries and disciplines

❑ Industry-specific XML vocabularies, perhaps shared by different applications within the same industry

XML Vocabularies

As you can see in Figure 14-1, there are a multitude of different XML vocabularies, applying to specific types of applications and specific industries.

Further details on vocabularies shown in Figure 14-1 can be found at www.service-architecture.com.

Let's pick one of the vocabularies shown in Figure 14-1. The MathML (or Mathematics XML) seems like a sensible choice, given the material presented in this book. Even though the topic of mathematics can seem incredibly complex in some ways, the interpretation of mathematical formulae and calculations, expressed in XML, can be very simple. In other words, you don't have to understand the meanings of mathematical formulae to write them out in XML, using MathML. As opposed to being written down in English, or some otherwise abstract scientific notation, formulae are recorded as XML. One does not have to have much of an understanding of the content and semantics of a mathematical formula. Each part of a formula has a specific tag in MathML and can thus be easily converted. Some of the elements of MathML are shown in Figure 14-2.

Application XML Vocabularies	Industry XML Vocabularies
Address XML	Accounting XML
Computing Environment XML	Advertising XML
Content Syndication XML	Astronomy XML
Customer Information XML	Building XML
Electronic Data Interchange (EDI) XML	Chemistry XML
Geospatial XML	Construction XML
Human XML	Education XML
Localization XML	Food XML
Math XML	Finance XML
Open Office XML	Government XML
Topic maps XML	Healthcare XML
Trade XML	Human Resources XML
Translation XML	Instruments XML
Universal Business Language (UBL)	Insurance XML
Universal Data Element Framework (UDEF)	Legal XML
	Manufacturing XML
	News XML
	Photo XML
	Physics XML
	Publishing XML
	Real Estate XML
	Telecommunications XML
	Travel XML

Figure 14-1: XML vocabularies for applications and specific industries

Element	Description
math	The root element for a Math XML (MathML) document
mrow	Group expression with operators
mfrac	Fraction
msqrt	Square root
mroot	Everything but a square root, such as a cubed root
menclose	Encloses an expression with specified notation
msub	A subscript such as for a base in a logarithm
msup	A superscript such as for raising an number to a power
msubsup	Adds a subscript and a superscript such as for integration in calculus
mfenced	Adds parentheses for expression precedence
mmultiscripts	Presubscript and tensor notations
mtable	Defines a matrix (a matrice)
mlabeledtr	A single labeled row in a matrix
mtr	A single unlabeled row in a matrix
mtd	Single cell in a matrix
mpadded	Padding is adding of space characters around textual content
munder	Under accent limits
mover	Over accent limits
munderover	Both under and over accent limits
mstyle	Make style changes
merror	Return an error message
mphantom	Contains expressions invisibly
maction	Bind actions to expressions

Figure 14-2: The elements of MathML (Mathematics XML)

Figure 14-2 shows some of the Mathematics XML elements as listed on the W3C specification website for MathML. The elements important to your understanding in this book are as shown in Figure 14-3.

Basic Element	Description
mtext	A text value
ms	A string value
mn	A number
mspace	A space character
mi	A variable
mo	An operator such as +, or a separator such as (
mglyph	Specialized mathematical characters

Figure 14-3: The basic elements of MathML

The topics of this book are XML and databases, not mathematics. This why many of the items in Figure 14-2 are grayed out, and also why only a small number of all the elements in MathML are covered here. I am simply trying to demonstrate a vocabulary for specific tasks—in this case, mathematics! Figure 14-3 shows the basic elements that make up MathML. Here's an example:

```
x + y
```

The preceding expression can be represented in MathML with the following steps. First, you need the namespace and the root element:

```
<math xmlns="http://www.w3.org/1998/Math/MathML">
</math>
```

Next, you group the expression as an executable expression, which is not operated on with any other expression, or part thereof, at this level of precedence:

```
<math xmlns="http://www.w3.org/1998/Math/MathML">
    <mrow>
    </mrow>
</math>
```

Now you add the first variable, *x*:

```
<math xmlns="http://www.w3.org/1998/Math/MathML">
    <mrow>
        <mi> x </mi>
    </mrow>
</math>
```

Then you add the second variable, *y*:

```
<math xmlns="http://www.w3.org/1998/Math/MathML">
    <mrow>
        <mi> x </mi>
        <mi> y </mi>
    </mrow>
</math>
```

And finally, you add the operator between the two variables, yielding the entire expression:

```
<math xmlns="http://www.w3.org/1998/Math/MathML">
    <mrow>
        <mi> x </mi>
        <mo> + </mo>
        <mi> y </mi>
    </mrow>
</math>
```

This makes sense. All you are seeing here is that a specialized syntax of XML is being used to interpret a specialized topic or language. In this case, you are attempting to write mathematical expressions into

XML, using a specialized form of XML called MathML. The resulting MathML XML documents can be passed between many different mathematicians, and even computers, and be universally understandable by all (persons and computers). It certainly beats writing complex, mile-long equations down on paper, scanning them, e-mailing the images, and then expecting some mathematician on the other side of the world to read your writing, let alone interpret the symbols. And computer imaging? Not a chance. Still in the realm of science fiction at this level. And even if possible, much more expensive to implement. Mathematicians generally use a common system of symbols. Industry standards will likely vary. XML standards can certainly help. And if there are not any tools for constructing vocabulary-specific XML documents, then they will likely be built if someone is willing to pay for them. And there are always many people willing to build open source software.

As already stated *ad infinitum* throughout this book, the intention of this book is beginner level, and not to go into too much depth with something, such as describing the ins and outs of MathML. So, let's get away from the more technical coding aspects and look at some simple examples on the Internet. What about a news feed? This could be written in XML, with a specific XML vocabulary for news feeds. Figure 14-4 shows a website containing medical information news feeds.

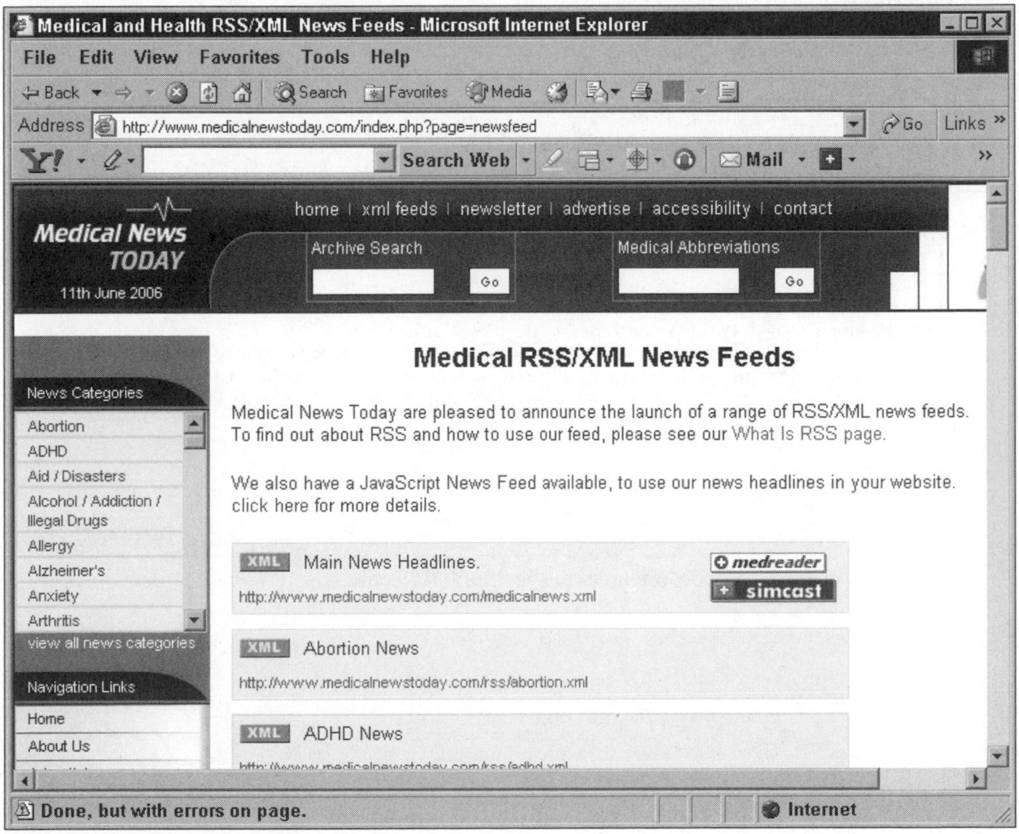

Figure 14-4: A news feed XML website

I clicked the first XML link, as shown in Figure 14-4, and got the result shown in Figure 14-5. You may get an error from clicking this link, depending on which browser and operating system you are using.

Figure 14-5 demonstrates an XML vocabulary that is universally understandable to a specific industry — namely, the medical news media. This specific vocabulary is a thing called RSS 0.91. RSS is actually a family of XML formats called Rich Site Summary (also known as Really Simple Syndication). RSS allows construction of XML in a specialized manner. RSS yields richly formatted and interpretable XML content for a specific application or industry. RSS is often used for news feeds on the Internet.

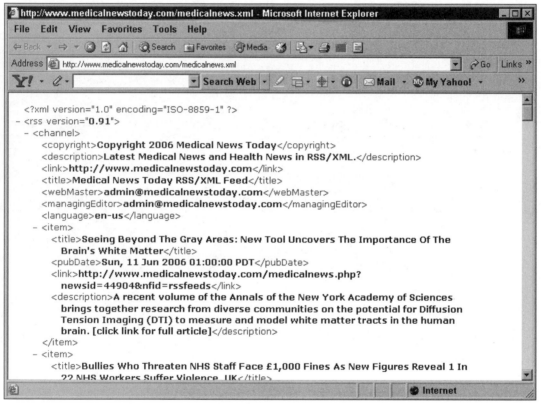

Figure 14-5: A news feed using an industry-specific XML vocabulary

Another, perhaps more fun example might be one called Astronomy Instrument Markup Language (AIML). AIML can be used to denote the way in which astronomical instruments are managed. This includes instruments such as telescopes, cameras (of any form one can dream up), and any other type of weird and wonderful instrument that might be used for *finding stuff* in outer space, from outer space, on land, and by civilian, military, or even more secretive organizations. Figure 14-6 shows an example NASA web page.

I then clicked in the example, as shown in Figure 14-6. I got an error because the DTD file is non-existent (even with the suggested change shown in Figure 14-6). So, I downloaded the XML document indicated by the link highlighted in Figure 14-6, commented out the DTD file specification in the XML file, and executed in my Internet Explorer, as shown in Figure 14-7.

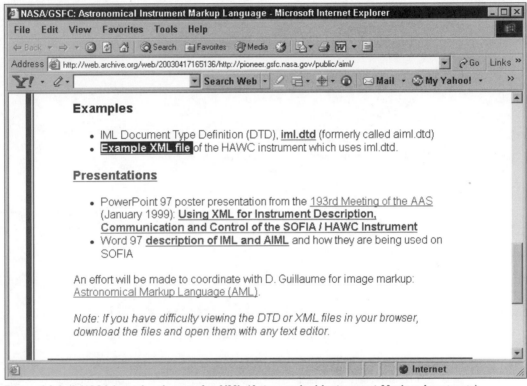

Figure 14-6: A NASA-based web page for AIML (Astronomical Instrument Markup Language)

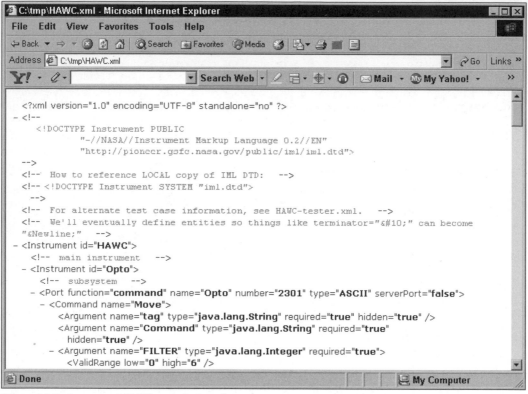

Figure 14-7: An example AIML vocabulary document

Commercial Implementation of XML

A multitude of industries utilize XML in one form or another, and often for different reasons:

❑   Some industries use XML because of its standardization of information transferal. In other words, information sent between different people, computers, or companies can be easily understood by all parties. They all use XML, and perhaps some type of specialized XML vocabulary to interpret data.

❑   The other obvious reason is the natural object and hierarchical structural aspects of XML documents. Object methodologies lend themselves to management of complex information much better than do relational database modeling techniques. Why is this the case? The answer is simple. The more an object data model is divided into its smallest divisible parts, the simpler and more manageable it becomes. When dividing a relational database model into its simplest and most detailed parts, the relational model can begin to fail. This failure is often seen only in commercial environments. Commercial environments usually have massively uncontrollable quantities of data. The more a relational database is divided into self-contained elements, the larger and more complex the queries against that data can become. The result is nearly always abominable performance. Poor performance is unacceptable in industry because companies must turn a profit in order to remain viable concerns.

The result is that, commercially, XML is more likely to be used in order to simplify data transfer operations. There are many commercial environments that do utilize XML to handle complex data issues. However, they tend to be either bleeding edge technology, such as bioinformatics and genetic engineering, or perhaps smaller parts of larger database implementations. For example, some military applications include native XML database installations for a specific function on a naval vessel, for instance — as opposed to *running the entire ship*. In other words, XML is used specifically where it can provide the best benefit.

Common industrial and commercial uses of XML and XML databases are as follows:

- ❑ **Data Transfer and B2B (Business to Business):** Information portals or data transfer mechanisms in the corporate world.

- ❑ **Catalog and document management:** Catalogs of data such as storage of scientific textual documents and research papers, requiring extensive searching facilities both as document titles and within those documents.

- ❑ **Manufacturing:** Manufacturing has always been a complex issue for relational databases and any application development. A high degree of complexity is one of the primary motivating factors for use of XML. The mind boggles at the complexity of all the parts that go into manufacturing a commercial aircraft. This could include manufacturer suppliers, even their suppliers, pricing, where parts are located, how and where parts fit, and measurements. A list like this can go on and on. Even manufacturing something as simple as bricks will likely involve raw materials, where they come from, oven temperatures, a multitude of types of bricks. Again, the list can go on and on.

- ❑ **Medicine:** Medical information often includes diagnoses with specialized multimedia data, such as imaging, and even imaging annotations. Again, complexity is the issue for use of XML.

- ❑ **Personalization:** Whenever you go to a website, such as Amazon or eBay, you might get a personalized web page — if not now then in the future. XML can handle this personalization by providing a generic framework for interpreting what is specific to yourself. When you surf to that web page you will get something that says *Hi* specifically to you, and the site might try to *market at you* based on what you have purchased in the past (even from other vendors). This type of web page could probably be more irritating than anything else — a little like junk email. It might be more useful than you think, working on a subliminal level.

- ❑ **Web services and feeds:** Any kind of Web Service providing real-time data can utilize XML to standardize both transfer and display (see Chapter 7). News feeds, stock market feeds, flight information and booking systems are some more common examples of many other varying applications.

- ❑ **Bioinformatics and genetics:** This type of data is particular complex and highly volatile. Volatility implies that these fields of research are still very much research, and they can change dramatically, and repeatedly. The flexibility and complexity-handling capabilities of XML can benefit these fields immensely.

- ❑ **Incomplete and inconsistent data:** Any information, including data such as customer profiling and entertainment data can often be incomplete, and is potentially inconclusive. XML is flexible enough to allow you to leave stuff out and mix different things together. For example, entertainment could include data about restaurants, night clubs, hotels, or even the crumbly candy bars you purchase in a movie house. In other words, describing the flavor and ingredients of goodies purchased in a movie house is very different from the swimming pool and restaurant facilities of a swanky downtown hotel. XML allows for this type of flexibility because both its data and metadata structure are both flexible and directly available. In other words, data and metadata are both in the same place (in the same XML document).

❑ **Geographical, geospatial, and geological data:** Geographical data is locational data such as countries, cities, population, and demographics (used in this book) data. Quite often, this information involves one thing inside another, within a multiple-layered hierarchy. Generally, one does not necessarily need to access this type of data, unless one is looking through the parent information. This is not always the case. Geospatial data applies to locations in three-dimensional space, such as both above and below the earth's surface. For example, known oil and natural gas deposits are below the earth's surface. Climatological data is above the surface of the earth. Geological data might be about mapping prospective resources based on satellite data (visible and otherwise) — even ground-based data, such as geophysical research. A large part of geophysical data is putting sticks of dynamite into holes in the ground, and then lighting the fuses, running away — fast! — and measuring the vibrations through different densities of materials (using special instruments, of course). For example, shock waves produced by dynamite pass through granite differently as compared to passing through oil. Earthquakes produce shock waves as well. Just much bigger ones.

❑ **Cartographical data:** Cartography is the science of drawing maps. It can be quite complex. Given the capability of online mapping services to provide detailed driving directions between two points anywhere in America, the complexity of these systems is quite unimaginable. Often mentioned with the subject of online cartography are subject areas and buzzwords, such as XML Topic Maps (XTM) and Global Positioning Systems (GPS). There are also many different types of maps, and also different types of projections. For example, a political map shows capital cities and the borders of countries. A topographical map concentrates on elevations and topography. Topography includes things such as rivers, mountain ranges, valleys, and anywhere that it might be good to go swimming or skiing. Topography is the lay of the land with respect to the inorganic part of the natural world. The organic parts are the fauna and flora, and thus represented. A topographical map might show countries, borders, and cities but they are less of a priority than the topographical features. Back to projects. Different types of projections are vastly different. If you take a globe and flatten it out onto a two-dimensional map, the picture is quite different from reality. To make it look nice, you get what is called a mercator projection, which spreads things out more the closer you get to the poles. The result is that the distances at the poles, on the flattened out map, look much greater than they are in reality. Traveling from pole to pole, according to the map, has no distance whatsoever if you go from one map edge to the other. This is quite obviously completely silly. To the untrained eye, why not? This can be done from left to right. So why not up and down? If one can go from side to side instantaneously, why not up and down? A road map is just that: a road map where online services provide directions as well. Just imagine trying to figure out all directions between all addresses in every country in the world. Yoiks! The point I am trying to make is that cartography is far more complex and far more data intensive than it might seem at first glance.

When to Use a Native XML Database

In general, XML documents can be used as, or within, a database when the overall physical size of the database is small. Additionally, some types of datasets can be so incredibly complex that a relational database model might stumble. XML, being naturally an object modeling derivative, can be highly effective at handling highly complex data modeling. However, even a highly complex database model, within the scope of a very large set of data, will very likely still be far more efficient if implemented in a relational database.

The advent of object databases was supposed to unseat the marketing positions of the relational database vendors. This did not happen. This unseating did occur in previous decades with respect to the development of hierarchical, network, and relational database technology. Relational databases vendors tend to rapidly incorporate some of the aspects of new technologies. They often do this in a kludgy manner. However, when it comes to fighting off the competition of object database vendors, the relational database vendors won that little battle hands down over a decade ago. Will native XML databases unseat relational database vendors? This is unlikely because some of the more rapid development relational database vendors, including Oracle Database (see Chapter 5) and SQL Server from Microsoft (see Chapter 6) already incorporate XML data types.

In Chapters 5 and 6, it was adequately demonstrated that an XML data type is effectively embedding a native XML database into a relational database. Yes, it is a bit of a kludge. And the same thing was done when incorporating object methodologies into relational databases. The underlying structure remains relational database technology. However, it does work. And the commercial users of these relational databases are not shifting to XML in significant numbers yet, if at all. As with object database technology, XML is being used quite extensively, where it can be, and where it is most usefully employed. These implementations are quite typically new implementations (newly built software), or situations that can easily resolve age-old problems, such as transferring data between disparate metadata structures. B2B data transfers is a good example of this type of activity. The biggest issue with legacy software, and currently used things is as it always was. Changing everything across the board is simply too expensive. If new technology is useful it will be utilized where it makes financial sense. If new technology is better, then it will gradually take over.

One of the biggest issues with object databases and object methodologies, in general, is that of reporting. Performance is so poor that it makes object database storage pointless, where any kind of output of more than a single data item (a row or record) is required. The same would apply to XML documents, when reading those documents not in the sequence or hierarchy that they are created in. Reporting is an essential commercial requirement.

One could dictate many pros and cons when discussing the capabilities of relational databases, as compared to native XML databases. Additionally, XML documents are somewhat similar in structure to object data models, and thus these two can also be compared against relational modeling techniques. There is much to be said for relational and object (including XML) technologies. Both are good and bad. Anything further written by myself on this topic may very well deteriorate into personal opinion. My only comment is that if a new technology is good, it will gradually come into general use. It will eventually succeed its predecessor. So watch this space!

The power of XML may be unlimited in some respects. It is flexible and thus adaptable, perhaps to any situation and any requirement. So, it may very well be inevitable that XML will, some time in the future, become an integral factor in the way in which data is stored and manipulated. In other words, XML may be the future of both applications and databases, in one way or another. The only question that remains is to a degree that is yet to be seen. Where some XML standards fail to gain a foothold via popularity of use, others succeed. The future of XML is already determined. As already stated, the only question that remains to be seen is how far will XML be utilized? How far will it go? What do you think?

Summary

In this chapter you learned that:

- ❑ XML is capable of managing complexity.

- ❑ XML is not capable of scalability (it can't handle large data volumes).

- ❑ XML data structure is similar to object database modeling.

- ❑ XML allows for schema flexibility. This is not necessarily an advantage.

- ❑ There are many native XML database products but initial investigation is encouraged.

- ❑ Not much is known about native XML databases because they are new to the commercial world in comparison to relational databases.

- ❑ Relational databases are extensively industry tested over decades of commercial use.

- ❑ Specific XML vocabularies cover both application types and specific industries.

- ❑ A native XML database can be used when it is appropriate.

- ❑ An appropriate use for a native XML database is in an environment of high structural complexity and small physical size.

Glossary

.NET: Software strategy and suite of tools, implemented by Microsoft Corporation. Used for development and executing Web Services over the Internet.

Absolute Path: XPath search expression starting at the root node of an XML document.

Abstracted Class: An abstraction is created to generalize attributes, values, and methods that are common to multiple classes.

Active Server Pages: A Microsoft Corporation, server-side Internet scripting language.

Algorithm: A set of computational steps, implemented to solve a problem.

Alias: An assumed name or label assigned to some type of token or object, such as a table in a relational database query.

ALTER INDEX: A command used to change the structure and/or content of an index in a relational database.

ALTER TABLE: A command used to change the structure and/or content of a table in a relational database.

Alternate Index: An index created on one or more fields of a relational table as an addition to any existing primary or foreign key indexes.

Amazon: Globally present Internet company that primarily operates as an online book retailer.

Ancestor: Any node above the current node in an XML hierarchical tree. For example, the parent, grandparent, great-grandparent, or the root node are all ancestors of a node within an XML document.

Ancestor Node: See *Ancestor*.

Ascending Index: An index that is built sorted in ascending order, such as A, B, C.

Glossary

ASP: See *Active Server Pages*.

Atomic Value: A text value, having no children or parent node.

Attribute: In XML, an attribute is a specific value assigned to an element. In an object world, an attribute defines specific slots within classes. Attributes are the equivalent of a relational entity column or field.

Auto Counter: Allows automated generation of sequences of numbers, usually one after the other, such as 101, 102, 103, and so on. Some database engines call auto counters sequences.

Backus-Naur Form: A syntax notation convention.

BETWEEN: Verifies expressions between a range of two values.

Binary Object: Stores data in binary format, typically used for multimedia, such as images, audio, video, and so on.

Black Box: Objects or chunks of code that can function independently, where changes made to one part of a piece of software will not affect others. Object methodology allows black boxing. Relational database design and procedural coding do not allow black boxing.

Browser: A program used to surf the Internet, such as Internet Explorer or Netscape.

BTree: See *BTree Index*.

BTree Index: A binary tree. If drawn out on a piece of paper a binary tree index looks like an upside down tree.

Calling Loop: See *Parent Loop*.

Cardinality: Cardinality determines how many times a specific item can occur within a given set of items. Low cardinality implies there are few unique values within a large set. High cardinality means many unique values within a set of values.

Cascading Style Sheets: The HTML form of XSL for XML. CSS is used to provide formatting and processing capabilities to HTML pages.

Case Sensitive: XML documents are case sensitive. For example, `<root>` is different from `<Root>`.

Central Processing Unit: The processor or chip in your computer.

Child Loop: A programmatic loop, executing within, and possibly dependent upon, the results of a parent or calling loop. The parent loop may be dependent on the child loop. There can be only one child loop per parent loop.

Child Node: A child node is a non-atomic value, and a node with a parent node. A child node can have zero or more child nodes of its own.

Class: A class defines a structure into which data is stored, and is the object methodology equivalent of a relational entity or table. A class contains attributes for storing values in, much the same as a table uses fields for storing values into.

Client-Server: Client-server environment was common in the pre-Internet days where a transactional database serviced users within a single company. The number of users could range from as little as one, up to thousands of users. Number of users depended on the size of the company. The critical factor was a mixture of both individual record change activity and modestly sized reports. Client-server database models typically catered for low concurrency and low throughput at the same time, because the number of users was always manageable.

Client Side Scripting Language: Scripting language running in a browser, on an end user computer (client side). Used to create interactive application environment with end users.

CLOB: Character large binary object (binary object for storing large strings).

Coding: Programming code in whatever language is appropriate. For example, C is a programming language.

Collection: In XML a collection is also known as a sequence, which is a group of elements contained within a parent element. A collection is a special type of attribute, and is the term applied to a repetition of elements of one class contained within another class. At run-time that collection becomes a collection of objects. A collection effectively defines a one-to-many relationship between a parent class and a child class. A collection is similar to a relational entity on the many side of a one-to-many relationship.

Column: See *Field*.

COMMIT: Completes a transaction by storing all changes to a database.

Compiler: A programming tool used to parse program language command sequences. When all commands are assessed as valid, the program is converted to binary (0's and 1's) or machine language. A computer can execute machine language much faster than having the computer read all the commands in a language such as English, every time the program is executed (see *Interpreter*). A programming language is compiled and a scripting language is interpreted.

Complex Data Type: Typically used in object structures, consisting of a number of fields. Used to describe a multiple field structure using XSD.

Compression: A term often used to describe some form of compaction of physical space used.

Concurrency: A measure of the amount of processing that can be performed at once. Typically, for an Internet servicing architecture, concurrency is the number of user connections that can be serviced at once. See *Concurrent*.

Concurrent: More than one process executed at the same time means two processes are executing simultaneously, or more than one process accessing the same piece of data at the same time. See *Concurrency*.

Constraint: Constraints constrain, restrict, or apply rules both within and between relational database tables. The term also applies to restrictions, such as a data type, placed on an element (equivalent of a field) in XSD definition.

Context Index: Many documents are indexed by creating an index containing some value that uniquely identifies subject matter of each XML document. The indexed values are stored in a side table, and then an index is created on the side table. The result is fast indexed access into a large collection of XML documents, based on whatever indexed values are created for each XML document in the collection.

Control Structure: A programming term referring to program coding statements controlling which line of code is executed next. For example, a loop determines that all lines within the loop are executed until the loop is terminated somehow. Thus a loop is a control statement, controlling what to execute next.

CPU: See *Central Processing Unit*.

CREATE INDEX: A command used to create and index in a relational database.

CREATE TABLE: A command used to create a table in a relational database.

Cross-Join: A join where all records in one table are matched with all records in another table. The result is every record in one table joined with every record in the second table, regardless of any relationship between the two tables. The result can be meaningless except under special circumstances, and usually in data warehouses.

CSS: See *Cascading Style Sheets*.

Custom Data Type: A custom data type allows a developer to create a data type of their own definition, usually as a refinement of an existing data type, or a composite of a number of objects. Also known as a user-defined data type.

Data: A term applied to organized information.

Data Centric: A data-centric XML document in its purest form uses XML data as a method of transporting data between computers. In reality, XML is often a mixture of data-centric and document-centric data. Data-centric XML is generic and program accessible because it is repetitive.

Data Integrity: The processes and mechanisms where data is maintained in a sensible and usable state. In other words, child records are deleted before parent records. Also, changes made to parent records, affecting child records can sometimes be propagated into child records.

Data Warehouse: A large transactional history database used for predictive and planning reporting.

Database: A database is a collection of information, preferably related information, and preferably organized.

Database Model: A model used to organize and apply structure to otherwise disorganized information.

Database Procedure: See *Stored Procedure*.

Data Type: A simple data type restricts values in fields, such as allowing only a date or a number. More complex data types can comprise a composite of many simple data types, or even binary objects containing multimedia, and otherwise.

Date Data Type: A special data type for storing dates and times.

Decimal: Decimal data types contain decimal numbers, usually with fixed position decimal points.

Default: A setting used as an optional value for a field in a record when a value is not specified.

DELETE: An SQL command used to destroy records in relational tables.

Demographics: The science of breaking a population into groups, which can provide useful analytical results. Demographics is the study, characteristics, and distribution of human populations. Distribution can be according to whatever criteria are specified. For example, population can be described through (divided up by) language distribution, occupation distribution, infant mortality rates, economics, and so on. Demographics is a science applying to subject areas such as geography, marketing, consumer activities, medicine. Essentially anything, depending on what questions are asked of a population.

Denormalization: Denormalization is most often the opposite of normalization, more commonly used in data warehouse or reporting environments. Denormalization decreases granularity by reversing normalization, and otherwise.

Descendant: Any node that is a child, grandchild, and so on of the current node.

Descendant Node: See *Descendant*.

Descending Index: An index that is built sorted in descending order, such as C, B, A.

DHTML: See *Dynamic Hypertext Markup Language*.

DNS: Directory names service, converting names such as yahoo.com to an IP address.

Document: See *XML Document*.

Document-Centric: A document-centric XML document suitable for human consumption is essentially not really easily understandable by a computer, if at all possible. Document-centric XML is essentially the type of documents that would normally be written by hand, by an author, such as a Word document, a PDF document, or even something like this book.

Document Type Definition: The DTD allows the definition for the building blocks of an XML document. In other words, you create a DTD document. That DTD document contains the structural definition for the data in an XML document. That DTD definition can be used as a mapping structure, mapping between the metadata, plus data mix in an XML document, and the metadata table structure of a relational database model.

DOM: See *Document Object Model*.

DROP INDEX: A command used to drop an index in a relational database.

DROP TABLE: A command used to drop a table in a relational database.

DTD: See *Document Type Definition*.

Dynamic: In computer jargon this term is used to describe something that changes frequently, or something that can be created depending on the current state of data in a database.

Dynamic Data: Data that changes significantly over a short period of time.

Dynamic HTML: See *Dynamic Hypertext Markup Language*.

Dynamic Hypertext Markup Language: The dynamic of HTML where HTML, CSS, and scripting languages such as JavaScript are combined. All these things are combined to create HTML pages that can change dynamically in real time.

Document Object Model: All browser languages such as HTML and XML are interpreted when loaded into a browser. In other words, there is a program in the browser (it's called a parser) that not only validates web page content, but also executes any commands contained in those pages. The DOM is the structure of something such as an HTML or XML document, which the browser interpreter uses to parse those web pages.

eBay: An online auction web site.

Element: A term used to describe the nodes in an XML document.

Embedded Loop: A loop executed within another loop (see *Child Loop* and *Parent Loop*).

End User: The ultimate client user of software. For example, a global Internet user population buying products online, such as on sites like Amazon or eBay. Also the clients and staff of a company who actually use software to perform business functions, such as sales people, accountants, and busy executives.

Entity (DTD): An entity is essentially a reference, including an escape sequence such as & or an included DTD definition, which has been given a name, and is referenced elsewhere by that name, as in `&entity`.

Entity (Relational): See *Table*.

Event: Something occurs in an application or a database that causes some process to execute, performing some kind of event responsive functionality.

Expression: In mathematical terms, a single or multi-functional (or valued) value, ultimately equating to a single value, or even another expression.

Extended XLink: Extended XLink types establish multiple connections between multiple resources.

eXtensible Markup Language: The long-winded name for XML. XML is extensible meaning that XML is like HTML, except that XML can have any tag created for it. In HTML, all tags are predetermined and HTML is not extensible or flexible as XML is.

eXtensible Style Sheet Transformations: This is the transformation aspect of the eXtensible Style Sheets XML language.

eXtensible Style Sheets: XML allows for creation of any tags, and thus transformations of XML content require a specifically designed and crafted style sheet scripting language.

Field: Tables are divided into fields and records. Fields impose structure and data type specifics onto each of the field values in a record. Fields can even be used to attach some processing to (specific to that field). Changes can be used to trigger events to occur.

Field List: This is the part of a SELECT command listing fields to be retrieved by an SQL query. When more than one field is retrieved then the fields become a list of fields, or field list.

File System: A term used to describe the files in a database, or on a server computer, at the operating system level.

Filter: See *Filtering*.

Filtered Query: See *Filtering*.

Filtering: Retrieve a subset of records, or remove a subset of records from a data source. Filtering is done in SQL using the *WHERE* clause for a basic query of records retrieved, and using the HAVING clause to remove groups from an aggregated query.

Flat File: A term generally applying to an unstructured file, such as a text file.

Flattened Structure: This generally refers to a database model structure consisting of one, or at most very few, hierarchical layers. For example, a data warehouse star schema consists of fact tables and some dimension tables (all on the same level). The result is only two levels, flattened out from a normalized (multiple layered) table structure of an OLTP database. Some applications and databases, when working with XML, do not have the capability to deal with XML object-hierarchical structure, and tend to flatten out XML documents into one or two hierarchical layers.

Float Data Type: A floating point data type allows a number where the floating point can be anywhere in the number. Mathematically, a floating-point number is a real number.

Floating Point: A real number where the decimal point can be anywhere within the number.

FLWOR: See *XQuery FLWOR*.

For Loop: A programming looping construct used to execute a sequence of programming or scripting commands a specified number of times.

Foreign Key: A foreign key is a type of constraint where foreign key columns contain copies of primary key values, uniquely identified in parent entities, representing the child or sibling side of what is most commonly a one-to-many relationship.

Fragment: A small section of an XML document, consisting of properly formed XML. A fragment could be the entire XML document, or a small subtree (node and all children) of an XML document.

FROM Clause: The part of a query SELECT command that determines tables (or other data source) to be retrieved from. The FROM clause can also be used to syntactically describe and dictate how tables are joined (using the JOIN, ON, and USING clauses).

Front End: Customer-facing software — usually applications purchased either online over the Internet, or in-house as custom written applications.

Function: A function is a programming unit or expression returning a single value, also allowing determinant values to be passed in as parameters. Thus, parameter values can change the outcome or return result of a function. The beauty of a function is that it is self contained and can thus be embedded into an expression.

Generic: See *Dynamic* and *Generic Database Model*.

Generic Database Model: A database model usually consisting of a partial set of metadata about metadata. In other words, tables that contain tables. In modern-day large and very busy databases, this can be extremely inefficient.

Global Definition: Global data types and global variables are available, as in they can be set and retrieved at all program levels.

Granularity: Granularity is a term used to describe multiple scenarios. In a relational database model, granularity describes how much normalization is applied. In a data warehouse, granularity describes how much detail of transactions is retained for future analysis.

GROUP BY Clause: A clause in the query SELECT command used to aggregate and summarize records into aggregated groups of fewer records.

Hardware: The computer or machine that software runs on (see *Software*). Hardware includes the computer, disk drives, CPU, memory, and so on.

HAVING Clause: A specialized SQL query filter applied only to the results of a GROUP BY clause (see *GROUP BY Clause*).

Heterogeneous System: A computer system consisting of dissimilar elements or parts. In database parlance, this implies a set of applications and databases, where database engines are different. In other words, a company could have a database architecture consisting of multiple database engines, such as MSAccess, Sybase, Oracle, Ingres, and so on. All databases, regardless of type, are melded together into a single, and apparently one and the same, transparent database-application architecture. This can obviously become incredibly complex and is, in reality, an unlikely scenario.

Hierarchical Structure: A structure where there is a root node, which contains one or more child nodes, where each child can contain one or more child nodes, and so on. XML documents are hierarchically structured in this fashion.

Homogeneous System: Everything is the same, such as database engines, application SDKs, and so on (see *Heterogeneous System*).

HTML: HyperText Markup Language.

HTML DOM: The HTML Document Object Model.

Hypertext Markup Language: The most basic of all Internet browser scripting languages. HTML is inflexible but relatively powerful and unlike XML, has a set number of allowable tags.

Hyperlink: Refers to a link between web pages. In HTML a hyperlink (or link) is defined using a tag. In XML, hyperlinks can be defined dynamically using XLink and XPointer definitions.

I/O: I/O means Input/Output, which refers to the activity of reading from, and writing to disk. Disk storage access speed is much slower than communication between RAM (Random Access Memory) and the CPU (Central Processing Unit — the processor) of a computer. I/O is very significant for overall computer performance and should always be considered seriously.

If Statement: A programming control structure allowing the selection of different options, depending on criteria.

Implementation: The process of creating software from a design of that software. A physical database is an implementation of a database model.

INCITS: International Committee for Information Technology Standards.

Index: An index is usually and preferably a copy of a very small section of table, such as a single field, and preferably a short length field.

Indexing: See *Index*.

Inheritance: One class can inherit structure (attributes) and even methods from another class. In fact during execution, an object that inherits structure from a parent class can even inherit attribute values. Again the object model tends to make the difference between data and metadata more of a gray zone. Inheritance allows the application of any structure (attributes), values (attribute values), and functionality (methods), all the way down through a class hierarchy. A class inheriting from a parent class can use what is defined for a parent class, or can even redefine some or all of what is inherited. In very advanced definitions of XSD, XML documents can include inheritance.

In-House: A term applied to something occurring or existing within a company. An in-house application is an application serving company employees only. An intranet application is generally in-house within a company, or within the scope of its operational capacity.

INSERT: An SQL language command used to add new records to a relational table.

Instantiate: To create a copy of something from a definition, usually programmatically. So, an object is instantiated from a class, and a variable is instantiated from a data type (being defined as being of a specific data type).

Instantiation: Create a copy or duplicate of a definition. See *Instantiate*.

Integer: A whole number. 555 is an integer. 55.43 is not.

Internet Browser: See *Browser*.

Internet Explorer: See *Browser*.

Interpreter: Interprets programming language commands in their raw form (as written by a programmer, and not compiled in binary machine language — see *Compiler*). Scripting languages such as HTML, JavaScript, and XML are all interpreted by a browser when loaded into a browser (see *Browser*), because they are interpreted every time they are read. Thus they are scripting languages and not programming languages. A programming language is compiled and a scripting language is interpreted.

Intersection: An intersection is a term from mathematical set theory for items common to two sets (existing in both sets). An SQL intersection join finds all records that are common to two tables.

Item Value: This can be an atomic value or a node.

Iterate: See *Iterative*.

Iterative: In computer jargon, iterative means that a process can be repeated over and over again. When there is more than one step, all steps can be repeated, sometimes in any order.

Java: Java is a powerful and versatile object-oriented application programming language. Java is an SDK.

Java Virtual Machine: The JVM executes in memory in a multitude of environments, effectively allowing platform independence for Java-written software.

JavaScript: A client-side scripting language loosely based on the Java object programming language. JavaScript is, in reality, quite powerful and can even be used to build object-oriented coding.

Join: A joined query implies that the records from more than a single record source (table) are merged together. Joins can be built in various ways including set intersections, various types of outer joins, and otherwise.

JOIN Clause: This clause is the most up-to-date SQL standard, used for coding join queries.

Join Query: See *Join*.

JVM: See *Java Virtual Machine*.

Key: A key is a specialized field determining uniqueness or application of referential integrity through use of primary and foreign keys.

Kludge: Kludge is a term often used by computer programmers to describe a clumsy or inelegant solution to a problem. The result is often a computer system consisting of a number of poorly matched elements. Too many kludges can shorten the useful life of a system, but sometimes they offer the cheapest remedy to otherwise irresolvable problems or unacceptably costly solutions.

Legacy System: A database or application using a very out-of-date database engine or application tools or SDKs.

Local Definition: Local data types and local variables are available only within the scope and context of which they are defined. So if one procedure defines a variable *abc*, then the variable *abc* will not exist with the procedural set value outside of that procedure.

Locking: A concept applying to the sharing of data, in that as one process changes data, that data must be partially or completely locked, thus maintaining consistency of the data in a database.

Loop: A programming construct used to execute a sequence of one or more commands, repetitively.

Metadata: The tables and the fields defining the structure of the data. The data about the data.

Method: A method is equivalent to a relational database stored procedure, except that it executes on the data contents of an object, within the bounds of that object.

Microsoft Windows: The Microsoft Windows operating system.

Multiple Inheritance: Some object models allow multiple inheritance. Multiple inheritance allows a class to inherit details from more than one class at the same time. The result is a hierarchy that goes both upward and downward. Thus a class can become both a parent and a child of the same class, and a specialization and abstraction of the same class as well. Multiple inheritance can create a dual direction hierarchical structure, which is flexible, but can also become exceedingly complex.

Multiple Loop: A loop executed within another loop (see *Child Loop* and *Parent Loop*).

Multiuser: A computer environment allowing multiple end users to access the same software, hardware, and/or database, all at the same time (see *Concurrent*).

Namespace: URI available on the Internet containing XML functionality.

Native XML Database: An XML document is a database. Some example purpose-built native XML databases are Tamino, eXist, TigerLogic, Xhive, and XIndice.

Netscape: See *Browser*.

Network: A system of connected computers. A LAN is a local area network contained within a single company, in a single office. A WAN, or wide area network, is generally distributed across a geographical area — even globally. The Internet is a very loosely connected network — usable by anyone and everyone who has an Internet connection.

Node: A point in a tree containing either or both one parent node, and zero or more child nodes.

Normalization: Normalization is the process of simplifying the structure of data. Denormalization is the opposite of Normalization. Normalization increases granularity and Denormalization decreases granularity. Granularity is the scope of a definition for any particular thing. The more granular a data model is the easier it becomes to manage, up to a point, depending of course on the application of the database model. OLTP databases generally perform well with much granularity. Data warehouses perform best with less normalization granularity, but often require more granularity with respect to detailed transactional histories.

Notepad: A Windows basic text editor.

Number: A numeric data type allowing only numbers, of various formats.

Numeric Data Type: A specialized data type used for storing different variations of numbers.

Glossary

NXD: See *Native XML Database*.

Object: An object in object methodology is the iteration of a class at run-time, such that multiple object instances can be created from a class. And object is also a generic term applied to anything tangible, such as a table in a relational database.

Object Database Model: An object database model provides a three-dimensional structure to data where any item in a database can be retrieved from any point very rapidly. Whereas the relational database model lends itself to retrieval of groups of records in two dimensions, the object database model is very efficient for finding unique items. Consequently the object database model performs very poorly when retrieving more than a single item, which the relational database model is very good at.

Object-Relational Database Model: The object database model is somewhat spherical in nature, allowing access to unique elements anywhere within a database structure, with extremely high performance. The object database model performs extremely poorly when retrieving more than a single data item. The relational database model, on the other hand, contains records of data in tables across two dimensions. The relational database model is best suited for retrieval of groups of data, but can also be used to access unique data items fairly efficiently. The object-relational database model was created in answer to conflicting capabilities of relational and object database models — and also as a commercial competitor to the object database model.

OLTP: See *Online Transaction Processing*.

OLTP Database: See *Online Transaction Processing*.

Online Transaction Processing: OLTP databases were devised to cater to the enormous concurrency requirements of Internet (online) applications. OLTP databases cause problems with concurrency. The number of users that can be reached over the Internet is an unimaginable order of magnitude larger than that of an in-house company client-server database. Thus, the concurrency requirements for OLTP database models explode well beyond the scope of previous experience with a client-server database.

Open Source: A term applied to software that is free to use, but often more complex and less reliable to develop with. MySQL and Postgres are open source databases.

Open Standard: A standard applying to open source software (see *Open Source*).

Operating System: The lowest level of software on a computer, generally managing the interface and the hardware. Windows, UNIX, and Linux are all operating systems.

Operations: A term applied to the operations of a company. What does a company do to make a profit?

Operator: In programming terms an operator is a special type of operation operating on two separate expressions. For example, in the expression (p AND q), AND operates on both p and q, requiring that both are true to return a true result to the expression of both p and q at the same time. Also, in the expression (3+4) the plus sign is the operator that adds together the values 3 and 4.

ORDER BY Clause: Query SELECT command adjustment allowing re-sorting (reordering) of records as they are returned from a query to a database.

Outer Join: An outer join finds the intersection of two tables using an SQL join query, plus rows in one table and not the other. The result depends on whether the outer join is a left outer join, a right outer join, or a full outer join.

Parent: See *Parent Node*.

Parent Loop: A loop containing a single child loop (the child can contain a child loop of its own). There may be dependencies between the parent loop and child loop.

Parent Node: A parent node is a non-atomic value, which can have one or more child nodes.

Parse: The act of analyzing data, scanning for tokens, validating syntax, and so on.

Parser: A program that parses as its primary function (see *Parse*).

Partial Result: A term used in this book to describe output from a query (against a database). That output includes only a portion of the results (a partial result).

Path: A route or expression determining where something can be found within a structure of nodes (in a file system or an XML document).

Pattern Matching: A process where an expression is matched as a pattern against elements in a text file (such as when an XML document is parsed).

Performance: Performance is a measure of how fast database services applications, and ultimately end-users, get responses from a computer system.

Performance Tuning: The art or act of making a computer system provide better response to end users.

PHP: Called Hypertext Preprocessor and used to create dynamic web pages, based on flexible database content .

PL/SQL: Oracle Database stored procedure language (Programming Language for SQL).

Platform: A computer system, usually including both hardware and operating system.

Platform Independent: XML is platform independent because it consists of text files, where those text files can be interpreted by any browser, on any operating system, as long as the browser software keeps pace with XML standards as released by the W3C.

Precedence: Precedence is the order of resolution of an expression, and generally acts from left to right, across an expression.

Predicate: In programming terms, a predicate is a single expression comparison in a WHERE clause of an SQL query command. For example, WHERE p=q contains one predicate, and WHERE p=q AND x=y contains two predicates.

Glossary

Primary Key: A primary key uniquely identifies each row in a table. The entity on the many side of the relationship has a foreign key. The foreign key column contains primary key values of the entity on the one side of the relationship.

Processing Instruction: An XML term describing a specialized XML tag used to submit a processing request to the XML parser in a browser. In other words, a processing instruction is executed, and a non-processing instruction is not executed, but simply validated as being properly coded XML. The <xml> tag is an XML processing instruction because it determines that all text to follow should be validated as being XML data.

Program: A piece of coding that, when executed, performs a set of steps or actions.

Programmer: A person who writes (types) computer programs.

Programming: The art and science of writing programs.

Programming Language: A computer language used to write programs. C is a programming language. So is Java. A programming language is compiled (see *Compiler*) and a scripting language is interpreted.

Pseudocode: Pretend or make believe code. Used to put forward a concept or idea. The coding is not necessarily syntactically verified in any environment, SDK, programming language, database, and so on.

QName: Qualified name. A QName contains a namespace URI. A QName is an optional prefix and a colon, followed by a local name, or a URI plus a local element or attribute name.

Query: A query is a statement interrogating a database (or data source) and returning information. SQL executes queries against relational tables and XQuery executes queries against XML documents.

RAM: Random access memory. RAM is the memory chips inside our computer. RAM provides an ultra fast buffering storage area between CPU (the processor), and your I/O devices (disks).

RDBMS: See *Relational Database Management System*.

Real Simple Syndication: The latest version of RSS implies syndication and standardization of Web Services and web feeds online. See *Rich Site Summary*.

Record: Tables are divided into fields and records. Fields impose structure and data type specifics onto each of the field values, in each record.

Referential Integrity: Referential integrity is a process (usually contained within a relational database model) of validation between related primary and foreign key field values. For instance, a foreign key value cannot be added to a table unless the related primary key value exists in the parent table. Similarly, deleting a primary key value necessitates removing all records in subsidiary tables, containing that primary key value in foreign key fields. Additionally, it follows that preventing the deletion of a primary key record is not allowed if a foreign key exists elsewhere.

Relational Database Management System: A relational database contains tables with data. The management system part is the part allowing you access to that database, and the power to manipulate both the database and the data contained within it.

Relational Database Model: The relational database model provides a two-dimensional structure to data. The relational database model more or less throws out the window the concept and restriction of a hierarchical structure, but does not completely abandon data hierarchies. Any table can be accessed directly without having to access all parent objects. Precise data values, such as primary keys, are required in order to facilitate skirting the hierarchy, to find individual records, in specific tables.

Relative Path: A path through data from a specified point within that data (usually the currently actively accessed node).

Repository: Another term for a storage medium, such as a relational database, an XML document, or a native XML database.

Reserved Character: A character that is reserved by a compiler or interpreter, as having s specific meaning. For example, in the expression x+y, the plus sign means addition, and not the word "plus."

Reserved Word: This is a special word, in programming syntax known as a token that has special meaning to a programming language.

Restriction (DTD): See *Constraint*.

Rich Site Summary: RSS allows construction of XML in a specialized manner. RSS yields richly formatted and interpretable XML content for a specific application or industry. RSS is often used for news feeds on the Internet. RSS is also known as Real Simple Syndication. See *Real Simple Syndication*.

ROLLBACK: This command undoes any database changes not yet committed to the database using the COMMIT command.

Root: The root or topmost element of an upside-down tree.

Root Node: See *Root*.

Row: See *Record*.

RSS: See *Rich Site Summary* and *Real Simple Syndication*.

SAXON: A program allowing execution of XQuery queries. Saxon software can be downloaded at the following URL: http://saxon.sourceforge.net.

Saxon: See *SAXON*.

Scalability: Used to describe and define how much data volume and processing or throughput an architecture, application, or database, or all three, can manage before being overwhelmed. A scalable architecture is one that will either not react badly to, or will be easily adaptable to an exponential increase in size over a short period of time. An architecture that is not scalable will likely be rendered useless in a production scenario in a very short period of time.

Schema: A schematic or logical structure applied to data stored in a database. Essentially, a schema is defined as the set of tables in a single database model for a relational database.

Glossary

Script: A script is a sequence of commands written in a scripting language (see *Scripting Language*).

Scripting Language: A scripting language is similar to a programming language but is usually simpler syntactically (fewer commands). The result is usually less capability. A programming language is compiled and a scripting language is interpreted (see *Interpreter*).

SDK: See *Software Development Kit*.

Secondary Index: See *Alternate Index*.

SELECT Command: A query is executed using a SELECT command. A SELECT command contains all the fields to be retrieved when reading tables in a relational database.

Self Describing: 1) A term often applied to XML in that an XML document includes data, metadata, and relationships between elements within the XML document. And these three things do not require definition of DTDs or XSDs. 2) Self describing implies that something describes its own structure. XML documents are self describing because they contain data in the form of text values. That data is then described by XML elements, attributes, and the hierarchical relationships between all elements in the XML document (the metadata).

Sequence: See *Auto Counter*.

Server Side Scripting Language: Scripting language running on a server, not directly accessible by end users. Used for serving up web pages based on dynamic content (see *ASP*).

Sibling: See *Sibling Node*.

Sibling Node: A sibling is a node in the same collection, which has the same parent node.

Simple Data Type: See *Data Type*.

Simple Object Access Protocol: Protocol (a standard) used for passing universally understandable XML messages over the Internet.

Simple XLink: Simple XLink types establishes a connection between two resources.

Single Line Entry: In a relational database, an SLE form essentially adds a single object, usually a single row to a single table.

SLE: See *Single Line Entry*.

SOAP: See *Simple Object Access Protocol*.

Software: Describes the architectural part of a computer system that is programmed or scripted. For example, the Windows operating system is software. Oracle Database is also software. Any XML documents stored on a computer are software. XML is a gray area because depending on how XML is used, that XML data can be either data or scripting. Technically, data and metadata are not software but just data. However, XML is executed as an interpretation by a browser and in that respect is software .

Software Development Kit: A suite of programs used for application development.

Sorted Query: See *ORDER BY Clause*.

Specialized Class: A specialization of a class is an inherited, specific type of a class. Specializations often substitute for what are usually called types in a relational database.

SQL: See *Structured Query Language*.

SQL/XML: The SQL Standard for XML is a standard created and supported by INCITS.

Static Data: Data that does not change significantly over a long period of time, if ever.

Stored Function: A stored function is precisely the same as a stored procedure except that it returns a single value. See *Stored Procedure*.

Stored Procedure: A stored procedure, also sometimes called a database procedure, is a chunk of code stored within and executed from within a database, typically on data stored in a database but not always.

String Data Type: A simple data type containing a sequence of alphanumeric characters.

Structured Query Language: SQL is a non-procedural (or scripting) language. A non-procedural language does not allow dependencies between successive commands. SQL is an abbreviation for Structured Query Language, the language used to access data in a relational database. Generally, for any relational database other than Microsoft SQL Server, SQL is pronounced "ess-queue-ell" and not "sequel." The term "sequel" or "seekwl" was chosen by Microsoft because "ess-queue-ll" Server probably sounded a little odd.

Subquery: A special type of SQL query, which is called by another query, possibly passing values between calling query and subquery, helping to determine results for the calling query.

Substitution: A process of taking one thing, such as a chunk of code, of a chunk of XML data (and XML fragment) and replacing the chunk with another.

Surf: See *Browser*.

Surfer: See *Browser*.

Surrogate Key: Used as a replacement or substitute for a descriptive primary key, allowing for better control, better structure, less storage space, more efficient indexing, and absolute surety of uniqueness. Surrogate keys are usually integers, and usually automatically generated using auto counters or sequences.

Syntax: Any language has rules governing what words are valid, and to a certain extent the sequences in which those valid words are allowed to occur. For instance, the English language syntax dictates that the word "an" always precedes a common noun beginning with a vowel (an apple). When the common noun begins with a consonant then the word "a" is used (a dog). The same rules of syntax apply to programming and scripting languages. For example, *<a tag>* is a valid opening element in XML, but *a tag* without the <> characters is not a valid XML element.

Table: "Table" is the term used to describe the primary structural and data storage container in a relational database. A table is the definition of data, or the metadata. Tables are divided into fields and records. Fields impose structure and data type specifics onto each of the field values in a record.

Tag: See *Element*.

Tertiary Index: See *Alternate Index*.

Text: In XML, text items are the values between the start and end tags.

The Web: See *Internet* and *Browser*.

Throughput: A term often applied to data warehouses, as a measure of how much data a database can process in a given period of time.

Timestamp: A data type used to store date values, with a time of day attached as well.

Token: A term used to describe a word object. For example, elements or attributes in an XML document are sometimes described as tokens. Also, syntactical elements in programming and scripting languages are known as tokens.

Transaction: A transaction in SQL is a sequence of one or more commands where changes are not as yet committed permanently to a database. A transaction is completed once changes are committed or undone (rolled back). See *Transactional Control*.

Transaction Control: A transaction comprises one or more database change commands, which make database changes. A transaction is completed on the execution of a COMMIT or ROLLBACK command, manually or automatically. The concept of transactional control is that SQL allows sets of commands to be permanently stored all at once, or undone all at once. See *Transaction*.

Transactional Control: See *Transaction Control*.

Transactional Data: Data about the day-to-day dynamic activities of a company, such as invoices.

Transformation: A process of changing something from one thing into another. XSL can be used to transform XML data into something visually appealing in a browser. XSL does this beautification process by adding HTML commands in with the XML data.

Truncate: The term truncate implies removing characters from a value, typically a number, where no rounding occurs. Truncation is colloquially known as chopping off.

Tuning: See *Performance Tuning*.

Tuple: See *Record*.

UNION Clause: An SQL clause used to merge the results of two queries into a single set of records.

Unique Key: Like a primary key a unique key is created on a field containing only unique values for a specific field, or composite of fields, for all records throughout an entire table.

Until Loop: A special type of loop that will test for continuation of loop processing at the end of the loop, executing the loop at least once.

UPDATE: An SQL command used to change values in table fields in a relational database.

URI: Universal Resource Indicator (can be on a LAN, WAN, or the Internet).

URL: Universal Resource Locator (address on the Internet).

User: See *End User*.

User Defined: Something defined by a user or developer, usually a developer, for making the coding process easier.

User-Defined Data Type: See *Custom Data Type*.

User Friendly: Describes a software application, or otherwise that allows ease of use for the computer illiterate (the end user population). The more user-friendly software is, the easier it is for anyone to use.

Value Index: An index on text and attribute values (one or a combination thereof)—perhaps with a filter applied to those values, reducing the set of values in the index.

Variable: A programming term for an empty memory slot that can be set to a specific value for subsequent use at a later time, somewhere else in the program. Variables can be used to pass values on, either changed or unchanged, to other parts of application coding.

VBScript: A client-side scripting language similar in function to JavaScript. ASP uses a server-oriented version of VBScript.

Very Large Database: Very large databases (VLDB) are presently in the terabyte range. Ten years ago a VLDB might have been a few hundred gigabytes.

VLDB: See *Very Large Database*.

W3C: See *World Wide Web Consortium*.

Web Browser: See *Browser*.

WHERE Clause: The *WHERE* clause is an optional part of the *SELECT* statement, the *UPDATE* command, and the *DELETE* command. The *WHERE* clause allows inclusion of wanted records and filtering out of unwanted records.

While Loop: A special type of loop that will test for continuation of loop processing at the start of the loop, possibly not even executing the loop once.

Wildcard: Allows a string to contain any value, usually determined by an asterisk or star character (*).

Windows: The Windows operating system.

Glossary

Windows Explorer: A Microsoft Windows tool used to view and access files on disk in the Windows operating system (or the Windows file system).

World Wide Web Consortium: The standards organization responsible for the specification of XML standards, as well as other standards.

XForms: An XML flexibility-driven application that can be used for generating dynamic web pages input and display screens. All this from XML documents.

XHTML: A more restrictive but also more accurate and precise form of HTML.

XInclude: An XML standard allowing inclusion of one XML document or script within another at execution time. XInclude effectively merges multiple XML files at run-time.

XLink: XLink defines the standard by which web page hyperlinks are created from XML data in XML documents. Those XLink hyperlink standards are thus universally understandable for all XML documents.

XML: See *eXtensible Markup Language*.

XML Data Type: A data type that can store XML data as XML data, including the XML DOM and all XML capabilities and attributes. In other words, an XML data type stored in a relational database could have XML standards such as SQL/XML executed directly against that data type from within the relational database. Oracle Database and SQL Server Database allow use of and access to these data types (XMLType data types). DB2 Database also allows storage of XML data but is far more complex to use than XML data types used in Oracle and SQL Server.

XML Document: A term used to describe a self-contained, well-formed set of XML data.

XML DOM: XML Dynamic Object Model.

XML Fragment: See *Fragment*.

XML Schema Definition: XML Schemas are used to define logical structure onto XML data, much like defining a mapping between XML data and relational table structures (tables from a relational database). In addition, XML Schemas are also used in hand with other XML technologies, including XPath 2.0, XQuery, and even things such as SOAP.

XML Vocabulary: Specific syntax in XML used to describe a specific application or industry. For example, MathML for representing mathematical expressions, functions, and whatever in XML.

XML-FO: XML-FO or XML Format is used to format and beautify the output of XML for output display to the user. In reality, XML-FO is the formatting aspect of XSL. XSLT is the transformation aspect of XSL.

XPath: XPath is used to navigate through XML documents based on an absolute path (from the root node) or a relative position of a node (from the currently active node) in an XML document.

XPath 1.0: Version 1.0 of XPath, See *XPath*.

XPath 2.0: A vastly improved and much more powerful successor to XPath 1.0. XPath 2.0 and XQuery 1.0 support all of the same functions and operators, and they share the same data model. XQuery queries of XML documents are built using XPath expressions. Seventy-five percent of XQuery functionality is actually XPath 2.0 functionality. Large parts of current XML standardization, including XQuery, XLink, XPointer, and XML Schema are all linked to, and built upon, the expressive parsing power of XPath 2.0 (integration).

XPath Expression: XPath is all about expressions. An XPath expression is essentially a pattern used to search for matching patterns of elements, attributes, and values of both elements and attributes inside XML documents.

XPointer: XPointer refines an XLink definition, allowing for pointing of hyperlinks to XML fragments within larger XML documents. See *XLink*.

XQuery: XQuery is to XML as SQL is to relational databases. XQuery is used to read XML documents with the help of XPath expressions to select and filter data from XML data. XQuery is designed to query anything appearing as XML data, even XML data type structures (or otherwise) stored in a database, as something like an XML data type. XQuery syntax is not written in XML (it is not an XML document).

XQuery 1.0: The current version of XQuery. See *XQuery* and *XPath 2.0*.

XQuery FLWOR: FLWOR stands for "For, Let, Where, Order By, and Return." The XQuery FLWOR statement is a form of a *for* loop. In programming parlance, a *for* loop allows repetitive processing of all the items in a collection of items. In other words, a *for* loop allows the same processing to be executed against every item in a collection.

XQueryX: An XML document query language similar to XQuery, but written as XML scripting.

XSD: See *XML Schema Definition*.

XSL: See *eXtensible Style Sheets*.

XSL-FO: The formatting aspect of XSL (as opposed to XSLT).

XSLT: eXtensible Style Sheet Transformations. See *eXtensible Style Sheets*.

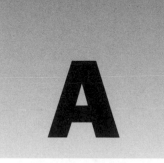

Exercise Answers

This appendix contains all the answers to the exercises that appear at the end of each chapter.

Chapter 1

Exercise 1 solution

e. None of the above. All tags are correct and there are no missing tag delimiters.

Exercise 2 solution

There are two errors in the XML document. The first error is that the first line, containing the `<xml>` tag, should look like this:

```
<?xml version="1.0" ?>
```

The second error is that the closing `</customer>` tag is missing from the end of the second customer entry. XML strictly enforces the tag (element) hierarchy.

Exercise 3 solution

It's an XML data island, embedding an XML data/metadata page directly into an HTML web page script.

Exercise 4 solution

e. None of the above. XSL is a formatting language that allows application of templates to consistent data repetitions in XML documents. That means that for tags that are duplicated in an XML document, their content can be displayed consistently, when one or more repetitions are displayed in a web page.

Chapter 2

Exercise 1 solution

a. Node class. Many of the other classes in the XML DOM inherit both attributes and methods from the Node class.

Exercise 2 solution

Choices b, c, and d are all true. A class defines structure and programmatic definition. One or more objects can be created from a single class making an object an iteration. Saying an object is a copy of a class is not strictly correct but it gets across the concept that the class and object are two different things. In a relational database a table could be a class, and the rows in the table the objects created against that class (the table), using the structure of the table as a blueprint from which to copy or duplicate from.

Exercise 3 solution

b. It's loading a .txt file. The file loaded should be an XML file with an .xml extension, such as customers.xml, and not customers.txt. d. The keyword *new* is missing before ActiveXObject. The script should look something like this:

```
<HTML><BODY>

<SCRIPT LANGUAGE="JavaScript">

var xmlDoc;
xmlDoc = new ActiveXObject("Microsoft.XMLDOM");
xmlDoc.load("customers.xml");

</SCRIPT>

</BODY></HTML>
```

Exercise 4 solution

a. returns an element. b. returns the first item in a collection. c. is the correct answer returning a Document class object. d. returns an attribute name. e. returns an attribute value.

Chapter 3

Exercise 1 solution

e. None of the above. xls:text is a data retrieval element, dumping text into the output.

Exercise 2 solution

c, d, and e are all correct. For a and b, the operative term is eXtensible, and not eXtendable. The word "extendable" means to stretch, make larger, or even richer and more comprehensive. XML is not quite an expanded form of HTML, but rather a modification of HTML with specialized features. Thus the word "extensible" as opposed to extendable applies to the difference between HTML and XML.

Exercise 3 solution

a, c, d, e, and f are all correct. b. xls:foreach is incorrect because the for loop element is xls:for-each (hyphenated).

Chapter 4

Exercise 1 solution

e. ORDER BY. The ORDER BY clause is added to the end of a query SELECT statement to re-sort records after the WHERE and GROUP BY clauses have been applied to the selected records.

Exercise 2 solution

e. All records and all fields in the CUSTOMER table. The * (asterisk or star character) means that all fields are retrieved from a table. The lack of a WHERE clause filter or a GROUP BY clause summary means that all records are retrieved. In other words, all the data contents of the entire table are retrieved.

Exercise 3 solution

f. All but b. Answer f is correct because b is a query that retrieves data from a database. The UPDATE statement changes records in a table. The CREATE TABLE statement creates a new table. The ALTER TABLE changes an existing table. The INSERT statement adds records to a table.

Exercise 4 solution

d. 4. Answer d is correct because there are three JOIN clauses and four tables shown in the query.

Chapter 5

Exercise 1 solution

d. SQL/XML is a standard established by INCITS (the International Committee for Information Technology Standards). This standard is established in order to attempt to standardize XML use with SQL in relational databases.

Exercise 2 solution

e. All of the above. PL/SQL can be used to call functions provided in the DBMS_XMLGEN package. PL/SQL can also be used to generate XML documents using SQL, cursors, and stored procedures, both as output display and as XMLType data (see Appendix B). The SYS_XMLGEN function allows for limited XML data generated, as does the DBMS_XMLGEN package. The easiest method of generating XML documents is to use PL/SQL code because PL/SQL allows for full program control. Full program control allows for the easiest method of converting between relational table structures into XML object hierarchical structures.

Exercise 3 solution

d. Retrieves all the content of an XML document from an XMLType stored in an Oracle database, in a more readable, properly organized format. Without use of the EXTRACT method, the output will be a single string, with no indenting at the start of each line for each subtree, and no line breaks.

Exercise 4 solution

a. 0. The query will finding nothing because the and, not the or, operator is used. The two countries cannot be retrieved because they are in two different regions of the world, and each country is a child of one other region node. If the or operator were used instead then both countries would be retrieved, including all subtree data for each country, within each country.

Exercise 5 solution

a. is correct because the EXTRACT method finds the subtree for the country China. b. is incorrect because being an UPDATE statement, it retrieves nothing, changing content only in a table. c. is incorrect because the EXISTSNODE method returns a 0, meaning nothing is found, or 1, indicating a node was found. The EXISTSNODE method does not actually return a node, but only an indication that the node does or does not exist. d. is also incorrect because the GETROOTELEMENT method returns the root element only, excluding its subtree, which happens to be the rest of the XML document.

Chapter 6

Exercise 1 solution

e. None of the above is the correct answer. The document physical size limitation on XML data types in a SQL Server database is 2GB. I did manage to bulk load an XML document of over 4GB but I had a few problems with some aspects of SQL Server functionality other than loading.

Exercise 2 solution

d. modify() is the correct answer. The modify() method allows changes to the XML document data stored within an XML data type.

Exercise 3 solution

a. exist() and d. query() are both correct answers. The exist() method checks for the existence of XML data type data. The exists() method is a misspelling of the exist() method and thus does not exist. The modify() method allows changes to XML data type data, and thus c. change() and e. update() are both non-existent methods. The query() method allows retrieval and data from XML data types.

Exercise 4 solution

e. All of the above is the correct answer. RAW mode returns a single XML element for each record returned by a query. AUTO mode is more sophisticated than RAW mode, returning a single layer of nested elements for each table in a join query. EXPLICIT mode allows for complete control over how XML is displayed, allowing for return of properly structured XML document hierarchical data. PATH mode is a more sophisticated and easier to use option than EXPLICIT mode.

Exercise 5 solution

c. XML Schema Definition is the correct answer. Obviously all other answers are therefore incorrect. An XSD (XML Schema Definition) can be used to generically impose schema structure onto an XML data type, using a SQL Server schema collection.

Chapter 7

Exercise 1 solution

d. SOAP is used to send context-rich messages between computers. SOAP is used as a universally understood set of XML tags to send context-rich messages between computers, even in heterogeneous environments.

Exercise 2 solution

a. A body section, containing the XML document to be sent, c. A header section, containing specifics of the body section, and d. An envelope section, constituting the root node of a SOAP XML document.

Exercise 3 solution

e. None of the above. XSD stands for XML Schema Definition—allowing for specification of a table, fields, and inter-table relationships definition.

Exercise 4 solution

c. SOAP wraps XML documents into specialized XML tags and a Web Service can provide answers to functional expressions. Option a. is incorrect because SOAP is rather used to send messages. A server process or web server will send those messages. b. is correct but c. is a better answer.

Exercise 5 solution

d. is the appropriate answer because the body tag closing element is incorrect and there is nothing wrong with the envelope tag. a. and c. are incorrect answers because the header section is optional. b. is a poor answer because there is nothing wrong with the envelope tag, but the namespace is missing from the body tag.

Chapter 8

Exercise 1 solution

The answer is False. A class defines the structure of an object where the object is the copy or iteration of that class, as created at run-time. A class is therefore the structural definition for an object.

Exercise 2 solution

The answer is True. Object models tend to allow for more in the way of containment of data within other items of data. A relational structure, when output to an XML structure can be generated using a simple SQL query. Simple queries joining two tables produce the data from both tables, mixed into each row of the output, a flattened structure. Some relational databases can produce hierarchical output using specialized functionality.

Exercise 3 solution

e. All of the above. A class is the basic metadata structure in the object model. A table is the same thing but in the relational data model. An object is an iteration or copy of a class's structure. A row in a table copies the structure of the fields in a table, over and over again. Class and table are metadata. Object and row are data. Tables in relational databases contain fields. Fields contain data values. Attributes in classes, copied as objects, contain data values as well. A stored procedure can be loosely equivalent to a method as long as one pictures both as coding within a database structure.

Exercise 4 solution

e. All of the above. Technically, any form of inheritance can be pictured as either abstracted or specialized. Semantically, the abstracted and specialized classes are created last because they attempt to generalize or refine on some other class or classes, respectively. However, in general, specialized classes often stem from relational data model types and many-to-many relationships. Abstracted classes are usually a purely object modeling creation, where the object model allows for reduction in both metadata structural complexities and method coding.

Exercise 5 solution

e. XML documents contain both metadata and data is the best answer because c and d are incorrect and a and b do not pertain to XML. In its simplest form, an XML document contains metadata in its tags and data in the value of the tags. An XML document can provide much of the storage capability to be a database all by itself. Tags and hierarchical structure contain metadata defining the structure of data. Values and attributes contain the actual data.

Chapter 9

Exercise 1 solution

Very Large Database

Exercise 2 solution

Online Transaction Processing

Exercise 3 solution

Native XML Database

Exercise 4 solution

d. The typical sizes of a modern day VLDB is terabytes and NXD is megabytes. This answer is correct for both data warehouses, as well as for some very large OLTP databases. Native XML databases are not implemented beyond megabyte sizes.

Exercise 5 solution

c. Both of the above. Both a and b are correct. Flattened XML documents contain only a root level and a single layer underneath. Hierarchical XML documents contain multiple hierarchical layers, describing structure with respect to relationships between different classes and types of metadata.

Exercise 6 solution

e. All of the above. XML documents and XML fragments can be stored in native XML databases as collections. Those collections can be validated against schemas, or not. Schemas increase data integrity but reduce flexibility. Not using schemas for collections allows fragments to differ both structurally and on content.

Exercise 7 solution

a and b are both correct. c is just completely silly because concurrency has little to do with indexing in this case. d is even more ridiculous because there is no such thing as a transactional index, in any database, and creation and destruction of XML data may be transactional but have nothing to do with a non-existent index type.

Chapter 10

Exercise 1 solution

The first expression is an absolute path and the second is a relative path. An absolute path scans from the specified node, generally the root. A relative path scans from the current path. The current path is the current point to where any processing has scanned to, within an XML document.

Exercise 2 solution

e. None of the above. The expression //country/../@name searches for country nodes anywhere in the document. Then the two dots move upward to the parent node (that could be a region node), where the parent node has an attribute called name.

Exercise 3 solution

d. The second last city for every country is the best answer because we are not specifically sure of the structure of the XML document. Assuming the demographics node is the root node, the XPath expression finds all cities, within countries, within regions. The predicate applied to the city finds the last city in the collection of cities, less 1 (the seconds last city).

Exercise 4 solution

d. All countries with at least 1 attribute. The entire contents will not be found because [@*] is a predicate, and any data outside of the path /demographics/region/country will be missed. Countries beginning with the letter A is completely nonsensical because nothing in the expression gets anywhere near specifying that particular restriction. The predicate [@*] implies all attributes within the country element, and thus at least 1 applies in this case.

Exercise 5 solution

a. Get all attributes of a node called bigthings is a good answer because the expression includes bigthings/attribute::*. Answer b is incorrect because parentofcollectionofthings is actually a sibling of collectionofthings (child finds the child of the former) — there is no parent node in this picture at all. Answer c is incorrect because it contradicts the first two, and it's simply wrong. The same applies to d. Answer e (Get zip!) implies get nothing. Actually this could be a good answer as well because you don't know the content of the XML document anyway.

Chapter 11

Exercise 1 solution

d. For, Let, Where, Order By, Return is the correct answer. The other answers are all silly.

Exercise 2 solution

XQuery is not written in XML so the answer is False.

Exercise 3 solution

The answer is True. Saxon allows for execution of XQuery queries in a shell.

Chapter 12

Exercise 1 solution

d. 3 is the correct answer because the XLinks are all simple types links (one source to one target). There are three XLink definitions from the current document and thus the current document is excluded because it is not linked back to.

Exercise 2 solution

e. arc is the correct answer. An arc XLink type describes the route between two resource links, and thus the arc proceeds from one resource link to another resource link.

Exercise 3 solution

The answer is True. XPointer points to an address, whereas XLink only links to a file.

Exercise 4 solution

f. None of the above is probably the best answer. XForms does have greater functionality, but only in the form of a few more built-in functions. However, look at the functionality and flexibility in HTML and XForms becomes solely data centric. HTML encompasses much, much more than just data-driven display. XForms absolutely does not have all the functionality of HTML because there is much more to HTML than just forms. It might be debatable as to whether XForms is more complex than HTML or not. From a programmer's perspective, the flexibility of XForms, and the rigidity and coding intensity of HTML, XForms is much easier to deal with.

Chapter 13

Exercise 1 solution

Document Type Definition.

Exercise 2 solution

XML Schema Definition.

Exercise 3 solution

False. XSD uses XML syntax and DTD does not.

Exercise 4 solution

a. is correct because DTD entities are functionally richer than calls to previously constructed script sections of XSD. b. is correct. c. is incorrect because XSD is the next generation of DTD.

The Sample Database

This appendix contains the initial version of the demographics database used throughout this book in examples. Any changes made throughout this book are not necessarily reflected in this appendix unless absolutely necessary. In other words, this is the clean version of the demographics database.

All diagrams are drawn in Erwin, a database modeling design tool, using the Information Engineering (IE) methodology. The database used to write this book was initially an Oracle10*g* Database and an SQL Server Database. Figures B-1 and B-2 show the logical and physical relational ERD model, respectively.

Scripts for creating schemas in Oracle and SQL Server databases, as used in this book, can be found at www.oracledbaexpert.com/oracle/beginningxmldatabases/index.html.

The database is too large to include actual table insertions in this book. Scripts for the Oracle and SQL Server database table insert commands can be found at www.oracledbaexpert.com/oracle/beginningxmldatabases/index.html.

> *Depending on what version of each database engine you are using, you may have to alter script syntax to make the script function properly.*

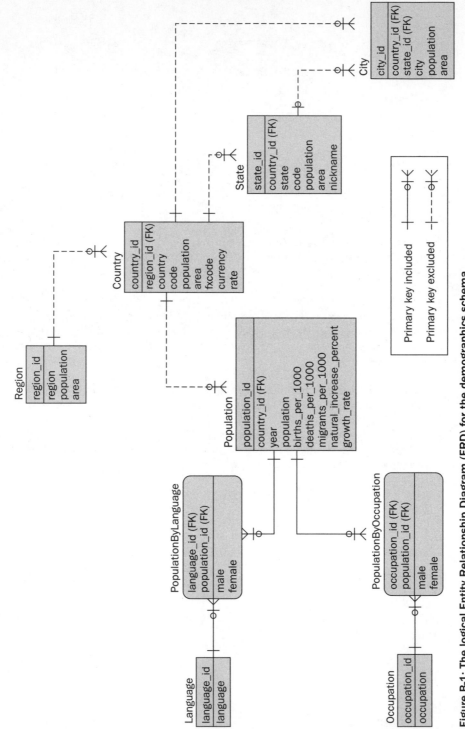

Figure B-1: The logical Entity Relationship Diagram (ERD) for the demographics schema

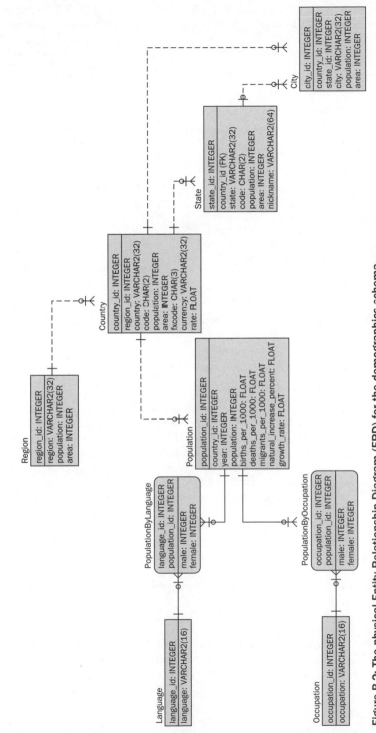

Figure B-2: The physical Entity Relationship Diagram (ERD) for the demographics schema

Figure B-3 shows an object equivalent model for the relational model ERD. The object model is used as a basis to create an initial XML document object for the entire demographics database.

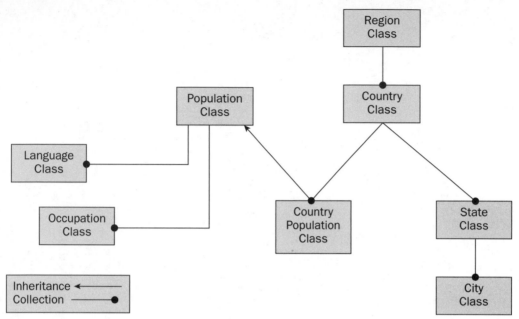

Figure B-3: The XML object model for the demographics schema

There are various ways to represent the object model for the demographics schema. However, the model shown in Figure B-3 should be familiar when compared with the relational model shown in Figure B-1. In general, the object model for data removes types and many-to-many relationships from the relational model. Types are removed by creating multiple collection contained classes (the language and occupation specialized classes are collections within the population class). The many-to-many relationship entities of POPULATIONBYLANGUAGE and POPULATIONBYOCCUPATION are catered for by the inheritance from the population class into the four specialized population classes for the regions, countries, states, and cities.

The XML document for the demographics database is much too large to include in this book in printed form. Both scripts to create the XML document (using Oracle Database PL/SQL) and the XML document are available at www.oracledbaexpert.com/oracle/beginningxmldatabases/index.html.

The XML version of the demographics database (demographics.xml) does not include languages and occupations because the XML documents are simply too large.

A script was used to generate the demographics database as a single XML document from an Oracle database. This script is written using Oracle Database PL/SQL, and will function only in Oracle Database. However, PL/SQL is a cinch for any programmer to understand, and this script should be easily recoded into any programming language for XML document generation from either SQL Server or DB2. This script can also be found at www.oracledbaexpert.com/oracle/beginningxmldatabases/index.html.

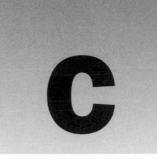

Syntax Conventions

Syntax diagrams in this book use Backus-Naur Form syntax notation conventions. Backus-Naur Form has become the de facto standard for most computer texts:

❑ **Angle brackets: < ... >.** Angle brackets are used to represent names of categories and are also known as *substitution variable representation*. In this example, `<table>` will be replaced with a table name:

```
SELECT * FROM <table>;
```

The preceding code becomes:

```
SELECT * FROM country;
```

❑ **OR: |.** A pipe or | character represents an OR conjunction meaning either can be selected. In this case, all or some fields can be retrieved, "some" meaning one or more:

```
SELECT { * | { <field>, ... } } FROM <table>;
```

The preceding code becomes:

```
SELECT name, id, population FROM country;
```

❑ **Optional: [...].** In a SELECT statement, a WHERE clause is syntactically optional:

```
SELECT * FROM <table> [ WHERE <field> = ... ];
```

The preceding code becomes:

```
SELECT * FROM name WHERE name='England';
```

❑ **At least one of: { ... | ... | ... }.** For example, the SELECT statement must include one of *, or a list of one or more fields:

```
SELECT { * | { <field>, ... } } FROM <table>;
```

The preceding code becomes:

```
SELECT name, id, population FROM country;
```

This is not a precise interpretation of Backus-Naur Form where curly braces usually represent zero or more. In this book, curly braces represent one or more iterations, never zero.

XML Technology

- **Document Type Definition**: Also known as a DTD, this is used to define structure and permissible parts contained within an XML document.

- **Native XML Database:** A specialized type of database using an XML document as a basis for storage of both data and metadata (structure and definition). Typically, an XML document contains more than one XML document in a collection and usually more than a single collection. A Native XML database is used to store, maintain, and allow access to data directly from XML data.

- **SOAP:** This is the Simple Object Access Protocol used to allow for universally understandable transfers of XML document data, typically using another universal tool, an HTTP connection.

- **WSDL:** This is the Web Services Description Language, which is used to describe a Web Service in XML, effectively allowing for sharing of both data and functionality across the Internet.

- **XForms:** XML Forms is used to define form data for input format into a screen.

- **XHTML:** HTML is the HyperText Markup Language used for creating static web page content. XHTML is the eXtensible HTML, which is a stricter and cleaner version of HTML.

- **XInclude**: XInclude allows the inclusion of one XML document inside another, irrespective of validation.

- **XLink:** This is the XML Linking Language, which is used to allow for the creation of hyperlinks inside XML documents.

- **XML DOM:** This is the XML Document Object Model, which allows programmatic access to XML documents.

- **XML Editor:** These are specialized editors that will usually perform some kind of interpretation from a text document into an XML structure. Generally, these editors require a properly structured XML document and obviously force the construction of properly structured XML documents. To be able to write error-free XML documents, you will need an intelligent or professional XML editor!

❏ **XML Schema Definition**: Also called XSD, this allows the definition of structure and data types against XML documents. XSD can provide a mapping between XML data and relational tables in a relational database.

❏ **XML:** XML is the eXtensible Markup Language.

❏ **XMLType Data Type:** Some databases allow storage of XML documents into a database in the native form of XML. In other words, the content of that XML data type can be accessed directly as if it were an XML document, include data, metadata structure, and things like the XML DOM. XML documents are stored in an XML data type inside a relational database in order to distinguish between XML data and non-XML data.

❏ **XPath:** A specialized and highly flexible expression language used for navigating XML documents. XPath and XQuery are both used together to access XML documents.

❏ **XPointer:** This is the XML Pointer Language, which allows XLink hyperlinks to point to more precise areas of an XML document.

❏ **XQuery:** This is the XML Query Language, which is used to query XML documents. Seventy-five percent of XQuery 1.0 functionality is contained within XPath 2.0.

❏ **XSL:** XSL is the eXtensible Style Sheet Language. XSL consists of three parts: XSLT, a language for transforming XML documents; XPath, a language for navigating in XML documents; and XSL-FO, a language for formatting XML documents.

❏ **XSL-FO**: This is the eXtensible Style Sheet Language for Formatting Objects. XML-FO allows for output display formatting.

❏ **XSLT:** XSL Transformations is used to transform XML documents into other XML formats, such as XHTML. XSLT to transform XML data.

XML Relational Database Technology

Figure E-1 shows the various stages of development for XML in various different vendor database engines.

This book initially contained a chapter that covered native XML capabilities in IBM DB2 Database. The XML native aspect of DB2 is covered by a DB2 option called DB2 XML Extender. DB2 XML Extender software was too complex, and the explanation too drawn out for what is essentially a beginner-level book that covers XML in databases, not DB2 Database specifically. This is not meant to imply that DB2 Database is inadequate. It is merely too complex for beginner-level explanation in this particular book. The basics of XML DB2 have been included in this appendix rather than as an individual chapter because details on the DB2 XML Extender option are not included.

Database	What's it Called?	Production Release?	How XML Handled?	Native XMLType Datatype	Verified?	Publish XML from Tables	Create Tables from XML	Change XML	Advanced XPath and XQuery?
Oracle	XML DB	Yes	Rich features	Yes	Chapter 5	Yes	Yes	Yes	Yes
SQL Server	FORXML, OPENXML	Yes	Rich features	Yes	Chapter 6	Yes	Yes	Yes	Yes
DB2	DB2 Extender	Yes	Useful but complex	Yes	Too complex	Yes	Yes	Yes	Unknown
Sybase	XML Management Package for ASE	Unknown	Java classes and perhaps otherwise	Possibly		Yes	Yes	Yes	Yes
MySQL			Nothing native						
Ingres			Basic						
Postgres			Experimentation only						
Teradata						SQL/XML only			

Figure E-1: The various stages of development of XML capabilities, in various databases. All timing aspects are directly related to when this book was written. This appendix was added in mid-May, 2006.

The Basics of XML in IBM DB2 Database

Once again, it was decided that DB2 XML Extender was too complex to install and manage for a beginner-level book so I moved the details into this appendix. This section covers the basics of XML in DB2 Database, without digging experimentally in the DB2 XML Extender software.

DB2 XML Datatypes

There are three available XML data types for use in DB2 database:

❑ **XMLVARCHAR:** XML documents less than 3KB.

❑ **XMLCLOB:** XML documents up to 2GB.

❑ **XMLFILE:** XML documents stored externally to DB2 on disk.

To enable a DB2 database for XML use, you need to enable the XML Extender by executing a script called getstart_prep.cmd.

An XML datatype in DB2 database either involves the DB2 Extender, or the use of a basic CLOB object to store an XML document as a string. A CLOB object is a data type used to store very large string values in binary format. Use the XML2CLOB function (superceded by the XMLSERIALIZE function) to convert an XML document into a string for direct database storage into a CLOB data type field.

See the section on SQL/XML later in this appendix. Coverage of the DB2 XML Extender is deliberately omitted from this book because this book is a beginner-level book. The manual covering DB2 XML Extender software is almost 350 pages long, just by itself. DB2 XML Extender requires far too much manual definition, including specialized tables and specialized structural enforcement metadata documents (DAD). Oracle Database and SQL Server database provides much of this functionality automatically, in the way of their particular implementations of an XML data type.

Document Access Definition (DAD) documents specify direct mappings between relational tables and XML documents. In other words, XML data is not stored in a relational database, but stored in relational tables where the DAD documents provide a real-time, overhead-consuming, direct mapping between XML document structure and relational table structures. It's a waste of resources because both the external XML and the tables contain the same data—even though that data is structurally different. This approach is also inefficient because a change to one requires a change to both. Native XMLType data types are much more effective. An XMLType data type effectively creates a form of a Native XML database (or a collection or multiple collections thereof) within a relational database.

Creating XML Documents from a DB2 Database

This section is divided into three separate sections:

❑ **The** REC2XML **Function:** Returns very basic record-by-record XML tagged record output from simple queries.

❑ **SQL/XML:** A large number of SQL/XML functions are in a DB2 database.

❑ **DB2 XML Extender:** This piece of software extends DB2 database, allowing generation of XML data in CLOB tables, utilizing Document Access Definition (DAD) files, and Websphere. Websphere is a DB2 front-end Graphical User Interface (GUI) package. Additionally, Websphere is a GUI front-end application. This book deals with XML capabilities at the database level (within the database), not front-end applications. The problem with using the DB2 XML Extender software is that it is tremendously complex. It even needs to be specifically installed. It is too complicated for a beginner-level book, which this book is, and DB2 XML Extender is thus deliberately omitted from this publication. The intention of this book is to present the reader with easy methods of resolving XML issues with various relational database engines. Much as I would like to describe, explain, and demonstrate DB2 XML Extender in this book, it is simply too complex for a beginner's book.

Using The REC2XML Function

The REC2XML function is a very simple method of returning the result of a query as an XML formatted string. The result is a simple field names and field data format. The syntax for the REC2XML function is a little over complicated for the purposes of this book. Essentially, the REC2XML function can be used to retrieve records from tables, producing a formatted, record-for-record XML tag structure. The following example displays regions:

```
SELECT REC2XML(1.0, 'COLATTVAL', '', REGION_ID, REGION, POPULATION, AREA)
FROM DEMOGRAPHICS.REGION;
```

This is a partial result where each row is output on a single line. I have reformatted the output with new lines to make it a little more readable:

```
<row>
    <column name="REGION_ID">1</column>
    <column name="REGION">Africa</column>
    <column name="POPULATION">789548670</column>
    <column name="AREA">26780325</column>
</row>
```

```
<row>
   <column name="REGION_ID">10</column>
   <column name="REGION">North America</column>
   <column name="POPULATION">331599508</column>
   <column name="AREA">18729272</column>
</row>
...
<row>
   <column name="REGION_ID">9</column>
   <column name="REGION">Near East</column>
   <column name="POPULATION">1499157105</column>
   <column name="AREA">4721322</column>
</row>
```

The REC2XML function is very basic.

The DB2 Implementation of SQL/XML

The DB2 SQL/XML functions get a lot better than using only the REC2XML function. Available functions are as follows:

❑   XMLSERIALIZE (CONTENT XML-function AS datatype): Applies an XML function (as detailed in the list below), producing XML content.

❑   XML2CLOB(XML-function): Converts an XML document to a string format for storage into a CLOB object field. The XML2CLOB function is superseded by the XMLSERIALIZE function.

The XML functions are as follows:

❑   XMLELEMENT (NAME element [, namespace] [, XMLATTRIBUTES (...)] value): Builds an XML element:

<element>value</element>

❑   XMLATTRIBUTES (value AS name [, ...]): Creates an attribute name-value pair within an element:

<element **attribute="value"**>value</element>

❑   XMLFOREST ([namespace] value AS element [, ...]): Can be used to build a sequence of elements on a single level:

```
<element>
   <element1>value1</element1>
   <element2>value2</element2>
</element>
```

❑   XMLCONCAT (XML-function [, XML-function ...]): Concatenates a variable number of elements, such as a number of elements in a subtree, passed back up to a parent element.

- ❑ XMLAGG (XMLELEMENT [ORDER BY column [, column ...]]): Concatenates and optionally orders a set of XML values into a parent element.

- ❑ XMLNAMESPACE (namespace AS prefix , ...]): Builds a namespace declaration.

Now let me explain each method by example, as I did with SQL/XML in Chapter 5, which covers Oracle Database's implementation of SQL/XML.

The first example uses the XMLELEMENT function to create XML elements (tags) directly from a query:

```
SELECT XMLSERIALIZE(CONTENT XMLELEMENT(NAME "region", REGION) AS CLOB)
FROM DEMOGRAPHICS.REGION;
```

This is the result:

```
<region>Africa</region>
<region>Asia</region>
<region>Australasia</region>
<region>Caribbean</region>
<region>Central America</region>
<region>Europe</region>
<region>Far East</region>
<region>Middle East</region>
<region>Near East</region>
<region>North America</region>
<region>Oceania</region>
<region>Russian Federation</region>
<region>South America</region>
```

You can't do this; DB2 will return an error:

```
SELECT XMLELEMENT(NAME "region", REGION)
FROM DEMOGRAPHICS.REGION;
```

In DB2, you have to cast the result into a data type, which is exactly what the XMLSERIALIZE function does. The XMLSERIALIZE function in the previous example typecasts the result of the query into a CLOB object.

Multiple XMLELEMENT functions can even be embedded within one another to produce a hierarchy of multiple layers, as an XML document should be constructed:

```
SELECT XMLSERIALIZE(CONTENT
XMLELEMENT(
    NAME "region",
        XMLELEMENT(NAME "name", REGION),
        XMLELEMENT(NAME "population", POPULATION)
    ) AS CLOB)
FROM DEMOGRAPHICS.REGION;
```

This is a partial result, reformatted on separate lines:

```
<region>
    <name>Africa</name>
    <population>789548670</population>
</region>
<region>
    <name>Asia</name>
    <population>47382633</population>
</region>
...
<region>
    <name>South America</name>
    <population>375489788</population>
</region>
```

This next example mixes elements and attributes together by adding in the XMLATTRIBUTES function:

```
SELECT XMLSERIALIZE(CONTENT
XMLELEMENT(
    NAME "region", XMLATTRIBUTES(REGION AS "name"),
        XMLELEMENT(NAME "population", POPULATION)
    ) AS CLOB)
FROM DEMOGRAPHICS.REGION;
```

This is the result with the name attribute highlighted for the first region:

```
<region name="Africa"><population>789548670</population></region>
<region name="Asia"><population>47382633</population></region>
<region name="Australasia"><population>24340222</population></region>
<region name="Caribbean"><population>40417697</population></region>
<region name="Central America"><population>142653392</population></region>
<region name="Europe"><population>488674441</population></region>
<region name="Far East"><population>2100636517</population></region>
<region name="Middle East"><population>294625718</population></region>
<region name="Near East"><population>1499157105</population></region>
<region name="North America"><population>331599508</population></region>
<region name="Oceania"><population>9133256</population></region>
<region name="Russian Federation"><population>258037209</population></region>
<region name="South America"><population>375489788</population></region>
```

And this query places all the fields applicable to each region into the element for each region:

```
SELECT XMLSERIALIZE(CONTENT
XMLELEMENT(
    NAME "region",
        XMLATTRIBUTES(REGION AS "name", POPULATION AS "population")
) AS CLOB)
FROM DEMOGRAPHICS.REGION;
```

This is the result with the attributes highlighted for the first region again:

```
<region name="Africa" population="789548670"></region>
<region name="Asia" population="47382633"></region>
<region name="Australasia" population="24340222"></region>
<region name="Caribbean" population="40417697"></region>
<region name="Central America" population="142653392"></region>
<region name="Europe" population="488674441"></region>
<region name="Far East" population="2100636517"></region>
<region name="Middle East" population="294625718"></region>
<region name="Near East" population="1499157105"></region>
<region name="North America" population="331599508"></region>
<region name="Oceania" population="9133256"></region>
<region name="Russian Federation" population="258037209"></region>
```

The XML_CONCAT function concatenates multiple XML fragments into a single XML pattern:

```
SELECT XMLSERIALIZE(CONTENT
XMLELEMENT(NAME "region", XMLATTRIBUTES(REGION AS "name"),
   XMLCONCAT(
      XMLELEMENT(NAME "population", POPULATION),
      XMLELEMENT(NAME "area", AREA)
   )
) AS CLOB)
FROM DEMOGRAPHICS.REGION;
```

This is a partial result, formatted for readability:

```
<region name="Africa">
   <population>789548670</population>
   <area>26780325</area>
</region>
<region name="Asia">
   <population>47382633</population>
   <area>657741</area></region>
...
<region name="South America">
   <population>375489788</population>
   <area>17545171</area>
</region>
```

The XMLAGG method concatenates with the added option of re-sorting child elements of the XMLAGG function:

```
SELECT XMLSERIALIZE(CONTENT
XMLAGG(
   XMLELEMENT(NAME "region", XMLATTRIBUTES(REGION_ID AS "id"),
      XMLELEMENT(NAME "name", REGION),
      XMLELEMENT(NAME "population", POPULATION),
      XMLELEMENT(NAME "area", AREA)
   ) ORDER BY POPULATION DESC
) AS CLOB)
FROM DEMOGRAPHICS.REGION;
```

This is a partial result showing regions sorted in order of descending population size for each region:

```
<region id="7">
   <name>Far East</name>
   <population>2100636517</population>
   <area>15357441</area>
</region>
<region id="9">
   <name>Near East</name>
   <population>1499157105</population>
   <area>4721322</area>
</region>
...
```

The XMLFOREST method allows you to create multiple XML elements in a single method. The following query creates multiple elements by selecting fields. It is not creating each field as an individual element:

```
SELECT XMLSERIALIZE(CONTENT
   XMLELEMENT(NAME "region", XMLATTRIBUTES(REGION_ID AS "id"),
      XMLFOREST(REGION AS "name", POPULATION AS "population", AREA AS "area")
) AS CLOB)
FROM DEMOGRAPHICS.REGION;
```

This is a partial result, formatted here for readability:

```
<region id="1">
   <name>Africa</name>
   <population>789548670</population>
   <area>26780325</area>
</region>
<region id="2">
   <name>Asia</name>
   <population>47382633</population>
   <area>657741</area>
</region>
...
<region id="13">
   <name>South America</name>
   <population>375489788</population>
   <area>17545171</area>
</region>
```

Working with XML in DB2 CLOB Objects

XML documents can be stored into a DB2 database using CLOB objects. As you already know, a CLOB object is simply a text object stored in binary form. Thus, a CLOB object allows storage of very large text strings into a DB2 database, in a field, in a table. Let's begin by creating a table containing a CLOB object field:

```
CONNECT TO NEWDEM;
CREATE TABLE DEMOGRAPHICS.XML(XML CLOB(5M));
COMMIT;
```

A simple method of loading an XML document into a DB2 database table is to use the LOAD command. Using the LOAD command might look something like this:

```
LOAD FROM '<path>\demographicsCLOB.xml' OF ASC INSERT INTO DEMOGRAPHICS.XML(XML);
```

Unfortunately, the LOAD command appears to be somewhat dated and functions only when attempting to upload a delimited file, or a file allowing locational specifications (positions of columns in a line). The XML document I am attempting to load is all a single line and the LOAD command is inappropriate.

Loading small strings is not an issue, as in the following command:

```
INSERT INTO DEMOGRAPHICS.XML(XML) VALUES('<root><region id="1"><name>Africa</name><
population>789548670</population><area>26780325</area></region><region id="2"><name
>Asia</name><population>47382633</population><area>657741</area></region></root>');
```

Loading an XML document of a few gigabytes as a string might be a slight problem using a command like that shown in the preceding code.

Also, using the LOAD or IMPORT options within the DB2 Control Center tool is limited by a number of bytes for each line. It appears that the only way to load a large XML document into a table, containing a CLOB field, is by inserting a string. The DB2 XML Extender software is far too complex for this book, and thus importing a very large XML document into a DB2 database is a little problematic, as shown in Figure E-2.

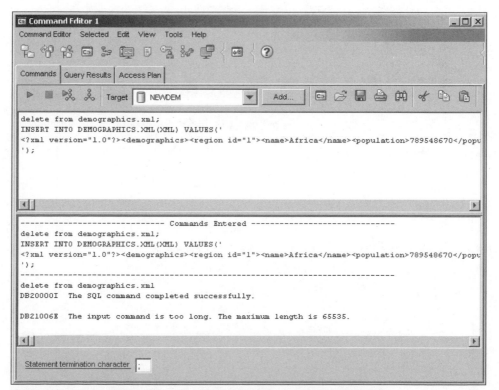

Figure E-2: Loading large XML documents into DB2 is a little problematic.

A shell SQL tool could probably be used to resolve this issue, but it might be best to comply with the 2GB size limitation for DB2 CLOB objects. What I will do is to recreate the XML table with a primary identifier as shown in the next section of code. Yes, a command tool could be used, but there is another way that will comply with the size limit on CLOB objects of 2GB. The first thing to do is to recreate the XML table with a primary key field:

```
CONNECT TO NEWDEM;
DROP TABLE DEMOGRAPHICS.XML;
CREATE TABLE DEMOGRAPHICS.XML(
    ID INTEGER PRIMARY KEY NOT NULL,
    XML CLOB(2M));
COMMIT;
```

Second, the XML data can be split into regions and each region can be added to a separate record. The result will be all regions stored in separate records as regional fragments of the entire demographics XML document:

```
INSERT INTO DEMOGRAPHICS.XML(ID, XML) VALUES(2, '<region><name>Asia</name> ...
<region>');
```

Yet another issue with DB2 and using the Command Editor tool is that it allows only a string of 64KB maximum. Only two of the regions in the demographics XML documents are less than 64KB. Only the region of Asia can be added to the database using the DB2 database CLOB field (in the XML table created previously) for the purposes of later testing, as shown here:

```
INSERT INTO DEMOGRAPHICS.XML(ID, XML) VALUES(2, '<region><name>Asia</name> ...
</regi
on>');
```

All the regional XML fragments are available on the website specifically for the DB2 database; the URL is http://www.oracledbaexpert.com/oracle/beginningxmldatabases/index.html.

Retrieving XML data is a simple matter of reading a CLOB object from a table. Additionally, the only method of changing XML document content is to read, change, and then update the entire CLOB object. Further demonstration is not required.

Index

Index